CHINESE DEFENCE POLICY

CHINESE DEFENCE POLICY

Edited by

Gerald Segal and William T. Tow

University of Illinois Press
Urbana and Chicago

© 1984 by Gerald Segal and William T. Tow

Manufactured in Hong Kong

Library of Congress Cataloging in Publication Data

Main entry under title:

Chinese defence policy.

   Includes bibliographical references and index.
   1. China—Military policy—Addresses, essays, lectures.
2. China—Defenses—Addresses, essays, lectures.   3. China
—Armed Forces—Addresses, essays, lectures.   I. Segal,
Gerald, 1953-   II. Tow, William T.
UA835.C448   1984   355'.033051   83-24229
ISBN 0-252-01135-X
ISBN 0-333-35132-0 (Macmillan ed.)

Contents

Acknowledgements		vii
Notes on the Contributors		ix
Introduction *Gerald Segal and William T. Tow*		xiii

PART I SOURCES OF STRATEGY

1. Strategic Doctrine — 3
   Georges Tan Eng Bok
2. Civil–Military Relations — 18
   Ellis Joffe
3. Towards a New Strategy? — 36
   Paul Godwin

PART II THE ARMED SERVICES

4. Ground Forces — 53
   Harlan Jencks
5. Air Forces — 71
   Bill Sweetman
6. Naval Forces — 85
   Bruce Swanson
7. Nuclear Forces — 98
   Gerald Segal

PART III THE ECONOMIC DIMENSION

8. Military Industry — 117
   Sydney Jammes
9. Aspects of Modernisation — 133
   Karen Berney

| 10 | Arms Sales to China
William T. Tow | 149 |

PART IV FOREIGN POLICY: THREAT AND PROMISE

11	China's Changing World View *Hammond Rolph*	167
12	The Soviet Union *David Armstrong*	180
13	The United States *Robert Sutter*	196
14	Western Europe *Douglas Stuart*	209
15	Japan *Joachim Glaubitz*	222
16	Southeast Asia *Larry A. Niksch*	234
17	South Asia *Yaacov Vertzberger*	247
18	The Middle East *Yitzhak Shichor*	263
	Index	279

Acknowledgements

Joint books are never easy to write, but serving as joint editors is often more taxing if only because of the proliferation of sensitive authors who view their every comma as sacred. Bill Tow and I at first decided to edit separate books on Chinese defence policy but some of the contributors who had been approached by both of us rightly suggested we pool resources. The result might have been more messy if Bill had not suggested at an early date that he concentrate on organising the conference and I take on editorial duties for the ensuing book. Therefore, my first debt of gratitude is owed to Bill and the excellent staff at the University of Southern California's German Graduate Program (Munich). With a special blend of American hospitality and German efficiency, the conference was held in Garmisch from 3 to 5 May 1983. Carolyn Kayser was especially sensitive to the international needs of the participants. We are of course also deeply indebted to the Ford Foundation for the generous grant that made the conference possible in the first place.

The final debt is owed to those people involved in the production of the book. Various specialists reviewed assorted chapters, but special mention must be made of the service, tasteful tact and, above all, the patience on the part of Tony Mason, Edwina Moreton and Anne-Lucie Norton.

The most important debt is owed to the sensitivities of the contributors. Some of the original papers for the conference were three times longer than the strict word-limit, and many people suffered as precious words were cut. As the editor, I am sorry for the pain, but in the final analysis it is hoped that the end justifies the means.

GERALD SEGAL

Notes on the Contributors

David Armstrong is a Lecturer in International Studies at the University of Birmingham. He is the author of various articles on Chinese and Soviet foreign policy and *Revolutionary Diplomacy* (1977) and *The Rise of the International Organization* (1982).

Karen Berney is Assistant Editor, *Electronics* (McGraw-Hill). She received her MA in Chinese studies from the University of Michigan (1978) and served on the staff of the *China Business Review*, 1979–82, with responsibility for writing on Chinese high-technology developments.

Joachim Glaubitz is Senior Research Fellow, Stiftung Wissenschaft und Politik (Ebenhausen, Munich) and Professor of East Asian Affairs, University of Munich. He is the author of various articles on Chinese and especially Sino–Japanese policy and *Opposition gegen Mao* (1969) and *China und die Sowjetunion* (1973).

Paul Godwin is Professor at the Air University Center for Aerospace Doctrine, Research and Education, Alabama. He is the author of various articles on Chinese foreign and defence policy, as well as *The Chinese Tactical Air Forces* (1978), *Doctrine Strategy and Ethic* (1977), *The Chinese Defence Establishment* (editor, 1983).

Sydney Jammes is an analyst with the Central Intelligence Agency in Washington DC. His most recent unclassified publications have been in support of US Congressional Committees including *China's Military Capabilities* for the Senate Foreign Relations Committee and co-author of *China's Military Strategic Requirements* for the Joint Economic Committee.

Harlan Jencks is Adjunct Professor of National Security Affairs at the Naval Postgraduate School, California, and Research Associate at the Center for Chinese Studies, University of California, Berkeley. He is the author of various articles on Chinese foreign and defence policy, as well as *From Muskets to Missiles* (1982) and co-editor of *Chinese Communist Politics* (1982).

Ellis Joffe is Professor of Asian Studies at the Hebrew University of Jerusalem. He is the author of various articles on Chinese defence policy as well as *Party and Army: Professionalism and Political Control in the Chinese Officer Corps* (1971).

Larry A. Niksch is specialist in Asian Affairs, Congressional Research Service, Library of Congress. He is the author of various articles on Asian defence policies as well as *Fighting Armies* (1983).

Hammond Rolph is the Associate Director and Research Associate, School of International Relations, University of Southern California. He is the author of various articles on Asian, and especially Chinese defence policy, and *Communism in Vietnam* (1967) and *Vietnamese Communism and the Protracted War* (1971). From 1943 to 1964 he served as a US Naval Intelligence Officer, including assignments in Nanking and Tokyo.

Gerald Segal is Lecturer in the Department of Politics, University of Bristol. He is the author of various articles on Chinese foreign and defence policy as well as *The Great Power Triangle* (1982), co-author of *Nuclear War and Nuclear Peace* (1983), editor of *The China Factor* (1982), *The Soviet Union and East Asia* (1983), co-editor of *Soviet Strategy* (1981) and *Soviet Strategy towards Western Europe* (1983).

Yitzhak Shichor is Senior Lecturer in the Department of Asian Studies, Hebrew University of Jerusalem. He is the author of various articles on Chinese foreign policy as well as *The Middle East in China's Foreign Policy* (1979).

Douglas Stuart is Associate Professor of International Relations, Johns Hopkins University, Bologna, Italy. He is the author of various articles on Chinese foreign and defence policy as well as co-author of *The Limits of Alliance* (1984) and co-editor of *China, The Soviet Union and the West* (1982).

Robert Sutter is Specialist in Asian Affairs, Congressional Research Service, Library of Congress. He is the author of various articles on

Chinese foreign policy as well as *China Watch* (1978), *Chinese Foreign Policy After the Cultural Revolution* (1978) and *China Quandry* (1983).

Bruce Swanson is Strategy Analyst at the Center for Naval Analyses, Virginia. He is the author of various articles on Chinese defence policy as well as *Eighth Voyage of the Dragon: China's Quest for Seapower* (1982).

Bill Sweetman is a freelance journalist specialising on airpower. He is the author of various articles on Chinese and Soviet airpower as well as co-author of *Air Forces of the World* and *Soviet Airpower*.

Georges Tan Eng Bok is Research Associate, Atlantic Institute for International Affairs. He is the author of various articles on Chinese defence policy as well as *La Modernisation de la défense Chinoise* (1983) and *Chinese Military Modernization*.

William T. Tow is Visiting Assistant Professor, University of Southern California, German Graduate Program, Munich. He is the author of various articles on Chinese and American defence policy as well as co-author of *The Limits of Alliance* (1984), co-editor of *China, The Soviet Union and the West* (1982) and *US Foreign Policy and Asian-Pacific Security* (1982).

Yaacov Vertzberger is Lecturer in the Department of International Relations, Hebrew University of Jerusalem. He is the author of various articles on Chinese and Asian defence policy as well as *The Enduring Entente* (1983), *Misperception in Foreign Policy Making* (1984) and *Coastal States, Regional Powers and Superpowers*.

Introduction

GERALD SEGAL
WILLIAM T. TOW

How strong is China? The answer is not to be found by counting tanks and ICBMs, nor by repeating China's stated military doctrine, for the reality of defence policy is far more complex. For China, as for most other states, the answer lies in an analysis of defence policy, and especially of how foreign and internal politics interact. In the case of the superpowers, this complexity has not prevented some from analysing the problems of defence policy, but in China's case there have been few such attempts, and no current ones.

The last comprehensive analysis of Chinese defence policy is well over a decade old.[1] More recently there have been good article-length surveys,[2] but the subject none the less deserves more complete treatment.[3] Thus the over-arching purpose of this book is to provide a broad analysis of the nature of Chinese defence policy.

Because of the wide-ranging nature of defence policy and the need for detailed expertise on military matters, any analysis stands or falls on whether it manages to marry the skills of the specialist with the analysis of the strategist. The chapters in the book that follows are all relatively brief and concise, not because there was nothing more to be written, but rather because it was felt to be best to concentrate on the broader implications, and leave much of the nuts and bolts of military hardware to specialist journals. This project was conceived around five basic questions outlined below and the authors were encouraged to synthesise their detailed knowledge in order to provide a broader and more reflective analysis.

The conference preceeding this book drew together the authors so that the specialists and the strategists, the hardware buffs and the foreign policy analysts could bridge the gaps in each other's work. The book that follows is not meant to be the last word on Chinese defence policy, for one thing that did emerge from the conference was that there are important disagreements among the experts. Nor is this book intended as a great social-science synthesis of available knowledge. For despite some scholars' calls for such unification, it is plain that the subject of Chinese defence policy is too complex to fit into neat patterns or models. We strive to make matters as simple as possible, but not more so. To force common analysis and answers is to go beyond the evidence.

In this spirit of accepting debate and change in Chinese defence policy, the contributors addressed themselves to five main questions. Not all the answers were the same, but certain important trends were evident. Rather than run through each chapter in turn as is often done at the start of an edited volume, it was thought better to outline the basic questions and their answers. To the extent that there are common themes in this book, they are to be found in the five questions.

HOW STRONG IS THE PEOPLE'S LIBERATION ARMY (PLA)

It is conventional thinking that the PLA is weak. Some analysts suggest that despite having the world's largest standing armed forces, China ranks as no more than a middle-sized power.[4] There was support among the contributors to this book for the view that the PLA has serious weaknesses, but the general concensus was that the limitations should be kept in perspective. To be sure some contributors, notably Godwin, Jencks and Sweetman, emphasised the size of the task which remains to be done in modernising the PLA. But they, along with most of the others, suggested that a great deal had already been done to improve PLA fighting power. China may not be in the first rank of military power, but neither is it fifth rate.

This tone of relative optimism seems to be founded on several supports. First, as Tan Eng Bok, Joffe and Jencks point out, a great deal has already been done to improve those aspects of PLA power not tied directly to weapons procurement. The evolution of a new and more modern doctrine, new stress on greater professionalism and training, and the retreat from involvement in civilian politics have all helped increase the combat effectiveness of the PLA. A military force is often as dependent on intangible factors as it is on hardware. Morale, especially in a Chinese military régime indoctrinated to stress 'man over weapons', is still an important factor in the assessment of PLA power. This is not to say that relative inferiority of PLA equipment is unimportant, but merely that numbers and types of weapons are far from the total of military power.

Second, there is evidence that PLA defence spending on equipment is not as low as some had thought. Joffe, and especially Shichor, argue that the PLA is probably getting more of the equipment that it wants than has previously been thought. In part through arms sales abroad, in part through barter deals for latest model equipment, and in part simply through greater domestic efficiency, funds do exist for some modernisation of equipment. While the official PLA budgets indicate a fall in defence spending since 1980, the year after the Sino-Vietnam war, it is less clear that the budget has been cut when pre-1979 spending is considered.[5] What is more, if only part of the foreign currency earned in foreign arms sales is ploughed back into the Chinese military, then there are large and hidden sources of PLA funding.

Third, contributors to this volume were all at pains to stress that it is not always necessary to have *the* most modern equipment in order to have a useful fighting force. Certainly much of Soviet equipment is considered inferior to Western hardware, but if Soviet equipment proves to be more robust in combat, then 'low' technology may be preferable to high technology. Certainly not all combat is fought at the forefront of technology. In the 1979 Sino-Vietnamese war the weakness of Chinese airpower was not crucial because that service arm was less suited to the specific small-scale nature of the combat. What is more, evidence from the Iran–Iraq war suggests that Chinese equipment is at least reliable in a war where attrition takes a heavier toll on more modern and delicate hardware.

Fourth, it is clear that an ethnocentric analysis of Chinese defence policy will yield unduly pessimistic conclusions. Although defence policy may deal superficially with common territory or similar hardware, the special needs of China are not necessarily the same as those of the superpowers. The Chinese do not require sophisticated or extensive military equipment equal to that of the superpowers in order to carry out effective defence. The chapters on the services make it plain that even without the latest gadgets China can meet most of its defence requirements. Obviously a more offensive campaign, especially against a superpower opponent, would pose far more problems. The chapters on foreign threats make it equally plain that China faces no single 'model' threat, and therefore each particular military problem requires specific analysis. Those obsessed with military hardware would have us believe that technology determines military needs and performance. But, as usual, the Chinese reality is more complex, and in this case it leads to less pessimistic conclusions about Chinese power.

Fifth, some aspects of PLA power are being impressively modernised despite weakness in other areas. Most notably, as Swanson and Segal point out, the naval and nuclear forces have made impressive gains of late. The navy has been concentrating upon modern electronic war and with an increasingly maritimist capability. The nuclear forces are moving into more modern ICBM technology including an apparent MIRV capability, and the testing of an SLBM portends a more modern and secure second strike force. Spending in these two sectors is seen as likely to continue and both suggest an increasingly global role for the Chinese military.

In sum, China is not on a military par with the superpowers, nor is it likely to catch up in even the medium term. Needless to say the superpowers are not marking time waiting for China to close the gap. But the PLA does seem to be at least second rate in military power and this power is increasing more steadily than many had previously thought. That is not to say that China's planners necessarily feel confident about their ability to meet any military threat, for it is in the nature of military planners to be paranoid and able to point to new defence needs. But on balance the PLA is strong enough to deter threats to its security, and while it may not attain superpower levels, it is nevertheless unlikely to fall so very far behind.

IS THERE A NEW MILITARY DOCTRINE?

The PLA's new strength is only in part derived from modernisation of its doctrine, but this is an important element. However, there is a certain amount of uncertainty over over how far and in what direction the new Chinese doctrine is moving. China is said by some to have abandoned the concept of 'people's war', while others have suggested that the new strategy of 'people's war under modern conditions' has changed the meaning of the original term. What emerged from this study was a far more complex view of PLA doctrine. As Tan Eng Bok, Joffe, Godwin and the services chapters suggest, there can be no unanimity on the meaning of modern people's war.

First, the complexity in meaning of people's war is far from novel. As Tan Eng Bok in particular points out, it is important to note that people's war was always far more concerned with grand strategy than operational principles. At its roots was concern that war should not lose its relationship to politics, and above all should be fought with popular support. While people's war placed so high in the realm of first principles of politics, it remained both flexible and unaffected by specific changes in technology. Like any long-lasting ideology, it requires both these elements to survive change; at the same time it can rarely serve as an operational guide to policy. Thus people's war remains unchanging in its basic nature while allowing for natural change in its more operational sub-principles.

Second, the notion of 'modern conditions' is not a new addition to people's war. Indeed the phrase appeared during the height of the Cultural Revolution. Of course the definition of modern conditions has changed, but the need to have a flexible doctrine has long been accepted. While Chinese commentators may frequently suggest that there is only one doctrine, the reality of more than 30 years of the People's Republic proves otherwise. China has fought wars at its gates and beyond (Korea, India) and also chosen to sit behind the gates (Vietnam). China has fought positional war (Korea) and wars of greater mobility (India). Whatever the specifics of combat, it is plain that Chinese military doctrine has been flexible and has regularly sought to adapt itself to modern conditions.

However, it would be wrong to suggest that nothing has changed in Chinese strategy, for the process of change itself is normal. There are obviously new emphases on combined arms operations, improved logistics and more modern communication. The navy and the nuclear forces have been given new equipment, and seem to have adapted their strategy to suit their new capabilities. Certainly the navy has a more forward role than in the past, and the nuclear forces are heading towards more than a simple posture of minimum deterrence.

Thus there are changes in PLA strategy, but those in the West who expect a single new and coherent Chinese strategy to emerge will be disappointed. Such coherence never existed in the past, except in the ethnocentric or ethnic-chic images of some analysts. People's war was never simple or inflexible, and therefore can incorporate a great deal of change without changing its nomenclature. Much like the general foreign policy ideology of the Soviet Union or China, ideology can remain important in setting objectives, while not offering a clear road map to the goal. No doubt there will be those in the West who will expect pithy new phrases to replace people's war, or who will try to fit bits and pieces of changing Chinese operations into a pseudo-social-science interpretation. But to do so would be to oversimplify a more complex reality. The conduct of war is too pragmatic, and too closely related to changing political and military realities, to be analysed so simplistically. As the Chinese come to face this pragmatism more squarely, the least that foreign observers can do is abandon the search for a rigid doctrine.

IS THE PLA UNIFIED?

It is always easier to talk of the military as a single body, but it has long been recognised that the role of the military in politics is far more complex.[6] The question of the extent to which the PLA acts as a single entity or is riven by inter-service rivalry is tackled explicitly by Joffe and implicitly in the chapters by Jencks, Sweetman, Swanson and Segal. While some differences of emphasis emerge, the contributors did reach a broad consensus.

First, on some issues the PLA can largely be seen as a single unit. For example, as Joffe makes plain, in desiring greater professionalism or in urging a higher defence budget, the military is more or less united. However, as Joffe argues, these issues are no longer in serious debate in China. The question of professionalism in particular is one where the civilian leadership actively desires PLA specialisation and seems willing to grant the military areas of participation in politics as a matter of professional right.

Second, this unity on some issues should not mask evident splits over other issues, where the PLA cannot be regarded as a unified body. The chapters on the services come to no clear conclusions as to the implications of inter-service rivalry, but that there are conflicts seems undeniable. The air force, navy and nuclear forces require spending on electronics rather than steel, but even among the three more modern services there is competition for resources. Chapter 8 reinforces the point that differences cut across military as well as civillian lines.

While there are still divisions within the PLA, they are not always along the lines previously analysed. For example, Godwin argues that generational changes in the PLA are far more crucial today than the supposedly central–regional splits of the past. The old theories of Field Armies are just that – old. Central control appears to have become firmly established over the past few years, and while the PLA is far from unified, the cleavages within it now differ from those of old.

With increasing professionalism in the PLA, these splits are unlikely to disappear. To be sure the lines of power will be laid down in different ways, with traditional Party–Army differences less acute than before. The role of military–industry politics may well assume new relevance. The PLA itself seems unlikely to be able to decide on an equitable division of resources, and the modernisation process will make arguments along service lines more likely. This is not to suggest that the study of Party–Army relations ceases to be relevant – far from it – but the nature of the topics analysed will have to change with the times.

WHO THREATENS CHINA?

China, like the Soviet Union, is largely surrounded by hostile communist states. In fact this basic assessment of the source and nature of threat is as important for the study of Chinese defence policy as is the extent of the combat readiness of the PLA. China's increasing assurance about its defence position stems as much from its new confidence in the PLA as from an assessment that China is now less threatened than before. This is not to suggest that China no longer sees itself under any threat at all, but the threats have changed in nature and intensity.

Fifteen years ago, when China began normalising relations with the United States, Beijing faced an ominous series of threats around its borders. The Soviet Union not only deployed massive numbers of troops and modern equipment along the northern frontier, but in 1969 also rattled its nuclear sabre in China's direction. On the southern flank of China United States power in Asia was still well in evidence, though China could have confidence that the American threat was in decline.

The present Chinese perception of threat, as outlined by Armstrong, Sutter, Glaubitz, Niksch and Vertzberger in succeeding chapters, is less pessimistic. To be sure the Soviet presence is acutely felt along the border, but the threat is reduced and certainly less imminent. Similarly, United States power was greatly reduced with the end of the Vietnam war, though rivalry between Washington and Beijing does continue, and not merely on the Taiwan issue. In Southeast Asia the Chinese remain almost as concerned about the unfavourable situation as they were in the 1960s, but this time the threats come from communist Vietnam and to a large extent China is responsible for maintaining whatever high tension persists. Finally, other conflicts on the Chinese periphery have fluctuated in intensity. Although the Soviet invasion of Afghanistan for a time caused anxiety in Beijing, it is no longer seen as a particular problem for the Chinese; it is rather seen as a quagmire for the Soviet superpower. The Korean conflict is certainly under greater control than it was 15 years ago, when mini-crises did erupt, although Korea still remains a potential source of danger for a China seeking the environment of a stable foreign policy.

This overall improvement in China's perceptions of the threats it faces goes a long way towards explaining increased confidence in its defence policy. Beijing's assessment of its diplomatic position has always played a crucial role in China's attempt to make up for military weakness. But to a large extent in recent years China has suffered self-inflicted wounds in this respect as it exaggerated the extent of the Soviet threat and thereby encouraged Soviet hostility. China's responses to Soviet overtures in 1982, however tentative, do mark an important new shift in China's threat assessment. In the period of absurdly intense anti-Sovietism, China only succeeded in reducing its own freedom of manoeuvre as it obsessedly concentrated on building anti-Soviet coalitions. As the Chinese military grows in strength, and Beijing abandons its acute anti-Sovietism, China may well be opening up a new, more balanced phase in its efforts to deal with the two superpowers.

It is certainly clear from the contributors to this volume that Sino–American relations are no longer as crucial as they were to a calculation of Chinese defence policy. The improvement in Sino–Soviet relations has helped to offset the earlier excessive concentration on America. With the reduction in Chinese concern over the Soviet threat, and the more balanced view of the continuing United States threat, new possibilities have opened up for Chinese foreign policy. This new flexibility derives in part from more realistic threat assessments, and in part from a real sense that China's military power has increased. In the final analysis both internal and external factors are crucial to an assessment of China's perception of threat. But what is equally clear is that, precisely because China is feeling more confident, it is unlikely to raise the priority accorded to defence modernisation. As the fourth of the Four Modernisations, defence remains crucial, but there is now less pressing need than ever for Beijing's to alter its order of priorities.

WHO AIDS CHINA'S SECURITY?

Ten years ago, when playing 'China cards' was all the rage, this question might well have prompted praise for the role of western states in Chinese security. It is now obvious that hopes of a strategic alliance with China were as ill-founded as the previous century's dreams of the vast China market. Stuart, Tow, Sutter and Glaubitz make it clear that while various western states may still hope for close co-operation with China, there can be little prospect of a straight forward relationship.

These chapters make plain that there are various reasons for China's failure to incorporate other states into its security programme. First, it is evident that China and the western states still have important incompatibilities in strategic outlook. Not only do the United States and China continue to disagree over Taiwan, but there are broader conflicts as the United States under the Reagan administration reasserts its Asian role.[7] Similarly, Japan and China retain many common interests, yet important disputes, for example over contested territory still remain to be settled.

Second, there had been hopes in the West, and no doubt also in some Chinese circles, that the West could sell arms to China to help deter a Soviet threat. As is pointed out in other chapters of this book, China cannot afford to buy sophisticated weapons in sufficient numbers and is unwilling to rely on foreign sources for such vital aspects of its defence. As Defence Minister Zhang Aiping made plain in the spring of 1983, arms purchases can only provide assistance at the periphery Chinese defence, and the main effort will come from China's own development programme. It seems more than likely that the largely secret, but widespread Chinese arms deals in the Middle East – described by Shichor – will provide China with some of the new cash for these solo efforts, and above all will help provide the latest models upon which Chinese industry can base the reverse engineering[9] of its military technology.

Third, there is less need from the Chinese viewpoint for outside aid in security matters since China has scaled down its assessment of foreign threat. The foundations of western hopes for alliance with China have been undermined by signs of Sino–Soviet détente. With a reduced sense of threat, there is less need for China to compromise with western powers. Obviously the implications of this new Chinese confidence are widespread, with China's hardening of attitude on Taiwan only one of the more obvious manifestations. Certainly the prospect of major western arms sales or talk of China as NATO's 16th member are subjects of the past.

In sum, China is both stronger and more independent than many people had thought. The two characteristics, strength and independence, are obviously closely intertwined. China can feel more independent because it feels stronger, and similarly it can spend less on defence because it feels less threatened. While the precise balance of these emotions cannot be fully understood, it is plain that, contrary to much previous analysis, China is stronger in reality and self-perception than previously thought.

However, if analysts seek to make too much of this new reality they will be as disappointed as their predecessors. Chinese defence policy has clearly changed, but it remains just as complex. Therefore those seeking neat coherent models or pithy descriptions of defence policy will be disappointed. One of the hallmarks of current policy is pragmatism. Foreign analysts would do well to heed the lessons of the past, where both Chinese and foreign analysts suggested greater coherence or rigidity than actually existed. It should be plain that the currently stronger and more confident defence policy can easily change. Such change could come about as a result of renewed domestic instability, or a perception of increased external threat. The only certainty can be uncertainty, and analysts of Chinese defence policy should be wary of expecting anything more.

NOTES AND REFERENCES

1. William Whitson (ed.), *The Military and Political Power in China in the 1970s* (New York: Praeger, 1972).
2. John Baylis, 'China' in *Contemporary Strategy*, 2nd edn (New York: Holmes & Meir, 1984) and Wallace Heaton, 'China', in Douglas Murray and Paul Viotti (eds), *The Defense Policies of Nations* (London: Johns Hopkins University Press, 1982).
3. Gerald Segal, 'Chinese Defence Policy', *International Affairs*, vol. 59, no. 4, Autumn 1983.
4. Ray Bonds (ed.), *The Chinese War Machine* (London: Salamander, 1979).
5. CIA, NFAC, *Chinese Defence Spending, 1965–79*, July 1980; Ronald Mitchell, 'Chinese Defence Spending in Transition' in *China Under the Four Modernizations*, Part 1, 97th Congress, 2nd Session, Joint Economic Committee, 13 August 1982.
6. Dale Herspring and Ivan Volgyes (eds), *Civil–Military Relations in Communist Systems* (Boulder, Colorado: Westview, 1978); Timothy Colton, *Commissars, Commanders and Civilian Authority* (Cambridge: Harvard University Press, 1979); Gerald Segal, 'The PLA as a Group' in David Goodman (ed.), *Groups in Chinese Politics* (forthcoming, 1985).
7. William Tow and William Feeney (eds), *U.S. Foreign Policy and Asian–Pacific Security* (Boulder, Colorado: Westview, 1982).

Part I
Sources of Strategy

1 Strategic Doctrine

GEORGES TAN ENG BOK*

China's military doctrine is well-known under the general term of People's War. However, the Chinese concept of their military doctrine is more complex. In fact, the resulting confusion affects both Western and Chinese commentators. Not only have foreigners used the term People's War loosely, but so have some Chinese leaders, most notably Lin Biao.[1]

By and large, the Chinese, as well as the Soviets, use a highly structured terminology in their military affairs. The similarity is so close that analyses related to Soviet military thought could also be applied to that of China:

> Terms such as *military doctrine*, *military science* and *military strategy* have carefully defined meanings and relationships that should be appreciated ... Ideas tend to flow downward; discussions at one level (e.g. strategy) involve considerable refinement and restatement of higher level discussions (e.g. ideology and doctrine). Ideas are restated and reinterpreted to suit the subject under discussion and, in effect, to justify it by tying it to a higher authority, which ultimately is Marxism–Leninism.
>
> Throughout this examination, it is important not to impute Western ideas and practices to the Soviet in interpreting their literature.[2]

Such a recommendation is not out of place *vis-à-vis* Chinese military thinking, and is especially useful in pointing to the changing nature of Chinese military thought. Thus our analysis must begin with how the Chinese military thought was formed, how the People's War is structured, and how has China adapted People's War to the nuclear age?

---

* The author would like to thank General Guillermaz for his comments on an earlier draft of this paper. Professor Tsien Tche-hao's review of Chinese transcriptions in the text is gratefully acknowledged also.

FORMATION OF THE CHINESE MILITARY THOUGHT

The present Chinese military thought mainly results from three constituents: (1) China's ancient military thought; (2) Mao Zedong's contribution; (3) the Soviet influence through Marxism–Leninism. However, the reality is less simple. For example, one could wonder either if some kind of *force des choses* has contributed to blend these three constituents, or if cultural and historical legacies have tended to facilitate the Chinese receptiveness to the Marxist–Leninist considerations on war – especially the Soviet approach to military affairs. In addition, Mao Zedong's own personality and the specific conditions experienced by the Chinese communist movement are far from straightforward.

Apart from Mao Zedong's works in the military field, Sun Zi is the only Chinese strategist who has ever gained much cognisance in the West.[3] Indeed, Sun Zi apparently had an appreciable impact on Mao. In 1968 however, the latter denied such an influence. He only agreed to having had a quick look at Sun Zi's *Art of War* when he wrote his *Problems of Strategy in China's Revolutionary War*.[4]

The intellectual basis for Sun Zi's importance derives from the philosophical thought of both Lao Zi and Zhuang Zi, considered by General Wei Rulin as the founders of the psychological element in China's military thought.[5] This common conceptual nucleus rests on three principles: (1) mind is superior to matter (*gingshen dayu wuzhi*); (2) thought is more powerful than weapons (*sixiang zhongyu bingqi*); (3) doctrine overcomes (bare) strength (*daoshu shengyu qiangquan*). Such considerations serve to explain why, from Sun Zi to Mao Zedong, there is 'one important cultural trait of the Chinese in their military conflicts: a stress on the importance of man over machine'.[6] As a corollary, war, in Chinese traditional acceptance, does not constitute an end in itself, but fits into a greater design dominated by politics. Furthermore, according to Sun Zi, to subdue an enemy without fighting reflects the acme of skill: '... those skilled in war subdue the enemy's army without battle. They capture his cities without assaulting them and overthrow his state without protracted operations.'[7]

Such a traditional conception casts useful light on Mao Zedong's insistence on compelling an aggressor to fight a protracted war, thus denying him the ability to win. What is more, in terms of warfare conduct, the stress on winning without fighting tends to favour *deception*[8] in order not only to exploit the adversary's weakness but to *produce* such situations. In this respect, Mao Zedong's texts contains numerous word-for-word citations from Sun Zi's *Art of War* such as: 'avoid strength and strike at weakness', 'appear when the enemy does not expect it', 'cause an uproar in the East, strike in the West' etc. These, and other similar strategems, have been popularised in the *Three Kingdoms Romance*, a book known to also have influenced Mao.[9]

Beside the philosophical environment of ancient China's attitude *vis-à-vis* military affairs, one also has to recall the no less important role played by the traditional peasant struggles against the Confucian social order.[10] On one hand, such a tradition of the *lülin* (the Chinese version of Robin Hood) and their saga belongs to the Chinese popular culture, especially in the *Water Margin*, a favourite subject for the storytellers. On the other hand, peasant insurrectionary movements, such as those of the Taiping and the Nian, have contributed to an overall catalogue of experiences and traditions for the Chinese conduct of guerrilla warfare.[11] Moreover, these uprisings embody a social character which has been relevant to the development of Mao Zedong's thesis on the Chinese peasantry's revolutionary potency and its corollary, the close co-ordination between a full time guerrilla and a sympathetic civilian population.[12]

If one refers to the background enunciated above, few elements contained in the military principles, strategy and tactics formulated by the 'Great Helmsman' are original.[13] Similarly, Mao Zedong was not the sole theorist of People's War in China. For example, one could also mention in this respect Zhu De (*On Guerrilla Warfare*), Ming Fan (*A Textbook on Guerrilla Warfare*), Guo Huaruo (editor of *Tactical Problems in Guerrilla Warfare*), and Peng Dehuai (editor, with Mao Zedong, of *Strategy and Tactics of the Eighth Route Army*).[14] However, these similarities in thought do not minimise Mao Zedong's importance in developing the People's War doctrine. Rather, Mao Zedong should be praised for his synthesis of China's intellectual and popular traditions in military affairs *according* to the Marxist–Leninist world view, at a conceptual as well as pragmatic level.[15]

Mao was also deeply influenced by at least two external pressures. First, Marxism–Leninism brought to China a new emphasis on the social dimension of strategy. When Mao Zedong pointed to the peasantry's revolutionary potential during his famous investigation of the rural movement in Hunan – January and February 1927 – he did so from a class viewpoint. Therefore the revolutionary path he chose was aimed at the *whole* Chinese society. In contrast, the traditional peasant insurrections had generally been limited to border regions, where the administrative control was loose.[16] Moreover, it should be noted that these traditional rebellions were essentially produced by local conditions – in particular large-scale famines – and were without precise aims.[17]

Second, People's War differs fundamentally from ancient Chinese warfare in relying on *organised armed forces* under a 'centralised strategic command'. On the one hand, this implies that People's War is not restricted to guerrilla warfare. Furthermore, as will be developed later, the existence of such forces means that guerrilla warfare has, in People's War, 'to support regular warfare and to transform itself into regular warfare'. On the other hand, such concepts owe a great deal to the Soviet military system and experiences, which have inherited many of the Russians' strategic traditions and problems. Of course, one has to be cautious when mentioning the USSR's influence on Chinese military affairs, as it has varied considerably according to the period.[18] However it is obvious that People's War embodies many principles outlined in the Soviet *Unified Strategy*: a defensive strategy of mass mobilisation, of 'luring the enemy deep', and reflecting the military weakness of the USSR before 1925.[19] To a lesser degree, People's War also reveals the ascendancy of the Soviet *Integral Strategy* which emphasises, within an ideological and political subordination to the Communist Party, a centralised chain of military command and a greater autonomy for the army, previously confined to the conduct of military operations.[20]

PEOPLE'S WAR: DOCTRINE AND APPLICATIONS

A common assumption tends to summarise People's war as a defensive military strategy relying on mass mobilisation, 'trading space for time' and 'luring the enemy deep', then 'drowning him in a sea of people'. Although accurate to a certain extent, such a presentation could be misleading as it mostly refers to general statements, irrespective of specific situations.[21] Furthermore, this approach too often supports a common tendency, in the West, to stress the obsolescence and ineffectiveness of Chinese military strategy.

In fact, mainland China's strategic thought divides into Military Doctrine (*Junshi Xueshuo*) – better known as People's War – and Military Science (*Junshi Kexue*) (see Figure 1.1). Within this framework, Strategy belongs to Military Art (*Junshi Xueshu*), the most important branch of Military Science. The distinction among these levels is crucial,[22] for misperceptions about the obsolescence of People's War derive from a confusion between Military Doctrine and Strategy.

Military Doctrine in China, as well as in the Soviet Union, is determined at the highest level of the political and military leadership. Therefore it bears a dual character. First, Military Doctrine provides the accepted views on the nature of war, especially of 'future conflicts'. Thus, it not only reflects the CCP's Military Line (*Junshi Luxian*) or, in other words, its *military policy*, but is also part of its ideological global strategy. In this regard, Military Doctrine stresses the *primacy of politics* in the sense that war, viewed as a continuation of politics, is to serve political aims.[23] The subordination of military affairs to politics also implies the *primacy of men over weapons*.[24] Second, Military Doctrine constitutes *guidance* for the military to follow in preparing the armed forces for war. But one thing should be clear in this respect – preparing the armed forces for war, according to the Marxist–Leninist ideology, presupposes a war initiated by 'Imperialism' and 'Hegemonism'. Such an assumption introduces the *defensive essence* of People's War. Moreover, the related Chinese expression for 'war preparations' (*zhanbei*) also reflects this intention of *protection*. In this respect one could question whether People's War also describes the cases where China used force more offensively than defensively.[25] But even in offensive terms, China's use of force is aimed at altering 'the opponent's will, and not necessarily its capability, to carry out adverse policies'.[26] For example, a limited and carefully weighted military initiative could *deter* enemy actions and thereby obtain Chinese security by virtue of an 'offensive' action.[27] Whatever the case, whether defensive or offensive, the concept of People's War remains valid in many respects.

At the lower level, in accordance with the ideological and political framework instituted by Military Doctrine, Military Science provides a 'unified system of knowledge' aimed at studying 'war and laws directing the conduct of war', especially the 'theory of war and strategy'.[28] In less esoteric words, Military Science considers, within the guiding principles defined by Military Doctrine, all the problems raised by the means and conditions of waging armed conflict. To this end, it considers a series of academic topics in which Military Art constitutes the most important branch. Among the other topics, the Chinese particularly include Military System and Military Geography.[29] Military Art studies the various aspects and problems related to Strategy (*Zhanlüe*), Operations (*Zhanyi*) – also translated as Campaigns – and

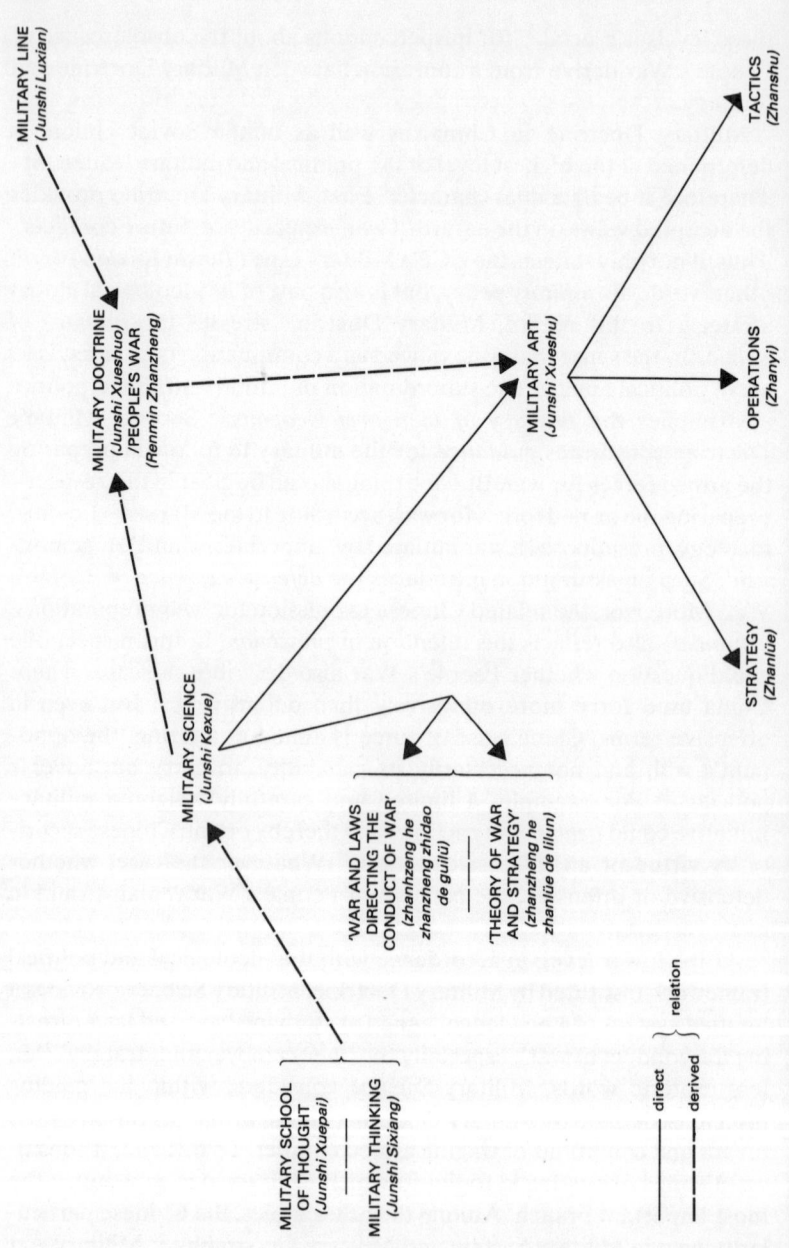

FIGURE 1.1 *Hierarchical relations among the Chinese military concept levels*

Tactics (*Zhanshu*), a three-level classification[30] that reflects, even now, a close Soviet influence on mainland China's military thinking. Strategy is concerned with the preparation and the conduct of the overall war (*zhanzheng*), while Tactics deals with all the aspects of combat operations for units (*budui*) – up to regiments and divisions – at the battlefield (*zhanchang*) level. 'Active Defence' (*Jiji Fangyu*), in order to fight a 'protracted war' (*Chijiuzhan*), provides the guiding principles of China's military strategy. It comprises three stages:

> The first stage covers the period of the enemy's strategic offensive and our strategic defensive. The second stage will be the period of the enemy's strategic consolidation and our preparation for the counter-offensive. The third stage will be the period of our strategic counter-offensive and the enemy's strategic retreat.[31]

The emphasis on the defensive in the first strategic phase is intended to reflect the Chinese assumption of their *material inferiority*, at least during the 'early stages of war' (*zhanzheng chuqi*). However, China's military strategy does not rely mainly on guerrilla warfare, but on regular warfare:

> ... the existence of war depends mainly on regular warfare, especially its mobile form, ... *guerrilla warfare cannot shoulder the main responsibility in deciding its outcome*. ... In saying this, we also have in mind the strategic task of developing guerrilla warfare into mobile warfare ... Thus, *the strategic task* of guerilla warfare is ... to support regular warfare and to transform itself into regular warfare.[32]

Neither is there a necessity to favour 'mobile warfare' (*yundongzhan*) instead of 'positional warfare' (*zhendizhan*) as the accent on either will depend on the objective and the available means. Tactics essentially rests on the principles of 'pit ten against one' (*yishi dayi*); an alternative formulation could be 'evading the strong and attacking the weak' (*biqiang daruo*). In order to attain a 'local superiority', Tactics notably resorts to 'human waves tactics' (*renhai zhanshu*), 'encirclement and outflanking tactics' (*yuhui baowei zhanshu*) and 'close and night fighting tactics' (*jingzhan yezhan zhanshu*). The art of Operations, a link binding Strategy to Tactics, relates to the preparation and the conduct of the 'co-ordinated combat of combined forces' at the Front (*zhanxian*) and Theatre (*zhanlüequ*) levels.[33] Mao Zedong's

Ten Great Military Principles (*Shida Junshi Yuanze*) form PLA's operational principles, with the emphasis on 'one basic principle: to strive to the utmost to preserve one's strength and destroy that of the enemy'.[34] Up to now Chinese strategists do not seem to have attached much importance to the operational level. But since 1977 there have been signs to indicate that this level has been given greater attention, possibly equivalent to that presently enjoyed by its counterpart in the Soviet Military Art.

TRENDS IN STRATEGIC AND OPERATIONAL CONCEPTS

From a global point of view, China is entering the 80s in a better position than during the previous decades. Among the internal elements in this respect, one could first indicate a more stable political situation coupled with a quite pragmatic economic programme. If it lasts, such stability will most probably help to create a social climate favouring economic growth, which in turn could assist in scientific, technical, and military modernisations.[35] Second, the 70s saw the normalisation of China's relations with Japan and the United States, at just the time when East–West *détente* began to fade. Third, China has been continuing to improve its nuclear arsenal.[36] Fourth, within the premisses envisaged by People's War and despite the obsolescence of its equipment, the PLA now seems credibly able to deter an all-out attack aimed at conquering the entire Chinese mainland.[37]

However, the improvement of China's global security may also induce reverse effects. First, the PLA Second Artillery's growing potential could tempt the Soviet Union to launch a pre-emptive surgical strike. Although the probability of such a contingency has been diminishing as the Soviet decision-makers seem to consider it no longer feasible,[38] strategic planners in Beijing cannot ignore such a risk. Second, improved ties between China and the industrialised democracies, especially the United States, may well worsen the Kremlin's paranoiac fears of having to fight a two-front war.

None the less, whatever the military options the Soviets might choose against China,[39] at least two things ought to be clearly understood. First, in the case of a global confrontation one could presume China would not constitute the major objective for the Soviet military planners. On the other hand, the Kremlin could not neglect the politically and psychologically counter-productive effects that aggression against China may bring about for East–West relations. Within these two sets of constraints, limited Soviet actions remain conceivable.

Since 1977, such considerations have induced Chinese strategists to review some of their military concepts. Song Shilun, for example, wrote in this respect:

> the theory of strategic offensive, the theory of co-ordinated fighting among different types of armed forces and services, the military principles of people's war under modern conditions, especially the principles of campaign and the tactical principles and so on are all subjects which need to be studied systematically, developed and updated.[40]

First, this evolution concerns the land-border defence strategy. Second, the implementation of these strategic arrangements calls, in turn, for some modification of the operational level.

In broad strategic terms, the military planners in Beijing have adopted a balanced attitude which is neither 'luring deep' the Soviets, nor meeting them 'at the gate' or beyond. As far back as 1978 Xu Xiangqian stated that:

> ... *luring the enemy in deep does not mean allowing the enemy to go wherever he likes*; it means forcing him to move in the direction we want, *organising a strong defense* with our priorities well-placed, *preventing the enemy from driving deep into our areas, leading him to battlefields prepared and organized in advance*, and in accordance with actual conditions, concentrating our superior forces on wiping out the enemy's troops one by one ...[41]

Thus China can foresee a certain amount of flexibility and pragmatism in its defence doctrine.[42] First, unlike NATO which needs to adopt an immediate frontal defence in order to avoid fighting in highly urbanised areas, the wide, unoccupied spaces of Manchuria and Xinjiang offer China various manoeuvring possibilities.[43] Second, any Soviet strike would probably be so massive that China would be forced to retreat on a wide front.

The main mission for the PLA in such a case would be to deny the Kremlin any possibility of a quick *fait accompli*. Hence, the Chinese 'Active Defence' would consist of a twofold strategy. On the one hand, there would be a *mobile defence* in order to avoid the invasion forces' main strength during their breakthrough, and to seek 'local superiority'[44] against their array. Since 1980 the *Jiefangjun Huabao* has been giving detailed reports of manoeuvres performed in accordance with such imperatives.[45] These counter-strikes would be supplemented with a series of attritional operations against the attacking forces' supply and communication lines in order to restrict the high speed of advance which is an essential part of the Soviet offensive doctrine. In addition to this, Chinese strategists have been envisaging the conduct of *positional warfare* on selected points such as mountains and vital communication junctions.[46] It should be also noted that, within these strategic plans, Beijing has been considering the use of theatre nuclear forces. However, available Chinese texts in this respect have not specified whether the PLA Second Artillery would take the iniative of an *ultimate warning shot*, or only respond to the Soviets' first use.[47]

Thus, the present trends in Chinese strategic thought require the PLA to adapt its operational concepts. This is especially true in terms of new stress on the regular army organisation, the C^3 structures (Command, Control, Communication), and the logistical system. In 1978, the Military Affairs Committee (MAC) announced two decisions, focussing respectively on army training and the cadre formation systems.[48] Among the themes that were developed, the main emphasis has been on the conduct of combined operations with more flexibility, and the improvement of C^3.[49] The 1979 Sino–Vietnamese war encouraged this process of adaptation and modernisation.[50] Logistics seemed to pose an especially difficult problem:

> If replenishment of manpower and material needed for fighting a war should depend solely on those captured from the enemy, how could the two parties in the 18-day Fourth Middle-East War, in which more than 600 aircraft and 3,000 tanks were lost, replenish themselves? Furthermore, should a war be fought between two countries, it will be impossible to replenish the strength of one side with the other side.[51]

Clearly some steps are under way in the process of updating China's Military Art. The pace will be protracted, but a great deal has already been done to fill the most obvious gaps in PLA strategy.[52] Some Western observers also seem to expect a replacement military doctrine for what they view as 'outdated People's War'. But such a hope underrates the flexibility of the Chinese military thinkers, and the pragmatic possibilities always inherent in people's war. Just as Chinese strategists now become more open about the chances for change within their new military doctrine, it would be ironic in the extreme if the last supporters of an unchanging view of people's war were to be found among Western analysts and not Beijing's policymakers.

NOTES AND REFERENCES

1. Generally, see 'China Tests New Military Strategy', *New York Times*, 14 July 1982. On Lin Biao's 'deviation', in addition to his 'Long Live the People's War' (*Peking Review* – hereafter *PR* – 36. 3 September 1965, 9–30), consult David P. Mozingo and Thomas W. Robinson, *Lin Piao on People's War: China Takes a Second Look at Vietnam*, Santa Monica (Calif.): RAND (RM-4814), November 1965; Ralph L. Powell, 'The Increasing Power of Lin Piao and the Party Soldiers, 1959–1966', *The China Quarterly* (hereafter *CQ*) 34, April–June 1968, 49–50; Donald S. Zagoria, *Vietnam Triangle. Moscow, Peking, Hanoi: A Classification of the Factors Governing the Relationships among the Communist Parties and States Involved in Vietnam*. (New York, Pegasus, 1967), 78–83 & 87–91.
2. Joseph D. Douglas, Jr., *Soviet Military Strategy in Europe*. New York: Pergamon, 1980, 1. Emphasis added.
3. In his interesting essay, Major Henning points at Qi Jiguang, whom he presents as Sun Zi's complement. Cf. Major Stanley E. Henning, US Army, 'Chinese Defense Strategy: A Historical Approach'. *Military Review* (hereafter *MR*) LIX(5), May 1979, 60–67. Among related Chinese sources, see Hong Chen, 'Qi Jiguang de Zhijun Sixiang' (Qi Jiguang's concepts of Military Management), *Lishi Yanjiu* (Historical Research) 6-1975, 20 December 1975, 88–96; Xie Chengren and Ning Ke, *Qi Jiguang* (Shanghai, Renmin Chubanshe, 1959).
4. Especially the chapter devoted to 'Sun Tzu and Mao Tse-tung' in Samuel B. Griffith's introduction to his translation of Sun Zi's writings (Sun Tzu, *The Art of War*. Trans. with an Intr. by Samuel B. Griffith. Foreword by Basil Liddell Hart. (Oxford, Clarendon, 1963), 75–88 (French edn); William Long, 'Mao Tse-tung as a Strategist', *Army*, April 1972, 10–17. I am indebted to General Guillermaz for this precision. For further details, see Jacques Guillermaz, 'The Soldier' in Dick Wilson (ed.), *Mao Tse-tung in the Scales of History* (Cambridge, Cambridge University Press, 1977), 128.
5. 'Xinli Zuozhan de Bizu', Cf. Wei Rulin, *Zhongguo de Junshi Sixiang Shi* (History of China's Military Thinking), (Taibei, Guofang Yanjiuyuan, 1968), 16–18.
6. Edward S. Boylan, 'The Chinese Cultural Style of Warfare', *Comparative Strategy* 3 (4)–1982, 353.
7. Sun Zi, *The Art of War* (see note 4), 114 (French edn).
8. Consult Scott A. Boorman, 'Deception in Chinese Strategy' in William W. Whitson (ed.) *The Military and Political Power in China in the 1970's* (New York, F. A. Praeger, 1972), 313–337.
9. Edgar Snow, *Red Star over China* (New York, Modern Library, 1938), 131.

10. For example: Etienne Balazs, 'Tradition et révolution en Chine', *Politique Etrangère* XIX(5), July 1954. 291–304; Jean Chesneaux, *Peasant Revolts in China, 1840–1949*, (London, Thames & Hudson, 1973); Jacques Guillermaz, *Le rôle militaire du paysan chinois*, (Paris, EPHE, 1959); *Mouvements populaires et sociétés secrètes en Chine au XIXe et XXe siècle.* Volume collectif préparé par Jean Chesneaux, Feiling Davis, Nguyen Nguyet Ho (Ouvrage publié avec le concours du CNRS. Paris): F. Maspéro *La Découverte*, 1970; Yuji Muramatsu, 'Some Themes in Chinese Rebel Ideologies', in Arthur F. Wright (ed.), *The Confucean Persuasion.* (Stanford California, Stanford University, 1960), 241–260; Stuart R. Schram, 'Mao Tse-tung and Secret Societies', *CQ* 27, July – September 1966, 1–13.
11. In this respect, one could indicate Teng Ssu-yu, *The Nien Army and their Guerrilla Warfare, 1851–1868.* (The Hague, Mouton, 1964).
12. On this latter point: Chalmers A. Johnson, 'Civilian Loyalties and Guerrilla Conflict', *World Politics* XIV(4), July 1962, 646–661.
13. Equally discussed in Ralph L. Powell, 'Maoist Military Doctrines', *Asian Survey* (hereafter *AS*) VIII(4), April 1968, 247.
14. *Chinese Communist Guerrilla Warfare Tactics.* Ed. with an Intr. by Gene Z. Hanrahan. Foreword by William R. Heaton, United States Air Force Academy, Colorado. Preface by D. J. Alberts, Captain, USAF, Dpt of Political Science and Philosophy, United States Air Force Academy, Colorado. 1st Ed. (New York, Columbia University, 1952. Boulder Colorado: Paladin, 1974). Respectively, 63–69, 75–93, 94–112, 113–115.
15. A bibliographical selection of works on Mao Zedong's military thinking: Cai Xiaoqian, *Mao Zedong Junshi Sixiang he Renmin Zhanzheng zhi Yanjiu* (Analysis of Mao Zedong's Military Thinking and People's War), Taibei, Studies on Communist China, 1971. 13–18; James E. Garvey, *Marxist–Leninist China: A Military and Social Doctrine.* (New York: Exposition, 1960), 243; Mao Tse-tung, *Basic Tactics.* Trans. and with an Intr. by Stuart R. Schram (New York: F. A. Praeger, 1966), 13–48 (Introduction); *Mao Tse-tung on Guerrilla Warfare.* Trans. with an Intr. by Brig. Gen. Samuel B. Griffith (New York, F. A. Praeger, 1961) 20–24; Stuart R. Schram, 1) *The Political Thought of Mao Tse-tung* (New York: F. A. Praeger, 1963), 193–211; 2) 'The Military "Deviation" of Mao Tse-tung', *Problems of Communism* (hereafter *PC*) XIII (1), January–February 1964. 49–56; 3) 'On the Nature of Mao Tse-tung's "Deviation" in 1927', *CQ* 18, April–June 1964. 55–66.
16. Cf. Jean Chesneaux, *op. cit.* note 10, 72–73 (French ed.).
17. For this latter point, cf. Yuji Muramatsu, *op. cit.* note 10.
18. Harlan W. Jencks, *From Muskets to Missiles. Politics and Professionalism in the Chinese Army, 1945–1981* (Boulder, Colorado, Westview, 1982), 15.
19. William W. Whitson, *The Chinese High Command. A History of Communist China Military Politics (1927–1971).* With the collaboration of Huang Chen-hsia (New York, F. A. Praeger, 1973), 14–15.
20. Ibid.; for an analysis of the difference between *Unified Strategy* and *Integral Strategy*: Raymond L. Garthoff, *Soviet Military Doctrine.* (Glencoe, Illinois, Free Press, 1953), 26 and next.

21. Refer, for example, to: Jonathan D. Pollack, 'The Evolution of Chinese Strategic Thought' in *New Directions in Strategic Thinking.* Ed. by Robert O'Neil and Major David Horner. (London, G. Allen & Unwin, 1981), 137–152.
22. A Chinese source precisely establishing this distinction could be found in: Ye Jianying, 'Developing Advanced Military Science of Chinese Proletariat'. *Renmin Ribao* (hereafter *RMRB*), 15 March 1979.
23. Mao Zedong, 'On Protracted War' (May 1938) in *Selected Military Writings of Mao Tse-tung* (hereafter *SMWM*) (Beijing, Foreign Language Press, 1967), 226–227. Emphasis added.
24. Ibid, 217–218.
25. Beyond the abundant literature in this respect, see Kim Yu-nan, 'China's Response to India and Vietnam: A Comparative Analysis'. *Sino–Soviet Studies* V (2), April 1981, 189–220 (in Korean with a substantial summary in English). On China's use of force in international relations, see: Kenneth E. Bauzon, 'China and the Use of Force in International Relations', *Asian Thought and Society* V (15), December 1980, 259–281; Davis D. Bobrow, 'Peking's Military Calculus', World Politics XVI (2), January 1964, 287–301; Angus M. Fraser, 'Use of the PLA in Foreign Affairs', *PC* XXIV (6), November–December 1975. 13–25; Gerald Segal, 'The PLA and Chinese Foreign Policy Decision-Making'. *International Affairs* 57 (3), Summer 1981, 419–456; Allen S. Whiting, 'The Use of Force in Foreign Policy by the People's Republic of China', *The Annals of the American Academy of Political and Social Science* 402, July 1972, 35–62. On Beijing's crisis management practice: Steve A. Chan, 'Chinese Conflict Calculus and Behaviour – Assessment from a Perspective of Conflict Management', *World Politics* XXX (3), April 1978, 391–410; Robert B. Mahoney, Jr. and Richard P. Clayberg, *Analysis of the Chinese Crisis Management Experience: Summary Report*, Arlington (VA): CAC1 (AD-A071-483/2GA), 1979; Edward Ross, 'Chinese Conflict Management', *MR* LX (1), January 1980. 13–25.
26. Steve A. Chan, ibid., 401.
27. According to John K. Fairbank, this seems to be a Chinese traditional attitude: '... China's invasion of South and Southeast Asia by land (Nepal, 1792; North Burma, 1766–70; and North Vietnam, 1788–89) were not attempts of conquest but merely over-the-border chastisements to re-establish the proper order ...' John K. Fairbank, 'China's Foreign Policy in Historical Perspective', *Foreign Affairs* 47 (3), April 1969. 463.
28. '*zhanzheng he zhanzheng zhidao de guilü*' and '*zhanzheng he zhanlüe de lilun*', Ye Jianying, *op. cit.* note 22.
29. *Jun Zhixue* and *Junshi Dilixue.* Ibid.
30. 'The science of strategy, the science of campaigns and the science of tactics are all components of Chinese military science. The science of strategy deals with the laws that govern the war situation as a whole. The science of campaigns deals with the laws that govern campaigns and is applied in directing campaigns. The science of tactics deals with the laws that govern battles and is applied in directing battles'. Note 2 in Mao Zedong, 'Problems of Strategy in China's Revolutionary War' (December 1936). *SMWM, op. cit.* note 23, 147.
31. Ibid, 210–211.

32. Ibid, 246. Emphasis added.
33. *'hecheng jundui xietong zuozhan'*
34. *'baocun ziji, xiaomie diren'*
35. For example, see: *China Under the Four Modernizations.* Part I. Selected Papers Submitted to the Joint Economic Committee. Congress of the United States. 97th Congress. 2nd Session. 13 August 1982. (Washington (DC), USGPO, 1982).
36. Consult: Gerald Segal, 'China's Nuclear Posture for the 1980s', *Survival* XXII (1), January/February 1981, 11–18, and Chapter 7 in this volume.
37. In this respect, refer to well-balanced argumentations respectively developed by June Teufel Dreyer, Sydney Jammes and John J. Sloan in *The Implications of US–China Military Relations*, A Workshop sponsored by the Committee on Foreign Relations, United States Senate, and the Congressional Research Service, Library of Congress. 96th Congress, 1st Session. 28 October 1981 (Washington (DC): USGPO, January 1982), 6–9, 22–23, 31–32.
38. Cf. the analysis developed by Paul H. B. Godwin, *The Chinese Tactical Air Forces and Strategic Weapons Program: Development, Doctrine and Strategy.* (Maxwell AFB, Alabama): Documentary Research Division, Air University Library, Air University (*Air University Documentary Research Study*, AU-201-78 AUL), April 1978, 48–50.
39. See William C. Green and David S. Yost, 'Soviet Military Options Regarding China' in *China, the Soviet Union and the West. Strategic and Political Dimensions in the 1980s.* Ed. by Douglas T. Stuart and William T. Tow. (Boulder, Colorado, Westview, 1982), 135–144 and the enlarged version of this text that appeared in *Issues and Studies* (hereafter *IS*) XVII (4), April 1981, 10–31.
40. Song Shilun, 'Mao Zedong's Military Thinking Is the Guide to Our Army's Victories' (originally carried in *Junshi Xueshu* 7–1981), *Hongqi* (hereafter *HQ*) 16, 16 August 1981, 15 (*Daily Report China* FBIS-CHI-81-180, 17 September 1981, K22).
41. Xu Xianggian, 'Heighten Vigilance, Be Ready To Fight'. *HQ* 8-1978. 48 (*SWB* FE/5881/C/7. 6 August 1979. Emphasis added.
42. Gerald Segal, *The Soviet 'Threat' at China's Gates.* (London: Institute for the Study of Conflict *Conflict Studies*, 143, 1983).
43. A similar thesis is developed by Paul H. B. Godwin, *Doctrine, Strategy, and Ethic: The Modernization of the Chinese People's Liberation Army.* (Maxwell AFB (Ala.): Documentary Research Branch, Academic Publications Division, 3825th Academic Services Group, Air University (*Air University Documentary Research Study*, AU-202-77-3825 ASG), June 1977. 77–78.
44. In this respect, the Chinese envisage opposing a PLA Infantry Corps against one Soviet Motorised Rifle Division. See 'Gongshi Xingdongzhong de Liliang Duibi he Yunyong' (Contrasts and Applications of Offensive Forces in Move), *JFJB* 30 October 1981, Cited in *Zhonggong Yanjiu* (hereafter *ZY*) 16 (3), March 1982. 94–95.
45. *Jiefangjun Huabao* (hereafter *JFJHB*) 7-1980. 10–11; *JFJHB* 11-1980. 13; *JFJHB* 1-1981. 2–5; *JFJHB* 5-1981. 12–15; *JFJHB* 1-1982. 2–5; *JFJHB* 4-1982. 8–11 etc.

46. Cf. Yan Wu, Xiong Zhengyan, and Peng Ziqiang, 'Mighty Troops Shake the Mountains – The People's Liberation Army Marching Toward Modernization', *RMRB*, 23 October 1981 (*Daily Report China* FBIS-CHI-81-211, 2 November 1981, K.4).
47. See Xu Baoshan, 'We Must Be Prepared To Fight Nuclear War in First Stages of Any Future War'. *JFJB*. 16 September 1979 (*China Report* 88/JPRS 7 58 25, 6 April 1980. 97–99).
48. 'Decision for the Efficient Working of the Military Academies', *NCNA*, 24 April 1978, and 'Decision on Strengthening the Army's Education and Training', *NCNA*. 3 May 1978.
49. Gong Gan, 'To Realise Modernisation in National Defence', *RMRB* 31 May 1978, Emphasis added.
50. *Beijing Radio*. 16 May 1979 (*Daily Report – People's Republic of China* FBIS-CHI-79-55. L1).
51. 'We Must Conscientiously Explore New Operational Methods'. *JFJB*. 9 April 1979. Cited by Chien T'ieh, 'Modernization of Peiping's National Defense', *IS* XVIII (12), December 1982, 45–46.
52. See generally: Gerald Segal, *The Soviet ...*, *op. cit.* note 42. Also: PLA Political Academy, 'A Preliminary Discussion of the Application and Development of the Ten Major Principles of Operation in Future Wars'. *JFJB*. 18 October 1979. Cf. ibid., 47. On the Army regularization, chronologically see: 'Make Fresh Contributions to the Modernisation of the National Defence', *JFJB* Ed. 27 September 1981; 'Build a Modernised and Regularised Powerful Revolutionary Army', *JFJB* Ed. 1 October 1981; Yang Xiushan, 'It Is Necessary To Reinstate the Regularisation Content in Army Building', *JFJB* 22 January 1982. For an excellent analysis based on these sources, consult Zhang Tianlin, 'Dui Zhonggong Chongxin Qiangdiao "Xiandaihua, Zhengguihua" Jianjun Fangzhen zhi Yanxi' (Analysis of the Chinese communist Army-building's Strong New Stress on 'Modernisation, Regularisation'), *ZY* 16 (3), March 1982. 98–106. On the PLA's large scale manoeuvres of September 1981: see a series of reports by the Chinese medias in *Daily Report China* FBIS-CHI-81-187. 28 September 1981, K1–K10. Among the analyses and comments, consult Michäel Weisskopf, 'Chinese Armed Forces Combine To Stage Largest Known Maneuvers in Peacetime'. *International Herald Tribune*, 28 September 1981.

2 Civil–Military Relations

ELLIS JOFFE*

The professed principle governing civil–military relations in the People's Republic of China has always been that 'the Party commands the gun', but the reality of these relations has been much more varied and complex. Although the basic framework of civil control of the military has been maintained throughout the history of the regime, its effectiveness has been uneven. Over the years the People's Liberation Army has moved across the entire spectrum of roles assumed by armies in politics – from political quiescence to political ascendancy, and then back again, though not to the starting point. As a result of these changes, the balance of power between the Party and the PLA has shifted sharply several times. The purpose of this chapter is to examine the changes in the role of the military and their effect on civil–military relations in the People's Republic.[1]

POLITICAL QUIESCENCE

Until the early 1960s, civil–military relations were marked by the political quiescence of the PLA.[2] This does not mean, of course, that the PLA was passive or apolitical, but that it operated under two constraints. First, it did not intervene by direct action in national politics to promote its institutional interests. Second, it did not intervene in issues outside the sphere of such interests to resolve leadership conflicts. Aside from these constraints, the PLA was highly active both

---

* The first part of this chapter is based on a paper which I delivered at a conference on 'The Analysis of Power and Policy in the PRC Since 1949' which was held in Saarbrücken, Germany on 22–27 August, 1982. I would like to thank the Truman Research Institute of the Hebrew University for support and Pamela Lubell for research assistance.

as a civic force implementing national policies and as a pressure group advocating its views in policy-making councils.

In the performance of non-military tasks the PLA acted as an arm of the Party according to the tasks assigned to it, whether these were in land reform, emergency aid, or the Great Leap Forward. These tasks contracted or expanded in line with the direction of the Party leadership, and at no time did the PLA attempt to take over positions of power on its own. This was most clearly demonstrated by its willingness to relinquish military domination of local administration in 1954, once the civil organs were ready to assume these duties.

If the military made no attempt to overstep the limits of political activity set down for it by the Party, it did not hesitate to clash with the Party leadership when its professional interests were involved. Such clashes began in the mid-1950s and reached a climax during the Great Leap Forward – arising from the Party's efforts to reverse the trend toward military professionalism and from differences over strategic issues. There is no doubt that the military leaders vigorously propagated their views in inner Party circles, as attested by the vehemence with which the Party rejected these views in the press. There is also no doubt that with regard to some areas which were in dispute the military took steps to put their views into practice by limiting the activities of political commissars and by letting Party organisations in the army fall into disarray. At no time, however did the military make a direct move to force the adoption of its views nor, as far as is known, did it threaten to do so. Despite the frictions between the Party and the PLA, civilian supremacy over the military was never in doubt.

Nowhere was the restraint of the military better demonstrated than after the dismissal of the Defence Minister, Peng Dehuai, at the Lushan Plenum of the Central Committee in August 1959. Granted that conflict over military issues was not the only, and perhaps not the central, reason for Peng's downfall, there is little doubt that the build-up of tensions deriving from this conflict played a key role in the showdown. As the chief spokesman of the officer corps, Peng had stood in the forefront of its resistance to the Party's crackdown on military professionalism. Although some of his colleagues may have disapproved of his political tactics, it is certain that Peng's views on military matters were widely shared in the armed forces, as evidenced by the periodic resurfacing of such views in subsequent years, and their full-scale adoption in the post-Mao period. Despite this, the military made no overt move to rally to Peng's support. Why?

The answer to this question has to be sought in the basic factors which govern the relations of the Chinese military with the civil authorities. These factors not only accounted for the political quiescence of the PLA at the time of the Peng Dehuai affair, but also decisively affected its behaviour after it intervened in politics. One central factor has been the great integrative power of modern Chinese nationalism. Fueling this nationalism is the searing memory of China's impotence and humiliation by foreign countries, especially during the warlord period; memories which doubtless inhibit China's military leaders from taking any step which even remotely smacks of 'warlordism.' Another factor has been the commitment of China's military leaders to the principle of civilian supremacy over the military, a commitment born out of their nationalism and buttressed by their indoctrination, training, and experience. This premise has been so deeply ingrained that the military have never violated it of their own accord, and even when they were forced by circumstances to do so, most of them obviously regarded it as an exception to their perceived role. Adding organisational strength to these factors has been the network of controls instituted by the Party in the armed forces which, despite its weakness during certain periods, has acted as a powerful check on military officers. A further check has been the innate conservatism of the professional military as well as their discipline. Finally, forged out of all these factors has been what is probably the most elusive and yet the most elemental constraint on the military: the ethic of professionalism and of non-intervention in political affairs by direct action. Given these factors, why then did the Chinese military intervene by force in the political process several years later, and did this intervention signify the collapse of civil supremacy over the military?

FROM INVOLVEMENT TO INTERVENTION

The Chinese military moved into the political arena not because the factors governing the Party–PLA relationship broke down, but because of developments extraneous to this relationship. These developments are well known and need not be recapitulated in detail. They were dominated by an intra-Party conflict that was triggered by the failure of the Great Leap Forward and centred on the fundamental issues relating to China's development strategy. The conflict entered a crucial phase after 1962, when Party leaders opposed to Mao's concepts sought to evade the Chairman's directives on the level of policy implementation. As the gap between declaratory policy and actual implementation by the Party bureaucracy widened. Mao and his supporters became increasingly alienated from the Party and its leaders. By the middle of the decade Mao concluded that it was necessary to shake up the Party and to reinfuse it with revolutionary values in order to overcome its resistance to revolutionary policies.

To accomplish this, Mao turned to the PLA, which under Lin Biao's leadership had curbed its professionalism and revived its revolutionary qualities. While Lin's efforts took professional interests into consideration, the revolutionary vigor of the PLA contrasted sharply with the bureaucratism and unresponsiveness of the Party. Consequently Mao began to use the PLA in order to prod the Party, a process that began in 1963 with campaigns that reached a climax a year later when the entire nation was exhorted to 'learn from the Army', and military officers were assigned to civilian organs.

Although the aim of these campaigns was limited to reforming the Party rather than replacing it with the PLA, they marked the start of the PLA's involvement in politics. This involvement radically, if still subtly, changed the role of the PLA. For the first time it was pulled into the political arena not to carry out the policies of a united leadership, but as an ally of one group against its opponents in a leadership that was becoming increasingly divided.

The PLA thus did not intrude into politics against the wishes of the civilian leadership, but was brought into the political arena by this leadership. To be sure, Lin Biao and other senior military leaders readily responded to Mao's initiative, whether out of conviction or calculation – or a mixture of both – but there were misgivings. One who voiced them was the Chief-of-Staff, Luo Ruiqing, who opposed the army's new role on the grounds that it damaged professional competence. However his opposition, which became bound up with power relations and strategic differences, was overridden without any disruptions and he was dismissed. The way was clear for Mao to launch the Cultural Revolution with the support of the PLA.

If other army leaders viewed such use of the PLA unfavorably, they kept their views to themselves – then and, with few exceptions, later. One reason for their silence was unquestionably their discipline. Another was doubtless that during the initial stages of the Cultural Revolution the army, as distinguished from its leadership, was kept out of the struggle. While the PLA leadership intervened in the conflict, the public manifestation of this intervention was chiefly verbal. Army units remained on the sidelines, apart from providing logistic support to the Red Guards. During this period, Lin Biao and his colleagues could reap the political benefits that accrued from backing the Maoists without subjecting the PLA to the bruising consequences of becoming entangled in the political battles that were raging throughout China. This situation, however, did not last long. As the Cultural Revolution escalated, so did the involvement of the army.

This escalation occurred owing to the inability of the Maoists to purge the Party organisations by using the Red Guards. Thwarted in their efforts by the unexpectedly forceful resistance of the Party Bureaucracy, and faced with mounting chaos as a result of these efforts, the Maoists decided that the only alternative to terminating the Cultural Revolution was to commit their remaining asset – the PLA – in support of the 'revolutionary' forces. Embroiling the army in political struggles, however, was an unprecedented move that was opposed by some senior military leaders on the grounds that it would subject the PLA to dangerous strains. After these leaders were purged the PLA was ordered, in what was undoubtedly the single most important decision relating to the political role of the military, to intervene in the Cultural Revolution in order to 'support the Left.'

This decision, as predicted by its opponents, indeed subjected the army to intolerable strains, which became apparent from the outset of its entry into the political fray in January 1967. Confronted with contradictory directives to maintain order and to support the Left, regional military commanders generally opted for stability rather than revolution. To fill the vacuum created by the paralysis of Party and administrative organs, military commanders established, in coordination with moderate leaders in Peking, Revolutionary Committees, ostensibly made up of veteran cadres, representatives of revolutionary organisations and the army but which, in effect, the army dominated. Where such Committees were not set up, the PLA ruled directly through Military Control Committees.

The army's preference for order and for working with old-time cadres aroused the opposition of revolutionary activists, to which the army responded in accordance with the shifts in the balance of power among the radical and moderate wings of the Beijing leadership. As the balance shifted, the behaviour of the PLA alternated between repression and restraint. Eventually, proponents of the hard line toward the anarchic 'revolutionary' elements won, and by the time the Cultural Revolution was terminated in April 1969, the Red Guard organisations had largely been broken up, and the power of their mentors in Beijing appreciably diminished. As the Party organisations were still in disarray or were defunct, the PLA became the supreme political and administrative authority in the provinces and, largely as a consequence of this, a central force in Beijing politics. The Cultural Revolution thus completely shattered the structure of civil–military relations in China.

What it did not shatter was the principle of civilian supremacy over the military which had governed civil–military relations prior to the intervention of the PLA in politics. Throughout the upheaval, powerful commanders in China's far-flung regions continued to accept Beijing's authority even when that authority had been greatly weakened by internecine strife and when the Party's political control organs in the army had ceased functioning. Many commanders, to be sure, circumvented central directives when these were confused or contradicted their desire for stability, but they never openly defied Beijing's authority. The one commander who broke this rule, Chen Zaidao of Wuhan, was not supported by his colleagues, although he did overtly what most of them did covertly. This fundamental commitment of the military to the principle of civilian supremacy, even when practice did not conform to it, was essential for the subsequent relinquishment of political power by the military.

If the principle of civilian supremacy withstood the terrible stresses of the Cultural Revolution, the unity of the army did not. Never monolithic to begin with, the PLA had until the Cultural Revolution been divided by disagreements over military policy and strategy between officers whose main orientation was professional and others who were more politically inclined. However, the intrusion of the army into the political struggle created new rifts which were much deeper than previous divisions and had nothing to do with military affairs. The main rift was between Lin Biao and some of his colleagues in the high command who had become identified with the policies of the radical left, on the one hand and, on the other hand, most regional commanders and professional military leaders who had to bear the bitter consequences of these policies. Not only had Lin failed to protect his regional commanders from Red Guard attacks, but he dispatched main force units to support radical organisations which the regional military were trying to suppress, thereby exacerbating intra-army rivalries. These rivalries isolated the Lin Biao group within the military establishment and undercut Lin's power base in national politics. Paradoxically, they also eased the eventual transfer of power from the PLA to the Party, for had the PLA been united under Lin Biao its withdrawal from politics would probably have been a much more difficult process.

DISENGAGEMENT FROM POLITICS

Although the Cultural Revolution catapulted China's military commanders to positions of regional rulers, the end of the upheaval did not lead to a relinquishment of these positions. On the contrary, the military continued to consolidate its political power by directing the process of Party reconstruction, which got under way after the turmoil. Since the reconstituted Party Committees were supposed to have higher authority than the army-dominated Revolutionary Committees, the Party leadership viewed the reconstruction process as a way of getting the military out of politics and reasserting civilian control over the army. The military, however, did not co-operate. Instead of stepping aside in favour of civilians, the military used their political posts to ensure that their representatives would be appointed to leading positions in the new Party Committees, either as first secretaries (21 out of 29) or as members of provincial Party secretariats (62 per cent). China's political system thus became military-dominated, and Mao's time-honoured dictum that 'the gun shall never be allowed to command the Party' was left by the wayside in practice.

If the professional values of the military had remained intact, and if the military had been reluctant to intervene in politics in the first place, why did they refuse to withdraw from the political arena? The simplest explanation is that power, once acquired whatever the initial impetus, is not easily given up. This explanation, however, is too simple, given the readiness of the military to do just that a short time later. A more specific explanation has to take into account the hostility of most military commanders to the radical Left, and their determination to block radical representatives from gaining positions of power. As long as this possibility existed, the military were not prepared to surrender their posts and to expose China again to the threat of disorder, for it was the breakdown of order that had impelled them to intervene in politics in the first place. What they were prepared to do, as later events indicated, was vacate their posts in favour of veteran cadres, but these cadres were prevented from returning to political activity by the Left in the immediate aftermath of the Cultural Revolution.

Internal PLA rivalries also contributed in the short run to its continued hold on political power. In order to strengthen the PLA as his power base in national politics, Lin Biao sought not only to strengthen its political position but also to replace most regional commanders, who had ' accounts to settle' with him, with his supporters during the reconstruction of the Party. These attempts not only injected an additional element of conflict into the process of reconstruction, but also strengthened the determination of regional commanders to hang on to their positions. Rival PLA groups thus had different motives for remaining in the political arena, but the result was a failure to return power to the civilians.

This failure united the moderate and radical wings of the Beijing leadership in a coalition against Lin Biao, who was held responsible for the domination of the military. Crucial to this coalition was the support or acquiescence of Lin's opponents among the regional commanders and professional military leaders at the centre, as evidenced by the ability of Mao and Zhou Enlai to isolate Lin with relative ease. Also working against Lin were his political ambitions and Mao's disillusionment with Lin as the Chairman's successor-designate. As a result of his isolation, Lin and his close colleagues acted in desperation, and Lin was apparently killed in a plane crash in Mongolia after allegedly planning to assassinate Mao.

The ignominious downfall of Lin Biao, and with him the chief-of-staff and other members of the General Staff, had an immediate impact on the political status of the PLA. It removed a major obstacle to the reassertion of Party primacy over the military. It deprived the PLA of a powerful voice at the centre, and left it without an effective outlet for channeling its demands. And it discredited the military, putting it on the defensive, even though the Party leadership drew a distinction between the Lin Biao group and the rest of the PLA. In these propitious circumstances the Party leadership intensified its efforts to chip away at the political power of the PLA.

These efforts took several forms. First, the political profile of the PLA was lowered considerably; its prestige as a political force was diminished, and Party supremacy over the military was stressed. Secondly, the importance of the PLA's concentration on military tasks and raising its professional standards was emphasised, presumably both to placate the military and to justify its withdrawal from political functions. Thirdly and most concretely, the political power of the PLA as measured by military representation in national and regional ruling organs was reduced. Thus, in the period between the fall of Lin Biao and the death of Mao, 9 of the 21 officers who were also first secretaries of the provincial Party Committees gave up their concurrent posts; PLA representatives in provincial Party Committees were reduced by some 16 per cent, in the Central Committee by about 14 per cent, in the Politburo by some 17 per cent; Military Control Committees were abolished; and 8 of the 11 Military Region Commanders were reshuffled.

The trend toward disengagement was inseparable from developments on the political scene. The fall of Lin Biao and the consequent weakening of the radical Left were used by moderate leaders to pursue policies which downplayed Maoist values, and to rehabilitate veteran cadres who were indispensable to the implementation of these policies. To these cadres military commanders were prepared to hand over power, but their position was far from secure owing to periodic radical assaults on the moderate leaders and their policies. The radicals also attacked the PLA and its veteran leaders. In this state of leadership instability and PLA antagonism toward part of the leadership, their withdrawal from politics stopped short of full-scale relinquishment of positions of power.

AFTER MAO: PROFESSIONALISM AND POLITICAL DISSENT

That the military remained a key force in politics in the twilight of the Maoist period was demonstrated in the succession struggle that broke out after Mao's death. The outcome of this struggle, which pitted the radical leaders against a coalition of moderates led by Hua Guofeng, was decided swiftly and without any disruptions owing to the intervention of the military on the side of the moderate coalition.

Military intervention in the succession struggle had several aspects. The army carried out a coup against the radical leaders – now labelled the 'gang of four' – and put them under arrest. It mounted a major propaganda effort after the coup in order to strengthen Hua's position by declaring the support of the PLA for the new leadership. And it was poised to intervene against radical resistance had the need for such action arisen. The military thus became the main prop of the Hua Goufeng leadership in the transition period, gaining a central position in the post-Mao power structure.

This position was reflected in the patronising attitude of the military press towards Hua and in the deference of the new leadership towards the military. It was also reflected in the remarkable outburst of professional demands from the military and in the receptivity of the leadership to the basic arguments of the military, if not to its priorities. More concretely, military representation in the Politburo elected by the 11th Party Congress in 1977 rose to 12 out of the 23 full members (as compared with 7 out of 21 in the previous one), while its strength in the Central Committee remained at about 30 per cent.

The pivotal role of the military in the power structure began to decrease with the emergence of Deng Xiaoping as the dominant figure and the revitalisation of the Party apparatus, staffed increasingly by cadres who had been purged during the Cultural Revolution. Much more assertive than Hua and less dependent on the military oligarchy for support, Deng has strengthened political and personal control over the armed forces. First as chief-of-staff of the PLA and vice-chairman of the Military Affairs Commission, and since 1980 as the Commission's chairman, Deng has appointed his supporters to key posts, reshuffled regional commanders to reduce their political power, and completed the process of returning the PLA to the barracks. Under Deng, in short, the imbalance in the Party–PLA relationship which had existed during the transition period has been redressed in favour of the Party.

While this shift may have been distasteful to some military leaders, it has not constituted a visible source of tension between the Party and the PLA. For one thing the military, as has been emphasised, are committed to the principle of civilian supremacy and have not resisted its implementation when the civilians have been in a position to lead effectively. For another, while some officers may have developed a taste for political power and its perquisites, the bulk of the professional military has probably welcomed the disengagement of the army from political affairs, since this has freed them from troublesome pressures and has enabled the army to concentrate on its military mission. Furthermore, political control under Deng has not been tantamount to interference in the activities of the officers, for it has been exercised in a cautious manner at all levels of the hierarchy so as not to hinder the performance of the military's professional duties.

Reassertion of Party control over the PLA, however, has not prevented the appearance of dissent in the armed forces as a result of Deng's policies. None the less, Deng and his colleagues have not had to confront a united and hostile military, as some observers have suggested, because opposition in the military to the Party's policies has been diffuse. This opposition has derived from different issues backed by different groups in the military, but owing to conflicting interests these groups have not coalesced against the Party leadership. On the contrary, opposition of one group in the military on certain issues has not precluded its support for the leadership on additional issues against other groups in the military. Coalitions, in short, have been issue-oriented and have cut across institutional lines. This disparity among military groups has been a vital source of strength for the Party leadership. An assessment of civil–military relations under Deng, therefore, requires an effort, even if partly speculative, to sort out the issues in dispute and the groups behind them.

One cluster of issues concerns the technological modernisation of the armed forces and involves the professional military. How disruptive these issues have been of civil–military relations depends on the depth of the differences between the Party leaders and the professional officers. At first glance, these differences are not easily reconcilable. Demands from the military, especially during the transition period, for a sweeping renovation of conventional weapons systems was rejected by the leadership on the grounds that economic modernisation must precede the procurement of weapons, and that only after a solid industrial and technological infrastructure has been laid can there be significant improvements in weapons. This rejection has been reflected in the published military budgets of the post-Mao years: expenditure reached a high point of 22.3 billion yuan in 1979 as a result of the Vietnam war, but was reduced to 19.3bn in 1980 and again to 17.5bn in 1981, rising slightly to 17.9bn in 1982. It has also been reflected in the extremely limited purchases of weapons systems from abroad, despite a flurry of visits by Chinese military delegations to various countries in the late 1970s.

On closer scrutiny, however, the gap between the Party leadership and the professional officers is narrower than initially appears. Several reasons cumulatively lead to this conclusion. However grudgingly or reluctantly, the professional officers must realise that rapid and comprehensive re-equipment of China's conventional forces is simply not possible if modernisation in other sectors is to be given a reasonable chance of success. This is because since the late 1950s these forces, with the exception of select sectors, have not kept up with developments in weapons technology and are considered to have fallen 15 to 20 years behind modern armies. The only way to close this gap quickly is by massive purchases from abroad, but the costs of such purchases are awesome. Just how awesome was indicated in a US Department of Defense study in 1979, which estimated that the purchase by China of American weapons and services needed to give China a 'confident capability' against a Soviet conventional attack would cost US$41 to 63 billion[3] at 1977 prices.

Even if possible, massive imports of military technology involve risks which cannot be taken lightly by Party and PLA leaders alike. One is that such purchases would make China dependent on the supplier for know-how and spare parts, and would make it vulnerable to political pressures or sudden cut-offs, as occurred when the Soviets abruptly terminated their military assistance in 1960. Another is that imported weapons systems would be replaced by more advanced generations of weapons by the time the Chinese had assimilated them. A third is that the Chinese would find it difficult rapidly to absorb large amounts of sophisticated technology owing to the low educational level of their troops.

Given these considerations, it is inconceivable that even the optimal demands of the most extreme officers extended to the overall updating of China's armed forces. Statements to that effect, particularly notable shortly after the downfall of the 'gang of four' which released the military from constraints that had previously prevented them from voicing their views, should therefore be attributed to rhetoric and posturing rather than to realistic demands. What precisely these demands have been is difficult to determine, but they obviously lie between the extremes of extensive imports at one end and continued self-reliance at the other. The military has evidently demanded the selective import of weapons technology to undergird domestic weapons production, rather than the purchase of ready-made weapons systems in large quantities (although small purchases of this type have obviously been advocated).[4]

The Party leadership, while not averse to this demand, has put more emphasis on self-reliance and on making do with available weapons and equipment.[5] Secondly, while conceding the need to tie military modernisation to economic development, the military have pressed for accelerating this modernisation as the economy advances.[6] The Party leadership, on the other hand, while conceding the need for military modernisation, has stressed that this modernisation should be gradual lest it affect economic progress.[7] In short, the differences between the Party leaders and the professional military have been a matter of degree rather than dogma, and they appear to have been contained by an understanding based on a mutual recognition of objective constraints and possibilities.[8]

Contributing to this understanding is not only the prospect of better days in the future, but also developments in the present. Despite the economic limitations, procurement of weapons has not been frozen. Since 1975 China has maintained a 'low yet constant level of military production,' manufacturing almost 100 pieces of equipment ranging from rifles to ICBMs.[9] If reports that since 1980 China has supplied Iraq with military equipment worth about US$4 billion even approach the true state of affairs, then its level of production has hardly been low.[10] Moreover, some of the weapons supplied by the Chinese – such as the T69 tank, which is reportedly equipped with infra-red equipment and laser range-finders[11] – indicate that the Chinese have assimilated important technological advances and have put them into mass production. Assuming that the PLA's most urgent needs are met before weapons are exported, and that at least part of the earnings from these exports are earmarked for the military sector, then the Party has done much to satisfy the military.

In areas not limited by economic considerations, it has done a great deal. Training has been upgraded with an emphasis on operations of combined forces. Organisation has been streamlined and discipline has been tightened. Educational and technical levels have been raised. Military academies and officer training have received special attention. Logistics have been improved and geared to the needs of modern warfare. The military role of the militia has been downgraded. And PLA participation in non-military duties has been reduced.

The dominant considerations in these far-reaching reforms have been professional, and their aim has been to enhance the combat capability of the armed forces. Political work has been explicitly subordinated to the attainment of this objective, and the role of political commissars has been implicitly downgraded. Not since the mid-1950s, and in many ways more than at that time, have professional officers carried so much weight in moulding the character of the Chinese armed forces. In short, the professional military seem to have little grounds for serious disaffection with the Deng leadership. They apparently regard Deng's policies as acceptable, if not satisfactory, and have found it possible to work out their differences not by intensifying disputes, but by restraint and rapport.

The same does not hold true of another, more politically oriented, segment of PLA officers. Unlike the professional military, these officers have found the Party's policies unpalatable, and unlike the professional military they have intervened in issues which lie outside the corporate concerns of the PLA. In short, while the PLA as an institution has returned to the barracks, and while its professional commanders have confined their activities to internal military affairs, this group of military leaders has intruded into the political arena and has publicly expressed its dissent from national policies.

Centred in the PLA's General Political Department and its subordinate organs, this group has apparently coalesced around the old marshal Ye Jianying. Ye undoubtedly does not view himself, and is not viewed by others in China, solely as a representative of the military, but as a national leader whose concerns are not limited by institutional boundaries. Although Ye has been identified in the past with the professional military and was a prime target of the 'gang of four,' closely connected personal and political reasons have apparently turned him into a focus of opposition to the policies of Deng Xiaoping. The personal reasons presumably stem from the fact that, despite radical attacks, Ye weathered the Cultural Revolution and his stature is linked to Mao's legacy. Furthermore, in the transition period Ye was the central pillar in the coalition led by Hua Guofeng, who not only symbolised continuity with the Maoist era but who unlike Deng, had been heavily dependent on Ye because of his own precarious political position. Ye's political motives presumably derived from his abiding belief in central facets of the Maoist ideology, and his concern for the future of the Chinese revolution as a result of Deng's dilution, if not abandonment, of this ideology.

The evaluation of Mao's role in the history of the Chinese revolution has clearly been a divisive issue between Deng and the military. The Resolution on this question finally adopted after the Sixth Plenum of the Central Committee, in July 1981, is generally considered by observers to have been watered down compared with statements reportedly made by Deng, and this modification is attributed to pressure from the military. Even if this is true, there is no doubt that the Resolution's verdict is much harsher than that given by Ye Jianying in his important article marking the 30th anniversary of the regime in October 1979.

Related to the treatment of Mao's legacy has been the discontent of the military with the consequences of what it has perceived as the drift away from Maoist values in Chinese society. Many articles reflecting such discontent have been published by the *Liberation Army Daily*.[12] Specifically, Party policies in two areas have come under attack: ideology and economics. In the ideological sphere, the object of attack has been what the military has regarded as the trend toward 'bourgeois liberalism' and its deleterious effects on the nation's moral fibre and social discipline.[13]

A dangerous symptom of this liberal trend from the military's viewpoint was the film script *Unrequited Love* by Bai Hua, an intellectual who worked for the army. His script was a bitter portrayal of a patriotic young artist who was hounded to death by radical ultra-leftists. The film and its author became a focus of attack by the army paper, which denounced it for 'negating patriotism' and reflecting 'bourgeois liberalism'.[14]

The most serious expression of ideological dissent emanating from the military was contained in an article published in the Shanghai *Jiefang Ribao* of 28 August 1982 which, as it later turned out, was reprinted from the previous day's army paper, and which explicitly attacked the Party leadership for slack ideological guidance and failure to stop the spread of pernicious ideas.[15] Published on the eve of the 12th Party Congress, the article was clearly designed to provide ammunition to Deng's opponents.

The reaction of the Deng leadership was forceful. On 27 September the army paper published an abject self-criticism for printing the piece in the first place, and refuted its arguments at length.[16] On the same day Wei Guoqing, the director of the PLA's General Political Department, which is responsible for the paper, was dismissed.

Criticism from the army was also directed at the Party's economic policies, which were viewed as another manifestation of the departure from socialist values, leading to moral laxity and corruption.[17] One target of attack was the Party's pragmatic policy of decentralising agricultural production down to the family level.[18] Others objected on the more practical grounds that the income of army men's families would be adversely affected by the system of production responsibility.[19]

How should the dissent from the Party's policies be assessed in terms of its impact on civil–military relations? Such an assessment depends on several interrelated questions, the answers to which cannot be given with certainty. The first question is the extent of dissent. Judging by the efforts of the leadership to refute it and to indoctrinate officers in study classes,[20] dissatisfaction with Party policies has been extremely widespread. This does not mean, however, that all those participating in such classes had disagreed with the policies of the Party. Furthermore, not all disagreements derived from the same reasons. For instance, on the issue of family farming, those who criticised Party policy for negating Maoist values could hardly be the same officers who were dissatisfied because the policy hurt the income of peasants handicapped by having a son in the army.

More important, it is unlikely that many professional commanders were among the dissidents, given their long-standing doubts about the applicability of Maoist principles and their concern with material development as the basis for military modernisation. At any rate, no high-ranking officer associated with the professional military has publicly spoken out against the leadership's economic or ideological policies. In fact, these officers have probably supported Deng and his colleagues, thereby creating a coalition that transcended institutional lines and brought together, as has happened in the past, moderate Party leaders and the professional military against their more politically minded military colleagues, who were allied with other Party leaders.

The significance of the dissent also depends on the form of its manifestation. At the lower levels of the armed forces, dissent from Party policies was presumably manifested in discussion sessions and speeches. At the national level, the most obvious voice of the dissidents was the army paper, but they doubtless made their views known in inner Party circles as well. Whatever the form, there is not the slightest indication that the military made any move to press their views by direct action of some kind. In the case of military policies, officers have the risky option, to which they have resorted in the past, of sidestepping or sabotaging distasteful directives in the course of implementation. To officers dissatisfied with national policies, such an option is hardly open. Their dissent, therefore, has been solely verbal. The question then is: have they been able to influence Party policies in this way?

In the final analysis, the answer is no. Although some of the professional military have spoken openly about the need for change on specialised issues, and received a large degree of satisfaction, the same degree of success has not been achieved by these PLA men more concerned about affecting Deng's strategy of national development. Although marginal policy changes may have been made as a result of pressure from the military, the main thrust of Deng's policies not only remains unchanged, but has been consolidated and extended. The reaction of the Deng leadership to criticism from the military on core questions has been not to make basic concessions, but to crack down on the critics through indoctrination campaigns and dismissals. While this criticism has strained civil–military relations, it has neither diverted Deng from his course, nor cast doubt on the supremacy of the Party over the PLA.

NOTES AND REFERENCES

1. The section on the Maoist period is based on several of my articles: 'The Chinese Army Under Lin Piao' Prelude to Political Intervention', in John M. H. Lindbeck (ed.), *China: Management of a Revolutionary Society*, (University of Washington Press; 1971), 343–347; *Current Scene*, Hong Kong, vol. VIII, no. 18, 7 December 1970, 1–25; 'The Chinese Army After the Cultural Revolution: The Effects of Intervention', *The China*

Quarterly, no. 55, July–September, 1973, 450–477; (with Gerald Segal), 'The Chinese Army and Professionalism', *Problems of Communism*, November–December 1978, 1–19.
2. I have taken the term 'political quiescence' and some of the ideas associated with it from Timothy J. Colton, *Commissar, Commanders, and Civilian Authority: The Structure of Soviet Military Politics*, (Harvard University Press: 1979).
3. *New York Times*, 4 January 1980.
4. See, for example, the article in *Hongqi* no. 10 by the then defence minister Xu Xiangqian, in *FBIS* (Foreign Broadcast Information Service), 18 October 1979, L-14.
5. See for example, article in *Hongqi* no. 21, in *FBIS*, 19 November 1982, K-22.
6. See, for example, statement by the defence minister Zhang Aiping, Xinhua Domestic Service, 18 October 1982, in *FBIS*, 19 October 1982, K-1
7. Ibid.
8. For an important statement by the Defence Minister Zhang Aiping reflecting this understanding see his article 'Several Questions Concerning Modernisation of National Defence,' in *Hongqi*, no. 5, 1 March 1983, in *FBIS*, 17 March 1983, K-2–7.
9. *Allocation of Resources in the Soviet Union and China – 1981*. Hearings Before the Sub Committee on International Trade, Finance, and Security Economics of the Joint Economic Committee, Congress of the United States, part 7, Executive Sessions, 8 July and 15 October 1981, (Washington, US Government Printing Office, 1982), 153
10. I have worked out the US$4 billion as follows. On 22 November 1982 *Newsweek* quoted United States intelligence officials as saying that Iraq buys a quarter of its weaponry from China. A week later it reported that Iraq was spending about US$1 billion per month on the war effort against Iran. Over about two years that amounts to US$24 billion. If only one-half of this sum was spent on weapons, China's share comes to US$3 billion. In addition, the *Far Eastern Economic Review* reported on 3 February 1983 that Iraq concluded a deal to buy tanks from China worth US$1 billion. The total figure for China's supplies since the start of the Iran–Iraq war is thus US$4 billion, although this figure, of course, is highly tentative.
11. *Far Eastern Economic Review*, 3 February 1983.
12. For one example see, Beijing Domestic Service, 2 January 1981, in *FBIS*, 6 January 1981, L-25.
13. See, for example, Shijiazhuang Hebei Provincial Service, 14 April in *FBIS*, 28 April 1982, R-1.
14. See, for example, Beijing Domestic Service, 19 April 1981, in *FBIS*, 20 April 1981, K-1.
15. In *FBIS*, 29 September 1982, K-4–6.
16. This article was reprinted in the Shanghai *Jefang Ribao* of 28 September 1982, in *FBIS*, 4 October 1982, K-1–8.
17. Beijing Domestic Service, 27 March 1981, in *FBIS*, 1 April 1981, K-5.
18. Haikou Hainan Island Regional Service, 13 February 1981, in *FBIS*, 18 February 1981, P-1.

19. Beijing Xinhua Domestic Service, 5 April 1981, in *FBIS*, 9 April 1981 P-1.
20. Beijing Xinhua Domestic Service, 24 April 1981, in *FBIS*, 1981, K-19.

3 Towards a New Strategy?

PAUL GODWIN*

Since the mid-1970s, the modernisation of the Chinese People's Liberation Army has once again become a major issue in China, and following the 1979 border war with Vietnam the defence establishment has focused its attention on improving the armed forces' capability to conduct combined arms warfare. With the introduction of combined arms warfare as the central focus of training and tactics, modernising the PLA became distinctly more complex. Updating the PLA's equipment, improving its logistical support capabilities, and increasing the proficiency of the officer corps in properly utilising these capabilities are all specific aspects of the broad and difficult problem of determining the PLA's future strategies.

The question raised by the debates and discussions in the Chinese press in recent years is whether the defence establishment seeks only to modernise the current equipment of the Chinese forces. However, given repeated references over the past four years to the necessity of restructuring the armed forces, it would seem to be self-evident that simply upgrading the equipment of the current force structure is not the sole objective of current modernisation programmes. Also anticipated, and perhaps even now under way, is a revision of the way in which the service arms and branches of the PLA are to be redesigned to meet the demands of combined arms operations. The primary purpose of this essay is to suggest what appear to be the most likely changes that will occur over the next few years.

THE LEGACY OF THE PAST

As the Chinese wrestle once again with the complex and interrelated problems associated with modernising their armed forces, issues from

---

* The opinions expressed in this paper are those of the author and are not intended to represent the official policies of The Air University, the United States Air Force, or the Department of Defense.

the past have re-emerged. The past eight years have been marked by disputes over doctrine, strategy, and the allocation of resources between the military and civil sectors of the economy. Even as these continuing issues are debated and the problems associated with determining the appropriate manner of viewing Mao's concepts of war and strategy and the need for a 'revolutionary' army are debated in the press, China is deploying its first generation of intercontinental ballistic missiles (ICBM) and testing its sea-launched ballistic missile (SLBM) from a submerged submarine. In fact, there is a Janus-like quality to the Chinese defence establishment, for it reflects two aspects of war and strategy. One face looks back to the people's war tradition of PLA's past, while the other faces the complexities of strategic nuclear warfare and deterrence in the latter part of the twentieth century.

China's current military elite has within it the same potentially conflicting experiences. Their most successful military experiences were in conducting protracted revolutionary war, but as they moved into leading positions within the military hierarchy, changes in military technology required them to face the complexities of strategic nuclear warfare and the conduct of military operations on technologically advanced battlefields. The force structure they have to utilise is itself a clumsy mix of two sets of capabilities derived from uneven progress in developing the technology of war and a continuing commitment to Mao Zedong's principles of people's war. It is this mix of traditional Red Army values, the demands of current and future wars, and the essentially *ad hoc* development of the current force structure that has led to many problems in the defence establishment.

Within the military leadership, however, there is a major faction that seeks a thorough revision of the current force structure and strategies for its employment. A November 1982 article in the Party's authoritative journal *Hong Qi* stated explicitly that the impact of modern weapons, science and technology on warfare has 'presented new problems to the patterns, strategy and tactics of warfare as well as to military organisation. The PLA is now engaged in the world of readjusting, reorganising and restructuring'.[1] Unfortunately, no precise outlines have yet appeared to indicate what 'readjusting, reorganising and restructuring' the PLA means, but inferences can be drawn from the discussions in the Chinese press and the experience of China's military elite.

The present force structure simply grafted air and naval forces to a pre-existing ground force. The ground forces are deployed into geographical areas determined by provincial boundaries. Provinces are the basis of Military Districts (MD), and two or more MDs are usually combined to form a Military Region (MR). MR headquarters command their subordinate MDs. Air force units are deployed into Air Districts (AD), whose geographical boundaries are coterminous with those of the MRs. The underlying strategic concept was to defend China by falling back into the interior and conducting a protracted war until the adversary was exhausted. The MR/MD deployment permits China to be defenced regionally, and allows the MR/MD commanders to fight independent or semi-independent campaigns during the protracted phase of the war. Under these conditions naval forces, deployed into three fleets, function primarily as a coastal defence navy complementing the continental defence of the ground forces. Air forces are intended to support ground operations in addition to their air defence role, as their AD alignment with the MRs indicates. The bomber force (Il-28 & Tu-16) supplied the initial structure of a long-range attack capability. Even as more aircraft, armoured fighting vehicles, artillery, and other supporting arms have entered the inventory, the defensive and protracted war character of the underlying military strategy remains evident. The rhetoric supporting the strategy emphasises the total mobilisation of the society to 'drown the enemy in the ocean of people's war'.[2]

The initial break in this basic concept of war and strategy came in the middle 1970s as nuclear weapons, although limited in numbers, accuracy, and reliability, began to assume more the character of a strategic deterrent. Nuclear deterrence brought China into a new category of strategic thought. The full-range ICBM test of 1980 and the development of solid fuels, used in the SLBM test of late 1982,[3] demonstrate Beijing's intent to raise the capability of the nuclear force to the point at which it can become China's primary deterrent against the USSR or any other nuclear power. None the less, as the architects of China's military modernisation programmes have indirectly noted, the existence of strategic nuclear weapons and a modernisation programme designed to increase the range, accuracy, and survivability of strategic weapons stands in stark contrast to the ossified general purpose forces deployed in their static roles in the MRs.[4]

Nuclear tipped missiles are so distinctly different from conventional forces in terms of their range and lethality, however, that they require different strategic concepts for their use. The common characteristic of *deterrence* links all the service arms of the PLA, but the conventional forces deter by raising the cost of a massive invasion *into* China, while the strategic forces are designed primarily to strike at the homeland of the aggressor. Granted, massive destruction will be the fate of both aggressor and defender in the event of a nuclear exchange, but with the current force structure and deployment of the conventional forces it is China alone that will accept the destruction of war if it remains below the nuclear threshold. By the late 1970s, this concept was already being challenged in the debates surrounding the modernisation of the conventional forces, as the modernisers argued that it was now necessary to 'win in a war against aggression at smaller cost and in less time'.[5]

As 'people's war under modern conditions' entered the lexicon of strategic analysis, it soon became evident that the Chinese recognised that a massive invasion from the USSR was unlikely. The need to defend against more limited Soviet objectives, particularly in north and north-east China, became a common concern. Defence against the highly mobile and lethal forces of the Soviet Union seeking only limited objectives was seen to be exceedingly difficult. The Chinese have sought to exploit Soviet dependence on the logistic support required for its highly mechanised forces through the development of strategies designed to weaken this support system and render the advancing forces impotent and susceptible to a Chinese counteroffensive.[6] The distinct problem with this strategy, also recognised by the Chinese,[7] is that their own forces are also becoming increasingly dependent upon logistic support as they absorb more armoured fighting vehicles (AFV) and artillery, and try to integrate air power into the land battle. When current Chinese analyses of combined arms warfare are taken at face value, maintaining high sortie rates for combat aircraft, sustaining AFVs and artillery in combat, and generally supporting even the relatively light forces of the PLA in combat would be very difficult tasks for its rear services.

It would seem to be self-evident that there are severe limitations on the kinds of military operations the Chinese can conduct against forces superior in weapons and equipment. Yet because the Chinese forces are themselves becoming increasingly dependent upon logistic support as they begin to organise for combined arms operations, the kinds of strategies and force structure changes they can realistically contemplate are extremely limited. References to 'fewer troops and simpler administration' as a way of slimming down the force structure make economic sense, but changing the force structure and deployment in a radical manner seems to be out of the question in the short run. None the less, changes can be made that 'fit' the military elite's past experience and would not require a radical change in current deployment practices.

TOWARDS NEW FORCE STRUCTURES

Enduring Problems

Defending China provides quite specific constraints that are functionally permanent. The Sino–Soviet border is extremely long, especially when the Mongolian People's Republic (MPR) is included. The area to be protected is large, and the road and railroad networks have only limited capacity to move military equipment rapidly over long distances. Limited strategic mobility for the ground forces is compounded by their low tactical mobility. Trucks, armoured personnel carriers (APC), and tactical airlift are in extremely short supply, and this condition will not change for some time to come. Low tactical mobility is compounded by the obsolescence of practically all of the major weapon systems deployed by the PLA. This weakness is aggravated by poor C^3I (command, control, communications and intelligence) capabilities. The ability to co-ordinate within the same military arm not only units, but also two or more service arms operating jointly, is critically dependent upon command and control facilities, which, in turn, depend upon effective communications systems to co-ordinate operations on widely dispersed battle areas and within given battlegrounds. Intelligence, both tactical and strategic, needs to be collected and quickly disseminated. In all of these areas the PLA can anticipate only slow improvement, although tactical communications could quickly be improved through battlefield radios of domestic design.

A final constraint is the lack of experience at all levels of command with the intricacies of planning and utilising combined arms operations. In many ways, the application of combined arms forces to a given problem is more difficult to master than the employment of strategic nuclear forces. The need for skilled commanders to manoeuvre and sustain air and ground forces containing diverse weapon systems in swiftly moving battles is an absolute requirement for current warfare. As the mobility and lethality of the ground forces and the range and effectiveness of combat aircraft increase, so the battlefield commander's task becomes increasingly complex and difficult. When his combat experience is restricted to light infantry operations with only limited tank and artillery support, continuous training and exercises in combined arms warfare can seek to correct this lack of experience. It must be noted, however, that this training is not only important for unit commanders and senior staff officers involved in force planning. Planning and command at higher levels, such as the General Staff and

Logistics Departments and in the Military Commission/Ministry of National Defence, also require a thorough understanding of the demands of combined arms warfare.

The force structures that follow take these limitations into account, and will assume only gradual changes in weapons and equipment. Such changes that do occur will not, in the short run, lead to any major improvements in the lethality and mobility of the armed forces. Precision guided munitions (PGM) will continue to be introduced, for they offer relatively cheap solutions to glaring weaknesses. Improvements in mobility for the ground forces will occur as more trucks and armoured personnel carriers are introduced. Similarly, tactical airlift will increase through the introduction of more helicopters and perhaps aircraft dedicated to troop and equipment mobility. C^3I will improve at the strategic level as the space programme's satellites begin to fulfill military requirements, and at the tactical level as domestic industry begins to improve battlefield communications equipment. The assumptions underlying these anticipated changes are that improvements in such areas are far cheaper than acquiring new weapon platforms (tanks, aircraft, ships), and that modifying existing platforms lowers training and logistic support costs while increasing the lethality and mobility of the forces.

Overall Structure

Balancing continuing constraints with anticipated improvements leads to the conclusion that the Chinese will remain dependent upon forces in being located in those areas considered to be the most likely avenues of attack. Low strategic mobility means that the Chinese cannot 'swing' sizeable ground forces from one part of the country to another; therefore pre-positioned forces will be required. These forces will have to consist of combat-ready combined arms 'packages' fully prepared for sustained warfare. Assuming that deterrence is their primary function in national strategy, readiness and sustainability are critical. This is necessary not only to fight effectively, but also to demonstrate to a potential adversary the capacity to fight. Here exercises have a dual importance, for they serve not only to test the readiness of the forces, but also to demonstrate a high state of readiness to the adversary.[8]

Given the current military elite's experience with ground forces, especially massed infantry, the central goal is to build upon this experience. The ground force corps deployed in the military regions are the most adaptable units of deployment. In addition to service and support units, each division will have attached armour and artillery units according to their tactical requirements. With attached units, a corps will approximate 42 000 personnel.[9] The usefulness of the corps as a primary unit of deployment within a military region is that it continues current practice and can provide tactical training in the terrain where it is most likely to fight. The corps assigned to the MRs in the north and northeast, for example, would be trained and equipped for warfare quite different from combat in southwest China and northern Vietnam. Thus both the corps and the military region concept of deployment are likely to be retained as the heart of the future force structure and its deployment.

Aviation

The military region's air force equivalent is the Air District (AD), with its borders coterminous with those of the MRs. This relationship establishes the organisational base for air/ground co-ordination through an adaptation of the Soviet concept of Frontal Aviation (FA).[10] Given that ground forces are the dominant factor in the experience of the Chinese military elite, the MR headquarters will function as the operational centre for air/ground co-ordination. The mission of frontal aviation will be to provide support for ground operations through aerial reconnaissance, battlefield interdiction, localised air superiority, and close air support. The basic command unit will be the Air Army, but the manoeuvre units will be based upon the Air Division. Each Air Army contains three divisions of approximately 100 aircraft.

A given Air Army will support three corps, which will form an Army Group. The combination of an Air Army and an Army Group will become the Composite Army.[11] The number of composite armies in any given MR/AD can be expected to be a function of the task assigned to the region.

While composite armies under the command of the MR headquarters will provide the core of the ground force/combined arms force structure, air defence of the region will be the direct responsibility of the AD commander. To distinguish between the missions of air support for the ground forces and air defence,[12] we will adopt the Soviet concept of PVO Strany – *Voyska Protivorozdushnoy Oborony Strany* (National Air Defence Forces). Following current Chinese practice, ground-based air defence systems (AAA, SAM) will be placed under the new Air Defence Forces (ADF). Following Soviet practice, defence of naval shore installations will be the responsibility of the ADF, and naval interceptors will be transferred to the People's Liberation Army Air Force (PLAAF) ADF.[13]

With ground and air defence missions defined, the role of the woefully inadequate bomber force must be considered. Slow and vulnerable though they are, the Tu-16 and Il-28 have combat radii that give them capabilities beyond the tactical uses of frontal aviation. 'Strategic' bombing is clearly far too ambitious for such a force, but the mix of approximately 100 Tu-16s and 450 Il-28s can be assigned a mission if the Soviet term Long Range Aviation (LRA) is applied. LRA will be given the mission of attacking targets beyond the range of frontal aviation. In fact, with air-to-surface missiles, the Tu-16 and Il-28 could be used to attack targets while remaining outside local ground-based air defence networks.

The final basic mission the air force can fulfil is a minimal strategic and tactical airlift capability. The PLAAF's lift capability is extremely limited, but a Military Air Transportation (MAT) command is feasible. That the Chinese think in these terms is indicated by the existence of the PLAAF air-mobile and paratroop forces.[14] Within the basic design, however, these units would be transferred to the ground forces. Responsibility for moving them would remain with the PLAAF MAT, but their deployment would be a ground force decision. The primary MAT mission would be to support all airlift requirements for the armed forces and mobilise civil aviation capabilities during war or national emergencies.

CONTINENTAL DEFENCE

The force structure outlined in this essay links air and ground forces to defend continental China. The composite army has been designated the basic deployment element. By aligning ground and air forces and specifying mission responsibilities for the PLAAF through particular commands (Frontal Aviation, Air Defence Forces, Long Range Aviation, and Military Air Transportation), a preliminary force structure using existing forces begins to take shape. This force structure provides the basis for a transition from strategies based upon concepts of people's war to strategies in which combined arms forces are structured to increase the combat effectiveness of available units. It permits strategy and tactics to be developed with combined arms forces while staying within the senior commanders' experience with large ground armies. The composite armies are perhaps best viewed as an extension of the old Field Army.

Using the composite army as the basic element of deployment also permits the problem of limited tactical mobility to be approached. An army group would deploy its forces to cover the same area that a modern corps would protect using its greater tactical mobility and lethality. The divisions of the attached air army would supply some of the missing mobility by permitting MR commanders to concentrate their air power on the most threatened areas. Additional lethality and tactical mobility could be provided to the ground forces by assigning additional armoured fighting vehicles (AFV), precision-guided munitions (PGM), and motorised infantry as they become available. Such weapons and equipment would be assigned to those areas where their tactical utility would have the greatest effect. The composite army concept, in fact, requires the strategist to think in terms of mobility and firepower because his forces are structured to make the most effective use of all available resources. It also requires planning staffs to think in terms of combined arms forces because they have to sustain combined arms packages in combat. These requirements extend up to the highest levels of defence planning, for the posture of the Chinese force must be viewed as the result of combining the capabilities of all service arms and branches rather than relying on the capabilities of each.

In defending continental China, the current MR/AD organisations would be seen as theatres of operation. Forces assigned to them would be viewed as Unified Commands, including naval assets when they were to be used in coastal defence. The size of the theatre would depend on the location of the 'threat', but it is not the purpose of this essay to analyse the required command structures when MR/AD commands are combined to form larger theatres. It is sufficient to state that the MR/AD is a unified command responsible for all theatre forces, with the ground commander as the senior officer. Long Range Aviation, Military Air Transportation and the three fleet commands of the navy are Specified Commands retained at the highest level of authority, as are the nuclear forces of the 2nd Artillery Corps. Elements of LRA, MAT, and the naval fleets would be assigned to the unified theatre commands when the tactical situation made such assignments necessary.

FORCE PROJECTION

The projection of military force differs distinctly from defensive operations, but this basic sketch of a likely future Chinese force structure provides the underpinnings for force projection. The design does enable the military hierarchy to plan in terms of mixing combined arms forces for operations in different terrains and weather conditions, and against different adversaries. Once force planning for readiness and sustained combat is integrated into effective planning for combined arms operations, then the step to force projection is relatively small. The essential questions are those of distance and the potential intensity of the combat, and for the Chinese defence establishment these are crucial limitations.

Currently, the PLA does not have the capability to project conventional forces much beyond China's borders. This will not change for some time to come without a specific decision to enhance projection capabilities. There is no evidence that the Chinese are preparing to invade Taiwan, for example. None the less, the PLA has been used to project force in the past, the most recent example being its expedition into Vietnam. The design outlined in this essay will improve the capability of the Chinese armed forces to do more effectively what they have done in the past – project forces limited distances across China's borders. Once force planners have adjusted to preparing logistic and combat support requirements for a variety of composite army types, planning for force projection becomes an extension of current planning procedures, especially when the distances involved are small.

Of far greater importance would be the political consequences of demonstrating an ability to project forces effectively. Such a capability would change the image of China held by its neighbours. The Vietnam incursion of 1979 may have demonstrated China's willingness to use force, but the results of its combat operations raised questions about the effectiveness of the forces it projected. A demonstrated capability to project force may be a useful tool in international politics; but, if the threatened country were an ally or 'friend' of either of the two superpowers, the consequences for China could be extremely complicated. A demonstrated increase in the capability of the PLA's conventional general purpose forces to conduct sustained combined arms warfare would have consequences similar to those for an increase in China's strategic nuclear forces. What is the intent behind these increased capabilities? In face of the combined dual capabilities of both the strategic and conventional general purpose forces of the PLA as they improve, this will be one of the major questions to be faced by Asia in the future.

THE MILITARY ELITE AND REFORM

The current military elite is taking a holistic view of modernising the Chinese defence establishment. Frequent references to 'leftism' inside the military hierarchy are clear evidence that there is continuing resistance to the implications of these policies, if not to the policies themselves. The weight of evidence, none the less, shows modernisers in influential positions in the Politburo, Military Commission (MC), Ministry of National Defence (MND), the new Commission in Charge of Science, Technology and Industry for National Defence, the service arms, and the military region commands.

At the Politburo, MC, MND level, Zhang Aiping is a vocal advocate of defence modernisation who served as chairman of the National Defence Scientific and Technological Commission (NDSTC) prior to his appointment as a deputy chief of staff and then defence minister. Yang Dezhi, the new chief of staff and a member of the Politburo and the MC, was Marshal Peng Dehuai's deputy commander in Korea, where he witnessed not only the stunning early successes of the Chinese People's Volunteers (CPV) but also the disastrous costs of the later phases of the war when mass failed to overcome firepower. It was Peng who led the first stage of China's military modernisation efforts in the 1950s, and his views were presumably influenced by his Korean War experiences. The Director of the General Logistics Department, Hong Xuezhi, was Marshal Peng's rear services chief in Korea and has a career pattern centred on logistics. The air force has been headed by Zhang Tingfa since 1977, but he has served in the PLAAF since 1956, when he was a deputy chief of staff. Liu Huaqing, the new navy commander, has a continuous career in both naval affairs and defence modernisation through his years in the NDSTC. Xiao Ke, commandant of the PLA Military Academy, has been an outspoken critic of the remnants of 'leftism' in Chinese professional military education (PME). He is a powerful advocate both of revising the PLA's approach to problems of military strategy and of improving the educational level and technical proficiency of the officer corps.

At the MR level (our new theatre commands), seven of the commanders about whom we have fairly complete biographical information served as division and corps commanders in the Korean War. As combat commanders they experienced combined arms warfare where artillery, close air support and battlefield interdiction inflicted, to Western eyes, incredible losses on their forces. They also commanded the first projection of force by the PLA.

The weight of the newly promoted career soldiers in the military hierarchy is manifestly behind the modernization movement. Although advanced in years as members of the Long March generation, this new elite may well represent its transitional generation. Command experience in the Korean War will serve as the key to this group's cohesion.

The major problem faced by this new elite of modernisers is to overcome the inertia of the past when faced with limited economic resources. A concentrated effort is being made towards what Xiao Ke refers to as the PLA's 'capital construction'[15] by improving the skills of the officer corps at all levels of the hierarchy. New officers are to be selected from the military academies, rather than recruited from the enlisted ranks. Junior officer 'command schools' are to be improved and their graduates will receive college degrees. The current officer corps is to be refurbished by requiring attendance at relevant PME schools before they are promoted. Xiao's most bitter comments have been directed at those 'comrades who always look back at the past. They even take pride in it. Didn't they command troops and fight in past wars despite the lack of culture?'[16] That was the past, and the future requires a highly trained and technically competent officer corps skilled in the demands of combined arms warfare.[17]

This pressure to improve the quality of the officer corps extends to training, where the emphasis has been on combined arms operations since 1980. The Chinese military elite saw the massive combined arms exercise conducted northwest of Beijing in the autumn of 1981 as the turning point in their revised training programme.[18] Perhaps 100 000 troops participated in what is believed to be the largest military exercise ever conducted by the PLA.[19] Impressive though this exercise may have been to the Chinese, Western military analysts viewing the documentary film made during the manoeuvres were not impressed. What they saw were weapons whose vintage years were the 1950s and the 1960s. Such weaponry is perhaps effective on clear days when visibility is good and you can see the enemy. Today's battle, one analyst in Hong Kong noted, 'is beyond the horizon'.[20] This is the PLA's dilemma: does its outdated weaponry so restrict its battlefield performance that no amount of reorganisation, training, and professional military education will do more than make a marginal increase in its combat performance?

CONCLUSION

This essay has outlined the probable direction of changes in the PLA's force structure. Such changes will permit the armed forces not only to make better use of combat capabilities that currently exist, but also to prepare the way for the necessary transition away from the influences of a restrictive people's war. It can be argued that 'people's war' is not a stragegy, which is true. None the less, thinking in terms of people's war and trying to modify Mao's concepts of war and strategy does not necessarily highlight the demands of two- and three-dimensional warfare. The Janus-like quality of the Chinese military establishment reflects the tension between these two approaches to war and strategy. Harlan Jencks has written that, in the 1960s Lin Biao was the architect of a 'balanced strategy' in which a modified concept of people's war was associated with a slow, self-reliant modernisation process.[21] In Maoist terms, this is a policy of 'walking on two legs'. It was this balanced approach that led to the two aspects of war contending in Chinese debates over both strategy and military modernisation. It is the contention of this essay that there is now sufficient evidence that the current military elite seeks to reject people's war, however modified, as an approach to strategy and force structure requirements. While the label of 'People's War' may well be retained, the content of Chinese strategy is likely to be very different from what has gone before. I have suggested what appears to be the most likely path the Chinese will follow in future years. None the less, these changes will require of them an orientation toward more contemporary concepts of force structure and the employment of military forces. Past practice and experience create an inertia that is difficult to overcome, but the attitudes of the military elite that have emerged over the past three years indicate that significant movement has already begun.

NOTES AND REFERENCES

1. Shao Huaze, 'A Reliable Guarantee for Socialist Construction', *Hongqi (Red Flag)*, no. 21, 1 November 1982, in FBIS-CHI, no. 224, 19 November 1982, K-23.
2. Ibid., K-26. This example serves primarily to demonstrate that the rhetoric continues, even in the most forward looking discussions.
3. See the full page photograph, in colour, of the ignited missile in *Jiefangjun Huabao (Liberation Army Illustrated)*, no. 12, 1982. The burn pattern clearly indicates that solid fuel was used.
4. Shao Huaze, 'A Reliable Guarantee...', K-22.
5. Gong Xuan, 'Modernise Our National Defence', *Renmin Ribao (People's Daily)*, 31 May 1978, 2, in FBIS-CHI, no. 110, 7 June 1978, E-2.
6. Beijing, Xinhua Domestic Service, 7 August 1978, 'Nieh Jung-chen's (Nie Rongzhen) 4 August speech at the National Militia Conference', in FBIS-CHI, no. 154, 9 August 1978, E-7.

7. Ibid. Three years later, Song Shilun made the same point in, 'Mao's Military Thinking Is the Guide to Our Army's Victories,' *Hongqi*, no. 16, 16 August 1981, 5–15, in FBIS-CHI, no. 180, 17 September 1981, K-22.
8. Lewis Sorley, 'Technology, Mobility and Conventional Warfare', in Ellen P. Stern, *The Limits of Military Intervention* (Beverly Hills, California, Sage Publications, 1977), 194–195.
9. Defense Intelligence Agency, *Handbook on the Chinese Armed Forces* (Washington, D.C., Department of Defense, DDI-2680-32-76), Annex B, A-2.
10. All Soviet force structure concepts used in this essay are taken from the relevant sections of Defense Intelligence Agency, *Handbook on the Soviet Armed Forces* (Washington, D.C., Department of Defense, DDB-2680-40-70, February 1978).
11. Reference to a 'Composite Army' was made in a *Jiefangjun Bao* editorial on 4 March 1983. Commanders were urged to organise their commands 'so that the various services and arms can co-ordinate and bring their power into play'. Beijing Domestic Service, 4 March 1983, in FBIS-CHI, no. 045, 7 March 1983, K-17–18.
12. In his visit to a Chinese air base, Major Lennert Berns of the Swedish Royal Air Force was a guest of the 38th Air Defense Division. In its training, the division practised both ground attack and air defence tactical exercises. 'Tientsin Time Capsule ... a visit to a Chinese air base', *Air International*, vol. 24, no. 1, January 1983, 20.
13. Fighter aircraft from the Soviet navy were transferred to PVO-Strany in the years 1960–1962. Defense Intelligence Agency, *Soviet Armed Forces*, 11–1.
14. Harlan W. Jencks, *From Muskets to Missiles: Politics and Professionalism in the Chinese Army, 1945–1981* (Boulder, Colorado, Westview Press, 1982), 157–158.
15. Beijing Domestic Service, 22 February 1983, reporting a *Jiefangjun Bao* editorial by Xiao Ke, in FBIS-CHI, no. 037, 23 February 1983, K-30.
16. Ibid., K-31.
17. Ibid.
18. There were numerous reports on this exercise. See, for example, the *Jiefangjun Bao* editorial, 'Make Fresh Contributions to the Modernisation of the National Defence', in FBIS-CHI, no. 187, 28 September 1981, K-2–3.
19. Michael Weisskopf, 'China Reveals Military Manoeuvres, Believed Largest in 30 Years', *Washington Post*, 27 September 1981, 29.
20. Quoted in, 'China's army ill equipped', *Washington Times*, 28 July 1982, 5.
21. Jencks, *From Muskets to Missiles*, 259–260.

Part II
The Armed Services

4 Ground Forces

HARLAN JENCKS

The PLA ground forces are in transition from their traditional preoccupation with guerrilla and light infantry operations towards a modern combined arms capability. China intends to defend itself against Soviet attack by 'people's war under modern conditions,' a strategy combining guerrilla warfare, positional defence, and mobile operations principally conducted by the militia, regional forces, and main forces, respectively.[1] Guerrilla and light infantry operations are not to be abandoned by any means. The Chinese recognise, however, that positional and mobile defence conducted by modern combined arms forces would play the decisive role against a Soviet invasion.

Creation of all the elements of a combined arms defence is a complex and comprehensive undertaking. There is a high degree of interdependence among developments in strategy, tactics, organisation, logistics, weapons, equipment, and command-control-communications-intelligence (C^3I). 'Ground forces modernisation' is therefore interrelated with most of the subjects treated in this book.

Because combined arms operations are so vital to both current and future Chinese defence plans, four important changes in PLA training went into effect in 1981; (1) changing the main object of attack from enemy infantrymen to tanks; (2) changing from separate branch training to combined arms training; (3) changing the emphasis from training individual soldiers to training cadres: and (4) recognition that 'under modern conditions' the PLA can no longer live off captured enemy supplies, and so requires a modern logistical system.

These and other changes in the PLA are currently subsumed under the term 'regularisation' (zheng gui hua). 'Regularisation' is more than improved technology and changed tactics.[2] It entails such new (to the PLA) features as standardised procedures, rationalised organisation, and tightened discipline. In particular, it means curtailment of the decentralised, semi-autonomous, self-sufficient 'guerrilla war habits' that have long characterised the ground forces. The chain of command is to be both simplified and strengthened. To 'better strengthen the sythesis of the various branches,[3] the PLA needs to institute 'scientific management in accordance with rules, ordinances, and regulations', and 'a strict system of personal responsibility [to] build normal order in work, life, education, and training in order to regularise and standardise the management of the army'.[4] The PLA is supposed to march, salute, maintain its equipment, and administer itself 'by the book' *in order* to attain modernisation. Combined arms operations cannot be conducted unless the PLA is 'regularised'.

ORGANISATION

A practical example demonstates the importance of standardised combat units. Suppose an infantry regiment is ordered to form a combined arms task force by receiving an attached tank battalion, a battery of self-propelled (SP) howitzers, and a platoon each of engineers and anti-aircraft (AA) machine guns. The regimental commander and his staff must know the capabilities and limitations of these attached units in order to supply and employ them effectively. This task would be much easier if every tank battalion, SP howitzer battery, engineer platoon, and AA machine gun platoon were organised, equipped, and manned like every other. However, there is currently a very low level of standardisation in the PLA, even among main force units. The even more vital issue of higher-level reorganisation is discussed in chapter 3.

As part of 'regularisation' the army's non-military activities and units are being curtailed, and its overall size reduced. In 1980 there was reportedly a plan to cut manpower by 35 per cent.[5] There appear to have been substantial reductions in the number of Capital Construction Engineer and Railroad Engineer units, although both continue to draw praise in the military press.

In the early 1960s the army absorbed virtually all police, border, and internal security units and functions. Beginning in 1972, 'People's Police' began to re-emerge. Between 1981 and early 1983 all provinces organised People's Armed Police Forces for border and internal security duties. In most cases these are former PLA regional units which have been redesignated and placed under the Public Security system of the Ministry of Public Security. They are now being retrained for their new police functions.[6] In the interim, PLA troops and the militia continue to share public security and border guard duties with police.[7] Separating and defining the functions of PLA regional forces and the various types of 'armed police' is proving to be a long, difficult process. Partly, this is no doubt because their functions inherently overlap – especially in border districts. Another reason is that some Military Region (MR) and Military District (MD) commanders are reluctant to give up civil police powers they have exercised since the early 1960s. Divesting the PLA of police functions is an important aspect of 'regularisation,' however: It will tend to reduce the overall size of the army and, more importantly, to restrict it to a more purely *military* role in society.

The decision has been made to devote fewer military man-days to 'agricultural production for self-support.' Fewer units were engaged in such production in 1981 than in 1980, and further reductions were ordered in 1982–83. However, just as in military training, troop units are expected to work more efficiently. PLA food production is supposed to increase, even as fewer soldiers engage in it,[8] and PLA assistance to the civil economy and disaster relief continues to get extensive press coverage. Although the ideal is still to 'reduce the burden on the state and the people.' Chief of Staff Yang Dezhi has said, 'Getting involved in public welfare activities is our army's glorious political task . . . serving the people, however, basically requires us to do our own job well'.[9]

The missions of the militia in 'people's war under modern conditions' continue to include rural guerrilla warfare and the provision of replacement manpower and service support for the PLA. In addition, the militia has acquired the important new role of defending cities and other fortified places. In 1978 the Party Central Committee issued a directive on 'readjusting the militia organisations.'[10] Although details vary from place to place, it appears that, as in the regular PLA, militia units have been reduced in size and the scope of their non-military duties curtailed. In Shanxi, for example, 'after readjustment, the scope of construction by militia organisations was reduced by 13 per cent and the number of personnel was reduced by 58 per cent'.[11] Technical and tactical training has been improved in the militia, as have equipment storage and maintenance. However, these changes have naturally encountered confusion and misunderstanding.[12]

Although the militia's role appears secure for the time being, there are continuing references to a PLA 'reserve service system'. In the 1950s Defence Minister Peng Dehuai wanted to scrap the militia entirely in favour of a Soviet-style army reserve. This may be the intention of the current leadership as well, though evidence is lacking. Some observers speculate that the 'reserve' may merely be a ploy to encourage active cadres to retire, on the theory that they might be more willing to become 'reserve officers' than to retire outright.[13] Others predict the gradual evolution of the militia into a 'regular' reserve force.

TRAINING, EDUCATION, AND PERSONNEL

In May 1978 a major effort began to improve all aspects of personnel qualification, training, and education.[14] Schools, training facilities, and military academies have proliferated. Efforts continue to plan, standardise, and modernise military training. Periodic training conferences are now held at all levels of command, and formal unit training plans are required. (It is a somewhat shocking revelation that the latter did not exist before – and still don't in 'backward' units.)[15] Training time allotment varies, but is increasingly devoted to military (as opposed to political or 'cultural') training, which is supposed to be 'hard, strict, and geared to the needs of actual combat'.[16] In infantry units less emphasis is accorded to skills like grenade throwing and bayonet fighting, while more time is devoted to 'modern' skills like anti-tank gunnery.[17]

A severe constraint on training had been the tight military budget. Fuel consumption and wear and tear inevitably result from realistic training, yet the PLA is constantly admonished to economise and conserve. To some extent this has prompted increased efficiency in the use of equipment. When troops are allowed to learn from their own mistakes in the field, however, the lessons are better learned, even though time, fuel, and equipment may be 'wasted' in the process. There is currently a tendency to eliminate such 'waste' by overplanning and oversupervising exercises.[18]

Cadres are the focus of PLA training reforms for several reasons. One seems to be a widespread, and surprising, lack of 'regular' military knowledge. Owing to a combination of historical circumstances and neglect, some cadres do not understand such rudiments of their profession as marching, tactics, unit administration, map reading, and inspection procedures. A more general problem is that while cadres may have *ad hoc* ways of doing these things, different units' procedures may vary so widely as to make coordinated operations impossible. This situation is the product of the decentralised guerrilla tradition, reinforced by 30 years of unit insularity. A cadre typically has served his entire career in the same regiment, with little standardised training, and no rotation to other units or places.[19] Recent reports tell of MRs and MDs seeking to correct the situation with 'regular troop training' for cadres in such basics as drill and ceremonies, tactics, and rifle firing.[20] A more obvious deficiency of PLA cadres, especially in the ground forces, is their general lack of technical education. To correct this, military technical schools have expanded since 1978. Academies and schools enrolled over 15 000 more students in 1981 than in 1980, and graduated nearly 10 000 more; while training units turned out nearly 200 000 cadres, squad leaders, and technical personnel.[21]

Training and educational emphasis has been shifted somewhat away from purely technical subjects since 1979. During the war with Vietnam recent graduates of PLA training institutions tended to overemphasise technical matters, and to be weak on tactics and troop leading. 'Maoist' tactics were largely responsible for the very high casualties. PLA troops reportedly charged heedlessly into intense Vietnamese fire, shouting slogans. Cadres also lacked knowledge of enemy tactics, and so were insufficiently flexible in seizing the initiative by modifying tactics and procedures. The most generalised deficiency, at all levels, was the inability to control dispersed forces and properly to employ supporting arms, especially artillery.[22] This apparently led to the current stress on training cadres in combined arms operations. For the first time ever there are also reports that cadres are studying foreign armies – especially prospective opponents.

In November 1980 regulations were promulgated specifying the educational levels and training diplomas to be required for all cadres and staff personnel, from company up through corps levels.[23] It remains to be seen whether these ambitious standards can be enforced. Senior and middle-grade cadres recruited before 1954, and ground force cadres generally, are overwhelmingly of peasant origin and seldom have more than middle school educations. In fact, a 1981 circular from the general departments noted there are 'cadres . . . whose level of education is lower than junior middle school', and that there are still illiterate soldiers in the ranks.[24] In early 1983 there was a month-long all-PLA conference on academics and schools, which publicised several new policies: Formal professional education is to receive top priority, 'even if it means fewer soldiers and manning offices with fewer people'.[25] Instructors are to rotate between schools and operational units (as in most NATO and Warsaw Pact armies).

The PLA has discovered the training value and economy of modern computerised simulation. This is one area where there has been widespread application of sophisticated electronics in all the arms and services. Virtually every issue of *Liberation Army Pictorial* reports on new applications of simulation. The PLA has also greatly expanded its use of such simple simulators as weapon's subcalibre devices.

As important as academies, classes, and simulators may be, all the separate units, pieces of equipment, technicians, commanders, and staffs must ultimately put everything together and operate on real terrain against a live opposing force. Realistic field exercises drive home teaching points, turn complex procedures into routine, and build individual and unit confidence. They also expose errors and omissions as nothing else can. The exercises which are most valuable are generally not huge or widely publicised. The latter type, like the widely noted manoeuvres in northwestern Hebei in September 1981, do provide training for national-level staffs, but the actual manoeuvres are carefully staged to facilitiate film-making and to 'demonstrate progress'. Various operations in the 1981 manoeuvres were conducted in discrete segments, separated by administrative breaks for preparation and rehearsal. In the jargon of the profession, it was a highly 'canned' exercise. While some useful troop training did occur, any manoeuvre that draws a Xin Hua camera crew and a grandstand full of high-ranking observers may be presumed to be mainly a 'canned' demonstration.

One such demonstration in June 1982 provoked considerable foreign interest because it included detonation of a nuclear blast simulator. The training value of the exercise may be judged from the presence of the MR deputy commander, the local Party leader, and 'tens of thousands of persons who observed the exercise'.[26] Simulation of a tactical nuclear blast was also included in a paratroop exercise in July, which may have been a 'real' exercise rather than a demonstration. If so, it was an exceptionally large one, involving the entire Airborne Corps, transport planes and helicopters, attack aircraft, and an opposing force with tanks.[27]

Such major exercises should follow extensive exercises by smaller units. While a few divisions and regiments appear routinely to be conducting combined arms exercises, most still are 'experimenting' with them. The quality of this training is hard to assess, since it mostly goes unpublicised. Some regimental and battalion training is publicised, and it tells a good deal about what the PLA has, and has not, accomplished. Of special note are the remarkably basic things which are hailed as signs of progress. In 1980, for example, a rifle battalion 'broke a new path' when it received attachment of a tank company and 'artillery, communications, engineering and antichemical warfare detachments'. This sort of task organisation has been routine in NATO and Warsaw Pact armies for *decades*. *Liberation Army Pictorial* proudly pictured 'young commanders' who had achieved such 'combined arms' capabilities as a machine gun company commander learning to drive a tank, a tank company commander who had learned basic infantry tactics, a rifle company commander who could operate a voice radio and another who could compute artillery firing data. Any good sergeant in any NATO army can do all that.[28] The most basic of all 'combined arms' operations is the co-ordination of artillery fire support with manoeuvre units. This was one of the major failings of the PLA in the 1979 war, and has received considerable training emphasis. Press reports indicate that there has been shocking ignorance among PLA infantry commanders about the artillery, and vice versa.[29]

Still more surprising is the apparent lack of standardised PLA troop-leading procedures and formats. In 1979 Hu and Jiang wrote that 'the assignment of specific tasks, co-ordination of operations, and security measures should be transmitted simultaneously, instead of separately'. Evidently the PLA lacks (or just doesn't use) anything comparable to the American five-paragraph field order format. Neither, it seems, are there standard procedures or formats to disseminate combat intelligence.[30] Troop-leading procedures also seem slow and diverse.[31]

Although the Chinese are aware of modern planning techniques like computer optimisation and critical path analysis, they will remain unable to apply them until current procedures are simplified.[32] Judging by most reports, and the rudimentary reforms being suggested, even a battalion-level PLA headquarters must be a ponderous bureaucracy. In late 1981 an artillery unit was ordered to change position at night in the rain in the mountains. It took six hours for the staff to decide where to go and what route to take. This was hailed by *People's Daily* as a fine example of 'achieving success at one stroke'.[33] Clearly there is still a long way to go.

A major dimension of the problem is resistance to change by older cadres. 'Some people' resist even the notion that soldiers need to learn science and technology.[34] Resistance to change is only one of the problems associated with aged cadres. Some are too frail physically, or are just plain senile, yet they hang on to their positions, blocking advancement of younger men. Constant exhortation and publicity for 'good examples' have hardly made a dent in this problem.[35] A variety of strategies are now pursued to force old cadres to retire. One is the institution of annual cadre examinations which emphasise modern technology, administration, and tactices.[36]

The Twelfth Party Congress (September–October 1982) probably broke the impasse on retirement. While the highest and oldest 15 or 20 military men remained in position, there was a real housecleaning at the levels just below them. Many of the senior army men named to the new Central Council were not even Central Committee members before. Many military academy cadres were removed from the Central Committee, and a housecleaning began in the MRs. Five MR commanders have been replaced, while there have been sweeping retirements at the next levels down. Practically all the deputy commanders and commissars of the Guangzhou MR, for example were forced to retire.[37] The very old men at the top will be allowed to die in office. The clearing out of the next several levels down creates room for senior cadres who joined the PLA in 1952–62, and four younger cadres who are college and academy graduates. Supposedly, promotion will hereafter be based on 'regular' qualifications, rather than 'the decadent concept of appointing people to posts [solely] according to seniority'.[38]

These criteria were re-emphasised at the 1983 Schools Conference by General Political Department Director Yu Qiuli, who suggested even more fundametal changes: (1) cadres should no longer be recruited primarily from the infantry, but from the specialised service arms; (2) cadre assignment, reassignment, and promotion should be handled by military academies and schools acting as a 'collective cadre department'.[39] These procedures, if adopted, will profoundly alter the nature of the officer corps. The latter procedure, for example, would remove cadre career management from unit commissars and party committees, entrusting it instead to the most professionally oriented officers in the PLA. The long-term implications of this would be far-reaching, both militarily and politically. Infantry dominance of the officer corps effectively has meant *peasant* dominance, at least in the ground forces. Yu's first suggestion would change that. Ground units are in any case bound to contain a higher percentage of urban officers and recruits in coming years, because of higher educational requirements. This will contribute to problems of discipline and morale, since urban-educated soldiers are, universally, less amenable to military discipline and less adaptable to field conditions.

At least some upper-level cadres are already being reassigned periodically to new places and units, and the practice is projected to expand. This practice, plus the 'cross-attaching' of units for combined arms operations, will result in new cadres frequently joining or temporarily commanding units. Some visible mark of rank will be necessary for soldiers to tell who is in charge; the traditional reliance on personal recognition will no longer suffice. Yang Dezhi is pressing for the reintroduction of military rank, which will probably come as soon as the current wave of retirements is completed.[40]

Just as in civilian society, the current reforms in the PLA stress 'socialist legality'. The Chengdu MR is now enforcing the 'PRC provisional regulations on punishing servicemen for dereliction of duty'. There is a clear need for such formal regulations, because discipline among soldiers and cadres has become somewhat lax. The Cultural Revolution left soldiers in a highly privileged position which provoked considerable popular resentment, so 'regularised' discipline is also intended to strengthen 'army–government and army–people unity'.[41]

'Regularised' discipline will supplement, but not replace, such traditional PLA disciplinary measures as 'criticism and self-criticism,' emulation campaigns, political work, and Party organisation. Chief of Staff Yang Dezhi, a leading 'regulariser,' has repeatedly stressed the continued (indeed, increased) importance of strong Party and political work in the army.[42] There is no question of ignoring politics in the 'regularisation' process.

LOGISTICS

The logistical system, supervised by the General Logistics Department (GLD – often literally translated as 'General Rear Services Department'), has long been highly decentralised.[43] For historical reasons, 'leftist guerrilla mentality' is especially persistent in the GLD, where a thorough re-organisation has been ordered. An enlarged meeting of the GLD Party Committee in November 1982 was addressed by a parade of national leaders, including Deng Xiaoping. GLD Director Hong Xuezhi bluntly demanded, 'If the development of our thinking stops at the stage of 'millet plus rifles' mentality, how can we promote our work to suit the development of the situation?'[44] Recalcitrant GLD cadres are a particularly serious problem because modernisation of PLA logistics is prerequisite to modernising equipment and training in the rest of the army. Despite resistance, the high command is pushing ahead. 'Logistics work must be improved, and the key lies in improving the organisational system . . . so that it will be more streamlined, rational, and efficient'.[45] Efficiency and economy are also stressed in the recent emphasis in equipment maintenance, storage, and accountability. This is seen as a vital facet of making 'full use of existing equipment' to defeat a better-armed enemy. More immediately, it will enable the PLA to cut waste and extend the usable life of existing material.

The current PLA logistical system is quite ill-suited to mobile operations. There are depots and warehouses throughout the country to which combat units are required to return to pick up their supplies. There is no forward 'push' in the system at all. This hobbles tactical commanders by siphoning off their organic transport, diverting their attention from operations to routine supply matters, and slowing the flow of parts, fuel, food and ammunition. A completely new system is required if mobile combined arms operations are ever to be sustained.

It has been widely noted that the military budget was reduced in 1980, 1981, and 1982, and increased only slightly for 1983. It is less widely recognised that the current PLA reorganisation, if it succeeds even partially, will save billions of Renminbi in reduced waste and inefficiency. Moreover, a great deal of real modernisation can be and is being achieved at relatively low financial cost. The new GLD computer centre, which became operational in May 1981, is a good example of a modest investment in modernity which can pay for itself in increased efficiency.[46] The same can be observed in the current reforms in organisation, training, personnel practices, and even in some hardware acquisitions.

EQUIPMENT

To engage the Soviet Army in modern combined arms combat with reasonable confidence, the PLA needs to upgrade virtually every category of equipment from tanks to chemical decontamination kits. Drew Middleton has suggested a Chinese 'wish list' (costing roughly US$41–63 billion) calling for 3000–8600 improved medium battle tanks, 8000–10000 armoured personnel carriers, 16000–24800 heavy trucks, 720 mobile surface-to-air missile launchers, 240 fighter-bombers, 200 air-superiority fighters, and 6000 air-to-air missiles.[47] Inclusion of air-to-air defence weapons on this list is important. Integral to the air–ground battle are tactical air support for one's own operations and protection of one's own forces against air attack (see chapter 5).

One less obvious but vital requirement is for improved C^3I systems to make PLA forces more responsive, integrated, and efficient. For example, long-range surveillance, target acquisition, and night observation (STANO) gear is needed. If Soviet first-echelon forces were allowed to concentrate unmolested, there is little chance that any defender could hold in the breakthrough sector.[48] STANO capability is therefore vital for early identification of the breakthrough sector, location and targeting of manoeuvre and support units, and allowing time for the defender to shift forces to meet the threat. The Soviet second echelon also has to be located and targeted. Both echelons must be attacked early enough to reduce their momentum and their power before they reach forward defences.

Because PLA electronic C^3I has always been poor, the Chinese have retained and perfected older systems like signal flags, couriers, and human reconnaissance. As a result the PLA is, on balance, somewhat less vulnerable to Soviet radio-electronic warfare than are NATO armies, which depend heavily on radio. The PLA can rely on extensive nets of informers inside enemy-occupied areas of China, and upon the superb combat reconnaissance ability of Chinese infantrymen.

Most Chinese C^3I equipment is copied from old Soviet types, but there are a few exceptions. For example, there are now Chinese-designed laser rangefinders. In 1980 China purchased five Field Artillery Control Equipment sets from a British firm, which they may try to copy.[49] PLA tactical and strategic communications systems must provide rapid, secure, and reliable communications all the way from the General Staff down to platoon level. Significant progress in the electronics industry has given the PLA a long-range secure-voice capability, and a few relatively modern technical radios, but these, and all PLA radars, are extremely vulnerable to enemy monitoring, jamming, and deception. Chinese offensive electronic warfare (EW) capability is still rudimentary. There is better hope for rapid improvement in C^3I than in most categories of PLA need, however, because the army is likely to be a beneficiary of 'spin-off' from the advancing Chinese electronics sector.

Ground forces weapons, on the other hand, are likely to modernise only very slowly. In 1981–82 conventional weapons research and development was reduced, with emphasis restricted to only a few major projects. Incremental improvement and adaptation of existing systems will probably continue to characterise ground forces' equipment through the 1980s.[50] There are several recent examples of such inexpensive 'innovation'. The Chinese are well aware of the important role of mobile anti-tank (AT) precision-guided munitions (PGM) in modern warfare. Ideally, the PLA needs over 6000 AT PMGs comparable to the American TOW, the French–German HOT, or the Soviet SPANDREL. Instead, in 1979, they began producing a 'second best' weapon which is cheap, simple, and 'Chinese' – a copy of the 20-year-old Soviet SAGGER, which the Russians are now replacing. Once sufficient quantities of the SAGGER are deployed they will give the PLA a reasonably useful long-range (3000 m) AT system where there was none at all. The SAGGER has been mounted experimentally on PLA jeeps, thereby creating a simple (if vulnerable) mobile launcher system. A next logical step would be to try launching SAGGERs from helicopters. The Chinese have also adapted to their limited means the sophisticated concept of artillery-deliverable mines. They use their ancient Soviet-made BM-13 'Katyusha' multiple rocket-launchers (MRL) to fire rockets which scatter parachute-deployed AT mines. They also drop parachute mines from their old H-5 bombers and Z-5 helicopters. Despite these improvements in long-range AT weapons, the Chinese still plan, of necessity, to engage enemy tanks mainly at close range. Whenever possible, minefields and obstacles will be used to stop or slow the tanks, while artillery and small arms fire attempts to separate them from their supporting infantry and combat engineers. Then, PLA infantrymen will attack the tanks with a variety of light rocket launchers, recoiless guns, and demolitions.

Ultimately, PLA forces will need to counterattack, and 'the tank remains the peerless weapon of the offensive'.[51] The Chinese recently began producing a 'new' tank, the Type 69. It is an improved version of the standard Chinese Type 59, which in turn is a modified copy of the old Soviet T-54. The Type 69 has a laser rangefinder, IR drive, spotlights, and a new main gun (said to be a smoothbore) of about 105mm. It probably has internal improvements as well.[52] Just how many Type 69s are now in service is uncertain. It probably does not measure up to the Soviet T-62, let alone the newer T-64/72. There is little prospect for a really new PLA tank before 1990, if then. Efforts to acquire a really effective long-range AT PGM seem more likely.

Tactical mobility and logistical support are serious PLA deficiencies which also require some new equipment. A few inexpensive new pieces have been deployed recently, such as a copy of the excellent Soviet PMP floating bridge and a simple minefield breeching rocket.[53] Modern heavy truck acquisition has increased. French Berliet GBC and GBU-15 trucks (and probable Chinese copies) are more in evidence in the PLA.[54] Recent exercises have included parachute and helicopter operations for both tactical assault and resupply. New tactical pipeline and field medicine equipment was seen in the 1981 manoeuvres.[55]

Although the PLA has many artillery pieces, flexible accurate fire support remains a problem. There is only one Chinese-made SP howitzer, for example, but it mounts a Soviet gun dating from the mid-1930s and appears to be defectively designed. A Chinese-made 130mm MRL is now in service. Based on similar Soviet designs, and mounted on tracked or wheeled carriers, it enhances PLA firepower using simple, inexpensive technology. Typically, however, MRLs are not very accurate.

In terms of doctrine, training, and equipment, the Soviet Army leads the world in chemical and biological warfare capability. Recent PLA exercises have included chemical defence play, but methods and equipment are obsolescent. Chinese chemical weapons are probably the same ones provided by the Soviets in the 1950s. Vulnerability to chemical weapons, which the Soviets are sure to use in a major war, is perhaps the greatest single threat to PLA ground forces.

Air defence, airlift, and close air support are addressed in chapter 5, and tactical nuclear forces developed in chapter 7. Only one point must be emphasised here: integration of air, air defence, and nuclear forces into the land battle requires suitable doctrine and technical procedures, fast and accurate target acquisition, and contact among ground, air, and delivery units and headquarters by means of rapid, reliable, continuous, and secure communications. Since most of this is at least a decade away from the Chinese, they may have suitable weapons and aircraft before they have the doctrine, organisation, and C^3I necessary to use them.

A final factor regarding equipment is the PLA's limited 'absorptive' capacity. Neither soldiers nor cadres, especially in the ground forces, have the education to learn to employ, operate, and maintain very much sophisticated equipment.[56] This helps explain the priority accorded to training and education over hardware.

THE PEOPLE'S ARMY AND MODERN WARFARE

'People's war under modern conditions' requires an army unlike the traditional Chinese 'people's army'. As the army becomes increasingly specialised, it will have fewer domestic functions and responsibilities. Its reserve force – whether a revamped militia or a completely new organisation – will also be more 'regularised' and less intimately involved in internal affairs. In these changes the ground forces will be affected most profoundly, for they always have been closest to the people and the soil. The most difficult changes of all will concern personnel, organisation, command, and control, for these involve much broader economic, social, and political issues. 'People's war under modern conditions' is China's defensive strategy during its long transition from 'underdeveloped' to 'world-power' status – a transition that still has decades to go. During the transition period the strategy is necessarily pragmatic and highly *ad hoc*.[57] Regional differences are inherent in the strategy, and are likely to become more pronounced before they begin to fade. The Shenyang and Beijing Military Regions are converting to a fairly modern centralised strategy and force structure, while military threats in other areas are to be met by essentially regionalised responses.

This situation contains, *inter alia*, the seeds of conflict between short-term regional military requirements and long-term planning for a self-sustaining national defence industry.[58] Opposition to 'military modernisation' by civil and military leaders in the west, south, and southwest might well be anticipated, therefore, owing not to 'remnant Maoism' or 'guerrillaism,' but to defence of vested regional economic and political interests. Similarly, force modernisation is likely to provoke increased rivalry between main and regional forces; and among the air, land, sea, and nuclear branches of the PLA. Successful containment of all these political and bureaucratic conflicts depends upon workable solutions to China's basic requirement for a stable and legitimate system of political authority and civil–military relations. 'Military modernisation' and the transition to a new national defence strategy are inextricably connected with these larger issues, which go far beyond the scope of this book.

In 1981 John J. Sloan listed six major categories of Chinese military requirements: These are: (1) Improved weaponry (2) Improved training/unit readiness/ education (3) Improved doctrine and tactics (4) Improved defence technology/production base (5) Improved logistical system (6) Improved organisation/command and control.[59] Although it is already implicit in Sloan's requirements 2, 3, and 6, I would add (7) Improved officer personnel system.

In this and the other chapters of this book, we have seen that the PLA currently is making substantial progress toward requirements 2, 3, 5, 6, and 7. Prerequisite to progress in category 4 is the general modernization of all Chinese science, technology, and industry – which is now a major national priority (chapter 9). Only in category 1 (improved weaponry), therefore, is there slow progress *and* a low priority. Considering the massive constraints, the priorities of the army and the nation appear to be correctly ordered. While backward weaponry is the most obvious and widely noted aspect of the PLA's deficiencies, we should recognise that substantial progress in six out of seven categories is not bad at all. Finally, it is well to remember that emphasising 'people problems' is an ancient Chinese predilection. Mao's insistence that 'men are more important than weapons' reflected that tradition, as does the stress on modernising the skills and thinking of PLA cadres in the 1980s.[60]

NOTES AND REFERENCES

1. See Paul H. B. Godwin, 'China's Defense Modernization...,' *Air University Review*, 32, No. 7, November–December 1981, 2–19; Gerald Segal, *The Soviet 'Threat' at China's Gates* (Conflict Studies No. 143, London: Institute of Conflict Studies, 1983); and my 'People's War Under Modern Conditions...?' *China Quarterly* (hereafter *CQ*), forthcoming.
2. Yang Dezhi, 'On Several Questions Concerning Regularization', *Jiefangjun Bao* (*Liberation Army News*, hereafter *JFJB*), 22 January 1982, 1, trans. in *China Daily*, 4 February 1982, 1.
3. Yang Shangkun, *Hong Qi* (*Red Flag*, hereafter *HQ*), no. 15, August 1982, cited by *Xin Hua* (*New China News Agency*, hereafter *XH*), 30 July 1982, trans. in *Foreign Broadcast Information Service Daily Report–China* (hereafter *FBIS*), 82–148, K10.
4. *XH*, 29 May 1982, trans. in *FBIS* 82–105, K8–K9.
5. Douglas T. Stuart and William T. Tow, 'Chinese Military Modernization...', *CQ* no. 90, June 1982, 262.
6. *XH* 27 and 29 April 1983, trans. in *FBIS* 83–085, K21–K24; and Lhasa Radio, 21 April 1983, trans. in *FBIS* 83–085, Q5.
7. Harlan W. Jencks, *From Muskets to Missiles* (Boulder, Colorado, Westview, 1982), 166.
8. *XH* 22 and 24 February 1983, trans. in *FBIS* 83–039, K2–K4; and *XH* 28 February 1983, trans. in *FBIS* 83–41, K2–K3.
9. *XH*, 22 May 1982, trans. in *FBIS* 82–103, K12.
10. June T. Dreyer, 'The Chinese Militia', *Armed Forces and Society* 9, no. 1, Fall 1982, 63–82.
11. *Shanxi Ribao*, 22 May 1982, 1, trans. in *FBIS* 82–117, R5.
12. Shijiazhuang Radio, 16 November 1981, trans. in *FBIS* 81–228, R1.
13. *HQ* no. 21, 1 November 1982, 19–23, trans. in *FBIS* 82–224, K26; and *Far Eastern Economic Review* (hereafter *FEER*), 6 August 1982, 11. I am grateful to Captain Mark Coyle for drawing the latter to my attention.
14. *XH*, 14 May 1978, trans. in *FBIS* 78–094, E13.
15. *XH*, 29 May 1982, trans. in *FBIS* 82–105, K8.

16. Beijing Radio, 21 November 1980, trans. in *FBIS* 80-229, L24.
17. Hu Zicheng and Jiang Zongping, 'Use Scientific Methods to Organise Coordinated Combat Command', *JFJB*, 16 September 1979, trans. in *JPRS, China Report: Political, Sociological and Military Affairs* (cited hereafter as *China Report*), no. 88, 4 June 1980, 102-104.
18. This is implied in *XH*, 14 January 1982, trans. in *FBIS* 82-010, K7.
19. Jencks, (note 7), 225-230.
20. *Zhejiang Ribao*, 13 January 1982, 1, trans. in *FBIS* 82-018, 06.
21. *XH*, 17 January 1982, trans. in *FBIS* 82-012, K12. Also see *XH*, 29 July 1981, trans. in *FBIS* 81-146, K2-K3; and Jencks, 151-152.
22. Party Central Committee circular cited in *Zhonggong Yanjiu (Chicom Studies*, hereafter *ZGYJ)* September 1979, 13, no. 9, 7.
23. These regulations are reprinted in full by Tang Chi-ming in 'Military Affairs in 1980', *ZGYJ* 15, no. 1, 15 January 1981, 71-72. Also see William R. Heaton, 'Professional Military Education in China', *CQ* no. 81, March 1980, 122-128; and Wang Yong-yeh, 'Inquiry Regarding the Current Situation of Chinese Communist Military Academies', *ZGYJ* 14, no.12, 15 December 1980, 84-90.
24. Beijing Radio, 25 February 1981, trans. in *FBIS* 81-038, L18.
25. *XH*, 3 March 1983, trans. in *FBIS* 83-045, K15. Also see Xiao Ke, *XH*, 21 February 1983, trans. in *FBIS* 83-039, K5; and Beijing Radio, 4 March 1983, trans. in *FBIS* 83-045, K17-K18.
26. *Ningxia Ribao*, 27 and 28 June 1982, cited *Kyodo* (Tokyo), 1 July 1982, in *FBIS* 82-128, K1.
27. *XH*, 20 July 1982, trans. in *FBIS* 82-141, K4. This exercise may have been the same one reported in *Ningxia* in June, Ibid.
28. 'Combined Arms Drill to Educate Qualified Personnel', *Jiefangjun Huabao (Liberation Army Pictorial*, hereafter *JFJHB)*, no. 7, July 1980, 10-11. This article also showed antiquated T-34 tanks, still in service in the vital Beijing MR.
29. *JFJHB*, no. 7, July 1980, 4-5.
30. Hu and Jiang, (note 17), 101. A survey of three PLA tactics manuals published in 1973-78 found no evidence of either standard operations order or intelligence report formats.
31. Ibid.
32. Ibid., and 'Three Methods for Plans Explained', *JFJB*, 16 September 1979, 3, trans. in *China Report* No. 88, 4 June 1980, 107.
33. *Renmin Ribao (People's Daily*, hereafter *RMRB)*, 2 December 1981, 4, trans. in *FBIS* 81-234, K22.
34. *RMRB*, 19 October 1982, 1 and 4, trans. in *FBIS* 82-209, K11; and 'Three Methods for Plans Explained,' 102.
35. Tsou Sze-yuan, 'Survey of Bandit Army Demobilisation and Retirement in 1981,' *Feiqing Yuebao* 23, no. 8, February 1981, 54-59. Also see Hangzhou Radio, 20 April 1982, trans. in *FBIS* 82-080, 02-03; and *XH*, 3 August 1982, trans. in *FBIS* 82-151, P3; and *XH*, 20 July 1982, trans. in *FBIS* 82-141, K3.
36. *Yunnan Ribao*, 16 December 1981, trans. in *FBIS* 82-002, Q4.
37. *Nanfang Ribao*, 2 November 1982, 1 and 3, trans. in *FBIS* 82-213, P1-P2; and *South China Morning Post*, 6 November 1982, 5.

38. Ibid., Yang Dezhi, 1; Guangzhou Radio, 22 October 1982, trans. in *Summary of World Broadcasts*, III FE/no. 7169/BII/4; and *XH*, 15 January 1982, trans. in *FBIS* 82–012, K5. On the PLA personnel system up to 1981, see Jencks, (note 7), 223–247.
39. *XH*, 3 March 1983, trans. in *FBIS* 83–044, K2–K3. Also see *XH* in English, 3 March 1983, in *FBIS* 83–043, K1–K2. Note the English word 'officer' (not 'cadre').
40. Yang Dezhi's statement that, 'In order to strengthen the modernisation programme in the army, we are planning to reinstate a system of military rank', is in Beijing Radio, 9 August 1981, trans. in *FBIS* 81–153, K6–K7. On the rank controversy since 1975, see Jencks, (note 7), 244–246.
41. Chengdu Radio, 31 January 1982, trans. in *FBIS* 82–922, Q1. On lax PLA discipline, see statements by PLA leaders in *RMRB*, 30 July 1982, trans. in *FBIS* 82–148, K6–K7.
42. Yang Dezhi, *China Daily*, 4 February 1982, 1; Yu Qiuli, *XH* 1 March 1983, trans. in *FBIS* 83–043, K1; *XH* 9 March 1983, trans. in *FBIS* 83–050, K21; and *XH*, 26 February 1983, trans. in *FBIS* 83–041, K3–K6.
43. Jencks, (note 7), 108 and 144–146. Also see the detailed study by Wang Shih-hong, 'Inquiry into the Condition of Bandit Army Logistics and Supply', in *Feiqing Yuebao*, 23, no. 6, December 1980, 44–51.
44. Hong Xuezhi in *RMRB*, 19 October 1982, 1 and 4, trans. in *FBIS* 82–209, K10.
45. *XH*, 18 November 1982, trans. in *FBIS* 82–224, K2.
46. Beijing Radio, 2 December 1981, trans. in *FBIS* 81–232, K8.
47. Drew Middleton, *International Herald Tribune*, 17 April 1981.
48. Soviet doctrine envisages a breakthrough by two reinforced motorised rifle regiments on a divisional front of only 12–16 kilometers. The defenders of this sector would face up to 300 armoured vehicles in these two regiments, closely followed by about 120 more in the second echelon. This attack would be supported by at least 200 artillery pieces. On the application of this doctrine in Manchuria in 1945, see P. H. Vigor, 'Soviet Army Wave Attack Philosophy', *International Defense Review*, January 1979.
49. *Business China*, 19 January 1980, 2.
50. *XH*, 1 January 1982, trans. in *FBIS* 82–001, K2; and Beijing Radio, 21 November 1980, trans. in *FBIS* 80–229, L25. Defence Minister Zhang Aiping strongly emphasised the concentration of resources on a few 'Key projects' in *HQ*, no. 5, 1 March 1983.
51. Shi Fang, 'What are the Prospects for Tanks in the Missile Era?' *RMRB*, 24 March 1981, 7, trans. in *FBIS* 81–061, A2.
52. *Xiandai Junshi (Contemporary Military Affairs)*, no. 67, cover; and no. 68, July 1982, 19–23.
53. *JFJHB*, no. 7, July 1982, inside front cover.
54. *JFJHB*, no. 11, November 1981, 16–17.
55. *JFJHB*, nos. 11 and 12, November and December 1981.
56. Shao Huaze, 'A Reliable Guarantee of Socialist Construction', *HQ*, no. 21, 1 November 1982, 19–23, trans. in *FBIS* 82–224, K23.
57. Segal, (Note 1) 3–4,

58. Godwin, (Note 1) 17.
59. Testimony and comments by John J. Sloan in *The Implications of US–China Military Co-operation: A Workshop Sponsored by the Committee of Foreign Relations of the US Senate and Congressional Research Service of the Library of Congress* (Washington, D.C., GPO, January 1982), 32–33.
60. Edward S. Boylan, 'The Chinese Cultural Style of Warfare', *Comparative Strategy* 3, no. 4, 1982, 341–364.

5 Air Forces

BILL SWEETMAN

The sight of Polish cavalry charging the armoured columns of the Wehrmacht in September 1939 would probably offer the closest historical parallel to a meeting in battle between China's air forces and the air power of China's close and unfriendly neighbour, the Soviet Union.

Two decades of neglect have left the People's Liberation Army Air Force (PLAAF) in very poor shape. This situation results from three main factors: the problems inherent in the use of air power by a country with a land mass as large as China's, the power and effectiveness of the forces facing the PLAAF and the lamentably poor quality of China's own equipment. An examination of the service's present predicament, combined with an assessment of the minimum requirements for effective air power in the Chinese environment, leads to the conclusion that the resources required to bring about such an improvement are vast. However, there is still room for some optimism that with recent changes in Chinese foreign and defence, policy, China's airforce still can carry out an important role. But first the pessimism, and then the optimism.

THE PROBLEM

The size of the land mass which the PLAAF has to defend is a problem in itself. Most recent aerial conflicts have taken place where the defensive perimeter is small; forces operating in any part of the defence zone can be transferred quickly to provide reinforcement when needed. In fact, any combat zone which is narrower than the normal combat radius[1] of the average modern military aircraft is in practical terms a point target, because units based all over the area can be vectored into any specific action. Experience has shown that such a small defensive zone can be a tough and costly nut to crack, even by a force superior in numbers and technology to the defenders, because it can virtually be saturated with air defence systems such as fighters, surface-to-air missiles (SAMs) and anti-aircraft artillery (AAA).

Land masses the size of the Soviet Union, United States and China present a different challenge. Defensive resources must cover a large number of military and industrial targets, and it is impossible either to saturate the area around all of them, because the area is too large, or each of them, because they are too numerous. The United States and its allies have developed a deep perimeter defence of warning systems, SAMs and fighters. The Soviet Union, operating the most extensive air defence system of all, combines perimeter defences and short-range point-defence systems, all of which are constantly updated and improved.

But even these systems must content with only a limited number of targets, falling within a small and defined range of systems. The frontiers of the Soviet Union and the United States are so far apart that only the largest of long-range aircraft on either side present a threat to the adversary's air space. Not so the Chinese–Soviet border, where any conflict would see action between long-range and short-range[2] offensive and defensive systems in the same theatre. As in the central region of Europe, air power can take full advantage of its inherent mobility to deliver a concentrated assault in any part of the theatre, and defences must be prepared to protect vital, identifiable targets such as air bases and troop concentrations from such an onslaught.

Another aspect of the Sino–Soviet theatre is that weather conditions can vary considerably, so that great importance attaches to the ability to conduct air operations at night or in poor weather, when terrain and the target may be concealed. The northerly latitudes of Beijing and other major centres are also significant; unless a force is equipped to fly and fight in darkness, the number of sorties which it can mount in winter will be reduced as a function of the increasing hours of darkness.

Finally, it should be noted that topography favours the Soviet Union. Most major Chinese cities are within 60 to 90 minutes' flight time, at the most economical cruising speed of a military aircraft,[3] of Soviet-controlled bases in Siberia or Mongolia. The reverse applies to only a few Soviet industrial centres, mostly the new ones established in the Kazakh SSR, or Western Siberia, before China was perceived as a possible threat.

It would however be unduly pessimistic to focus only on China's less favourable air defence capability. Just as the proximity of Chinese cities favours a Soviet attack, so Indian cities are subject to Chinese attack. Indeed, apart from the Soviet Union, no other air power in Asia poses a serious threat to China. Many of these neighbours, including Taiwan, Vietnam and India, are all far more vulnerable to Chinese strikes. Nevertheless, the study that follows concentrates on the Soviet threat to China as the most pressing problem.

THE SOVIET THREAT

In recent years, almost every conflict fought primarily on the ground has turned into a stalemate. When air power has played a central role, however, the results have usually been decisive, more akin to a rout. Witness the battles over Sinai in 1967, or the Lebanon in 1982.[4] One blow by better trained and technically superior forces can, in the right circumstances, shatter the opponent's air power. His land forces are left naked to attack and reconnaissance and, in the absence of friendly air reconnaissance, are blind beyond the visual horizon. Defeat for the land forces at that point is almost inevitable; it can be brought about and completed without the use of nuclear weapons and with minimal losses for the attacker.

The Soviet air forces face potential opponents on two fronts, while China faces only one major adversary. But this has not been good news for China. In the past ten years, the Soviet Union has comprehensively overhauled its long-range and short-range aircraft and missile forces to meet the needs of the European theatre. China's total production of new-model military aircraft over the period 1972–82 has barely reached double figures;[5] the Soviet Union has fielded an arsenal of new weapons and built them in thousands.

This trend can be placed in a historical perspective. The Chinese and Soviet aircraft and missile forces were quite similar in their technical standards by 1960, with the Soviet Union maintaining a lead equivalent to a few years of development and production. By 1970 the gap had widened considerably in the specific case of long-range nuclear missiles – which had absorbed the bulk of the Soviet Union's energies in the 1960s – but relatively little divergence occurred in the balance of tactical forces. Soviet and Chinese units alike flew aircraft which, by Western standards, were deficient in warload and range, and were virtually useless at night or in bad weather.

But the 1970s have seen the Soviet Union making massive improvements, while technical development in China has stagnated. New systems have become standard throughout the Soviet forces; while units facing Nato took priority in re-equipment, these new weapons are now replacing older aircraft and missiles throughout the Soviet Union. Designed to foil Nato's defences, they entirely outclass anything which the Chinese forces can field in significant numbers. A brief review of some of the most important new weapons drives this point home.

Most Soviet developments in long-range missile systems have been directed at improving their position in the strategic nuclear balance with the United States. There is one important exception: the mobile SS-20 missile. While this weapon is a medium-range or theatre system in the Nato context, its range is quite sufficient to threaten Chinese targets from bases within the Soviet Union: in the Sino–Soviet context, therefore, it is a full-fledged strategic weapon. Fully mobile, truck-mounted strategic weapons are considered to be so dangerous that they have been outlawed by treaty between the Soviet Union and United States, and the development of a longer-range version of the SS-20, the SS-X-16, was suspended some years ago.[6] But China still faces a threat from such a weapon, and, paradoxically, that threat may increase if efforts to control such weapons in Europe are successful; there is a strong chance that, given a ceiling on missiles in Europe, the Soviet Union will simply relocate its SS-20s to the East.

The other new long-range system to be deployed in recent years by the Soviet Union, the Tupolev Backfire bomber,[7] is in a similar category to the SS-20 in that its production is not restricted by treaty between the USA and Soviet Union; it is exempt because its range is not sufficient for it to pose a threat to the United States. Like the SS-20, though, its range is quite long enough to hit Chinese targets. Backfire represents a tremendous advance over earlier Soviet bomber designs. Its advantages include the ability to fly at high speed, close to the ground, for long distances, so that it is concealed from radar by terrain or the horizon. It carries its own very powerful electronic jamming equipment, to confuse the defences while warning the Backfire's crew of any impending attack, and accurate navigation and bomb-aiming systems. Backfires in Soviet service are armed with both nuclear and conventional weapons, and the latter should not be ignored; a flight of four Backfires, for example, could deliver some 50 tons of high explosive on to a precision target at night or in bad weather.

Frontal Aviation, the air arm dedicated to the support of Soviet land forces, has seen improvements of a similar order. The most important development has been the production in vast numbers of Mikoyan Flogger fighter and attack aircraft. These fast, well-armed and well equipped tactical fighters are backed up by less formidable but still useful new developments in the Sukhoi Fitter series. A typical Frontal Aviation regiment[8] can now deliver three to four times as much ordnance per mission as it could have done a decade ago, and carry it twice as far. These weapons can also be delivered more accurately and with greater immunity from interception, thanks to the extensive jamming devices carried aboard the latest Soviet types. Even more formidable is the Sukhoi Fencer, a heavy strike aircraft capable of night and bad weather operations, but it is the smaller single-seat Flogger and Fitter types which make up the bulk of the force.

Even this generation of aircraft is now being followed by another new wave of fighter designs, which will be forming an increasing proportion of Frontal Aviation strength in the second half of the 1980s. They include the high-performance Fulcrum and Foxhound fighters, the Soviet answer to the newest American types.

Special mention in the Chinese context has to be given to two particular aircraft types, one about ten years old and the other on the point of large-scale deployment, because both have been combat-tested in Afghanistan and both are likely to be of special importance in Soviet contingency plans for conflict with China. The first, deployed in 1973, is the Mil Mi-24 Hind armed helicopter. This is a multi-purpose machine, designed to serve as an airborne escort for armoured forces or as a means of attacking enemy troops and armour on the move. It carries a heavy and accurate load of guided anti-armour missiles, rockets and cluster bombs, and is equipped with sophisticated night-sighting systems. It is also well protected against fire from the ground. Another relatively slow, but well equipped and heavily armed aircraft is the new Sukhoi Su-25 Frogfoot attack type, first used in 1982 in Afghanistan. Frogfoot carries a heavy internal gun and can lift about twice the weapon load of the Flogger or Fitter types. Both Hind and Frogfoot would probably be vulnerable to an effective air defence system, but in its absence their payload and accuracy would enable them to wreak havoc on ground forces.

Another aspect of the total threat is the ability of Soviet ground force to defend themselves against air attack, and this area has also seen a great deal of improvement in the last decade-and-a-half. As the Soviet forces advance, their air-defence system moves with them. It is built up in layers: the top layer consists of medium-range SAMs such as the SA-6 and the improved SA-11, carried on tracked vehicles which can keep pace with the armoured spearhead, and ready to be emplaced and in action at a few minutes' notice. The next layer of defence is provided by missiles with a shorter range but quicker reaction time, while automatic, radar-controlled guns and portable SAMs form the 'last ditch'. Among Western air tacticians, it is taken for granted that there will be no chance for a second-pass air attack against Soviet ground formations; the bombs must be dropped on the first pass, because an attack against forewarned defences would amount to suicide.

There is one other significant aspect of Soviet military capabilities and operational philosophy: the offensive and defensive use of C^3I resources. These include considerable reserves of reconnaissance satellites and launchers; reconnaissance aircraft capable of overflying large areas of territory with minimal risk of interception, and other aircraft equipped to monitor or jam an opponent's own communications and warning systems. Many of these resources are grouped under the heading 'radio-electronic combat' and are co-ordinated to achieve the greatest possible disruption.

CHINESE RESPONSES

What can the PLAAF accomplish against this sort of opposition? It is a problematical question. While the Chinese air arm certainly outnumbers the Soviet air regiments based in the Eastern theatre, possibly by a factor of four or five to one, there are two considerations which offset that advantage. For one thing, the Soviet forces could be reinforced rapidly from the West without rendering the European front in the least vulnerable: forces in the Western Soviet Union can be considered as a mobile reserve. Secondly, and more importantly, the huge advantage in electronic intelligence and reconnaissance enjoyed by the Soviet Union would mean that, in an actual engagement, the PLAAF units might well be outnumbered by forewarned and alerted Soviet regiments. But regardless of numbers, an assessment of PLAAF equipment against the tasks which it might be expected to attempt is hardly encouraging.

Long-range strike units, for example, would be assigned the task of neutralising some of the Soviet Union's more threatening weapons such as the SS-20s and Backfires based on Siberia and around Vladivostok. These forces have, it is true, taken a step in the right direction recently; the last of the ancient Tu-4 Bull bombers, Soviet copies of the

1942–vintage B-29 Superfortress bomber, have finally been retired, leaving the aircraft enthusiasts of the Confederate Air Force as the sole operators of the type. The primary long-range strike aircraft of the PLAAF is the H-61,[9] a reproduction of the Soviet Tu-16 Badger. At the time of its appearance in the early 1950s, the Tu-16 was a fast jet bomber, only 100 knots or so slower than the fastest fighters in service. But the Soviet Union retired its Badgers from bombing some two decades ago. Since that time, the Badgers have been used almost exclusively for maritime reconnaissance and as carriers for cruise missiles. The H-6 does not appear to carry any electronic countermeasures equipment beyond that visible on the 1960–model Tu-16 from which it was copied; in the face of modern air defence, its ability to penetrate and strike its targets is effectively zero. The only other medium-range combat aircraft produced by the PRC is the H-5, a copy of the older, slower and less well armed Il-28 Beagle. Its vulnerability to defences would be even greater than that of the Badger.

The principal fighter produced in the PRC is the J-6 Farmer, copied from the Soviet Union's first supersonic interceptor, the Mikoyan MiG-19.[10] Chinese J-6s have been delivered to Egypt and, in quite large numbers, to Pakistan. The J-6 is considered to be a competently designed aircraft for its day, with a high rate of climb and a heavy cannon armament, and is easy to maintain. These factors have encouraged the PRC to deploy it in very large numbers, and no less than 95 per cent of PRC fighter output has comprised J-6s and the related Q-5s. But while the J-6 can be deployed effectively by a country such as Pakistan, which faces an adversary equipped with aircraft of only slightly later concept, its age and small size lead to some problems. Its performance and handling decay at altitudes above 20 000 feet, and it does not possess an effective radar or medium-range missiles. Matched against a more modern and sophisticated aircraft such as the MiG-23 Flogger, the J-6 would be in a difficult tactical predicament. Even were the J-6s to outnumber the Floggers heavily, there would be no way in which the more modern fighters could be forced into an engagement, because of their higher speed and altitude capability and their greater detection range. On the other hand, a MiG-23 formation can choose the time, place and manner of combat – in tactical jargon, they possess the advantage of 'engagement control'.

The importance of engagement control can hardly be overstated. The MiG-23s could, for instance, loiter above the effective altitude of the J-6s, before making a hit-and-run attack, firing Apex missiles at five miles and launching short-range dogfight missiles as they pass among the surviving J-6s. While Pakistani pilots have found the J-6 to be an effective fighter in a low-speed, short-range manoeuvring engagement, Soviet tactics emphasise the avoidance of such combats; so after a single pass the Soviet pilots would probably use their superior speed and acceleration to leave the lethal envelope of their victim's weapons.

The precedent of Vietnam, where US fighters achieved disappointing results against less sophisticated aircraft, would probably not apply in this case. The technology of medium-range air-to-air missiles has advanced considerably, for one thing. More importantly, the Soviet Union would see no need to restrict the use of such weapons. Over Vietnam, American pilots were expected to identify targets positively as hostile before attacking, negating the advantages of their better radar equipment. Over China, the Soviet pilots would know that the odds in favour of a radar target being a Chinese aircraft would be at least ten to one. The 'exchange ratio' – the relationship of kills to losses – would be heavily in favour of the Soviet Union.

In the field of tactical support – the launching of air strikes against enemy ground forces – the PLAAF is similarly ill-equipped, despite the development of the Q-5 Fantan attack fighter[11] from the J-6. The crucial shortcoming of the Q-5 is not its speed or weapon load – in fact, thanks to its internal weapon bay, it is probably as fast with weapons carried as most modern strike aircraft – but its ability to find and strike its targets. One look at a photograph reveals the limited extent of the Q-5's sensors, which appear to comprise Doppler radar for measuring groundspeed and a radio altimeter. The only conclusion to be drawn from this is that the Q-5 has only one way of delivering free-fall weapons accurately: in a diving attack from medium altitude against a target which has already been visually identified and located on a first pass. As noted above, such an attack would have virtually no chance of success, or even of survival.

It is true that the PLAAF does possess some fighters of more modern design, in the shape of the J-7 – a copy of the early-model MiG-21.[12] But in operational terms this fighter represents only a small advance over the J-6, with similarly limited armament and equipment. Some J-7s are being supplied to Egypt, but on present plans they will be used only for training.

An unknown quantity among the fighter force is the newest product of the Chinese industry. This is the J-8, known to Nato as Finback; about 50 are believed to be in service, and the design is apparently based on that of the MiG-23 Flogger. One of these aircraft was delivered to China by Egypt, as part of an agreement under which China provided overhaul facilities and knowhow for the engines of Egypt's MiG-21s. A strong possibility is that the J-8 is a slightly smaller version of the MiG-23, powered by a Chinese-built Rolls-Royce Spey engine. Such an aircraft would represent an enormous advance on the J-6 or J-7. However, it should be noted that even a faithful copy of the original would not match MiG-23s in Soviet service, because the aircraft supplied to Egypt were deliberately downgraded export versions of the type.

The state of the PLAAF fighter/attack force reflects the mixed performance of the Chinese industry. While the J-7 and J-8 have been developed with apparent success, they have still been produced in far smaller numbers than the J-6 and Q-5. One possible reason for this is that the later aircraft are more difficult to produce by labour-intensive means than the early-1950s designs. Alternatively, the PLAAF may still stress the importance of numbers over quality. Another contrast is between the industry's ability to produce relatively modern engines such as the British Spey and its seeming inability to produce the other vital elements of a modern fighter – radar and missiles. The only air-launched guided weapon of any type produced in China is a copy of the Soviet AA-2 Atoll missile, which is itself a copy of an early version of the US Sidewinder, while radar equipment on Chinese aircraft appears to be based on late-1950s Soviet equipment.

Lastly, two glaring gaps in the Chinese aerospace forces should be noted. The only SAM in Chinese service is the CSA-1, copied from the Soviet SA-2 Guideline developed in the late 1950s. It has numerous drawbacks. It is not mobile, it is ineffective at low altitudes and, being of Soviet design, is highly susceptible to Soviet jamming. Organic air defence for the ground forces is restricted to manually aimed guns, which are unlikely to be effective against low-flying attack aircraft. Another total lacuna in Chinese capabilities is the lack of any means for gathering intelligence on its opponents or for preventing its adversaries from doing the same.

The depressing truth is that the outcome of a Sino–Soviet conflict at the present time would be disastrous. The PLAAF would be unable to defend its own airfields, let alone the Chinese ground forces. Armour, motorised infantry and artillery forces would systematically be sought out and crippled by Soviet attack aircraft, while the complete imbalance in intelligence information supplied by the two sides' aerospace forces would prevent the Chinese army units from bringing their numerical strength to bear.

TOWARDS A NEW AIRFORCE?

The picture painted so far is bleak. China's major adversary, the Soviet Union, seems to have an overwhelming advantage in the air. However, such pessimism is not necessarily unrelieved, nor is it permanent. First, it is plain that the Soviet Union constitutes only one (albeit the most crucial) potential threat. Worst-case planners, obsessed with the latest in technological wizardry, will never be happy unless the Chinese can match the Soviet Union in every category of weapon. But it should be obvious that wars are rarely fought at the full limit of the possible, and certainly international relations are not always resolved by recourse to war. Therefore there is much that even a limited air force can do for China without matching every Soviet nut and bolt.

Certainly in comparison to any other Asian power China can claim, if not superiority, then a lack of inferiority. Against the Soviet Union, China's main task is to raise the cost, risk and uncertainty for Soviet planners. War can be deterred by denial as much as by punishment. Obviously the tilt towards the Soviet side of the air balance is not something China can be proud of, but neither does it mean that Chinese military power has no use.

One need only consider the kinds of conflict in China's past thirty-five years to see that air power is not always crucial. In China's latest war, in 1979 against Soviet backed Vietnam, air power did not figure at all. Both China and Vietnam apparently calculated that the war should remain limited. That China failed to teach Vietnam a lesson in the war had less to do with Soviet (or Vietnamese) air superiority than with the lack of Chinese ground force power.

Second, it is arguable that China needs a first rank air force to keep the cost too high for the Soviet Union. It is noteworthy that in the last few years there has been a trend towards the development of slightly smaller and cheaper aircraft. This has been made possible mainly by developments in advanced electronics, with a contribution from new structural materials. Examples of these new fighter/attack types are the American Northrop F-20, the Swedish Saab JAS-39 Gripen and Israel's Lavi, all of which are smaller than Nato's F-16A – developed about a decade earlier – but which are claimed to have equal or better performance. They are not in the class of the newest Soviet fighters, such as the new MiG-29 Fulcrum, but are considerably cheaper to build and operate and are certainly capable of fighting effectively against such opposition. It should be stressed that it is not necessary to close the technology gap completely, but merely to reduce it to acceptable proportions.

Chinese designers have already demonstrated a remarkable ability to clone a design from a single specimen with no outside help. While not equivalent to the development of a brand new aircraft this is no small achievement, and the fact that China has managed to establish a small business as a supplier of 'bootleg' MiG components indicates that the copies match the quality of the original. Another successful programme has been the establishment of a production line for the Rolls-Royce Spey engine. While this is not representative of the latest military engines under development in the West, it is certainly comparable to the powerplant of the MiG-23.

Nevertheless, it is still a very long step from this sort of programme to the indigenous development of a truly competitive, fully equipped fight/attack aircraft, and it is probably not a step which the Chinese industry can expect to take without outside help. The experience of the Israeli industry, which in recent years has been the only successful new entrant into the manufacture of combat aircraft, may be instructive. Starting in 1967, with a reliable source of engines and a batch of purloined design data, Israel produced first a copy of the French Mirage 5 fighter, and then two successively improved Israeli versions of the design, the Kfir and Kfir C2. In parallel, the Israeli defence industry worked on an air-to-air missile, Shafrir, and a series of combat aircraft radars. All of these systems entered service between 1973 and 1978.

Despite the successful development of these systems, however, the Israeli aircraft industry has still turned to outside help in the development of the brand new Lavi attack fighter, seeking partnership agreements with US companies in such fields as composite structures and advanced microelectronic systems. The lesson for China is that full self-sufficiency takes a long time and a great deal of co-ordinated effort to attain, and that it is necessary to keep lines of technical help open. Against the Israeli example must be set the precedents of India, Egypt and a Jugoslavian/Romanian team; all three attempted to break into combat aircraft manufacture on their own, with results which have ranged from the mediocre to the disastrous.

So where does China go from here to help solve its air force problems. First, there is the option beloved of the China-market dreamers – large scale purchase of western equipment. But this can be quickly dismissed, as it has been by the Chinese, because of excessive cost and the lack of spin-off to China's own home industry. It would merely create external dependencies in crucial defence areas.

Second, there is the residual hope of China-marketeers that if they cannot sell the equipment, they will sell the know-how under licence and according to specific Chinese requests. This option still carries an element of risk, but retains a number of attractive features. For one thing, the resulting aircraft could be tailored closely to Chinese needs. Should the PLAAF decide to place a high premium on the ability of the aircraft to operate from short runways, for example, this could be taken into account at the early design stage. Another advantage of such a programme would be that it would make maximum use of China's investment in aircraft design facilities and expertise. It would also transfer the largest possible amount of technology into China, and leave the industry in excellent shape to undertake future projects – such as the provision of transport aircraft for internal services – on its own initiative and using its own resources.

Third, China can use only the smallest amount of external aid, in an essentially independent drive to self-sufficiency. The risks of the go-it-alone option are daunting. Development of a modern combat aircraft requires competence in a wide range of technologies, and an unforseen problem in almost any area can delay a programme or cause its costs to increase drastically. The price of failure – an air force equipped with J-6s and Q-5s in the late 1980s – does not really bear thinking about.

Nevertheless there is also much to commend this go-it-alone approach, and China seems to have been leaning in this direction since 1982. As the scale of the Soviet threat has been reduced in China's perception, and the costs of foreign technology have appreciated to their present high levels, China has come to look on this independent path with greater favour. By obtaining foreign models of equipment (see Chapter 18) and perhaps even with some aid from selected foreign arms manufacturers, China has been able to get a better start on military modernisation than many had previously thought possible.

Obviously there is a long way to go in this modernisation, but judgement of Chinese success seems to hinge on several factors that are in question. First, just how far does China have to go along the road to modernisation? If it is to the superpower position, then pessimism is in order. However, if China needs merely to raise the level of cost to any invader, then success is much closer to hand.

Second, how threatened is China? If the threat is imminent and from the Soviet Union, then pessimism is in order. However, if China perceives less of a threat, and an improved relationship with the Soviet Union, then China's air power predicament is not so serious.

Third, what kind of forces does China need? If it is the mirror image air force of the superpowers, then pessimism is in order. But if China can emphasise the durability of relatively simple and numerous aircraft then, as in people's war, numbers may count in China's favour. If China can concentrate on obtaining air defence, and like Nato seek to nullify Soviet power by raising the cost to any attacker, then a force concentrating on defensive air power and mobility for troops will be more likely to deter a potential threat.

As the Chinese air force moves into the 1980s, it has grounds for optimism and pessimism. Pessimism is properly justified by the lack of rapid growth in matching Soviet air power, and the relatively increased spending on China's naval and nuclear forces. However, a degree of optimism must also exist. The Soviet Union is no longer perceived as an imminent threat. What is more, China's aircraft, recently sold to Iraq, have performed well and there are signs that China itself is providing new and important elements of air power without foreign dependence. It is still too early to determine whether the optimists or pessimists are right, but only a full-scale war between China and the Soviet Union is likely to prove conclusively the pessimist's point. By then, it may be too late, both for the Chinese themselves and for western analysts.

NOTES AND REFERENCES

1. Combat radius is the distance from its base at which a military aircraft can engage in combat or strike a target and return. Realistically, few tactical aircraft have a combat radius of more than 250nm/450km.
2. The terms 'long-range' and 'short-range' are used in preference to the Western 'strategic' and 'tactical' which have no precise equivalents in Soviet or Chinese doctrine.
3. This is 70–80 per cent of the speed of sound, or around 450–500kt/800–900kmh.
4. Israeli forces achieved a reported kill/loss ratio of 80–2 in combat over the Beka'a Valley in 1982.
5. The J-8 Finback is the only aircraft in this category.
6. The first strategic arms limitation treaty (Salt I).
7. This is the 'reporting name' assigned to the aircraft by NATO, and applies to both the Soviet original and the Chinese copy. Chinese-developed types have NATO reporting names in the same series.
8. The regiment comprises 36 aircraft.
9. Chinese aircraft designations comprise the Pinyin initial signifying the aircraft's primary role – H for bomber, Q or attack and J for fighter – followed by a number which identifies the type. While the Western equivalents (B, A and J) have been used in the past, this practice will in time lead to confusion with the US Department of Defense's designation system.

10. The original MiG-19 was flown in 1953 and was in service by 1955. It is powered by two 8,800 pound-thrust Tumansky jet engines, carries a single pilot and can be armed with two missiles – Atoll, Sidewinder or equivalent – in addition to its three 30mm cannon. Its maximum speed is around 800 knots (1400km/hr). Between 2000 and 3000 of the type have been built in China.
11. The Q-5 is a development of the J-6, using the same wings and rear fuselage. The forward and centre fuselage sections are redesigned to accommodate a small internal weapons bay, a unique feature in this class of aircraft.
12. The MiG-21 was designed as the simplest and cheapest fighter capable of twice the speed of sound. It has no search radar and a very small combat radius, confining it to target-defence operations in clear daylight. Later versions, in production in the Soviet Union and India, are very much better equipped.

6 Naval Forces

BRUCE SWANSON

The decade of the 1970s saw dramatic changes in China, not the least of which was a sustained effort to modernise its navy. In fact in each year of the decade approximately twenty per cent of the defence budget was dedicated to the naval forces.[1] The results have been impressive: China's conventional submarine force tripled from 35 to 100 vessels, and missile craft inventories grew from 20 ships to more than 200; a 12-missile tube, nuclear-powered missile submarine (SSBN) and two nuclear-powered attack submarines (SSN) were launched; guided missile frigates were commissioned; various auxiliary vessels were built; manpower doubled. Additionally, naval schools shook off the stifling, introverted effects of the 'Great Proletarian Cultural Revolution' (GPCR), and introduced modern curricula to the post-Civil War generation.[2]

The first two years of the 1980s saw these trends continue. The Chinese navy began to operate at greater distances from the coast and, in 1981, a twenty-ship task force sailed to the vicinity of the Fiji Islands where it supported a successful ICBM test launch from western China. Then, in the autumn of 1982, the Chinese startled the world with an apparently flawless firing of an underwater submarine-launched ballistic missile (SLBM). Although reports of this event remain obscure, it is now believed that the missile was fired from China's aging Golf Class (SSB) submarine, and travelled some 600–700 nautical miles.[3]

THE FACTORS OF CHANGE

China's naval renaissance was induced by a confluence of decisions and events which turned the country away from its traditional continentalist philosophy to one which was decidedly more maritime in nature. Foremost among the factors of change was China's decision in the late 1960s to revise its foreign relations *vis-à-vis* the West, and particularly the United States and Japan. Shortly thereafter, in the early 1970s, the PRC gained entry to the United Nations – a membership that it has used effectively.

Second, there was a transition of power in China in the 1970s. With Mao's death and the suppression of the radical power base, new leaders emerged who place politics and ideology second to economics and national modernisation. For the moment, it is far better to be 'expert' than 'red'. While many old-time Long Marchers remain in high posts, their power has been heavily eroded, and the accent is on technocrats.

Third, the emphasis on improving China's economic system has been of particular significance. Eschewing the traditional Soviet-style planned system the Chinese, in the 1970s, made bold moves which highlight the growing importance of maritime affairs in China's modernisation plans. For example, one of the earliest decisions involved the rapid build-up of the merchant marine. The PRC had two very good reasons for doing this: first, as the nation moved toward a trade-oriented system, it found that it was almost wholly dependent on an expensive charter system run by European shipping firms; and, secondly, modernisation in the highly populated, industrial coastal regions required more ships and efficient ports to move goods. Chinese efforts in this sphere have been massive, and nothing short of astounding. Between 1970 and 1980 nearly ten million dead-weight tons of merchant ships were either purchased or built by the Chinese. Every major port also underwent a facelift, and many added modern container and petroleum-handling facilities.

Chinese shipbuilding also made impressive gains as old-line yards like Jiangnan (Kiangnan) have re-entered the international shipbuilding and repair market. Since 1979 contracts have been signed for the export of ships built in the PRC totalling more than 900 000 tons. Customers include Singapore, Malaysia, Rumania, Poland, the United States, Italy, the Federal Republic of Germany, Hong Kong, and Macao.[4]

Underlying the effort to modernise China's port and shipping system was Beijing's decision to open up special economic zones at various coastal sites. Several in the south are now in operation and they are attracting foreign investors. The PRC leadership has given them much economic autonomy, as well as high priority for raw materials, power, and labour.

Offshore oil and gas development is also of paramount concern to the Chinese. Wells have been sunk and are successfully extracting petroleum in the Gulf of Bohai, East China Sea, and South China Sea. While Western estimates of China's offshore reserves vary, all agree that they are significant and, thanks to a shallow continental shelf, relatively easy to exploit.[5]

Aquatic food production is also being expanded by the Chinese. More efficient fishing boats and equipment have been added, and with the advent of the Law of the Sea Treaty, Chinese fishing fleets will be much more in evidence at greater distances from the coast. An indication of China's intense interest in exploiting and utilising its ocean resources, can be seen in its current involvement in a comprehensive, six-year survey of the coastal zones.[6]

China stands to gain a great deal from the Law of the Sea Treaty. For instance, key provisions of the treaty will allow Beijing to claim economic control over vast ocean and sea regions. There are problems, however. For example, China claims some 160 islands, reefs, and islets in the South China Sea which are also claimed by other nations, such as Vietnam and the Philippines.

There are also important military–strategic motives for Chinese Naval expansion. Despite recent ongoing efforts by China and the Soviet Union to improve relations, there remains wide disagreement between the two. Standard among Chinese charges is that Soviet hegemonism is one of, if not *the* greatest threat to world peace. Beijing invariably cites three key complaints – the large deployment of Soviet forces (an estimated 50 divisions) along their common border; the Soviet invasion of Afghanistan; and the Soviet support for Hanoi and the Vietnamese-backed Heng Samrin regime in Kampuchea.

Soviet naval activities in the South China Sea, Malacca, Indian Ocean, and Persian Gulf are another favourite target of the Chinese media. In early 1980, the *People's Daily* noted the following:

> What deserves attention is that the Soviet Union established a new command organ and noticeably strengthened its navy in the Far East, war theatre in 1979. In 1978 it sent some submarines, large vessels capable of water–surface operations, and auxiliary vessels from Europe. In 1979, it officially included the carrier *Minsk* in its Pacific fleet. Since the outbreak of our country's self-defence counterattack against Vietnam, the vessels of the Soviet Pacific Fleet have stepped up their activities and gained the right to use the naval and air bases in Cam Ranh Bay, Danang, Ho Chi Minh City and Haiphong.[7]

Deng Xiaoping has explained the Soviet naval expansion in the Pacific as being part of the Kremlin's 'dumbbell strategy'. According to Deng, the Soviet navy is bent on controlling the Pacific at one end, and the Indian Ocean/Persian Gulf at the other. Joining the two regions is the critical bar of the Malacca Strait.[8]

China's concerns over Soviet naval operations near its coast are not unwarranted. During the late 1960s and the 1970s, as Sino-Soviet relations steadily deteriorated, the Soviet navy conducted provocative operations in China's adjacent seas. Intelligence collectors appeared in the Yellow and East China Seas, and Soviet naval squadrons, including the carrier *Minsk*, crossed the East China Sea near Shanghai. Undoubtedly, Soviet submarines carry out surveillance activities along China's coast, much in the manner of their operations against Sweden.

The Chinese are especially alarmed over the Soviet naval presence in Vietnam. Since 1979 the USSR has maintained a naval squadron at Cam Ranh Bay, and TU-95/Bear-D reconnaissance and TU-142/Bear-F ASW aircraft at Danang.[9] The air missions carried out by these planes are principally aimed at surveillance of China's southern coasts, as well as the large Chinese submarine force based in the South China Sea. The Chinese are also unhappy with the Soviet Union's attempts to upgrade the Vietnamese navy. In 1982-3 the USSR has given Hanoi four Petya I, one ex-Barnegat frigate (now fitted with SS-N-2/Styx SSMs), one Admirable class corvette, four SO1 PCs, a Shershen class PTF, and eight Osa II class PTGs.[10]

Finally, there have been important changes in China's leadership leading to a new emphasis on the navy. The PRC navy is making a concerted effort to broaden the experience of its officer corps through more frequent rotations in assignment. Lately, fleet commanders (that is, the North Sea Fleet, East Sea Fleet, and South Sea Fleet) and their staffs have been rotated every two to three years. This is a big change considering the PLA's past record of keeping senior officers in the same billet for years.

At the high command level, changes have been made which are very favourable to the navy. For example, in November 1982 General Zhang Aiping was named China's new defence minister. From 1975 to 1982 Zhang had been chairman of the influential National Defence Scientific and Technological Commission (NDSTC). In this capacity he played the key role in the development of China's SSBN. Apparently, in early 1979, he impressed upon Deng Xiaoping the need to speed up efforts to develop the submarine-launched missile which had been lagging for years. With Zhang's urging, funding was arranged for the navy's research institute to upgrade the critical computer capability necessary to test the missile.[11]

Zhang's interest in naval matters stems from previous important assignments with the navy in the 1950s. Although a Long Marcher (he is 72 years old), Zhang helped organise the East Sea Fleet in 1949 and, in 1955, planned and directed the PRC's capture of the Dachen Islands, the PLA's first combined air-land-sea operation.[12]

The other important personnel change occurred in October 1982. At that time, Admiral Liu Huaqing became China's 'chief of naval operations', replacing Ye Fei. Liu's previous assignment was that of assistant chief of staff of the PLA (1979–82), an office of considerable importance. Liu also has strong navy credentials, having served in a variety of naval posts from 1950 to the mid-1960s. Liu was purged in 1968 during the Cultural Revolution, and did not reappear until 1975 when he was identified as being Zhang Aiping's vice-chairman of the NDSTC.[13] Liu undoubtedly played a principal role in supporting the navy's modernisation programmes, including submarine missile development.

TECHNOLOGICAL MOTIVATION

All of the foregoing factors have acted to raise the PRC navy's technological consciousness. In May 1982 the navy held its first scientific symposium, where several hundred papers were presented on topics such as natural science, mathematics, and statistics. Others addressed the application of science in naval modernisation, and strategic and tactical concepts under wartime conditions.[14]

Later, in August, the navy held its annual congress, which was prominently reported in the *People's Daily*. Unlike past congresses, where politics and ideology always preoccupied participants, this one emphasised the many technological advances being made by the navy. The Maoist doctrine of 'man over weapons' was not in evidence as the navy representatives listened to speeches describing their warships as 'scientific fortresses, moving on the sea'.[15] The delegates were also reminded of a recent visit to the fleet by the old-time military hero Marshal Ye Jianying. According to the *People's Daily*, Ye had advised the navy to 'make vigorous efforts to catch up with the advanced world standard. Only by making vigorous efforts can we catch up'.[16] The article goes on to trumpet the virtues of scientific knowledge, describing it as the 'gold key' to success in the navy's many material achievements.[17]

The Chinese have done more than just pay lip service to their new-found technological percipience. Since 1981 education and training programmes have expanded at a rapid rate, with naval schools adding courses in operational research and military science and technology. The Falklands war received a great deal of attention and study in PRC naval schools, and in fact is being used to re-educate personnel on modern naval tactics and strategy.[18]

NAVAL REFORM – THE IMPACT ON TACTICS AND STRATEGY

The Chinese recently have devoted a great deal of attention to reassessing their traditional coastal defence doctrine. In the past, most ships and aircraft were given local defence responsibilities, and were expected to defend a sea region not much beyond land radar range; that is, out to about fifty nautical miles. That thinking has changed. The navy now views itself as a combined service made up of a main surface force, a submarine force, a naval air force, and a coastguard force.[19] The first three are evolving into a navy with regional responsibilities out to at least the limits of China's continental shelf and exclusive economic zone (ranging between 200 and 350 nautical miles).

As a result of this, more advanced operational activities have been noted. For example, Chinese naval squadrons have been observed operating further at sea for longer periods of time. In May 1981 three PRC destroyers and two replenishment auxiliaries left Qingdao in the Yellow Sea and sailed eastward beyond the Okinawa chain, and thence south to the Tonkin Gulf. After anchoring off Hong Kong, the vessels returned to Qingdao via the Taiwan Strait. During these sorties, ships refuelled in alongside manoeuvres.[20] Ship-based helicopter operations were also conducted under the most adverse of weather conditions.[21]

The emphasis on extended at-sea operations, the new ordering of forces, and advanced weapons development obviously reflect a keener appreciation of sea power by the PLA high command. In fact the Chinese, whose ability to counter a limited Soviet ground attack is severely restricted, may be in the process of building a SSBN force which would ensure that such a hypothetical Soviet invasion is an expensive one. The potential costs would of course be even higher if the enemy was one of the other regional naval powers, including the United States, Japan or Taiwan. It is rumoured that the PRC now has six SSBNs under construction at a cost of 10 billion yuan (roughly $20 billion US).[22] When these are completed at the end of this decade,

China will be able to put eighty-four 200 kiloton nuclear missiles at sea. No matter what type of attack might be launched against China, the PRC's small SSBN force will loom as a significant deterrent.

In terms of Chinese wartime contingency planning, there are at least five conventional scenarios in which the navy would play a significant role. Three involve the Soviet Union which might attempt limited invasions of Xinjiang (China's far west), the Beijing–Tianjin corridor, or Manchuria. In the latter two of these scenarios, the Chinese believe that Soviet naval infantry would attempt landings to link up with ground forces. A Beijing–Tianjin attack would probably originate from Mongolia, whose border is only 300 miles from the Chinese capital. Subsequently a Soviet naval force would attempt to enter the Gulf of Bohai and put troops ashore near Tianjin. By Chinese reckoning, a Soviet thrust into Manchuria would also be accompanied by a Soviet amphibious landing on the Liaodong Peninsula.

The PRC navy conducts tireless training to thwart these anticipated amphibious landings. And it is well organised to interdict a Soviet naval invasion force in the Yellow Sea and Bohai Gulf approaches. An estimated sixty conventional submarines, well suited for shallow-water operations, are divided into squadrons at Shanghai, Qingdao, and Lushun. Each of these bases also possess main-surface force squadrons of missile destroyers and frigates. Other minor bases and islands have contingents of small missile and torpedo craft numbering several hundred vessels. Ashore there are many air bases which have M16 fighters and TU-16 and IL-28 bombers, and, along the coast there are numerous missile batteries and gun emplacements which are in hardened sites.

China's fourth scenario involves 'protecting' its island claims, offshore petroleum holdings, and fisheries in the South China Sea. It views Vietnam and its patron, the USSR, as threats to its interests in this region. As stated previously, the PRC is most unhappy about Soviet naval activity in the area and the assignment of ships to Vietnamese bases. Further exacerbating relations in the area are conflicting claims between Beijing and Hanoi over territorial rights and island ownership. The Vietnamese and Chinese frequently engage in verbal clashes over ownership of many of the islands in the South China Sea and occasionally fighting erupts, especially among fishermen – the latest shoot-out occurred in July 1982.[23] Several years ago the Vietnamese captured a Chinese tug towing an oil rig north from Signapore and held it for a number of weeks for violating Hanoi's claimed territorial waters.

Since the early 1970s China has been carefully improving its naval posture in the South China Sea. First, it began increasing its order-of-battle by moving submarines and main surface force ships to the bases on Hainan Island and the Leizhou Peninsula. Finally, in 1974, it attacked the Paracels Islands (China calls them the Xisha Islands), defeating the few South Vietnamese defenders stationed there. Over the next eight years China added many new buildings, pier facilities, and radar surveillance sites in these islands, and a permanent naval force is now in residence. Additionally, ships and aircraft have been added to bases on Hainan Island and the expanding naval facility at Zhanjiang.

China's fifth contingency scenario involves an attack against Taiwan. The PRC fully realises the enormous cost in manpower and equipment that such an invasion would entail. Moreover, there is a strong possibility that the PLA would not be successful. For domestic political purposes, however, recovery of Taiwan remains a national policy goal and, on occasion, Beijing conducts naval exercises in the Taiwan Strait. Moscow, which likes to keep the pot stirred over China's weakness *vis-à-vis* Taiwan, recently reported that the PRC is planning to update its small, vintage amphibious force. According to the report, China will soon build heavy-tonnage landing vessels and high-speed hydrofoil landing craft.[24]

It is not thought likely that China will attempt during the next fifteen years to solve the Taiwan problem through military action. One major reason is Hong Kong. Beijing wants the world, and Taiwan in particular, to view the return of that island to Chinese control as a model event. China also has economic reasons for refraining from turning the Taiwan Strait into a war zone. It has need to keep the route open in order efficiently to use its growing merchant fleet for overseas trade. Also, it wants to open a large special economic zone at Amoy, five miles distant from the Nationalist-held island of Quemoy. If the Chinese expect to attract foreign investors to Amoy, they will have to keep the peace in the area. Thus, over the next decade, it is believed that the PRC navy will appear only periodically in the Taiwan Strait, avoiding any hostile acts.

DEFICIENCIES

Despite its accomplishments, China's navy remains constrained by lack of technology and low technical education standards and facilities. Many of the navy's deficiencies are readily identifiable.

Weapons and Electronic Systems

For some years the PRC navy has struggled to build an adequate surface-to-air missile (SAM) for its destroyers and frigates. Recently the Chinese opted to solve this persistent problem by turning to the West. In November 1982 China concluded a $160 million contract with two British defence firms, Vosper Thornycroft and British Aerospace, for the purchase of an undisclosed number of Sea Dart SAMS for installation aboard Luda class destroyers. However, shortly after the contract had been agreed, the Chinese cancelled it. The official reason was that the PRC Central Committee had decided to spend the money on crew habitability programmes. The more likely reason was a budgetary one, with higher priority ground forces or air requirements pre-empting the navy SAM programme.[25] It is believed that, in time, the Chinese will attempt to renegotiate the Sea Dart contract with the British.

With the successful underwater missile launch in October 1982, China apparently overcame its longstanding SLBM problems. The next SLBM testing phase will be a delicate one, however. For the Chinese must test fire the missile from a nuclear-powered submarine, and it may be some time before that event occurs. One reason for this is that the navy may still be experiencing difficulties with the engineering plant aboard its nuclear submarines. Since about 1972, when the first SSN was launched, there have been rumours of serious propulsion problems.[26] The Chinese could well turn to the West for help in troubleshooting these recurring technical and design failures.

Anti-submarine warfare is a main weakness of the PRC navy. Weapons are vintage 1950 Russian models, and it is believed that sonars are equally primitive. The Chinese continue to shop in the European defence markets for replacement systems, but have made no major purchases to date.

Although Chinese naval electronic systems are old and much less advanced than systems used by China's potential adversaries, the Chinese are being very selective as they continue to travel about Europe looking at available radars, sonars, and ECM equipments. They will probably make necessary purchases when they feel ready.

Mine Warfare

The China coast is susceptible to mining, but only recently has the Chinese navy begun to show interest in mine warfare. Training has been conducted where aging mine sweepers have carried out synchronous sweeping exercises – a procedure well known among Western navies. However, Chinese equipment is very old and will have to undergo significant improvement before the navy can be expected effectively to open coastal sea lanes in wartime.

Aircraft

Chinese naval aviation lags far behind in at-sea capability. Its aircraft are old and have little ability to carry out ASW or anti-ship operations. The Chinese also need maritime patrol planes which can extend their current short-range surveillance and intelligence horizon. The navy is looking at the Western market, however, and is interested in the French Exocet missile, the British Nimrod, and various maritime patrol airplanes. If China wants to improve its ability to control and patrol its vast offshore economic zones, sooner or later it will have to consider improving its naval aviation.

Personnel and Training

Since 1982 the Chinese navy has made great strides in raising personnel technical standards. Sailors no longer spend long periods engaged in ideological training and seminars, but rather concentrate their energies on mastering technical skills. The Chinese are still far behind, however, and it will take a major overhaul to reach Western levels. It will also require an expensive investment in computer-assisted training aids, as well as other education and training materials.

THE FUTURE

For the moment, all indicators point toward China's conversion to a regional navy with limited blue-water capability. However, in order to move from its traditional coastal defence posture to one that is more flexible and versatile, Beijing is likely to continue looking to the West and Japan for help. The Chinese remain cautious, for they are keenly aware that past attempts at naval reform and modernisation foundered owing to over-dependence on foreign technology and advisors.[27] Thus Beijing has moved in a deliberate and selective fashion, only concluding armament agreements after full and lengthy investigation.

It will take money to enable the Chinese navy to make a shift in posture but, at present, the military budget is declining. Upon taking office as defence minister, Zhang Aiping warned that it would be necessary for the PLA 'to retrench expenditure in peacetime to ensure a rapid development of the national economy'.[28] The same theme is being disseminated elsewhere. For example, the *China Daily* wrote that 'the speed and scale of our national defense spending must not surpass state financial and material capabilities, nor must such spending be detrimental to the progress of economic construction'.[29]

These warnings may be intended for the army, which has been bloated for years by excessive manpower and a redundant organisational structure. It is well known that Deng Xiaoping has wanted to reduce the army and reorganise it into a leaner, more efficient force. The navy, which has been favoured for a number of years, is expected to continue steady growth and hold its own in the budget fights to come during the 1980s. Furthermore, the availability of funds is not all that uncertain. In fact, the Chinese economy is doing nicely by current world standards. Wharton Econometrics notes that balance-of-payments calculations show that China has become a net creditor in the world, with a large and growing current account surplus. Moreover, China's growth rate stood at 7 per cent in 1982, and its industrial output was at 10 per cent through June of that year.[30]

If China succeeds in restyling the navy into a limited blue-water regional force, several possibilities exist *vis-à-vis* Pacific naval affairs. First, if Sino–Soviet relations remain cool, the USSR can be expected to react to Chinese naval growth by expanding its Pacific fleet. In fact, Soviet naval expansion in Asia during the 1970s was due in no small part to China's naval build-up. Considering the size of the PRC's present submarine fleet and its plans to create a small SSBN force, the USSR will continue to monitor the activities of these forces closely. The Soviets are likely to improve their ASW posture, as well as perfect their defensive and offensive mining capability. They will also continue to help the Vietnamese expand their navy.

Because of its dependence on international shipping for raw materials and trade exports, Japan will also be interested in Chinese naval expansion. Considering past naval confrontations between these two nations, it will not be surprising if the Japanese Maritime Self-Defence Force begins to spend more on naval aircraft and ships.

Taiwan can be expected to use any PRC naval build-up as a bargaining point with Washington. The PRC's SSBN test has been a major news item, and Taibei is surely measuring its options for countering that threat.

Association of Southeast Asia Nations (ASEAN) have legitimate worries over a bigger, more active Chinese navy. The Philippines, for example, has claimed ownership of several South China Sea islands that China also claims. Indonesia, which worries more about Chinese expansion than Soviet ambitions in its regional sphere of interest, will be watching Chinese naval activities in the South China Sea islands with concern. In this regard, Jakarta has a large overseas Chinese population, and has been on the receiving end of Chinese aggression or subversion more than once. It is also mindful that history shows past Chinese maritime expansion always to have been southward through Malacca into the Indian Ocean. Any attempt by the PRC navy to send even a peaceful show-the-flag force beyond the South China Sea will be viewed with great alarm by Indonesia.

The United States must also calculate the consequences of a Chinese naval build-up. Each of the reactions postulated above would obviously complicate the western Pacific naval equation and force a new assessment by Washington. The biggest worry, however, will be how Sino-Soviet relationships evolve. If an *entente cordiale* results and current US economic trends continue straining defence spending, the US Pacific Fleet could find itself facing overwhelming odds.

In conclusion, China's naval and maritime successes over the past decade have placed the navy in a strong position at the highest leadership levels, both civil and military. A consensus seems to be taking shape and plans are being devised calling for even bolder maritime policies. Serious problems do exist and, as stated earlier, China has a poor record at maintaining constant growth or planned modernisation programmes in the naval and maritime spheres. The next two decades will tell whether Chinese efforts fail or succeed.

NOTES AND REFERENCES

1. 'Chinese Defense Spending,' CIA Research Paper SR 80-10091, July 1980.
2. For details, see Bruce Swanson, *Eighth Voyage of the Dragon* (Annapolis: Naval Institute Press, 1982), ch. 19. Also see 'PLA Navy Holds First Scientific Symposium', in Foreign Broadcast Information Service: China (hereinafter FBIS-CHI), 19 May 1982, K15.
3. The best description of China's submarine missile programme is contained in LCDR David G. Miller, Jr., 'China's SSBN in Perspective', *US Naval Institute Proceedings*, March 1983, 125-27. Also see the Chinese account in 'Radical Rejuvenation of PRC Navy Planned', in Foreign Broadcast Information Service: Soviet Union (hereinafter FBIS-SOV), 26 August 1982, B1. Chinese descriptions of the launch are carried in FBIS-CHI, 18 October 1982), K1-12.

4. 'China Daily Reviews Shipbuilding Industry', FBIS-CHI, 28 September 1982, K12–13.
5. The latest discovery is described in 'Wen Wei Pao On East China Sea Gas Discovery', in FBIS-CHI 11 August 1982, W6. Also see 'East China Sea Well Yields First Natural Gas', FBIS-CHI, 10 August 1982, K16.
6. 'Survey of Coastal Zones, Tidal Flats Under Way', FBIS-CHI 19 November 1982, K26–27.
7. 'Renmin Ribao Looks at Soviet Military Strategy', FBIS-CHI 15 January 1980, C5.
8. See Deng's interview in *Forbes*, 9 June 1980.
9. G. Jacobs, 'New Soviet Arms for Vietnam', *Pacific Defence Reporter*, September 1982, 51.
10. Ibid.
11. 'Newsletter on Launch', FBIS-CHI, 18 October 1982, K8 and K11.
12. 'Zhang Aiping on the New Constitution', *Zhongguo Xinwen She*, trans. in FBIS-CHI 14 December 1982, K62.
13. Wolfgang Bartke, *Who's Who in the People's Republic of China*, (New York, Armonk, M. E. Sharpe, 1981), 228.
14. FBIS-CHI (19 May 1982), K15.
15. 'Renmin Ribao Reports on PLA Navy Congress', FBIS-CHI 25 August 1982, K18.
16. Ibid.
17. Ibid.
18. 'PLA Naval Academy Studies Falklands Battle', FBIS-CHI 12 July 1982, K11.
19. FBIS-CHI 19 May 1982, K15.
20. See Jonathan Pollack, 'The men but not the guns', *Far Eastern Economic Review*, 18–24 December 1981, 28.
21. Qiu Weiming, 'First Group of Pilots Trained for Ship-Based Helicopters', *Renmin Ribao*, 13 November 1982, 4.
22. 'China's Nuclear Subs', *Defense and Foreign Affairs Weekly*, 22–28 November 1982, 1.
23. 'Xinhua Commentator Rebuts SRV on Xisha Islands', FBIS-CHI 11 June 1982, E1–3, and 'Militiamen Clash with SRV Gunboats in Beibu Gulf', FBIS-CHI, 27 July 1982, E1–2.
24. FBIS-SOV, 26 August 1982, B1.
25. Desmond Wettern, 'Letdown for Britain on China Arms', *The Daily Telegraph*, 2 March 1983, 28.
26. Ti Tsung-heng (Di Zongheng), 'Communist, Nationalist Naval Strength Assessed', *Ming Bao*, February, March, April 1977, trans. in Joint Publication Research Service (JPRS) 71527, July 1978, 37–38.
27. For details see Swanson, *Eighth Voyage of the Dragon*, Ch. 6–13.
28. Qtd in 'Asia: China's Military Posture', *Defense and Foreign Affairs Weekly*, 20–26 December 1982, 4.
29. Ibid.
30. Albert Keidel, 'China's Maturing Reforms: Regional Miracle Growth?' *Wharton–Pacific Basin Economic Review*, Fall 1982, vol. 2, no. 2, 73–76.

7 Nuclear Forces

GERALD SEGAL

The analysis of nuclear weapons strategy figures prominently in studies of the great powers, but in China's case nuclear weapons seem less crucial. We are thus confronted with a basic problem – the tendency to interpret Chinese nuclear doctrine primarily in terms of Western strategic thought, whether it be of the superpower or limited great power variety. The necessity to overcome ethnocentrism in strategic analysis is now well recognized.[1] Thus it is crucial to return to basics in assessing Chinese nuclear forces and doctrine. What is the Chinese perception of threat, what forces does it have, what are the sources of Chinese strategic doctrine, and finally what is the nature of Chinese deterrence strategy?

THE THREAT

China's assessment of the nuclear threat is obviously related to a broader assessment of trends in general international relations. Thus it should become immediately clear that China's nuclear threat assessment is regularly changing and rarely unchallenged. It is the nature of the changing international scene and the regular domestic debates that makes generalisations about threat assessment notoriously dangerous.[2] On balance, at present China has reason to be concerned with three potential nuclear threats.[3]

The Soviet Union poses the most varied types of threat, ranging from a direct clash along their long border, to an indirect confrontation, perhaps involving such Soviet allies as Vietnam. The other superpower, the United States, poses less direct, but no less important potential threats. Indeed it was precisely such indirect United States threats in the 1950–60s regarding Korea, and especially Taiwan, that probably encouraged China to seek its own nuclear forces.[4] The rationale for Chinese concern with similar threats from the United States has not entirely disappeared since the normalisation of relations. Real disputes continue to exist between the United States and China, and given Washington's unwillingness to withdraw from the Pacific theatre,[5] the potential for conflict is unlikely to decrease.

The third potential threat, from India, is obviously far less imminent, if only because of India's low key and uncertain nuclear future.[6] It is however important to consider potential non-superpower threats because, perhaps more than most aspects of defence, nuclear strategy needs to be concerned with future planning. In this context, the potential for other regional nuclear forces, especially in Pakistan and Japan, would make it clear to China that it could soon be part of a very complex Asian nuclear balance of power. While China has pledged itself not to be the first user of nuclear weapons, and thus implicitly offered solace to non-nuclear states,[7] there is good reason to doubt that this pledge has much operational importance. As is apparent from the current debate in Western Europe about pledges of no-first-use, it is clear that they provide no guarantee that nuclear weapons will not be used once a conventional war has begun.[8] It is equally clear that pledges of nuclear free zones, which China has also proposed, are empty promises. A nuclear free zone is not a nuclear safe zone. Thus China's assessment of potential nuclear threat needs to be broad, and above all flexible. Before assessing the extent of doctrinal flexibility, it is useful to outline briefly the nature of China's own nuclear forces.

THE NUCLEAR FORCES

By most measures, China is the world's third largest nuclear weapons power.[9] Its nuclear posture, like that of the Soviet Union, has three tiers. First, China has a passive programme of civil defence designed to reduce the effect of nuclear weapons that reach China. While one may question the effectiveness of civil defence, there is little doubt that China continues to see it as useful and worthy of expenditure. Second, China retains some active defence, especially in the air. Once again one may question its utility, but not China's determination to retain this tier.

Third, like both superpowers, China has offensive forces designed to carry a nuclear war to the enemy. While China may have fewer of each type of weapon, it does seem to have adopted a range of nuclear forces. At the top range it has recently developed a fully inter-continental ballistic missile (ICBM). In 1981 there was evidence that a MIRV capability was tested for an ICBM. More importantly, in 1982 China demonstrated an SLBM capability, and although the missile used was only of medium range, the mobility of the submarine clearly extends the range of this system to intercontinental distance. In the medium range China has long had a mix of systems, from missiles to bombers. At the tactical level there has been speculation about China's development of such weapons. While it is unclear whether China actually deploys such systems, by 1982 it was clear that PLA forces were training in a simulated nuclear environment resulting from the use of tactical systems.[10] Thus by 1982 China seemed to be well on its way to a full range of nuclear forces, although the actual numbers in each category will not necessarily be high.

These Chinese forces appear to be deployed in various modes, and as with the recent move to a broader range of forces, so China seems to adopt a more flexible approach to basing. The SLBM now completes the triad of forces, although they are unlikely to go in for the massive numbers in each environment as does the United States. Even the Soviet Union accepts an imbalance in favour of its land-based component. China, like the Soviet Union, has also tried to disperse its land-based forces.[11] Both are continental powers with paranoia about hostile neighbours, thereby encouraging such flexibility in forces.

Clearly the precise nature of forces deployed is due to a number of factors. It is now necessary to assess in greater detail the sources of Chinese strategic nuclear doctrine, and then offer some ideas on the more precise nature of Chinese strategy.

SOURCES OF NUCLEAR STRATEGY

The sources of strategy are myriad and complex. The selection that follows is not comprehensive, and above all omits one of the crucial motives for strategy, serendipity.[12] It should also be stressed that strategy is regularly changing often as a result of domestic debates.[13] It is for these, and other, reasons that it is best to adopt a flexible attitude towards the definition of key terms. Thus doctrine, strategy and policy are used interchangeably. This is not to suggest there is no important distinction,[14] but rather that Chinese nuclear strategy, like that of other powers, has complex origins. In order to understand the nature of strategy, it is best to keep an open mind on possible sources, deriving what one can from 'military strategy', 'military science' and 'military doctrine'.

Geography

It would be foolish to adopt a Mackinder-like determinism in arguing that geographic realities set enduring features of military strategy.[15] Yet the physical and human geography of a state is relevant in certain limited but important ways. Four aspects stand out as most relevant. First, with the world's largest population, the Chinese people are less likely to be entirely destroyed in a nuclear exchange. Despite a city-dwelling proportion of its population not dissimilar to that of the Soviet Union, China can have greater confidence of some sort of post-nuclear survival. In absolute numbers, many more millions reside in the countryside in China than in any other state.[16]

Second, China's economy is less industrialised than that of either superpower. This provides for weakness on the one hand as it will take fewer weapons to destroy Chinese industry, but it provides for strength in that the Chinese economy is more rural-based and less vulnerable to nuclear strikes.

Third, despite a lengthy coastline marked by thousands of islands, China is primarily concerned with land threats to its security. While this continentalist bias may now be changing,[17] it certainly has been historically true that China has been more concerned with its position on land. This leads to the fourth factor. China, much like the Soviet Union, perceives itself to be surrounded by hostile states (mostly communist). China's land boundaries, the second longest after those of the Soviet Union, offer more protection than in the Soviet case. Only in the north and west does geography work against China, and then not without grounds for optimism in defence.[18] However, unlike the Soviet Union, China is still involved in competition with neighbours over irredentist claims, including conflict with Taiwan, Vietnam and Japan.

In sum, China has less cause to be concerned with a general invasion of its territory or vulnerability to nuclear war. This is not to say that continentalist China has no fears. Indeed its major fears are of limited threats along its coastal and land frontiers. With its relatively backward economy, China's short-term growth could easily be set back by limited strikes.

Ideology

Ideology is not an instruction manual on defence policy for any state, but it is relevant as a prism through which perception of the external and internal reality are filtered, and often refracted. Like geography, ideology is not a rigid determinant of policy, but it does help shape the end product of military strategy. Four major aspects of ideology appear as most relevant.

First, like the Soviet Union, China continues to believe that conflict between capitalism and communism is inevitable. There was a time when China was more vociferous on this point than Moscow, arguing that the conflict would inevitably be military. Khrushchev abandoned the belief that the atom bomb 'obeys the class principle' but for a time China continued to argue that supposed Soviet nuclear advantages could be used to pressure the West. However, China never engaged in what it called 'nuclear fetishism', by exaggerating the utility of nuclear weapons. China's belief that military (conventional) struggle would continue and inevitably result in world war, was only abandoned in 1980.[19] Thus China, like the Soviet Union, had come to believe that although conflict will continue it need no longer be of the military kind. Therefore deterrence, in the military context in general and the nuclear sense in particular, took on new importance.

Second, China also shares the Soviet belief that the avoidance of war is best achieved by preparation for war. For example, in 1982 a Chinese statement decleared, 'Peace cannot be gained by prayer, and war cannot be avoided by concessions'.[20] This lesson of peace through strength was learned not only in terms of East-West confrontation, but also in terms of reliance on someone else's power for China's security. China's bitter experience with the Sino–Soviet defence alliance was perhaps the prime motive in Beijing's search for its own nuclear capability.

Third, with the Soviet Union China shares the belief that communism will truimph in the end. But in this case China was well ahead of the Soviet Union in arguing that nuclear war was not a useful instrument for obtaining this objective. China's long held belief that nuclear weapons were 'paper tigers', that their decisiveness was exaggerated, suggested that the triumph of communism would be achieved through more traditional and less devastating means.[21]

Fourth, like the Soviet Union, China believes in the absence of a dividing line between nuclear and conventional war. The social and political essence of war is consistent, and in Clausewitzian terms, China sees any combat as a continuation of the policy of furthering the communist cause.[22] Indeed Beijing has been less infatuated with the novelty of nuclear weapons for far longer than the Soviet Union. There was no Chinese equivalent of Khrushchev's 'nuclear fetishism' or the Soviet Union's relative disregard of conventional power during the first part of the 1960s.[23] In sum, while it is true that important elements of Chinese ideology have changed over time, they retain the view that peace must be kept through strength and pre-eminently a self-reliant strength. Wars can be controlled, but the end of international conflict will only come when the social structures of states are transformed towards communism.

Institutions

Despite the recent academic vogue to explain defence policy almost entirely with reference to institutional or bureaucratic politics, it is more useful to see institutions as only one of several determinants of strategy. In the very murky area of Chinese institutions,[24] three aspects stand out as most pertinent to nuclear strategy. First, as in the Soviet Union, the military is not a single coherent institution. Especially when it comes to foreign policy the PLA, as do various other groups in Chinese politics, tends to be divided. The resulting debates are no more unusual than they are in the Soviet Union where cross-cutting cleavages complicate the decision-making process.

Second, in part because of these complex cleavages, the PLA has little clear role in the formulation of foreign policy strategy. While the PLA may participate in decisions as does the military in the Soviet Union,[25] in China the choices are more clearly identified as political and not requiring the predominance of military expertise. This trend seems especially true in the realm of nuclear weapons strategy where the military involvement is far less direct.[26] China has no institution resembling the powerful Strategic Rocket Forces in the Soviet Union. The Second Artillery in China might fulfil some of the same roles, but it is far more dominated by civilian public security and scientific experts. The Second Artillery also seems to be far more tied to central foreign policy-making and might in some respects be seen as a shortcut, obviating the need for large spending on conventional forces. Neither does there appear to be anything like the powerful Soviet design teams and the military-industrial pressure groups involved in shaping Chinese strategic forces.[27]

Third, this greater political control in China is made possible in large part by the relatively backward nature of the Chinese defence economy and its strategic forces. China's 1982 testing of an SLBM was a startling leap into the superpower technology of the 1960s. While such leaps may be impressive in relation to the under-developed nature of the Chinese economy as a whole, this very distinctiveness makes them more easily controlled by the civilian leadership. The evolution of China's defence technology seems therefore to be more the result of precise civilian strategy than subject to the vagaries of institutional politics. This may well change as China modernises, but in the meantime China seems more content to persevere with, and overcome, specific technological problems over a long period, than to embark on expensive and urgent experiments without a clear idea of the outcome. Thus the long concentration on the development of solid fuel and improved guidance systems for the Chinese ICBM and SLBM may (for many years) have delayed progress in other aspects of nuclear weaponry. But it did have the advantage of in the end producing what the leadership probably wanted, and no doubt at a cheaper cost.[28]

In sum, military institutions seem to play a less crucial role in determining Chinese nuclear strategy. This is less due to the complexity of the decision-making process, although that is no doubt part of the story, but more essentially because of the relative state of Chinese underdevelopment. Therefore the political control and relative simplicity of doctrine is more easily maintained. This state of affairs may change with trends towards modernisation, but this is not necessarily so. It is possible that China, as a 'non-superpower', simply does not seek the massive overkill capacity possessed by the superpowers. In order to understand this problem, it is time to concentrate more specifically on the nature of Chinese strategic doctrine that results from the sources of strategy already outlined.

NUCLEAR WEAPONS STRATEGY

The assessment of China's nuclear strategy needs to fall between ethnocentrism and ethnic-chic – between the tendency to see China as any other nuclear power, and the tendency to see it as an entirely special case. Thus it is essential to emphasise that China, like other nuclear powers, sees these horrific weapons as essentially for deterrence. But definitions of deterrence are almost as abundant as the weapons themselves.[29] What all the definitions share is a belief that deterrence is the prevention of an action by making clear that its costs will outweigh its benefits. Beyond this generality, deterrence is defined differently in various nuclear states. A useful way of getting to the heart of the Chinese doctrine is to ask three key questions. First, is deterrence to be achieved by relying on threats of punishment or by denying the enemy victory? Second, is this deterrence achieved by using a broad range of weapons, or will a few types suffice? Third, does China need a large number of each type of weapon, or will a few be enough?

Deterrence by Denial

The most deeply rooted bias in strategic studies literature is the conception of deterrence as based on a threat of punishment. Western ethnocentrism in this regard has only recently been countered by those who point to the Soviet belief in deterrence by denying victory to the enemy.[30] Where does China stand?

China shares the Soviet belief that by emphasising the defensive component, victory can be denied the enemy.[31] It relys on the ability to show that it can fight and not lose a nuclear war. This is not to say that the 'war-fighting capability' is necessarily aggressive, for it is felt that the best way to prevent war is to show that it would be fruitless. As has been seen, China, like the Soviet Union, deploys three tiers of forces – (1) passive civil defence, in keeping with the Clausewitzian notion that the social and political dimensions of war must be ensured; (2) active defence to help minimise the potential damage; (3) offensive forces able to take the war to the enemy.

The reasoning behind this pattern is complex. First, there is the geographical–historical legacy of border threats. Vulnerability is most keenly felt in the north where traditional invaders were to be found. But the more recent sense of weakness is concerned with threats from the sea, including plundering western imperialists, Japanese militarists, and most recently the US-supported offshore threat. Mao Zedong declared in October 1949 that 'the Chinese people had stood up' and would no longer be molested by foreigners now that the Chinese could defend themselves.

Second, as in Soviet ideology, there is no room in Chinese thought for trusting foreigners, be they capitalist, or neighbouring socialists like the Soviet Union. One of the more bitter, but hard-learned lessons of the Sino–Soviet split and the Chinese vulnerability to United States nuclear threats in the 1950s was that China had to rely on itself for defence. In addition, as in the Soviet Union there is no distinction between nuclear and conventional war. Thus a war-fighting doctrine is more necessary when it is felt that any conflict is likely to escalate to the nuclear level.

Unlike the Soviet Union, institutional factors in China do not seem to add to the desire to develop an across-the-board war-fighting doctrine. As has already been pointed out, the military in China has less power than its Soviet counterparts. Nevertheless, China still seems to have adopted the notion of deterrence by denial.

The Range of Deterrence

Whether deterrance is by denial or punishment, a full range of weapons may not necessarily be required to meet a spectrum of threats. The perennial question of 'how much is enough' to deter has two parts – how many types of weapon, and how many in each category. China seems to have answered the first part by developing a wide range of forces.

On the intercontinental level, in the last two years China has tested its first full range ICBM and a shorter range but more adaptable SLBM. China's relative neglect of this tier until recently was apparently due mainly to technological problems in guidance and propulsion.[32] There had been expectations of a Chinese ICBM for well over a decade, but apparently the programme did not have top priority in China. The recent advances were no doubt encouraged by a desire to have a nuclear strike potential against the United States as well as the Soviet Union (already provided by medium-range forces) and a perception that nuclear deterrence might be a cheaper defence option than massive spending on dated conventional forces.

At the medium-range level China, like the Soviet Union, has long had such capability. As most threats were perceived at this level, and few technological problems were encountered with weapons delivered by aircraft or medium-range missiles, the needs in this tier could more easily be met. As in the USSR, the requirements of geography and the limits of technology were the most important factors in the evolution of such forces.

At the tactical level of nuclear weapons, China has only recently begun to extend its capability, thereby refuting Zhou Enlai's pledge not to do so.[33] Recent discussion in China has made it plain that, like NATO, China sees some utility in deterring Soviet convential and tactical nuclear superiority by using its own tactical nuclear weapons.[34] Some have argued that China's no-first-use pledge would prevent such an early use of nuclear forces, but it seems more likely that a Soviet invasion would provide sufficient excuse to cross the nuclear threshold first. Much as in the Soviet case, a no-first-use pledge seems less than reliable from a state that minimises the fire-break between nuclear and conventional war. Whatever the case, China is certainly now training for tactical nuclear war and has apparently come to see the need for fully ranged nuclear weapons.

Massive or Minimum Deterrence

The range of deterrent weapons can be broad, but the quantities in each category need not be large. This third aspect of deterrence is concerned with the second part of the question, 'how much is enough?'. Depending on whether you need a large or small number of weapons, you can be said to pursue minimum or massive deterrence. Obviously few states will admit that they have too much weaponry, especially as the requirements of different defence policies requires differing forces. For example, the precise definition of 'assured destruction' still remains contentious.

China's nuclear weapons strategy diverges sharply from those of the superpowers on this question. China seems to see no requirement for massive numbers in any category. In neither the defensive tiers of its denial deterrence, or in its offensive component, does China seem to embark on massive spending. Not even in the relatively long-established category of medium-range weapons has China built up more than a minimum capability.[35] The explanation for this falls into three parts.

First, the ideological notion that nuclear weapons are 'paper tigers' means that they cannot be the decisive force to defeat China. Unlike the Soviet ideology that accepted the decisiveness of nuclear forces back in the 1950s, China has never believed that these weapons were so revolutionary. As Zhou Enlai noted in 1964, 'the United States can't use the atom bomb to deal with a peasant war'.[36] In keeping with the Maoist dictum of 'despising the enemy strategically, but taking him seriously tactically', China sees the threat of nuclear war primarily in the realm of limited war. The Maoist line, still retained in contemporary Chinese defence policy,[37] argues that because of the nature of China's huge, rural population, the only way to defeat China is to invade, and such an operation is deterred by the non-nuclear people's war. Of course China's definition of people's war has undergone several changes to take into account 'modern conditions'.[38] As Yang Yong declared in 1983, 'Actually, when Comrade Mao Zedong was guiding Chinese revolutionary warfare, he never adhered to one pattern. He always adapted flexible, strategic and tactical principles in the light of the political, economic and military conditions of the enemy and ourselves'.[39] Thus with 'flexibility' China seems to feel it can deter general nuclear war with non-nuclear people's war.

This is not to say that China does not see any utility for nuclear weapons or fails to appreciate the power of their punch.[40] However, China's concern seems to be primarily in the realm of limited wars. China has appreciated its relative weakness in crisis management when facing a nuclear superpower while armed with little more than a 'paper tiger' doctrine.[41] But if nuclear weapons are only required to deter limited wars, then China requires only a limited number of weapons. It would be reasonably calculated that the enemy is less willing to run high risks on limited issues and therefore China would only require a limited amount of deterrence. The wide range of possible threats of limited war would however require a wide range of limited nuclear forces for deterrence.

The second and related reason for this minimum deterrence comes from human geography. Here lies China's real credibility in pursuing people's war as deterrence against general threats. China's large and dispersed rural population is a crucial characteristic. Ye Jianying declared that nuclear weapons.

> ... can only be used to destroy centres and the economic reserves of the opponent during the strategic bombing phase. After that, they are used principally as fire power preparations for assault. However, the army and regular weapons are necessary to terminate war ... (this) is to rely primarily on man ... They (US) also recognise that they cannot deal with China only by using nuclear weapons, because China possesses a large territory and lots of people, plus its complicated terrain ...[42]

Su Yu added in 1978,

> We do not deny that nuclear weapons have great destructive power and inflict heavy casualties, but they cannot be counted on to decide the outcome of a war. The aggressors can use them to destroy a city or town, but they cannot occupy those places, still less can they win the people's hearts ... (nuclear weapons) pose a much greater threat to the imperialists and social–imperialist countries whose industries and population are highly concentrated ... Our economic construction cannot therefore be destroyed by nuclear weapons.[43]

What is more, it also seems possible that the relatively poor state of the Chinese economy has tended to encourage Chinese leaders to see nuclear weapons as an economy measure in defence. Thus there is less reason to go in for anything but the most minimal level of nuclear forces required for deterrence.

Third, the apparent fact that the PLA is less involved in the making of nuclear weapons policy means that the military is likely to get fewer new toys. After all, the limited war threat assessment for nuclear weapons seems to be primarily a civilian doctrine. In sum, China parts company with the superpowers in adopting a minimum deterrence doctrine (for numbers of weapons, but not types).

CONCLUSIONS

Several key principles emerge in assessing China's nuclear posture. First, China's threat assessment seems flexible and pragmatic. Second, it therefore relies on a flexible deterrence doctrine. Third, and most important, the specific deterrence strategy is distinctive and suits China's needs. China sees deterrence as based on denial and a range of forces, but it rejects the need for massive numbers in each category. This distinctive doctrine also results from the complex sources of Chinese policy, including, geography, ideology, institutions and technological determinism. None of these factors on their own explains the resulting doctrine. But it is clear that the relatively higher concern with limited nuclear war and the relative unconcern with general nuclear war stands out as most distinctive.

Two possible areas of change in the future seem most crucial. First, greater spending on securing China's flexible second strike probably means more spending on top-of-the-range offensive weapons – ICBMs and SLBMs. At the lower end of the offensive spectrum, further development of tactical nuclear forces seems likely, given that no large scale conventional weapons programme is begun. Second, it seems unlikely that China will build up massive numbers of weapons in each category. Thus it will be unlikely to get involved in arms control, even though there are increasing pressures from other states to do so.[44] However, it is possible that a growing Chinese economy, and increased professionalism in a PLA more accepted as a participant in policy-making, will lead to a shift from minimum to massive deterrence. If this were indeed to happen, it would be a great shame, for it is precisely in this distinctive strategy of minimum deterrence that China seems to have the most to teach us.

NOTES AND REFERENCES

1. Ken Booth, *Strategy and Ethnocentrism* (London: Croom Helm, 1979). Colin Gray, 'Strategy and National Style', *International Security*. vol. 6. no. 2. Fall 1981.
2. Gerald Segal, 'The PLA as a Group in Chinese Politics' in David Goodman (ed.) *Groups in Chinese Politics* (forthcoming).
3. Gerald Segal, 'China's Nuclear Posture in the 1980s' *Survival*, vol. 23. no. 1. January–February 1981.
4. Jonathan Pollack, 'Chinese Attitudes Towards Nuclear Weapons, 1964–9', *The China Quarterly*, no. 50, April 1972. Jonathan Pollack, 'China as a Nuclear Power' in William Overholt (ed.), *Asia's Nuclear Future* (Boulder, Colorado: Westview, 1977).
5. William Tow and William Feeny (eds), *US Foreign Policy and Asian–Pacific Security* (Boulder, Colorado: Westview, 1982). Robert Scalapino, 'The US and East Asia', *Survival* vol. 24. no. 4. July – August 1982. Richard Solomon, 'Coalition Building or Condominium' in Donald Zagoria (ed.), *Soviet Policy in East Asia* (London: Yale University Press, 1982). David Armstrong, 'The Soviet Union and the United States' in Gerald Segal (ed.), *The Soviet Union and East Asia* (London: Heinemann, for the Royal Institute of International Affairs, 1983).
6. Leo Liu, 'Comparative Nuclear Policies: China and Other Developing Countries'. *Asian Profile*. vol. 6. no. 1. February 1978.
7. E. Ted Gladue Jr., *China's Perception of Global Politics* (Washington: University Press of America, 1982) Ch. 2.
8. Gerald Segal, Edwina Moreton, Lawrence Freedman, John Baylis. *Nuclear War and Nuclear Peace* (London: Macmillan, 1983).
9. Data in this section is based on *The Military Balance 1982–3* (London: International Institute for Strategic Studies, 1982).
10. Xinhua, 2 January 1982, *Nanfang Ribao*, 25 January 1982 in JPRS, China Report no. 80227 52. *Ningxia Ribao*, 29 June 1982 in no. 81432. 14–6. Xinhua 20 July 1982 in *FBIS*-CHI-82-141-K2-4. Also Jiefangjun Bao, 16 September 1979 in JPRS *China Report*. no. 75825, 4 June 1980. 97–9.
11. Georges Tan Eng Bok, 'La Strategie Nucleaire Chinoise', *Strategique* (Troisieme Trimestre, 1980). Dispersal remains a difficult task and one where the recent development of solid fuels should be of great help. For just one example of how China continues to see the need to guarantee assumed destruction see PLA Literature no. 3, 1 March 1978 in JPRS, *China Report* 74022. Like NATO and its cruise missiles, China perceives the need for medium range forces that are mobile and dispersable during the threat of war.
12. Robert Berman and John Baker, *Soviet Strategic Forces* (Washington: Brookings, 1982).
13. Gerald Segal, 'The Soviet "Threat" at China's Gates'. *Conflict Studies*. no. 143 (London: Institute for the Study of Conflict, 1983). Gerald Segal, 'China's Security Debate' *Survival*, vol. 24. no. 2. March – April 1982.
14. Georges Tan Eng Bok, Chapter 1 in this volume.
15. Colin Gray, *The Geopolitics of the Nuclear Era* (New York: Crane and Russak, 1977).

16. Segal, 'China's Nuclear Posture...' (note 3).
17. Bruce Swanson, *Eighth Voyage of the Dragon* (Annapolis, Maryland: Naval Institute Press, 1982).
18. Segal, 'The Soviet "Threat"...' (note 13).
19. 'Quarterly Chronicle and Documentation'. *The China Quarterly*, no. 85, March 1981. 211–2. Segal, 'China's Nuclear Posture'. John Wilson Lewis, 'China's Military Doctrine and Force Posture' in Thomas Fingar (ed.), *China's Quest for Independence* (Boulder, Colorado: Westview, 1980) 153. Also, Jonathan Pollack, 'China as a Military Power' in Onkar Marwah and Jonathan Pollack (eds), *Military Power and Policy in Asian States* (Boulder, Colorado: Westview, 1980).
20. *FBIS*-CHI-82-206-A1-4.
21. Leo Yueh-Yun Liu, *China as a Nuclear Power in World Politics* (London: Macmillan, 1972). Morton Halperin, 'Chinese Attitudes Towards the Use and Control of Nuclear Weapons' in Tang Tzou (ed.), *China in Crisis*. vol. 2 (Chicago: University of Chicago Press, 1968). Harry Gelber, 'Nuclear Weapons and Chinese Policy', *Adelphi Papers* no. 99 (London: IISS, 1973).
22. Lewis, 'China's Military Doctrine'; Pollack, 'China as a Military Power', (note 19).
23. On Soviet strategy generally see John Baylis and Gerald Segal (eds), *Soviet Strategy* (London: Croom Helm, 1981). David Holloway, *The Soviet Union and the Arms Race* (London: Yale University Press, 1983)
24. Gerald Segal, 'The PLA and Chinese Foreign Policy Decision-Making', *International Affairs.*, vol. 57 no. 3; Summer 1981. Segal, 'PLA as a Group' (note 2).
25. Timothy Colton, *Commissars, Commanders and Civilian Authority* (Cambridge: Harvard University Press, 1979). Dale Herspring and Ivan Volgyes (eds), *Civil–Military Relations in Communist Systems* (Boulder, Colorado: Westview, 1978). Thomas Wolfe, *The Military Dimension in the Making of Soviet Foreign and Defence Policy* (Santa Monica: The Rand Corporation, June 1978). Matthew Gallagher and Karl Spielmann Jr. *Soviet Decision-Making for Defence* (New York, Praeger, 1972). Edward Warner, *The Military in Contemporary Soviet Politics* (New York: Praeger, 1977).
26. Harvey Nelsen, *The Chinese Military System*, 2nd edn. (Boulder, Colorado: Westview, 1981). Harlan Jencks, *From Muskets to Missiles* (Boulder, Colorado: Westview, 1982). Also, Segal 'The PLA ...' (note 2).
27. Alexander, 'Decision-Making'; Holloway, *The Soviet Union*; David Holloway, 'Technology, Management and the Soviet Military Establishment', *Adelphi Papers* no. 76 (London: IISS, 1971). Karl Spielmann, 'Defence Industrialists in the USSR', *Problems of Communism*, vol. 25, no. 5. September – October 1976. Hannes Adomeit and Mikhail Agursky, 'The Soviet Military Industrial Complex and its Internal Mechanism', *National Security Series*, no. 1 (Kingston, Ontario: Centre for International Relations, 1978).
28. For recent insights into the development process for nuclear weapons see Xinhua, 17 October 1982 in *FBIS*-CHI-82-201-K7-12. Zhang Aiping on 18 October 1982 in no. 202-K1 and two Xinhua reports of 20 and 23 October in no. 207, K12-5.

29. Patrick Morgan, *Deterrence* (London, Sage, 1977). Alexander George and Richard Smoke, *Deterrence in US Foreign Policy* (New York: Columbia University Press, 1974). Robert Jervis, 'Deterrence Theory Revisited'. *ACIS Working Paper* no. 14 (UCLA: Centre for International Studies, May 1978). Robert Jervis, 'Deterrence and Misperception', *International Security*, vol. 7. no. 3. Winter 1982-3.
30. Glenn Snyder, *Deterrence and Defence* (Princeton: Princeton University Press, 1961). Dennis Ross, 'Rethinking Soviet Strategic Policy' in Baylis and Segal, *Soviet Strategy*. Booth, *Ethnocentrism*. Henry Trofimenko, 'Changing Attitudes Towards Deterrence', *ACIS Working Paper* no. 25 (UCLA: Centre for International and Strategic Affairs). John Erickson, 'The Soviet View of Deterrence', *Survival*, vol. 24. no. 6, November-December 1982. Shai Feldman, *Israeli Nuclear Deterrence* (New York, Columbia University Press, 1982) Ch. 1.
31. Segal, 'China's Nuclear Posture' and Lewis, 'China's Military Doctrine'. In the Chinese case there appears to be an important gap between deterrence definitions and deployment of forces. In general China only applies the term 'nuclear deterrence' when describing the doctrine of others. Deterrence in general in China means 'the power to force inaction by frightening' and deterrence in strategic policy is 'to force into a state of fear'. Implicit in these Chinese terms is the word 'contradiction', suggesting the ambiguity of deterrence. It also mirrors China's apparent uncertainty over the concept. On China's views of civil defence see Donald McMillen, 'Civil Defence in the People's Republic of China' *Australian Journal of Chinese Affairs* no. 8 (1982). Liberation Army Daily, 8 November 1978 in *BBC*/SWB/FE/5969/B11/8-9.
32. Apparently the problem with the shift to solid fuel propulsion is less with the fuel itself than that its less predictable burns require superior guidance to compensate. Whatever the reason, it is notable that China did not seem to take the more expensive Soviet method of coping with such technical problems and embark on several parallel and competing design projects. China seemed anxious about the speed of progress.
33. Zhou Enlai in late 1964, Edgar Snow, *China's Long Revolution* (Harmondsworth, Penguin, 1974).
34. See note 10 and Segal, 'The Soviet "Threat"'.
35. I am grateful to Paul Godwin for his suggestion that the small numbers of medium range forces may be due to a decision to keep spending to a minimum while developing new nuclear systems. While this may in part explain the small numbers, it does not take into account that most of the costs are in development, not deployment and China might have been expected to deploy larger numbers after having spent most of the funds on development.
36. *Selected Works of Zhou Enlai*, vol. 1. (Beijing: Foreign Languages Press, 1981) 313 Halperin, 'Chinese Attitudes' and Pollack, 'Chinese Attitudes' and Segal, 'China's Nuclear Posture'.
37. Segal, 'The Soviet "Threat"'.
38. Ibid.
39. *Guangming Ribao*, 22 January 1983 in BBC/SWB/FE/7253/BII/7.
40. J. Chester Cheng (ed.), *The Politics of the Chinese Red Army* (Stanford:

The Hoover Institution, 1966), 67–9. Edgar Snow 'Zhou Enlai in 1960', *Red China Today* (Harmondsworth, Penguin, 1970). Pollack, 'Chinese Attitudes'. Alice Langley Hsieh, *Communist China's Strategy in the Nuclear Age* (Englewood Cliffs, N. J.: Prentice-Hall, 1962).

41. Alice Langley Hsieh, 'China's Secret Military Papers', *The China Quarterly*, no. 18, 1967. 84–7. Mao Zedong, 16 June 1964 in *Miscellany of Mao Tse-tung Thought* (Arlington, Virginia: JPRS-61269, 1 and 2. Feb. 1974) 356–7. Hsieh Chan, 'The Atom Bomb is a Paper Tiger', People's Daily, 21 June 1977 in *SPRCP-* 77–29.
42. Hsieh, 'China's Secret Military Papers' 84.
43. *Fifty Years of the Chinese People's Liberation Army* (Peking: Foreign Languages Press, 1978) 44. Also, Fu Zhong, 'Mao Zedong Military Science is Forever the Chinese People's Treasure', *Red Flag*, August 1981 in *FBIS*-CHI-81-162-K5.
44. On the China problem in arms control with special reference to the European theatre see Lawrence Freedman, 'The United States Factor' and Gerald Segal, 'The China Factor', both in Edwina Moreton and Gerald Segal (eds), *Soviet Strategy Towards Western Europe* (London: George Allen and Unwin, 1984).

Part III
The Economic Dimension

8 Military Industry

SYDNEY JAMMES*

Over the decade of the 1970s, the defence industry has changed from the premier claimant on China's capital and labour resources to a lower priority sector that must bow to Beijing's overriding goal of building China into a major economic power by the end of the century. Moreover, the defense industry has been charged with unprecedented research and development and production responsibilities in support of the civilian economy. This does not mean that the Chinese have abandoned the goal of modernising their armed forces, but rather reflects the present leaders' recognition that they must correct fundamental weakness in the pattern and rate of national economic development before they can undertake any dramatic upgrading of defence capabilities.

China is a large, slowly developing country, with at least three-quarters of its labour force engaged in agriculture and with a low level of output per capita in industry. Nevertheless, it has advanced further towards military self-sufficiency than any other Third World state. In terms of output, the Chinese defence industry remains the third largest in the world – exceeded only by those of the superpowers – producing a wide range of weapon systems, including nuclear weapons and delivery systems (long range missiles, jet aircraft, and submarines). The sophistication of the military equipment produced and the technology used in its production, however, lag far behind that of the industrially-developed countries. Almost all of the output consists of copies or modifications of Soviet weapon designs of the 1950s, and a

---

* This chapter is a revised version of 'China' by Sydney Jammes in Nicole Ball and Milton Leitenberg (eds). *The Structure of the Defense Industry*. (London: Croom Helm, 1983). Gratitude is owed to the editors for their kind assistance. The views expressed in this chapter are those of the author, and not of any US government agency.

number of constraints – political and economic – prevent any major remedies to the industry's backwardness in the near future.

THE SETTING

China has a long history of arms production, but it was not until the Communist Party came to power in 1949 that attempts were made to develop a rational defence industry. Assistance on a broad scale was provided by the USSR in the 1950s, when a number of large Soviet-designed factories were built to make duplicates of then-current Soviet weapons. By the late 1950s these plants were producing a wide variety of military equipment, including jet aircraft. The aid, which left a characteristic and lasting imprint on Chinese design and production practices, ended abruptly in 1960, and the Chinese were left to make the best they could of the situation.

The Soviet departure, together with the Great Leap Forward, virtually stopped arms production in the early 1960s; by the middle of that decade, however, output of all types of arms had reached new peaks. In the mid-1960s the Chinese also launched an ambitious construction programme in the military machine-building industry. Under the general slogan of 'war preparation', the PRC constructed hundreds – possibly thousands – of small, medium, and large-scale industrial projects in every region of the country, including the remote interior. The size of that effort apparently caused severe dislocations in the economy.

In 1966, just when the Chinese armament industry seemed to have recovered completely from the difficulties attendant with the Great Leap, Mao Zedong launched his Great Proletarian Cultural Revolution. This was not basically economic in nature, as the Great Leap had been; nevertheless, it affected the Chinese defence industry in a variety of ways. Although the central authorities sought to insulate the industry from the troubles of the Cultural Revolution, political activity in the factories frequently caused disorders. Disruptions in the transportation and communications systems created bottlenecks in the delivery of raw materials, parts and sub-assemblies. During 1967, the first full year of the Cultural Revolution, the value of new military equipment produced fell by about 20 per cent.[1]

During the Cultural Revolution, the disruptions in military production were shorter and less severe than those of the Great Leap. By late 1968 there were signs that the worst effects on the weapons industries were over, and heightened tensions with the Soviet Union then began to spur another period of growth. Overall, growth in annual defence production for the period 1965–71 averaged 10 per cent.[2]

In 1972, defence output and the construction of new production facilities were again cut severely. Hardest hit was the aircraft industry, where output dropped about 70 per cent, but production of naval ships and land arms declined also.[3] Three factors apparently were responsible: the government's new emphasis on agriculture; the military's reduced influence in policymaking as the shattered party and government apparatus recovered from the Cultural Revolution and the fall of Lin Biao, and a realisation by the military that continued large-scale output of older weapons was taking resources away from its long-term efforts at defence modernisation. In early 1975, however, defence began to return to favour. As part of a major reassessment of economic policy, Premier Zhou Enlai presented to the Fourth National People's Congress a broad outline for revitalising the economy and raising the level of technology in China. In what is now billed the 'four modernisations', Zhou's long-range economic plan called for the modernisation of agriculture, industry, science and technology, and national defence with the aim of achieving developed-nation economic status for China by the year 2000.[4] Within this framework, the Military Commission of the party Central Committee proposed a comprehensive plan in mid-1975 for modernising China's military forces and defence industries.[5] In keeping with their opposition to the general modernisation programme, leftists in the leadership attacked the military plan for disregarding 'revolutionary' principles.

By early 1977 the leftists had been defeated, Hua Guofeng and his moderate allies were in control, and the military planners were moving quickly to modernise the military machine-building industry. In the brief period between mid-1975 and the end of 1977, Beijing started to expand a large number of military industrial facilities, made sweeping changes in the military and scientific/technological institutional structures, resumed testing of a variety of weapon systems (after a hiatus in some cases of as much as six years), and launched a massive study of foreign military technology and equipment.

The whole period was one of strong debate, however, over the appropriate level of defence spending, priorities within the military, and the role of defence in deciding what science and technology to acquire. The leaders of the People's Liberation Army, led by Defence Minister Ye Jianying, wanted larger allocations of resources for modernising the armed forces. These demands apparently conflicted with the development plans for the civilian sector, which were supported by a large part of the party leadership. The civilians did not deny the importance of a defence build-up but felt that China could best achieve it by first encouraging growth in non-defence investment. Moreover, because overall economic planning was inadequate, the leaders did not immediately understand the difficulties and costs of military modernisation. After Vice Premier Deng Xiaoping's return to power in August 1977, a compromise plan apparently was reached. The extent of the compromises and their impact on China's military machine-building industries can only be inferred. It is likely, however, that the military modernisation plan as it was envisaged in 1981 is considerably less ambitious than the one the military commission originally proposed in mid-1975 and that military production and the development of the military–industrial sector of the Chinese economy now have a relatively low priority in recognition of competing economic goals. According to present policy, a full-blown effort to modernise the military must await further development of agriculture and light industry and the development of greater skills in machine-building, metallurgy, electronics, and chemistry.

Even though definitive information on the compromises is lacking, a scaling back became apparent in February 1978, when Premier Hua Guofeng in his report to the Fifth National People's Congress called for a return to Zhou's 'four modernisations'.[6] Subsequently, Beijing selectively curtailed the expansion that had begun in military-related industries, established stronger control over the military–industrial bureaucracy, and increased the transfer of existing weapons manufacturing capacity to non-military production.

Overall, defence production increased 1 or 2 per cent per year between 1972 and 1979, and then soared to its highest level in 1979 as China engaged Vietnam in the border war. Production has since returned to the same level as the mid-1970s, well below the 1971 and 1979 peaks.[7]

THE DEFENCE INDUSTRY AND THE ECONOMY

Defence absorbs a substantial portion of China's economic resources, particularly its output of high-technology machinery, Despite its relative low priority, more than 10 per cent of the PRC's industrial output is believed to be in the form of military goods. (It should be pointed out that data are very rough, both on overall industrial output and on

TABLE 8.1 *Defense procurement and industrial production (indexed to 1967 levels)*

Year	Defence procurement	Industrial production
1967	100	100
1968	97	109
1969	115	132
1970	166	156
1971	172	173
1972	120	191
1973	123	216
1874	132	225
1975	143	248
1976	138	248
1977	129	284
1978	130	322
1979	162	349
1980	135	380
1981	119	395
1982 (tentative)	129	411

SOURCE: Statement by Major General Schuyler Bissell, Deputy Director Defence Intelligence Agency, before the Subcommittee on International Trade Finance, and Security Economics of the Joint Economic Committee, United States Congress, 28 June 1983.

defence industry production, so that the ratio of the two is subject to rather wide margins of error.)[8] The military's share of production, however, is currently much smaller than it was in the past, particularly during 1965–71. A comparison of their respective trends shows that defence procurement growth conformed closely to the growth of industrial output through 1971. Since 1972, however, industrial output has continued its upward trend, while defence procurement has increased only slightly.

No estimates are available on the size of defence industry's labour force. If employment is assumed to be proportional to output, and if defence output is assumed to be roughly 10 per cent of Chinese industrial production, the defence industry can be expected to include about one-tenth of China's industrial workers, or 4 million people.[9] The defence industry's production of military equipment, however, does not fully utilise its productive capability. Much of the excess capacity is devoted to producing civilian goods. The magnitude of this civilian production is not known with certainty, but some sources claim it to be as much as 30 per cent of the total output of the industry.[10] Using this figure to obtain total output – and assuming employment proportional to output – the number of defence industry workers could be almost 6 million.[11] These estimates are of necessity very rough and differ from each other by sizeable margins.

Similarly, no estimates are available on Chinese capital investment in the defence industry. It is clear, however, that military production consumes many of those resources needed for sustaining economic growth. A large share of the capacity to produce machinery and equipment is diverted away from civilian programmes. Furthermore, much of China's industrial sector devoted to the production of military equipment represents the nation's most productive capacity.

More important from the standpoint of economic growth, however, is the fact that the defence effort pre-empts a large share of the finest scientific, engineering, and managerial talents of the economy – assets that might otherwise improve productivity in the civilian sector. Indeed, American government sources believe that the proportion of China's advanced industrial sector committed to defence production is 'far larger ... than is the case in the US or the USSR'.[12]

The relatively low priority currently being given to military equipment modernisation reflects the present Chinese leaders' recognition that they must correct fundamental weaknesses in the pattern and rate of economic development before they can undertake any dramatic upgrading of defence capabilities.[13]

Moreover, the resource allocation policies adopted in December 1978 (with the establishment of the three-year programme of 'readjustment' by the Third Party Plenum) do not, at least for the near term, support defence modernisation. Investment in heavy industry – particularly the iron and steel industry – was cut back, and allocations to agriculture, light industry, and the building materials industry were increased.[14]

PROBLEMS IN THE DEFENCE INDUSTRY

Technological weaknesses in the Chinese defence industry are apparent throughout the entire system, from basic research to the maintenance of finished products. The most critical shortcomings are in the design of technology and manufacturing know-how. A key weakness at all levels of the military industry establishment is the rapidly growing shortage of well-trained scientists, engineers, and technicians.

The government is fully aware of the crisis it faces in training large numbers of new technicians. Until China has sufficient engineers and technicians trained in modern methods and conversant in modern technology, staffing for most major weapons programmes will include many engineers lacking needed design and production skills. Even with this weak cadre of trained engineers and technicians, China can nevertheless mobilise enough technical talent for selected high-priority projects in the strategic weapons, aircraft, and naval fields. Growing numbers of young students will begin to enter the defence industries in the next few years as the current emphasis on science and technology in the colleges and universities throughout China bears fruit. Additionally, several thousand engineering and technical students are abroad for advanced training.

In establishing China's defence industry during the 1950s, the Soviet Union seems to have purposely withheld the expertise and means to develop new weapon systems. Consequently, the Chinese have had to limit their research and development efforts to a few major projects. These have generally included one or two models in each major type of weapon system (such as aircraft, missiles, and ships). The systems being developed show a substantial technological improvement over those currently being produced, but they still only represent weapons technology levels achieved by the Soviet Union in the early 1960s. Progress in general has been slow, and many projects that were begun in the late 1960s are still under development.

The capabilities of the industrial infrastructure to support modern weapons development and manufacture are uneven. While China produces most of the materials and basic types of machinery required to support its current weapons production effort, any attempt to improve its military manufacturing processes will require the import of a variety of modern industrial technologies.[15]

Beijing has developed a substantial machine-tool industry made up of several thousand plants, which range in size from backyard shops to large, modern factories. This industry can meet the country's needs for low- and medium-grade machine tools and can produce some good-quality general purpose machine tools for export. It is far less capable, however, of making the precision tools needed in the production of sophisticated weapons. In numerically controlled machine tools and computer-aided manufacture, China is still in the early stages of development. It can be expected to continue to buy precision machinery and equipment from Japanese and Western suppliers.

China has developed a strong and rapidly expanding electronics industry. This industry has held a priority claim on the nation's resources because of the importance of its products to both military development and industrial production. An estimated one-half to three-quarters of its total output is procured by the military, with most of the remainder going to civilian industry. In terms of volume of production, China's electronics industry compares favourably with industries in some of the developed countries of Western Europe, such as the UK, France and West Germany. In technology, however, the industry still lags substantially behind world levels.[16]

CIVILIAN VERSUS MILITARY CONTROL

Expecting (perhaps with reason) a degree of military objection to their economic policies, the current leadership in Beijing has found it necessary to strengthen control over the defence industry. In a series of moves that underscores the determination to re-establish strong civilian control over the military, the bureaucracy that manages military production has been reorganised. Beginning in late 1977, the ministerial heads of the machine-building industries – the industries responsible for military production – were replaced. Five of the new appointees were civilians supplanting men formerly associated primarily with the PLA. By September 1978, all eight of the ministers of machine-building were civilians.

In May 1982, the Chinese announced more far-reaching organisational changes in the defence-industry sector. Under the new arrangement, several defence machine-building ministries have been consolidated into related civilian sector ministries in what appears to be an attempt to enhance civilian control and to foster greater integration of military and civilian production activities. The full details of the new organisational structure are not yet known. The implications of some of the changes will not be understood completely for some time to come.

The organisational changes of the past several years have consolidated China's military–industrial and scientific functions into a more manageable framework. The National Defence Industry Office (NDIO), which originally appeared in the Chinese media in the mid-1960s but then disappeared, re-emerged in 1976 as the principal co-ordinating unit between the State Council and the military machine-building industries and, in concert with the State Planning Commission, the arbiter on matters of production and allocation of funds – a function that had been handled by the Ministry of National Defence.[17] Additionally, the State Scientific and Technological Commission (SSTC) reappeared with seemingly broad powers over the planning, funding and supervising of all scientific and technological work including defence-related activities, while direct control over military research academies and institutes apparently reverted from the National Defence Science and Technology Commission (NDSTC) to the individual ministries. The NDSTC probably retained responsibility for defence-related scientific and technical projects.

A further consolidation of control over defence production occurred in June 1983 with the merging of the NDIO, NDSTC and the office of the science, technology and arms commission of the Central Committee of the Chinese Communist Party into a Commission in Charge of Science, Technology and Industry for National Defence.[18] The implications of this merger are not fully understood at this time, but Biejing's aim in all these moves appears to have been to erase past special treatment of the military in the allotment of scarce resources, to eliminate overlapping redundancies between civilian and military efforts, and – within the defence industry – to concentrate resources on the most important projects.

DEFENCE INDUSTRY CONTRIBUTIONS TO THE CIVILIAN ECONOMY

There is growing evidence that China's military machine-building base is much larger than is needed to support its present relatively modest rate of output. To better use this excess manufacturing capacity, Beijing has adopted a policy under which a sizeable and growing proportion of capacity at military plants is used for non-military production. The harbinger of this policy appears to have been Chairman Hua Guofeng's report to the Congress in February 1978, when he called for greater integration of military and civilian enterprises. He indicated that co-ordination of production would reduce the need for investment capital, but his speech did not provide any specifics on how this integration was to be accomplished.[19]

Under this policy, an increasing number of military factories are sending specialists to civilian organisations to familiarise themselves with the market for non-military items. The programme has led to new lines of production in military plants, ranging from cameras to mining equipment. The Xiangtan Tank plant, for example, has started to

TABLE 8.2 China's Industries of Defence Production

Ministry (pre-1982 name)	Minister and Career Experience, Current (C) and Former (F)[1]	Product Areas; Military (M) and Civilian (C)	Import and Export Corporation
Ministry of Nuclear Industry (2nd Ministry of Machine Building)	C: Jiang Xinxiong F: Han Xinan (f) manager in textile and nuclear industries. Liu Wei, brigadier general; Liu Xiyao	M: Nuclear weapon material, C: Nuclear power plant reactors, radiation measuring meters and instruments, isotopes, uranium survey and mining equipment, optical instruments; mechanical components, e.g. air filters, valves, heat exchanges.	China Nuclear Energy Industry Corporation
Ministry of Aviation (3rd Ministry of Machine Building)	Industry C: Mo Wenxiang, municipal party secretary F: Lu Dong, manager in metallurgical industry; Li Qitai, Air Force general	M: Jet fighters, ground attack bombers, transports, helicopters, engines. C: Agricultural planes, prototype commercial aircraft, washing machines, clocks, air conditioners, refrigerators, small cars and baking ovens.	China Aero-Technology Import and Export Corporation.
Ministry of Electronics Industry (4th Ministry of Machine Building)	C: Jiang Zemin. F: Zhang Ting Deputy director of planning in machinery, aviation and electronics industries. Qian Min, provincial party secretary Wang Zheng, lieutenant general	M: Avionics, radar, sonar, mobile command control and communications equipment, guided missile navigation systems, fire control and range-finding systems, ground station satellite communications equipment. C: consumer electronics including computers and peripherals and duplicating machines. Washing machines, electric meters, ice skates, lamps, and electric meters.	China Electronics Import and Export Corporation

Ministry of Ordnance Industry (5th Ministry of Machine Building)	C: Yu Yi, engineer and manager of provincial defence industry F: Zhang Zhen, manager in petroleum industry Li Chengfang, major general	M: Tanks, reconnaissance vehicles, armoured personnel carriers, anti-tank weapons, self-propelled artillery, mortars, rocket launchers, rifles, anti-aircraft and anti-ship weapons. C: High-precision forging and metal cutting tools, bicycles, chemical industrial products electrical appliances, steel and wooden furniture, oil-extraction pipes.	China North Industries Corporation
China State Shipbuilding Corporation (6th Ministry of Machine Building)	Chairman: Chai Shufan, vice chairman Capital Construction Commission F: Fang Qiang, admiral	M: Submarines, destroyers, frigates, fast attack craft, patrol escorts, ocean mine sweepers, hydrofoils, landing craft, navigational communications equipment. C: Bulk carriers, diesel engines, container vessels, offshore drilling rigs, engineering design and consulting services.	Chinese Shipbuilding Trading Co. Ltd.
Ministry of Space Industry 7th Ministry of Machine Building)	C: Zhang Jun, PLA political commissar F: Zheng Tianxiang, provincial party secretary Song Renqiong, lieutenant general	M: Strategic weapon systems: ICBMs (CSS-3 and CSS-X-4); IRBMs (CSS-2); MRBMS (CSS-1). Tactical missiles: CSS-N-2 anti-ship missiles; CSA-1 SAMS. C: Communications, meterological, earth resource satellites, remote sensing instruments, aerial cameras, expendable launch vehicles.	Great Wall Industry Corporation

[1] With regard to previous ministers, the names are in the reverse order of office holder in the recent past. The final name refers to pre-1977 ministers.

SOURCES: Files of the National Council for US–China Trade, Washington D.C.; *Jane's Weapons Systems, 1982*; *Jane's All the World's Aircraft, 1982*; *Jane's Fighting Ships, 1982*; and *The Chinese Armed Forces Today: Department of Defense Handbook on China's Army, Navy and Airforce, 1979* (Prentice Hall: Englewood Cliffs, New Jersey). Table compiled by Karen Berney.

produce sewing machines, electric fans, bulldozers, and tower cranes. And an ordnance factory in Wuxi reportedly has begun manufacturing equipment for use in ear surgery. The Chinese also claim that about 80 per cent of the defence industry enterprises in Liaoning Province have begun to produce daily necessities for local consumption as well as items for export.[20] Overall, production of civilian goods may pre-empt as much as 30 per cent of the defence industry's output.[21]

Also emphasised under the integration policy are joint defence and civilian research and development projects. The most notable project of this sort to be publicised involves a defence research institute engaged in the development of electronic circuits for the Ministry responsible for missile development (the Space Ministry).

The publicity about this project has underlined the benefits that have accrued to the defence institute from its cooperative relationship with the civilian sector – an emphasis possibly designed to persuade reluctant elements in the defence establishment to comply with the new policy.[22]

ARMS EXPORTS

China is a relatively minor exporter of arms with less than 3 per cent of the world military export market. Nevertheless, the People's Republic is the fifth largest weapons supplier to the world, ranking behind the USA, USSR, Britain, and France.[23] During the past five years the principal recipients of Chinese arms were Pakistan and a number of African states. The main exports have been aircraft, especially the Shenyang F-6 (the Chinese version of the Soviet MIG-19 fighter) and light coastal-defence craft. Tanks have also been exported, but in minute numbers compared with the exports of the USSR. The recipients have virtually all been 'uncommitted' countries'[24]

It should be noted that until recently China has not been a world leader in *sales* of arms, despite being a major *supplier*. For many years, China generally refused to sell military goods, but instead traded or gave arms in an effort to establish or enhance influence in the Third World. Over the past few years however, the need for foreign exchange to support economic modernisation has led to a reversal of this policy. Military sales are now a significant foreign exchange source and should become even more important in the future.[25]

Arms transfers account for a very small proportion of defence industrial output and are small relative to the nation's total exports and to its heavy industrial exports. Moreover, deliveries have fluctuated widely in response to political upheavals at home and to vacillating attitudes toward their costs and benefits. Until recently, arms transfers have declined over the past fifteen years – reflecting the ready availability of better and more modern Western and Soviet weapon systems.* The size of recent arms agreements between China and the Middle East suggests a reversal in this trend.[27] Although Chinese weapon systems are generally technologically inferior to those of the other major military exporters, Chinese arms – especially infantry weapons – do offer some advantages for Third World countries: they are simple and rugged, and getting arms from China is an alternative to tilting either to the West or to the Soviet Union.

OUTLOOK

Military modernisation is likely to remain slow and gradual, primarily dependent upon China's progress in lifting the levels of technology in its industrial base and in creating conditions for indigenous scientific and technological development. Some improvement in Chinese defence production capabilities can be expected on a selective basis; overall, however, the Chinese defence industry is likely to remain circumscribed by continued deficiencies in technology, personnel, and resources.

Even if China were to acquire foreign defence-related technology, the impact on production would not become apparent until the late 1980s. Time is needed to assimilate new technology into the existing production processes. The Chinese might participate in joint ventures or co-production programmes with other nations, but assimilation would still take time.

In any case, two fundamental imponderables affect all projections of Chinese economic and military development. The first is the ability of the present leaders to consolidate their hold on power and to implement their economic policies while at the same time placating a restless military. Their success in this endeavour is by no means assured, and it is further complicated by the factor of age – the likelihood that most of the present leadership will pass from the scene during the next five to ten years. The second is the government's ability to continue the

---

*Part of the decline is also attributed to the schism between China and Vietnam – formerly one of the prime recipients of Chinese arms.

gradualist approach to Chinese military modernisation by linking it to the eventual development of a modern industrial base. A serious deterioration in relations with the Soviet Union or renewed war in Vietnam could lead to increased allocations of resources to the military establishment at the expense of economic modernisation.

NOTES AND REFERENCES

1. Central Intelligence Agency, *Chinese Defence Spending 1965–79*, SR-80-10091, Washington, DC: Central Intelligence Agency, 1980, 2.
2. Ibid.
3. Ibid.
4. *Daily Report, People's Republic of China*, vol. 1, no. 13, Washington, DC: Foreign Broadcast Information Service, 20 January 1975, D20–D27.
5. *Peking Cieh-Fang-Chun Pao*, 27 August 1977, 1, 4.
6. *Daily Report, People's Republic of China*, vol. 1. no. 39, Washington, DC: Foreign Broadcast Information Service, 27 February 1978, D7–D10.
7. Statement by Major General Schuyler Bissell, Deputy Director Defense Intelligence Agency, before the Subcommittee on International Trade, Finance, and Security Economics of the Joint Economic Committee, United States Congress, 28 June 1983.
8. Because of a lack of data, all estimates of the defence burden on the Chinese economy are necessarily tenuous, and the one presented here is no exception. The only data generally available are the single-figure entries for 'defence and war preparation' in the Chinese state budgets for 1979, 1980 and 1981 (the first budgets revealed after a hiatus of almost twenty years) and the estimates presented publicly by the United States Central Intelligence Agency. The single figure presented in the Chinese state budget provides little insight into the problem. The figure is low, which suggests that it may include only defence operating expenditures – with military procurement, investment in defence industries, and research and development subsumed in such other budget accounts as 'capital construction' and 'science' in a manner similar to the Soviet practice. Other Chinese economic data seldom include any defence-related statistics. The Central Intelligence Agency data for China's defence expenditures are estimated on the basis of a 'building-block' methodology similar to that which the Agency has used for many years to assess the defence costs of the Soviet Union. It is based on a detailed list of the activities and physical components of the defence programme for each year. This list includes estimates of order of battle, manpower, production of equipment, construction of facilities, and the operating practices of the military forces. These estimates are then converted into monetary estimates. This costing is in yuan terms for some components and for others in US dollar terms. Estimates in dollar terms are converted to yuan using suitable yuan–dollar ratios constructed to reflect differences in the US and Chinese price structures for different goods and services. The published

Central Intelligence Agency data are more revealing than the official Chinese data, but they are still rather cryptic and provide only a limited view of the Chinese defence establishment. In the study presented here, the ratio of military production to overall industrial production presented in this chapter was derived by comparing estimated net Chinese military output (15 billion yuan) with the estimated value of overall net industrial output (143 billion yuan) for the year 1979. The estimated net military output was obtained by extrapolating from the figure on page 4 of Central Intelligence Agency, *Chinese Defence Spending*. The estimated net industrial output was obtained by multiplying the official announced gross value of industrial output by an estimated ratio of net value to gross value calculated by Dr Robert Michael Field in an unpublished paper based on data presented in *Jingjiyanjiu* [Economic Research] no. 4. (1975): 51, and *Jingjiyanjiu* [Economic Research] no. 12 (1979): 9. Possible definitional incompatibilities between the CIA's figures and the official Chinese data, as well as a problem of comparing current yuan with 1970 yuan, add to the uncertainty of the estimate. Nevertheless, despite the mental gymnastics used to arrive at it, the estimate appears reasonable in light of other official PRC statistics and the estimate of the percentage of a Chinese gross national product pre-empted by defence (8.5 per cent) presented in US Arms Control and Disarmament Agency, *World Military Expenditures and Arms Transfers 1969–78*, Publication 108, Washington, DC: December 1980.
9. Thomas G. Rawski, *Economic Growth and Employment in China*, New York: Oxford University Press, 1979, 163, estimates the number of Chinese industrial workers to be 40 million.
10. *Daily Report, People's Republic of China*, vol. 1, no. 159, Washington, DC: Foreign Broadcast Information Service, 14 August 1980, L1.
11. Rawski, *Economic Growth*.
12. Statement by George Bush (then Director of Central Intelligence), 26 May 1976, p. 31, in US Congress, Joint Economic Committee, Subcommittee on Priorities and Economy in Government, Hearings: *Allocation of Resources in the Soviet Union and China, 1976*, Part 2, Washington, DC: US Govt. Printing Office, 1976.
13. Central Intelligence Agency, *China: A Statistical Compendium*, ER 79-10374, Washington, DC: CIA, 1979, 3.
14. *Daily Report, People's Republic of China*, vol. 1, no. 248, Washington, DC: Foreign Broadcast Information Service, 26 December 1978, E4-E13.
15. China's drive to lessen dependence on foreign sources of steel is noted in an article on tank production in *Liberation Army Pictorial*, March 1980: China's successful development of armour plate and structural steel to replace various lines of chrome-nickel steel from abroad has been an important contribution and has resulted in the granting of first-class awards in national science and technology.
16. 'China's Defence Industries', *Strategic Survey*, London: International Institute for Strategic Studies, 1979, 70–1.
17. Ibid., 60.
18. Ibid., 69. Also *Daily Report, People's Republic of China*, vol. 1, no. 164,

Washington, DC: Foreign Broadcast Information Service, 23 August 1983, K–1.
19. *Daily Report, People's Republic of China*, vol. 1, no. 39, Foreign Broadcast Service, D7–D10.
20. 'China's Defence Industries', *Strategic Survey*, 72.
21. *Daily Report, People's Republic of China*, vol. 1, no. 159, L1.
22. *Daily Report, People's Republic of China*, vol. 1, no. 89, Washington, DC: Foreign Broadcast Information Service, 8 May 1978, E6. See also, *Daily Report, People's Republic of China*, vol. 1, no. 63, Washington, DC: Foreign Broadcast Information Service, 31 March 1978, E11.
23. Philip J. Farley, Stephen S. Kaplan and William H. Lewis, *Arms Across the Sea*, Washington, DC: The Brookings Institution, 1978, 13.
24. *The Chinese War Machine*, London: Salamander Books, 1979, 50.
25. See ch. 18. For a dated view of Chinese arms sales see John Copper and Daniel Papp, eds *Communist Nation's Military Assistance* (Boulder: Westview Press, 1983) Ch. 5.

9 Aspects of Modernisation

KAREN BERNEY

Chinese defence policy is more than just the sum of its weapons, quality of its soldiers or output of its military factories. Although it is beyond the scope of this book to assess the strengths and weaknesses of the Chinese economy as a whole, there are at least two other areas of Chinese constraint and advantage in modernisation that need to be assessed. First, what is the nature of the problem in China's economic modernisation in the defence field? Second, what natural advantages for modernisation does China have in the resource field, and what are their limitations? These questions are by no means comprehensive, but they are intended to help us focus on some of the broader aspects of Chinese defence policy.

MODERNISATION

The problems facing modernisers of military equipment are rarely assessed in any detail. While it is acknowledged that equipment is only one aspect of modernisation, it is still fairly crucial. What are the major roadblocks to the production of modern arms in China?

Industrial Reform

China's six defence industries face a host of technological, organisational, and managerial deficiencies that must be corrected before any real gains in production capabilities can occur. Briefly summarised, these are (1) lagging technical know-how, above all in rapidly changing disciplines such as microelectronics; (2) inadequate design–engineering and systems-integration capabilities; (3) an unbalanced approach to R & D and lack of co-ordination between research and production; and (4) management practices that overlook quality and innovation in pursuit of quantity. These not only bar implementation of more demanding domestic weapons programmes, but also adversely affect the prospects for successful absorption and diffusion of foreign military technology – if and when this happens.[1]

In October 1978 Beijing began experimenting with industrial reforms designed to counteract and gradually overcome the problems mentioned above. The initial target was the civilian industrial sector, but has since been expanded to include China's defence industries.

Chinese levels of technology in metallurgy, electronics, and machine tools lag behind the industrialised nations by ten to thirty years. This has been the most fundamental and often-noted impediment to the production of more sophisticated weapons.[2]

Though possessing large reserves of strategic minerals and metals, China's Ministry of Metallurgical Industry lacks the know-how for producing and processing crucial high-quality nonferrous metals. For example, the current glitch in Chinese production of the Spey turbofan engine is the failure of the Ministry of Metallurgical Industry to manufacture the nickel and chromium alloys needed for highly heat-resistant components.[3]

Economic readjustments have shifted emphasis from heavy to light industry. Sectors that support defence industries, such as steel, have been curtailed as a result. Plans for high-grade steel development and production, which are of great interest to the Ministry of Ordnance, have been downgraded as part of this readjustment. The six million tons a year Baoshan steel mill project, launched in 1978 and postponed a year later, is again on track, although many financial and bureaucratic issues remain unresolved.[4]

In contrast, expansion and development of China's electronics industry take high priority in the sixth Five-Year Plan. The state-of-the-art in Chinese electronics is perhaps best gauged by end-users. Reports from representatives of Western electronics manufactures, who have negotiated with both Chinese producers and users, confirm that whether consumer electronics, computers, or instrumentation, Chinese users loathe to buy equipment turned out by the Ministry of Electronics.[5] The reasons – poor quality and low reliability, exacerbated by the absence of repair and maintenance services. Disaffection with Chinese manufacturers also holds true for the telecommunications industry.[6] China's electronics weaknesses stem from the backward state of its semiconductor industry.

China has several thousand machine tool factories that adequately meet general-purpose needs and produce uncomplicated, high-quality products for export, but it is lagging in the development and use of numerically controlled and precision-guided machine tools. In addition, much of its inventory is obsolete. The Ministry of Machine Building conducted a survey on the technical levels of machine tools and power equipment currently in use and found that 25 per cent of the products dated from the 1940s, 40 per cent from the 1950s, 30 per cent from the 1960s, and only 5 per cent from the 1970s. The ministry claims that this pervasive obsolescence derives from the ten-year standstill in scientific and technological progress caused by the Cultural Revolution and the Gang of Four.[7]

Design and Application

Concomitant to the upgrading of basic industrial technologies is the acquisition of an indigeneous design capability supported by effective management. China's failure to generate truly novel weapons designs is evidenced by its inability, following an eight-year effort, to produce an airframe design that can accommodate the Spey engine at supersonic flight.[8] With the exception of nuclear weaponry, Chinese design engineers have demonstrated a talent only for modifying Soviet designs from the 1950s, particularly those for fighter aircraft. In some cases, Western experts question the degree to which Chinese adaptations represent major improvements over the original.[9] Moreover, since a majority of the factories under the defence industries possess large, specialised production lines acquired from the Soviet Union nearly thirty years ago, they are locked into producing outdated gear. The cost of refitting those factories with new assemblies would be astronomical.

While the training and skills of Chinese design engineers are not up to par for the job, neither are those of the project managers who lead them. The problem with managers, contends an analysis in *Jingli Guanli* in June 1980, is that they do not understand the interrelationship of scientific research and design work.[10]. Consequently, the article notes, designs enter into production before scientific research is complete, leaving unsolved the important problems in spare parts, components, and quality. The typical after-the-fact response: the launching of a crash programme for scientific research. The article goes on to argue that such experiences would not be repeated if China had greater appreciation of the role played by basic research.

Vertical integration of Chinese industries, however, has led to product-specific research and innovation. Because enterprises are largely self-sufficient, their research results are not usually transferable across enterprises and industries. In forfeiting basic research for applied research, China has lost important opportunities. Deprived of cumulative bodies of theoretical knowledge, Chinese scientists and engineers lack the basis for developing original and universal technological innovations.

While a proper blend of basic research, applied research, and testing and evaluation is essential to the formulation of operational designs, subsequent economic pay-offs are only obtainable when new designs are applied to production. This process, usually referred to as innovation, has been a key weakness of the Chinese industrial system.[11] Its roots are both attitudinal and organisational.

Until recently Beijing attached little importance to synchronising scientific and economic planning. Nor did it fully appreciate the role played by intellectuals in buttressing science and technology. Lacking precedent as well as incentives to tackle practical economic problems, China's scientists and engineers developed an elitist approach to their work, shunning mundane but useful projects in favour of more esoteric and less relevant endeavours.[12] According to Deng Xiaoping, 'This is the phenomenon of learning what is not to be applied and doing what one is not necessarily proficient in'.[13] The up-shot is that R & D is planned without regard to either specific application or follow-through to translate research results into usable technologies.

Though Chinese intellectuals have now regained the legitimacy and prestige denied them during the Cultural Revolution and are considered 'valuable and indispensable' assets to modernisation, lingering memories of how rapidly and unpredictably the political environment can change and offset their well-being continue to inhibit many from working to their full potential.

Production Problems

A related problem inhibiting innovation and its diffusion is the separation of research from production. The defence industries control at least fourteen research institutes specialising in prototype development and product development. They also maintain an undisclosed number of research academies that, in training scientific and technical manpower, work closely with experimental military factories. These are augmented by an unknown number of research institutes subordinate to the PLA's General Rear Services Department and General Services Department and to each of the armed services. Completing the network are research institutes under the Chinese Academy of

Sciences and research departments in major universities, which lend resources to defence-related projects, particularly those involving technology with civilian and military applications, such as computers, communications satellites, and expendable launch vehicles.[14]

This sizeable system has spawned quite a number of advances in military technology but, as in the civilian economy, when it comes to applying research results to production processes the system often breaks down. The Chinese journal *Si Kexuexue* (Scientology) reports that in Shanghai co-ordination between research and production units in preparation of new product designs occurs only 21.2 per cent of the time.[15] Though a similar analysis for the defence sector is not available, the fact that the problem is so deep-seated in China's most industrialised city suggests the existence of even worse conditions in other parts of the country.

At the production level, defence industries are severely hampered by ineffective management – a result of centralised economic planning. In its annual plan Beijing leaves the Chinese manager with little room for flexibility and creativity. Enterprises are given physical production quotas and detailed specifications on the output mix, consumption of raw materials, labour productivity, cost, and the amount of working capital used. In the past enterprise profits were remitted to the state, whereas firms operating at a loss received subsidies.

The impact of excessive centralisation of Chinese managerial behaviour has been similar to that in the Soviet Union. Essentially, managers pursue the fulfilment of physical output targets to the detriment of product quality, cost control, productivity and profitability. To guarantee plan-fulfilment and to guard against rising production targets or fluctuations in the availabililty of supplies, managers adopt such defensive measures as hoarding or stockpiling raw materials, either through barter arrangements or black market transactions. This is about the only instance in which Chinese managers show initiative. Basically they are conservative and cautious and averse to the kind of risk-taking associated with innovation. In addition, the traditions of vertical integration and self-reliance discourage managers from seeking out technologies available outside their immediate working environment.

Science and Technology

Finally, though deficient in many areas bearing on the sophistication and quality of weapons produced, defence industries – owing to their access to the country's best talent, material resources, and equipment –

have been China's prime movers in S & T. In terms of qualified personnel, the percentage of senior scientists and technicians employed in military industrial departments is three times that of the average civilian enterprises. Defence ministries can also claim more and higher-quality machinery and equipment. The Ministry of Ordnance ranks second in the country as an employer of metal-forging and cutting equipment. Its monopoly on precision-guided and numerically controlled machine tools enable it to carry out processing operations ranging from heavy machinery to electron optical instruments.[16]

Consequently, China's defence industries have been responsible for the country's most stunning S & T achievements – namely the development of strategic land and sea-based missiles and the launching and recovery of satellites. Its R & D has led to the creation of new materials and technology, 'some of which had never been in China before and have reached, or are near, advanced world levels'.

The defence industry's high concentration of scientific and technological resources in the face of declining orders for weapons from the PLA has been a primary impetus for integrating the military and civilian economies, an issue discussed in the following pages.

RESTRUCTURING INDUSTRY

To galvanise military suppliers into adopting management practices consistent with military–civilian integration, Beijing has linked the solicitation of civilian business to their overall welfare. The account of the Nanhua Power Machinery Research Institute reported in a July 1982 article in Beijing *Keyan Guanli* (Science Research Management) vividly explains why readjustment is a matter of survival. Because defence procurement was being trimmed back, explains the article:

> There were not many tasks, and for a while we were in a 'half-starving state'. Many jobs were unstable, discipline was lax, ideology was distracted. The entire institute was short of money ... We gradually realised that converting our purely military production structure in national defence scientific reserach to a structure that combined military and civilian endeavours, and expanding defence research are the objective requirements in the development of a Socialist economy and the long-run strategic measures to build up the four modernisations.[17]

As with all industrial reforms those imposed on defence industries have been characterised by forward movement, followed by periods of retrenchment during which evaluation and correction of mistakes takes place. According to an analysis in *Guangming Ribao* defence enterprises, eager to capture a share of the lucrative consumer market, are proceeding in an irrational manner; they are rushing to turn out certain 'hot-selling items', although production costs are too high to be competitive with their civilian counterparts.[18]

To ensure that military–civilian realignment will be grounded in reason, various Chinese commentators have recommended that it be guided by specific criteria.[19] First, in selecting consumer goods for production, military enterprises must ensure that they possess the appropriate technological processes. They should consider not only market demand but costs and quality as well, and refrain from competition with civilian producers when they are clearly the underdogs. They should also plan for full exploitation of comparative advantage by concentrating on precision products that fully exploit their superior technology. But in all cases they should not forget that 'the research, design experimentation, and verification of military products must be given priority for completion'.

In merging civilian with military production there should be both delegation and co-ordination. When the required technology is similar, manufacturing and processing equipment for both military and civilian customers should be done together, whereas design and assembly should be carried out separately. Military goods that demand special fabrication processes should not be forced into the same production line as consumer goods for the sake of gearing up for civilian markets.

In order to protect technological secrets, and thus competitiveness, business should be transacted on a contractual or licensing basis, or by joint ventures in which companies share the costs of investment and the resulting profits. The state can help here by promulgating laws and policies and establishing a nationwide patent system.[20] But technology transfer must stop short of personal shuffles between military and civilian units; rather, transfer should be confined to the free flow of knowledge based on the principle of 'learning, using, improving, and creating' through scientific exchanges, jointly sponsored training programmes, or the use of experts as temporary consultants.[21]

The Nanhua Institute established the 'four-services' criteria to guarantee the proper mix of civilian and military projects. National defence ranked as the top consideration. Military projects are to be carried regardless of loss or profit, whereas civilian jobs are geared toward domestic demands, advancing S & T, or increasing exports. Assigning responsibility for particular jobs is determined by the size and complexity of the projects.

It is difficult to determine the extent to which the Nanhua model has been adopted by the defence industries' research and design institutes and factories, but reform is centainly the order of the day and appears to be penetrating all sectors of the Chinese economy.[22]

THE ROLE OF ENERGY: BONANZA OR BUST?

China has recently adopted a 'Readjustment Programme' which is now slated to be extended through the completion of the current Five Year Plan for economic development, terminating in 1985. The programme calls for a moderate annual growth (4–5 per cent per year), gives high priority to light industries, and projects the decentralisation and rationalisation of enterprise management. Many development projects originally scheduled during the more optimistic days following the demise of the Gang of Four have since had to be postponed or rescheduled, among them the search for new non-ferrous mineral deposits.[23] Top priority has instead been given to energy conservation measures and to the increase of primary energy production: oil, coal, natural gas, and hydroelectric power. If relief from strategic resource shortages is achieved by 1985 (although based on the early returns the prognosis is not a hopeful one), off-shore petroleum resources will then be assigned greater priority, because without their development China will become a net importer of crude oil around 1990.[24]

In spite of its current limitations in both oil production and mineral extraction/trade (China's mineral exports total only about 17 per cent of its entire exports while its mineral imports account for about 35 per cent of all its imports), the PRC is clearly determined to garner increased strategic leverage from the petroleum and mineral networks already in place. The East/Southeast Asian regional security setting is certain to be affected by Chinese offshore oil development, both in the area of jurisdictional disputes concerning sovereign rights over coastlines and continental shelfs contiguous to the Yellow Sea, East China Sea, and South China Sea and in the realm of investment politics stemming from the question of Hongkong's political status and the effect of China's ideological positions on politico-economic relations with the region's newly developed countries (NDCs), including South

Korea, the ASEAN states, and eventually Taiwan. Western oil firms, for example, will certainly gauge their own future investment decisions involving China on the basis of Beijing's maturing ability (or continued inability) to smooth over present regional disputes. Diversification of China's offshore petroleum exploitation to the Yellow and South China seas will also make the PRC's future energy supplies less vulnerable to neutralisation by well-placed Soviet military strikes (and incidentally enhance the confidence of Western strategic and investment planners in China's overall development process). The obvious requirement here is to decentralise China's energy and industrial capacities, which are now bunched in the northeast corridor of the PRC. As recently concluded by Kim Woodward and Alice A. Davenport, ' ... successive offshore [petroelum] development will tend to integrate China more firmly into expanding commercial and political relations with the ASEAN states as well as with both Washington and Tokyo'.[25]

The Chinese pursuit of any significant petroleum fossil fuel recovery in conjunction with Western interests has natural 'spillover' implications for other sectors of China's resource development. For example, foreign corporations have already been invited to participate extensively in China's coal production. More than $3 billion has been allocated to ten different projects now in operation.[26] Japan is perhaps the leading capitalist partner in China's coal industry, since the 1978 Treaty for Friendship and Co-operation set the basis for the joint Sino–Japanese management of coal mining operations in Shandong (Yangzhou, Zhaozhuang) and Shanxi (Gujiao).[27] While extensive Chinese cuts or postponements of Japanese contracts were made in 1979 in the now infamous 'Baodong' episode, economic relations between Asia's two foremost powers are now largely restored – as related by Joachim Glaubitz in Chapter 15.

Joint Sino–American efforts in building up the PRC's coal industry are also strongly in evidence as a March 1983 agreement between Occidental Petroleum and the PRC concerning co-operation in exploiting the Pingsuo mines (in the Shanxi Province) graphically illustrates. Another agreement has been reached between the Chinese Government and the Fluor Corporation for building a 960 kilometre coal slurry pipeline that would carry fifteen million tons annually from Changzhi (Shanxi) to the port of Nantong, near Shanghai. Yet another American firm, the Bechtel Corporation, has agreed to conduct a feasibility study for the Chinese on the construction of a pipeline from Jungar in Inner Mongolia to the port of Qinghuangdao, northeast of

Beijing. This massive project, if pursued, would incorporate the eventual pumping of coal some seven hundred kilometres across China and would become one of the truly strategic components of China's industrial (and, by extension, military) development. Finally, China's imminent acceleration of co-operation in resource production with West European states should be briefly noted, as West Germany's Krupp Corporation and the United Kingdom's Shell Oil Company are currently negotiating for project contracts in the Inner Mongolia and Yunnan regions respectively.[28]

One can assert that the PRC has gained some bargaining leverage in international economic relations by what Kim Woodward has so aptly called 'the dual energy personality' of China. This means that while the PRC '... has the per capita energy life-style of a Third World country', it has 'the 'aggregate energy capabilities of an industrial country'.[29] While acting in the international economic system as a full member of the community of industrialised nations, China has simultaneously capitalised on its self-proclaimed identification and solidarity with the Third World. While it has emphasised its preferences for pursuing self-reliance in economic terms where possible, it has pragmatically rejected the adoption of extreme nationalist policies along xenophobic lines.

CHINA'S STRATEGIC MINERALS MARKET

There have been previous examples in China's economic history of the use of raw materials to satisfy specific global demands and incidentally enhance China's own strategic and economic welfare. Chinese national industries were strongly enhanced during the First World War by the exports of tin and antimony to belligerent countries, but the effects of this new-found prosperity were less than durable.[30] From such a historical perspective, one may ask whether the recent surge in Chinese mineral exports should not be considered as the consequence of some passing phase of the international market structure rather than as a lasting phenomenon within it.[31]

What does seem clear is that the West is once more assessing Chinese strategic mineral supplies as a growing power factor within the international system. In 1980, following a lengthy hiatus, the US Government decided to resume its purchase of Chinese minerals for its own national defence stockpile. Such purchases were to be governed by the newly passed Strategic and Critical Materials Stockpiling

Act and would be governed by the US General Services Administration (GSA). As a result of US trade liberalisation with the Chinese in this sector, China was able to supply the US with 25 000 tons of bauxite during 1980 alone and this category represented approximately 20 per cent of China's *total* exports to the US during that year.[32] In 1981 Washington started purchasing Chinese vanadium (used as an alloying element to strengthen steel). Chinese production of this metal (2900 tons per year) accounts for less than 10 per cent of the world's total, but the major part of this production is available for export, mainly to Western Europe. Most of China's vanadium export has been in the form of slag, but future sales of vanadium pentoxide and ferrovanadium are projected when they are improved to the point where they will become more competitive with other vanadium content alloys which are in high demand on the world market.

Western Europe and Japan are among the world's leading nations in minerals exploitation and metal refining technology. As such, they remain the key sources of Chinese diversification of some fifteen different materials which Beijing could export in order to earn enough foreign exchange to pursue its own modernisation efforts. 'Finished' or processed mineral supplies are also coming into China, largely from these nations. As Table 9.1 indicates, China's dependence on external (Western) sources for *finished* products remains quite high. It would be in Beijing's interest to improve its strategic minerals conversion capacity to remove the vulnerability of external dependence for such supplies.

Titanium supplies promise to be one means by which China may be able to rectify the raw material/finished product resource balance more in its own favour. China should be able to supply a portion of stockpile demand for titanium generated by US and West European aircraft or aerospace firms, although it may not retain the 15 per cent share of the US market which it suddenly gained in 1979–1980. China has a large reserve of titanium (estimated at 80 million tons, which is 10 per cent of the world's total). Beijing's production of titanium sponge is around 1000–2000 tons per year (less than 3 per cent of the world total) with about 30 per cent of this amount exported to the US. Since 1981, however, the titanium market became 'softer' as world supplies increased in relation to demand, and Chinese sales to the US declined abruptly.[33]

In general, Chinese foreign trade organisations have adopted noticably conservative strategies in responding to the widely variable conditions of the international mineral market. Their tendency is to

TABLE 9.1 Major Suppliers of Some Critical Materials to China

Material	Major Countries Supplying China
Iron and Steel	Japan, West Germany, Australia, Belgium, France, Italy, Netherlands, United Kingdom, Yugoslavia, Romania, Soviet Union
Aluminium	Canada, Japan, West Germany, France, United States, Italy, Australia, Norway
Copper	Chile, Peru, Canada, Japan, United Kingdom, Yugoslavia, Zambia, Philippines
Nickel	Canada, Albania, Cuba, Soviet Union, France, Netherlands, West Germany
Chromium	Albania, Iran, Pakistan, Turkey, Sudan, and probably southern African countries
Cobalt	Soviet Union, Belgium, Africa
Platinum	France, United Kingdom, West Germany
Lead	Peru, Canada, North Korea, Burma
Zinc	Peru
Natural rubber	Singapore, Thailand, Malaysia, Sri Lanka

SOURCE: National Foreign Assessment Center, *China: The Non-ferrous Metals Industry in the 1970's*, ER 78-10104U, May 1978.

withdraw from the markets almost completely when prices are falling, as evidenced by the trends established from 1979–1981. But such tendencies do not always follow predictable patterns. Chinese titanium and chromium sales developed rapidly, for example, during 1979–1980 even though worldwide marketing projections would logically have called for more cautious Chinese development of these exports. In other cases Chinese sales are determined by a simplistic response to immediate marketing trends. Before 1979 China hardly sold any germanium abroad. Owing to the rapid growth of the industries around the world which utilise this metal (in, for example, the construction of fibre optics) market prices increased sharply throughout 1980–1981 and Chinese germanium exports jumped accordingly.[34] Overall, China has thus far seemed to be a negligible influence in the determination of the prices of even those minerals which she possesses in abundance, such as antimony, tungsten, and tin. This hard reality is particularly significant when it is recalled that China was unable to use the witholding of mineral supply as a retaliation against unilateral curbs imposed on Chinese textile exports to the US by the Reagan administration. More sophistication in converting mineral supplies to strategic influence will need to be demonstrated by China's economic planners if this aspect of Chinese strategic resources is to be implemented effectively as a component of China's overall foreign policy.

CONCLUSIONS

For the pessimists, much of what has been presented above substantiates the view that improvement in China's defence position will be slow in coming. To be sure, there are serious limits on Chinese strategic resources and economic modernisation is hindered by important structural defects.

However, it would be wrong to leave the analysis on such a bleak note. In the first place, it is unfair to believe that China need match the superpowers in every category before it can be considered an important defence power. Such ethnocentrism fails to take account of the special needs of China. It also tends to miss other important trends that might lead to a more optimistic judgement. For example, China still remains in a class of resource power only matched by the superpowers. While obvious weaknesses exist for China, the essential autarky of a continental power should not be overlooked. Nor should it be forgotten that both superpowers also have serious gaps in their own resources. Thus Chinese military power in the end rests on the specific nature of China itself – its large population and its continental resources. To minimise these fundamental factors would be to miss the essential 'Chinese' character of its defence policy.

Similarly, despite limited investment in military industry, some important modernisation is taking place. Above all, there are some crucial signs of improvement in the economy as a whole, and that can only bode well for defence policy in the long run.

For the near term, or until economic conditions warrant a shift on investment priorities, China's defence industries can be expected to conduct business as usual: R & D that lends itself to unimaginative, but not insignificant, gains in existing weapons and equipment. Meanwhile, the PLA will concentrate on professionalising its troops with better training while Beijing continues its post-1979 practice of dispatching delegations to gather information on foreign military systems, establishing ties with Western military officers and business executives, and emphasising a S &T curriculum for Chinese students studying abroad.

How quickly Chinese defence industries generate the technological thrusts required for modern weapons production will depend not only on the availability of funds but on the success of management and organisational reforms. The six defence industries will have made substantial progress in removing the most serious constraints on modernisation – to the extent that 'civilianisation' of the military industrial machine results in: the sharing of technical information between civilian and defence entities, elimination of the boundaries between research, design and production, and a new emphasis on innovation and quality control.

Further driving the defence industries into efficient modes of operation will be the growing number of college graduates joining their staffs as managers and engineers conversant in state-of-the-art technologies. By being forced to compete for civilian business, albeit in a regulated context, defence industry personnel will acquire the necessary skills in project planning, systems integration and management to undertake large-scale and long-term weapons programmes. Technically competent Chinese managers will offset one of the greatest risks Westerners calculate when considering technology transfer to China; their interest in doing business with the defence industries will therefore be bolstered. Once technology is transferred, a solid managerial infrastructure will assure that it is absorbed and adapted by the S & T system for use in other areas of the economy.

Provided that China remains politically stable, 'civilianisation' of the military economy will spearhead the transformation of defence enterprises into more efficient and quality-oriented operations. If there is challenge to reforms it will come from factions of the PLA bitter over shrinking defence budgets and opposed to the reallocation of installed capital to the civilian sector. On the other hand, it is in their best interest to wait and see if economic readjustment bears fruit.

NOTES AND REFERENCES

1. Denis Fred Simon, 'China's Capacity to Assimilate Foreign Technology' in *China Under the Four Modernizations.* Joint Economic Committee, US Congress, 13 August 1982. 87–199.
2. Sydney Jammes and G. L. Lamborn, 'China's Military Requirements' in Ibid 597–605. Also. 'China's Defence Industries', *Strategic Survey, 1979.* (London: IISS, 1980) 67–72. Harlan Jencks, *From Muskets to Missiles* (Boulder, Colorado: Westview Press, 1982).

3. From the author's private discussions with Chinese officials representing the Ministry of Aviation Industry.
4. Martin Weil, 'The Baoshan Steel Mill' in *China Under The Four Modernizations*. 334–365.
5. Author's private discussions with project managers in US computer firms.
6. *Washington Post*, 7 April 1983.
7. 'Problems of Developing the Machinery Industry Studied' Beijing Jingji Guanli No. 6, June 1980 in JPRS, *China Report* no. 76217, 13 August 1980 34–42.
8. *Far Eastern Economic Review*, 10 April 1981, 24.
9. See note 2 and *Jane's All the World's Aircraft, 1982*.
10. Jingji Guanli, no. 6, 15 June 1980 see note 7.
11. Richard Suttmeir, 'Research, Innovation and the Chinese Political Economy', *China Under the Four Modernizations* 489–513.
12. *Beijing Review* no. 12, 12 March 1983 and no. 22, 30 May 1983 4. Also Leo Orleans, 'Science, Elitism and Economic Readjustment' in *China Under the Four Modernizations*. 475–488.
13. *FBIS*, 1 December 1982, K1–2.
14. Ibid.
15. Jencks, *From Muskets to Missiles* (see note 2), 202–7.
16. 'On the Shifting of Science and Technology from Military to Civilian Uses'. Beijing Jingji Yanjiu no. 11, November 1982 translated in JPRS, *China Report*. No. 82761, 31 January 1983 41–8.
17. 'Institute Urges Continuing Military, Civilian Research' Beijing Keyan Guanli no. 3, July 1982. JPRS, *China Report* no. 82108 28 October 1982 53–63.
18. 'Do the Work of Transferring Military Technology to Civilian Use Well', *Guangming Ribao*, 22 January 1982.
19. Ibid and 'The National Defence Industry Should take the Road of Integrating the Military and Civil' Beijing Jingji Guanli, no. 7. 15 July 1981 in JPRS *China Report*, no. 79262, 21 October 1981 42–7.
20. *The China Business Review*. vol. 8, no. 3, May–June, 1981, 39.
21. *Keyan Guanli* see note 17.
22. *Beijing Review* no. 5, 31 January 1983. 6.
23. A. Doak Barnett, *China's Economy in Global Perspective* (Washington: Brookings, (1981).
24. This prognosis has been offered by analysts of the International Monetary Fund. American officials have been quoted as contending that China's offshore oil deposits are not expected to yield 'significant' production until 1989. See *The Japan Times*, 3 April 1982, 5. China's current petroleum yield, incidentally, has stagnated at around 100 million tons per annum.
25. For a particularly illuminating analysis of the strategic aspects related to China's energy production, see Kim Woodward and Alice A. Davenport, 'The Security Dimension of China's Offshore Oil Development,' *Journal of Northeast Asian Studies* 1, no. 3, September 1982, 3–26.
26. Statement by Bai Xingjai, Director of the China Coal Society, reprinted in BBC, *SWB FE/W* 1222/A/21, 9 February 1983.
27. 'Sino–Japanese Coal Cooperation', *China Newsletter* (A JETRO 'Special Report'), no. 36, January–February 1982.
28. For a report on the German negotiations, see *Xinhua*, 1 March 1983 as

reprinted in BBC, *SWB FE/* W 1227/A/22, 16 March 1983. For the Sino–UK Shell transaction background information, see *Financial Times*, 16 November 1982.
29. Woodward, *The International Energy Relations of China* (Stanford: Stanford University Press, 1980), 49.
30. For a sophisticated evaluation of China's military expenditure trends from the mid-1960s onward, see Ronald G. Mitchell, 'Chinese Defense Spending in Transition', in Selected Papers submitted to The Joint Economic Committee, US Congress, *China Under The Four Modernizations*, 9th Congress, 2nd Session, 13 August 1982, 605–610.
31. *The Economist* (London) 23 April 1983 80–5.
32. Sabrina Brady, 'China's Strategic Minerals and Metals,' *The China Business Review* (September/October, 1981), 66–67.
33. *The Economist* (London) 23 April 1983.
34. Ibid.

10 Arms Sales to China

WILLIAM T. TOW

Access to advanced technology with military applications has been one of the most compelling reasons for the People's Republic of China to search for economic and political ties with the West and Japan since the end of the Cultural Revolution. Until very recently, China's basic strategic interests appeared to converge ever more closely with those of the industrial democracies in presenting the Soviet Union with a coalition of Chinese human resources and NATO/Japanese military and economic resources.[1] Beijing's current leadership probably hoped to obtain an arms and technology conduit without seriously compromising its own territorial claims and ideological interests. Until the Reagan Administration assumed power in Washington, the momentum of weapons and technology transfer was certainly working in China's favour, if not necessarily at a pace dictated or desired by Western defence firms. The 1975 Rolls Royce contract allowing China to acquire the Spey engine is still regarded as the bellwether of Sino-Western military co-operation. The PRC has similarly coveted access to Tokyo's advanced computer and electronics prowess which, over time, could be applied to selected Chinese space and guided missile systems.[2] While the United States failed to normalise relations with the PRC until 1979, or to establish direct military ties with it until early 1980, American policy planners have tacitly supported the European NATO states' efforts to sell weapons to the Chinese as a means of pressuring the USSR.

More direct Sino-American strategic co-operation during the early 1980s was induced by two key events: the February 1979 Sino-Vietnamese War (demonstrating the backwardness of China's military forces) and the December 1979 Soviet invasion of Afghanistan. By mid-1981, the US had reached an apex in its new China policy when Secretary of State Alexander Haig visited Beijing and talked of 'important opportunities' for the moving of Sino-American security co-operation 'onto a new plateau'.[3] Such hyperbole was offered in spite of President Reagan's pro-Taiwan sympathies. While revealing that the US would consider the sale of 'lethal weapons' to the Chinese on a 'case-by-case basis', even Haig (who was regarded as China's best friend in the Reagan Administration) tempered his assertions concerning the durability of US–PRC military relations by acknowledging that the Chinese had not exhibited much urgency about buying weapons.[4]

Following Haig's trip, however, old differences between the Americans and the Chinese began to return. Among other irritants, it seemed to China's leadership that Washington was overly presumptuous in defining China's own needs. Meanwhile xenophobic forces within the Chinese Communist Party (CCP) were becoming more open in their attacks on the Four Modernisations programme with its implicit reliance on foreign technology.[5] Even more important from China's perspective was the apparent disregard by the Reagan Administration for the PRC's demands that Washington more clearly cease supplying Taiwan with defensive weapons.

The result of Washington's failure to comply with Chinese territorial interests or defer to Chinese cultural sensitivities has been predictable and probably inevitable. By late March 1983, China's foremost political figure, Deng Xiaoping, intimated to a group of American Congressmen that relations between the PRC and the US had deteriorated almost daily since President Reagan took office.[6] Little doubt remains that the atmosphere conducive to Sino–American defence co-operation is undergoing a severe test. Neither the West European states nor Japan, moreover, have tried to mediate on Washington and Beijing's behalf or to fill the resulting military sales void.

While military sales remains only one component of more comprehensive geopolitical differences, both China and the United States tend to view them as an important component of their defence policies. With this assumption as a starting point, it would seem appropriate to evaluate the most salient factors concerning the PRC's military relations with the US and with other NATO countries. The most central questions are (1) how were high expectations for Western arms sales to the PRC dashed?; (2) what options are still available to China for obtaining the advanced weapons technology from Europe?; (3) what role might a western-armed China serve in global terms?

FROM ENTICEMENT TO DISENCHANTMENT:

When one assesses the deterioration of Sino–American relations since mid-1981, Taiwan can undoubtedly be seen as the major source of tension. But other factors directly related to the arms sales question itself should be taken into account. First, the PRC has by now realised that the West will not automatically bestow upon Chinese scientists and technicians its most advanced knowledge and technology. The 'heavenly mandate' is no more valid in barbarian eyes at present than when the Treaty of Nanking marked the superiority of European armaments over a century ago. There is little evidence that Western defence firms are inclined to enter into the type of co-production arrangements with China that would allow it to build formidable defence capabilities for a fraction of the time and cost originally incurred by their own countries.[7] A second problem has been the cost of those weapons systems. China's scarce capital and equally dear hard currency are largely assigned to sustain the country's latest Five Year Plan which was presented recently to the Twelfth CCP Congress. Within the current framework of Chinese economic priorities, defence allocations still take a back seat to the development of energy resources and consumer industries.[8]

Under such circumstances, it is not surprising that the Chinese would gradually drift away from a positive view of arms purchases. Beijing's current stance is underlined by two concurrent themes – American betrayal of diplomatic normalisation between the US and PRC brought about by the Reagan Administration's generous interpretation of the 1979 Taiwan Relations Act, and China's rising determination that it become self-sufficient in strengthening its own defences. These positions have intersected so that strategic relations with the US and its NATO allies have now been assigned a lower priority. Beijing is concentrating on indigenous efforts to establish credible military power. While not discounting the presence of at least some American or European defence technology in future PRC weapons production lines, China seems determined to develop *uniquely Chinese* defence products. In March 1983, Defence Minister Zhang Aiping elaborated upon the PRC's official policy course:

> ... Our country is a big country and it is not realistic or possible for us to buy national defence from abroad. We must soberly see that what can be bought from foreign countries will at most be things which are advanced to the second grade. This cannot help us attain the goal of national defence modernisation, nor will it help us shake off the possible state of being controlled by others ... if we are content with copying, we shall only be crawling behind others and will still be unable to attain our anticipated goal. The fundamental way is to rely on ourselves.[9]

The above remarks indicate that the Chinese have rejected the somewhat delicately calibrated American overtures concerning technology transfer policies to the PRC. Such a Western approach would have been regulated by the Committee for Export Controls to Communist Countries (COCOM) or through similar consultative bodies set up by NATO members and Japan. A predominant (though tacit) American assumption underlying any willingness to sanction the selling of 'dual use' or even 'lethal' military technology to the PRC was that West Europeans rather than Americans would be the most visible merchants, thereby preserving Washington's manoeuvrability in negotiating with Moscow. But the continuing legitimacy of such sales would eventually require a more open American commitment to liberalise its own regulations concerning the transfer of weapons and high technology to the Chinese.[10] The conditions for effecting this change materialised with the Carter Doctrine following Afghanistan and President Reagan's election signalling the American public's desire to assume a harder line toward the Russians. As a result, the US came to assign China a role in the Asian–Pacific area as a key opponent of Soviet military power.

The Reagan Administration subsequently hoped to balance off its geopolitical ties to China with its more accustomed role of supplying Taiwan with weapons needed to deter a takeover by the PRC. The Chinese, however, rejected the Administration's calculations by labelling its tactics as crude and unsophisticated as well as a direct assault on the PRC's sovereignty. As a result, China has let it be known that it '... would rather refuse to buy US arms than consent to a US arms sale to Taiwan, which is an interference in China's internal affairs ...'[11] This policy was obviously linked with China's determination to produce its own weapons, notwithstanding the obvious time and costs involved in such a venture.

President Reagan made several attempts to salvage his position. In January 1982 he rejected a Taiwanese request for the purchase of an advanced version of the F-5 jet fighter and this move seemed, for a while, to ward off a serious crisis in Sino–American ties at a time when Deng Xiaoping appeared particularly vulnerable to political rivals within the CCP itself. Yet the apparent benefits of this move were negated several months later when the Administration approved a $US 60 million spare-parts transaction for Taiwan.[12]

In February 1983 *Xinhua* reported that Chinese leaders complained to visiting US Secretary of State George Schultz that Washington was 'discriminating' against the PRC in economic and technical exchanges compared to the Nationalist regime and that 'the ceiling set by the US for its arms sales to Taiwan far exceeded the maximum annual figures published by US government departments'.[13] Three months later *Xinhua*'s Washington bureau chief commented that the deteriorating trend in Sino–American ties 'all boils down to the Taiwan question, or, to be more precise, hands off Taiwan'.[14]

In further efforts to reduce the impact of continued arms shipments to Taiwan, Reagan dispatched Schultz to China in an attempt to find a way to restore Sino–American security relations. The President followed Schultz's visit by sending two other American officials to China in May 1983 – his science advisor, George Keyworth, and his Commerce Secretary, Malcolm Baldridge. During their visits, signs of limited but important rehabilitation in security co-operation between the Chinese and Americans materialised.

It was widely speculated that they had agreed on measures to revive high level defence consultations which had been dormant since the cancellation of a scheduled September 1981 visit to the US by the People's Liberation Army Deputy Chief of Staff Liu Huaqing.[15] The cancellation had followed Chinese press criticism of various Chinese military and governmental figures acting, it was said, like tourists during past inspection trips to the US and thereby squandering national finances.[16] Keyworth signed several research protocols, including those applicable to joint Sino–American research in aeronautics and nuclear physics. He subsequently labelled the efforts of the US–China Joint Commission in Science and Technology as 'the most successful science and technology co-operation of any we have in the world'.[17] Such euphoria was to be considered, however, in the context of Beijing's consternation over the continued bureaucratic infighting between US agencies responsible for determining what US defence firms can or cannot sell to China.[18] The 'Category P' status assigned to China in 1981 for purposes of approving or restricting technology transfers remains largely ambiguous, although it seems clear that the PRC will be allowed to import more American technology than will the USSR or East European states, which remain under a more restrictive 'Category Y' classification.

After arriving in China on 23 May, Baldridge related to Premier Zhao Ziyang and other Chinese leaders that President Reagan had issued 'new orders' whereby China could expect to obtain 'significantly' higher levels of US technology more quickly by the simplification and reduction of existing restrictions on US products designated for the PRC, especially in the computer sector. But Chen Muhua, China's

Minister of Foreign Economic Relations and Trade, replied that 'many obstacles and difficulties still existed' in both trade and strategy between the two countries.[19]

Apart from an acceleration in official consultations and agreements over the first part of 1983 compared to the bleak pace of the previous year, other indicators of renewed US–PRC strategic collaboration are gradually appearing. Systems and Applied Sciences Corporation signed a contract effective in late January 1983 for the sale of an $11 million ground satellite tracking station to China as a follow-on to a January 1979 state-to-state agreement for the Chinese acquisition of Landsat's 'agricultural and geological' data base. While Landsat is usually described in terms of only civilian-related technology, the computer equipment actually involved is believed to have military applications. This point was driven home in February 1983 when China announced that it would launch its own permanently orbiting communications satellite above the Indian Ocean with a CZ-3 liquid fuelled rocket, complete with tracking and telemetry equipment.[20] Other relevant commercial activity is also being stepped up. American Motors has signed an agreement with the Chinese for the joint production of jeeps based on a 1954 design for a Soviet Army vehicle and officially designated by the United States Information Service as a 'military vehicle' for sale throughout the Far East.[21]

Finally, unnamed Pentagon officials have been quoted recently by Reuters press agency as anticipating an imminent breakthrough on negotiations for actual weapons production by joint Sino–American consortia, especially in the areas of anti-tank and anti-aircraft missiles.[22] Perhaps anticipating such a policy line, William Perry, former Under Secretary of Defense for Research and Engineering and still a DOD consultant, recently surmised before Congress that the US should consider a transfer of short-range, 'tactical' defence technology (as opposed to the outright sale of finished weapons systems) to the PRC – thereby allowing Beijing to build up its own defence infrastructure selectively and gradually so as to communicate credibly to the USSR that China's self-defence along the Sino–Soviet border is Washington's basic security objective. Perry further contended that the Chinese already have the capability to assimilate such technology.[23]

But recent discussions by Schultz and other US officials visiting China have not directly encompassed the question of US weapons transfers to the PRC owing to the continued sensitivity of the Taiwan questions and other Sino–American differences. Such roadblocks have also affected US nuclear technology sales to Beijing. In June 1982 the US Department of Commerce announced that the Reagan Administration was 'considering the possibility of a nuclear sharing/production agreement' with China without elaborating upon the specific form of agreement. In March 1983 the US Nuclear Regulatory Commission proposed the modification of nuclear exports rules which were clearly designed to facilitate the sale of atomic reactor components to China by the Westinghouse Electric Corporation. They were also designed to give a boost to a weakened American nuclear power industry which envisaged a China nuclear market of between $8 million and $25 million before the end of the century. American officials have continued to show concern, however, that China might be selling low enriched uranium to South Africa, Argentina, and to other countries in direct violation of US nuclear non-proliferation policies. The PRC also refuses to allow the inspection of its civilian nuclear facilities by outsiders and has yet to join the International Atomic Energy Agency. As will be noted below, the West Europeans have tended to capitalise on the Reagan Administration's indecision over the issue of nuclear exports to China by entering into their own arrangements with Beijing.[24]

During his China trip, Schultz was criticised by American businessmen for the US Government's lack of competitiveness *vis-à-vis* those of Europe and Japan in granting technology export licences. Schultz could only reply that '... maybe they are just better'.[25] With the announcement by Zhao Ziyang, that he was postponing his own return trip to the US owing to a lack of substantial positive relations between the US and PRC, it remained clear that the opportunities for an improvement in Sino–American relations, let alone arms deals, remained severely restricted.

CHINESE ARMS PURCHASES FROM WESTERN EUROPE

To what extent have the NATO European states been more successful than the United States in building up or sustaining arms sales to China? The British experience is instructive. During 1982 Marconi Avionics sold radars and airborne computers to the PRC for various Chinese jet fighters. Arabat, a British computer systems firm, won over $US 1 million worth of orders from the China Civil Aviation Administration applicable to aircraft maintenance and transport purposes. Vickers Ltd was reportedly producing turrets for China's more advanced (Type 59 and Type 69) tanks.[26] The most widely publicised British–Chinese arms deal, however, was an apparent failure. In November 1982 the UK announced that a consortium of British defence companies, led by Vosper Thorneycroft and British Aerospace, had signed a £100 million contract with China for fitting nine 'Luda' class destroyers with 'Sea Dart' surface-to-surface missiles along with radar and electronic equipment. A British Department of Trade official heralded the agreement as a forerunner of other anticipated contracts and as establishing a long-term trend for British exports of military technology to the PRC.[27] But the deal was cancelled at the end of February 1983 owing to China's funding shortages and because of fears by Chinese military leaders that the price of the British package would increase beyond the originally negotiated amount.[28]

As was the case with previous UK attempts to sell the Harrier VSTOL jet fighter, the Chinese seemed to be deterred by the high cost-per-unit of British products even though UK defence concerns are highly renowned for cost-effectively merging older equipment with the latest products of high defence technology. In interviews conducted with officials of the UK Defence Ministry's Sales Office during 1981, however, a sense of persistent optimism was conveyed to this author that the Chinese eventually would realise that British weapons technology can be made applicable to the PRC's needs and priorities.[29] Following the Sea Dart cancellation, PLA Deputy Chief of Staff Wu Xiuquan was quoted as arguing that the deal was only an 'isolated case' which would 'not concern future military co-operation with European countries.'[30] But the overall history of the Sino–British arms sales relationship has been characterised by frustration and dashed expectations on both sides.

Little in the way of military transactions has materialised between the PRC and France, which stands as London's primary West European competitor for any arms market with China. The PRC's lack of either a top-of-the-line fighter interceptor or strike aircraft spurred both French Foreign Minister Claude Cheysson and Defence Minister Charles Hernu to lobby for the sale of the Mirage 2000 to China, particularly since France announced in April 1982 that 150 units of this aircraft will be purchased by India. In May 1983 Zhao Ziyang announced that the Mirage was too expensive and that further negotiations were in order, despite the Mitterand Government's increasing propensity to sell advanced aircraft, anti-tank missiles, and other equipment previously considered too sensitive in relation to the USSR, Vietnam, and India.[31] Suspect French capability to supply spare parts is also a consideration. Dassault/Breguet's excessive dependence on export orders strongly implies a domestic production base without enough flexibility to meet the uncertainties and fluctuations of demand within the overall international arms market.[32] A more manoeuvrable aircraft such as the Harrier, or even medium-range fast, low-altitude penetrating bombers such as the F-111 or Jaguar would be more appropriate for a regional Chinese air defence role.[33]

China's arms sales relations with NATO states other than Britain and France have been even less noteworthy. From February through June 1982, Italian officials discussed Italian electronic systems for artillery and ground-to-air missiles already used by the PLA (on a Chinese modified version of the Soviet 'Sagger' anti-tank missile). But when China's ill-fated Hot/Milan co-production negotiations are recalled, it seems unlikely that the Italians would have anything more appealing to offer the Chinese than either French anti-tank and anti-air weapons, the American 'Redeye', the British 'Blowpipe', or Japanese equivalents. All these items could be sold to China, but the PRC seems unwilling to buy. West Germany currently remains aloof from China arms sales because of its geographic proximity and political sensitivity to Moscow. This remains true even though certain well-known conservative politicians within Bonn's present CDU/CSU/FDP coalition government have pressed for increased German security ties with Beijing to increase the FRG's leverage with the Soviet bloc.[34] Holland is still criticised in Beijing for recently selling submarines to Taiwan, while Belgium has made little effort to follow up its initial 1981 discussions with PLA officials concerning possible small arms transfers. Brussels was reportedly pressured by Washington not to follow through on a potential deal with the Chinese over a telecommunications computer system laden with US-made parts, which might have been relevant to military purposes.[35]

Bureaucratic and party politics in the United States, along with China's unwillingness to pay for modern US weapons and technology, have precluded the PRC from gaining access to the American defence market and have forced China to be highly selective as to what West European arms-related technology it actually buys. China's disillusionment with the European defence connection has not only compelled Zhang Aiping to infer that British, French, and other non-American weapons systems are 'second grade' but to call for the entire reorganisation of his country's military infrastructure along American and/or Soviet lines, thereby allowing the PRC to achieve a higher level of proficiency than Europe in defence technology.[36]

Yet upgraded relations between China and the so-called 'Second

World' (Western Europe and Canada and Japan) might still generate long-term benefits for the PRC. These states could help China meet important short-term needs while appearing as a good commercial partner rather than as an imposing would-be superpower. Forging a Second World connection might also create at least some leverage for China in its own strategic deliberations with the US.[37] Under conditions where the PRC was to emphasise its political and economic affinity with Europe and Japan, NATO's weapons inventories and Tokyo's technological fount may become more available to the Chinese.

China's purchasing credibility might be restored quickly if it were inclined to buy intermittently the most important systems needed for its defence modernisation in quantities which could serve as models for Chinese production. The frequency and volume of such purchases would have to be enough, however, to induce European defence firms to continue dealing with the PRC. A possible means to this end might be for China to use various Common Market offices. This would lend a particularly European identity to China's policy, although mechanisms would have to be derived to prevent China from circumventing US and NATO review procedures.[38]

EXTERNAL ASSISTANCE AND CHINA'S FUTURE MILITARY POWER

If there are such fundamental problems in Sino–Western arms deals, does China have any better options other than self-reliance? Does the Soviet Union have a role to play in Chinese planning? Historical experience will most likely temper most Chinese hopes for obtaining arms sales as part of the recent Sino–Soviet negotiations. It remains highly improbable that the Soviets would either offer or that the Chinese would accept arrangements similar to those of the early 1950s, when substantial Soviet nuclear and conventional military assistance was promised but only sometimes delivered to Beijing. Current Chinese policy statements reflect a widescale scepticism over the prospects that such relations could again occur. Such Chinese feelings are probably reinforced by the PRC's disillusionment over the almost equally unsatisfactory security relationship with the United States. As long as Soviet military forces remain massed along China's own boundaries and the bulk of Western forces are far removed from its shores, the appeal of renewed Soviet military ties should remain limited. Even if a partial political or ideological rapprochement is achieved between the two communist powers, the prospect of the Soviet Union declining to increase its own defence expenditures if Chinese offensive force capabilities were to increase substantially is improbable.[39]

However, if China does desire some sort of programme for the purchase of arms and technology, the West does look like a more hopeful option. For example, in its efforts to pursue a more viable nuclear deterrent, China's military could eventually benefit from a 'spill over' of Western commercial nuclear technology. The technology of American, British, and French nuclear power firms might allow China to cut through previous barriers to the production of more weapons-grade fuel with greater efficiency and at lower cost. Electronics and software technology could continue to be applied to Chinese satellite tracking and missile guidance systems. And US geodetic equipment – notwithstanding the assurances about Landsat's 'civilian applications' – can enhance the PLA's co-ordination of C^3 and target acquisition.

In sum, serious problems stand in the way of any major Chinese arms purchases from any source. First, China seems unwilling to buy technology on a large scale off anyone's shelf. Selected models may be purchased, but it seems that only those willing to help the Chinese help themselves are likely to sign deals with Beijing. Second, the West itself is by no means clear what weapons it wants to sell China, or what supervisory systems should be established to monitor what does take place. It should therefore not be surprising that China seeks a more independent foreign policy – one that avoids close strategic relationships with either superpower.

Despite current Chinese and American differences it remains true that neither the PRC nor the US have totally closed the door on some military relations. These possibilities may yet increase if Soviet military power were to be seen to grow rapidly at China's expense. Under such circumstances, some more tangible NATO–PRC security relations seem possible.[40] Such relations would significantly improve Chinese self-defence capabilities while hopefully, from a Western standpoint, sustaining a better equilibrium within an East Asian power balance. Whatever the case – increased Sino–Soviet détente, or a return to more Sino–Soviet tension – it seems clear that the dreams of a massive China arms market, much like nineteenth-century dreams of textile markets, are sorely misplaced. The common cause for the failure of both dreams, was to see the question from the point of view of what 'we can sell' rather than what China wants to buy.

NOTES AND REFERENCES

1. For background on the early development of Sino–Western arms ties, see William T. Tow and Douglas T. Stuart, 'China's Military Turns to the West', *International Affairs* (London), 57, no. 2 (Spring 1981), 286–300. Banning Garrett has offered the best assessment of the early US position in Gerald Segal (ed.), *The China Factor* (London: Croom Helm Ltd, 1982), 76–102.
2. For an account of emerging Chinese–Japanese strategic relations, consult Tow, 'Sino–Japanese Security Co-operation: Evolution and Prospects', *Pacific Affairs* 56, no. 1 (Spring 1983), 51–83.
3. The dynamics behind the Sino–American thaw which accelerated in concurrence with the Soviet intervention in Afghanistan are ably analysed in Strobe Talbot's, 'The Strategic Dimension in the Sino–American Relationship', Richard H. Solomon (ed.), *The China Factor* (Englewood Cliffs, New Jersey: Prentice-Hall, Inc., 1981), especially 91–93.
4. On Haig's remarks made in China and at a subsequent press conference in Manila, see *The Department of State Bulletin* 81, no. 2053, August 1981, 34–39 and 'A Green Light on Weapons', *Asiaweek* 7, no. 25, 26 June 1981, 16.
5. Don Oberdorfer, 'Haig Submits Proposal on Limiting US Sale of Weapons to Taiwan', *International Herald Tribune* (hereafter cited as *IHT*) 3–4 July 1982, 3; and Robert Manning, 'The Perils of Rhetoric', *Far Eastern Economic Review* (hereafter cited as *FEER*) 115, no. 8, 19 February 1982, 10.
6. Oberdorfer, 'US–Chinese Rift Over Defection: An Illustration of Imperiled Ties', *IHT* 9–10 April 1983, 5. For a fuller account of the discussions between Deng and the Congressional Delegation, see 'Reportage on US House Delegation's Visit–Meeting With Deng Xiaoping', *Xinhua*, 30 May 1983 and reprinted in Foreign Broadcast Information Service (FBIS), *China (Daily Report)*, 30 March 1983, B-1 through B-3.
7. This observation was strengthened by the author's interviews with US State Department officials in November 1979 and with representatives of British defence firms in September 1982. The US Defence Intelligence Agency (DIA) is concerned, however, that China might still be obtaining sophisticated high technology and equipment through firms in Hong Kong or through other 'unauthorised third parties'. Consult Teresa Ma, 'A Chinese Screen', *FEER* 117, no. 37, 10 September 1982, 73.
8. 'Report on the Sixth Five-Year Plan', *Beijing Review* 25, no. 51 20 December 1982, 10–35; Zhao Ziyang's address on 'A Strategic Question on Invigorating the Economy', ibid. 25, no. 46, 15 November 1982, 13–20; Tony Walker, 'China's Budget Deficit "Will Be About £918"', *The Financial Times*, 2 December 1982, 3; and David Bonavia, 'China Opts for Efficiency Instead of Rhetoric', *The Times* (London), 3 December 1982, 9.
9. 'Defense Minister Calls on China to Develop Its Own Weapons', *Xinhua*, 28 February 1983, and reprinted in British Broadcasting Corporation, *Summary of World Broadcasts Far East* (hereafter cited as BBC, SWB FE/7272/BII/I, 6 March 1983.

10. See the remarks of Roger Sullivan, a member of the Carter Administration's National Security Council and Assistant Deputy Secretary of State who was a key figure in formulating US guidelines for technology transfer, and COCOM review concerning the PRC that appears in Committee on Foreign Relations, United States Senate and the Congressional Research Service, *The Implications of US–China Military Co-operation* 97th Congress, 1st Session, January 1982, especially 49–50 and 106.
11. 'China Won't Accept US "Balanced Arms Sale"', *Beijing Review* 24, no. 25 22 June 1981, 11.
12. David Jenckins, 'Hawk and Chicken', *FEER* 119, no. 4 27 January 1983, 28–29; and a special report that Senator Barry Goldwater was advised by key Reagan Administration officials that the US Ambassador to Beijing (Arthur Hummel) was instructed by the President to advise the PRC that arms sales would not decline in volume over the near future. *Ashai Evening News* 16 July 1982, 4.
13. See the *Xinhua* report by correspondents Zhou Lifang and Zhu Minzhi reprinted in BBC, *SWB FE*/7252/A1/1, 8 February 1983.
14. Michael Parks, 'Dim Prospects Seen for US Ties', *IHT*, 3 May 1983, 3.
15. For the Chinese version of the Shultz–Zhang talks, see *Xinhua*, 3 February 1983 as reprinted in BBC, *SWB FE*/7250/A1/1, 5 February 1983. Western accounts include Bernard Gwertzman, 'US, China to Resume Military Contacts', *IHT*, 5–6 February 1983, 1, and Tony Walker, 'China–US To Renew Military Links', *The Financial Times*, 5 February 1983, 2.
16. For revealing analyses of the bureaucratic squabbling with the Chinese leadership concerning the issue of gaining defence technology through self-sufficiency rather than through assimilation from foreign sources, see Colina MacDougall, 'Chinese Political Row Leads to Loss of Order', *The Financial Times*, 24 March 1983, 6; and James Sterba, 'Chinese Press Criticises Inspection Trips to US', *IHT*, 3 February 1981, 4.
17. 'US, China Sign Pacts on Research', *IHT*, 12 May 1982, 5.
18. For background on Chinese frustrations over US bureaucratic intransigence, see Robert Manning, 'A Strategic Soft Sell', *FEER* 119, no. 7, 17 February 1983, 9–10.
19. See reports by David Bonavia in *The Times*, 24 May 1983, 8 and 25 May 1983, 10; *The Financial Times*, 24 May 1983, 6 and 25 May 1983, 6. Also see Michael Park, 'Baldridge sees US–China Trade Continuing Its Vigourous Growth', *IHT*, 24 May 1983, 11.
20. A Chinese announcement concerning the CZ-3 launching is 'Rapid Growth of China's Space Science', *Beijing Review* 25, no. 32 9 August 1982, 7–8. Western sources include Tony Walker, 'Chinese Building Satellite Launcher', *The Age* (Melbourne), 2 August 1982, 2; Walker, 'Chinese Plan to Launch Satellite', *The Financial Times*, 17 February 1983, 12; and Michael Weisskopf, 'China Plans Communications Satellite: Civilian–Military Applications Seen', *IHT*, 18 February 1983, 6. For an assessment on US technology transfers to China concerning overall satellite technology, consult Richard Homan, 'China Contracts to Buy US Satellite Station', *IHT*, 19 January 1983, 3.
21. USIS, *Wireless Bulletin* (Bonn Embassy Edition), no. 84 4 May 1983,

29–30 and John Holusha, 'AMC Expected to Sign Pact To Produce Jeeps in China', *IHT*, 4 May 1983, 13.
22. 'China May Co-Produce US Arms', *The Japan Times*, 10 March 1983, 1.
23. Hearings before the Subcommittee on Asian and Pacific Affairs of the Committee on Foreign Affairs, House of Representatives, *The New Era in East Asia* 97th Congress, 1st Session, 10 June 1981, 270–271. Roderick McFarquhar, in earlier testimony before the same committee, however, warned that the US should avoid 'taking up the role that the Soviet Union occupied *vis-à-vis* China in the mid-fifties ... to encourage business firms to do most of the sharp end work, because if one business firm falls foul of the Chinese, that is not the whole American effort', Ibid., 28 May 1981, 190.
24. On possible PRC transfers of enriched nuclear uranium to other nations, see Manning, 'The Nuclear Wild Card', *FEER* 115, no. 2, 8 January 1982, 28. Further background on US policies and concerns over the China nuclear supply question is to be found in Milton R. Benjamin, 'US Agency May East Nuclear Export Rules', *IHT*, 24 March 1983, 3; and Michael Parks, 'US Still Stalling on China Nuclear Deal', *The Japan Times*, 11 January 1983, 12.
25. Quoted in Daniel Sutherland, 'Shultz Glides Over Taiwan Issue to Get US–China Ties Flying', *The Christian Science Monitor* (International Edition), 4 February 1983, 4.
26. On the Marconi transaction, consult Shyam Bhatia, 'Marconi to Beef Up China MIGs', *The Observer*, 28 March 1982, 1; the computer deal is covered by Jason Crisp, 'UK Group Sells $1 million of Computers to China', *The Financial Times*, 16 August 1982, 3; and the Vickers Ltd assistance is reported by Claire Hollingworth, 'PRC: Report on Army Modernisation', *Defense and Foreign Affairs Daily* 11, no. 21, 21 February 1982, 1–2.
27. Bonavia, 'Britain Clinches £100m Weapons Deal with China', *The Times*, 12 November 1982, 9; Con Coughlin, 'Chinese Defence Deal Hailed As A Trail Blazer', *The Daily Telegraph*, 13 November 1982, 8; and Colina MacDougall, 'China To Buy British Missile', *The Financial Times*, 12 November 1982, 1.
28. 'Chinesisch–Britiseher Vertag geplatzt', ('Chinese–British Contract Abandoned,') *Suddeutsche Zeitung*, 9 March 1983, 8; *Defense and Foreign Affairs Weekly* 9, no. 13, 4–10 April 1983, 3; and MacDougall, 'Chinese Political Row ... *op. cit.* (note 16).
29. The interviews were conducted in September 1981. Britain also plans to continue displaying its products at Chinese international weapons exhibitions. See Desmond Wettern, 'China Mix-Up Hits British Arms Firms', *The Daily Telegraph*, 16 February 1983, 6.
30. *Defense and Foreign Affairs Weekly* 9, no. 17, 2–8 May 1983, 1.
31. *Defense and Foreign Affairs Weekly* 9, no. 18, 9–15 May 1983, 4 and ibid. 9, no. 19, 16–22 May 1983, 5–6.
32. For a short analysis of the French defence industries' production problems, see Andrew Pierre, *The Global Politics of Arms Sales* (Princeton, New Jersey: Princeton University Press, 1982), 97–99.
33. This point was noted by the US State Department's China expert, Chris

Johnson, in *The Implications of US–China Military Co-operation*, 100.
34. According to *Newsweek*, Franz Joseph Strauss, leader of West Germany's Conservative Christian Socialist Union Party, floated a post-election memorandum to newly elected West German Chancellor Helmut Kohl advocating closer ties with Beijing 'as a means of nettling the Kremlin'. 'Does Strauss Have the Veto Power?' *Newsweek* 101, no. 15, 11 April 1983, 12. In interviews with confidential sources in Bavaria, the author was able more precisely to discern the nature of Strauss' proposals. They included the increasing of economic relations, technical know-how, and joint ventures. The problem of West German 'high visibility' regarding any military interaction with China was reiterated in a 13 April 1983 interview with Col. Ulrich Schoffer (Ret.), West German Defence Attache in Beijing 1976–1980, by the author.
35. See note 19.
36. 'Defense Minister Calls on China ... *op. cit.* (note 9). A more extensive Chinese analysis recently weighing the problems of defence infrastructure development in graphic terms is Shao Huaza, 'A Reliable Guarantee for Socialist Construction', *Hongqi*, no. 21, 1 November 1982, reprinted in BBC, *SWB FE*/7188/BII/1–6, 20 November 1982.
37. The political conditions for implementation of this potential Chinese policy option have been admirably summarised by Douglas T. Stuart, 'Prospects for Sino–European Security Co-operation', *Orbis* 26, no. 3, fall, 1982, 721–747.
38. In May 1983, the EEC agreed to hold political talks twice a year with the PRC at Beijing's request. Hans Dietrich Genscher, West Germany's Foreign Minister, labelled this move as 'an important step toward developing relations' between the EEC and PRC and as a sign of China's willingness to 'assume worldwide political responsibility'. *IHT*, 14–15 May 1983, 2.
39. On 10 March 1983, the USSR and PRC agreed to increase their trade volume from about $300 million in 1982 to $800 million in 1983. But at the same time, Beijing turned down a Soviet proposal for a joint communiqué pledging both sides to non-agression against the other and to preserve mutual security along their common borders. See Xinhua's 'Reply to the Observer of the Soviet "New Times"', reprinted in BBC, *SWB FE*/7239/A2/1, 24 January 1983 as well as Takashi Oka, 'Peking Insists Military Issues Come First', *The Christian Science Monitor* (International Edition), 4 April 1983, 13.
40. As of this writing, movement was reported on the part of the Americans to ease up even further on trade restrictions against China. *IHT*, 6 June 1983, 1–2 reported that the PRC would heretofore be considered a 'friendly, non-aligned' nation in the category of Egypt or Yugoslavia.

Part IV
Foreign Policy: Threat and Promise

11 China's Changing World View

HAMMOND ROLPH

It may be trite to say that a nation's defence policy is critically influenced by its geopolitical[1] environment. Perhaps it is similarly commonplace to note that China's national defence problems, while not unique,[2] are more complex and intractable than those of most other states. Nevertheless, it is appropriate to consider the PRC's special defence problems in the light of both these basic factors, especially in view of the accelerating domestic policy revolution since the death of Mao and the developing change in the PRC's global posture.

There are certain environmental basics in the geopolitical setting that impinge on China's security problem, representing both opportunities and constraints. Her vast population, enormous and varied land area, rich resources, central position in East Asia, and long historical and cultural experience, give to China not only some innate sense of security but also provide her with a 'mystique' that enables the PRC to influence world affairs more substantially than the actual power at her disposal would otherwise support.

On the other hand, there are basic weaknesses which pose severe security problems for the PRC. The country's long frontiers, both land and maritime, are virtually as vulnerable as ever. China's economy, though making significant strides, remains fragile in terms of the population/agricultural balance, and backward in its industrial and technological base. Educational levels, even among the governing elites, are low. All these factors aggravate the difficulties faced by the military forces in planning for the defence of the country. They underlie the additional problems arising from the international environment and unresolved domestic political and economic issues.[3]

The PRC plays a distinctive role in the international system and is affected by the global political environment in special ways. Although China appears to have come to terms with the international system as it now exists,[4] there is considerable reason to suspect that Beijing would not be completely averse to significant change in that system, provided that the PRC's role, interests, and objectives were enhanced in the process. Cautious accommodation to the system, with its present rules and distribution of power, is the basis of present policy, but it would be safe to assume that Beijing is keeping its options open.

Despite the skill and sophistication with which the PRC has managed its increasingly complex foreign and security policies, it still functions in a relatively insecure international environment. While Beijing is presently navigating these waters rather adroitly, there still exist threats, actual or potential, on all sides. There is no regional security arrangement in East Asia in which the PRC can or will participate and China, virtually alone among the major states in the world system, is almost completely without any formal security ties, bloc memberships, or other political and security commitments.

While the PRC may have considered the possibility of seeking an American security umbrella in the late 1970s (perhaps following a modified and non-codified Japanese model), it appears in 1983 that she is attempting to achieve security by promoting reasonably good foreign relations *à tous azimuths*.[5]

Perhaps China perceives that she is farther along the road to achieving strategic independence that the actual situation warrants. Or is it possible that China's energies are so focussed on internal matters that international activity has become a secondary consideration for the leadership? Whatever the case, the PRC faces threats to its security and interests which the present policy of strategic self-reliance may not address successfully.[6] The informal 'international united front' against Soviet 'hegemonism', which figured so prominently in the security calculus until 1981, seems to have evaporated. Can the loss of a strategic understanding with the US, which now seems probable, be offset by détente with the Soviet Union, which appears difficult to achieve and may have little long-term value? Is there in fact a new coherent 'balanced' view of superpower threats?[7] What then are the specific settings in which PRC defence policy is being formulated and which will probably influence perceptions of security threat and opportunity.

RELATIONS WITH THE SUPERPOWERS – A DELICATE TRANSFORMATION?

For the better part of twenty years the principal 'enemy' of the PRC has been the Soviet Union, and since 1969 the Chinese have perceived the USSR as a direct military threat – in fact the only truly plausible threat to the territorial integrity of China.[8] This security problem was the primary motivation for Beijing's 'breakout' from global isolation in the early 1970s. It undoubtedly remains central to Chinese defence planning, despite some easing of tensions in recent years.

Whereas the Soviet threat to China was until the later 1970s largely a direct one, the menace of encirclement by 'projected' Soviet power has added a new dimension. Although the major reinforcement and modernisation of Soviet air and missile forces in the Far East, the rapid development of a Soviet 'blue-water' navy in the Western Pacific, and the deployment of Soviet air and naval forces to bases in Vietnam, are by no means exclusively directed at China, Beijing has quite obviously perceived them as major dangers. Furthermore, the Russians are engaged in a major long-term development of eastern Siberia as a self-sustaining base for the projection of Soviet power in Asia and the Northern and Western Pacific. As Thomas Robinson has pointed out, realisation of this goal will enable the Soviets to deal with the Chinese more confidently.[9] This Siberian build-up may not prevent improvement in Sino–Soviet relations over the next decade, but the longer-range scenario which Beijing might construct could be far more threatening. It is at least plausible to forecast that ultimately the Soviet Union is unlikely to accept the emergence of a powerful and modernised China on the doorstep of its Far Eastern empire.[10]

For the present, however, both of the Communist giants appear genuinely interested in lowering the high level of tension that has characterised their relationship for the last twenty years, especially since the armed border clashes of 1969. Several aspects of the situation favour the search for détente. Perhaps the most basic one is that so much of the earlier baggage carried by this conflict – the historical, cultural, ethnic, economic and ideological elements – has either been jettisoned or pushed aside. The security issues which now predominate, while difficult, are more straightforward problems. Both parties have made some concessions, the PRC rather more than the Soviets. The atmospherics of the relationship have improved. Furthermore, both Moscow and Beijing share an interest in developing greater leverage in the relations of each with Washington – almost a mirror image of the US–PRC relationship of the early to mid-1970s. It should also be recognised that the issue which a decade ago appeared most likely to lead to hostilities – the confrontation of large military forces – has now become a much more normal state of affairs with which both sides have learned to live. This stability is not unlike that which characterises the NATO–Warsaw Pact border in Central Europe, in contrast to some of the more volatile areas of tension around the globe. Furthermore, in the wider expanse of the Third World, the Soviet Union apparently looks less ominous to the Chinese than it once did. Moscow's political initiatives, such as Brezhnev's proposal for an Asian collective security scheme, have had little success. Soviet influence in the Middle East has declined, and the Kremlin's penetration of Africa seems less threatening to PRC interests than it did in the mid-1970s. All these factors, as well as the gradual revival of Chinese relations with the European Communist parties, tend to create a climate conducive to détente.

Nevertheless, resolution of the security issues that remain is proving to be a long and arduous task. Beijing has made it clear that China expects concrete Soviet concessions in three important security areas: the concentration of Soviet military forces on the Manchurian border and in Outer Mongolia, Soviet military operations in Afghanistan, and the Kremlin's establishment of a strategic military position in Indochina which threatens an 'encirclement' of the PRC. Moscow's reluctance to yield anything on these points since the recent series of talks began in October of 1982 may not be entirely due to typical Soviet stubbornness or to routine establishment of bargaining positions. The involvement of third parties to which the USSR is committed makes concession on some of these demands very difficult. Whereas it was earlier thought that the PRC considered the Southeast Asia matter to have the highest priority of the three, more recent reports indicate that the major Chinese concern is now the military forces on the northern borders.[11] One of the major problems is that the PRC has relatively little to yield on any of these issues – on the border forces, numbers but not much real power; on Indochina, few bargaining chips; on Afghanistan, essentially nothing.

There are obviously trade-offs for the PRC in any détente or rapprochement with the Soviet Union. However, on balance, a détente would seem to hold more advantages for China. A chance to pursue modernisation, both economic and military, without the present dangerous and costly burden of defending the borders in force, would be very welcome. An opportunity to make fuller use of the Soviet-style economic and technical infrastructure already in place in China would also provide a way to accommodate the vested interests of those who were trained in the 1950s to manage and operate it. In global terms, a more favourable PRC position in the 'strategic triangle' could result from increased leverage upon the US produced by better relations with the Soviet Union. Greater credibility with Third World countries may be generated by a more evenhanded policy toward the superpowers.

However, the question that must be addressed is whether these advantages would contribute sufficiently to China's security position to outweigh some of the drawbacks: revived suspicion of the PRC in the West and in some regional states, the weakening or loss of the only consistent PRC foreign policy line of the last twenty years, and the attenuation of a factor that has been a domestic unifying element over the same period.

THE WASHINGTON–BEIJING TIE: A MORIBUND RELATIONSHIP?

Whereas the United States was a key actor in Deng Xiaoping's 1978–81 pursuit of a 'global united front' strategy against Soviet 'hegemonism', relations with Washington are now, at best, 'dead in the water'. The trend toward downgrading American political ties, soft-pedalling the concept of any strategic understanding with the US, and generally treating the two superpowers more evenhandedly, has become quite evident both in PRC official statements and media output.[12] In contrast to the urgent tone of PRC statements of the 1978–81 period – designed to persuade the US and the West to step up their flagging defence efforts against the Soviet menace – today's Chinese comments denounce both Washington and Moscow for their pursuit of an 'absurd, barbaric,' arms race.[13] No longer is the American military position in East Asia and the Western Pacific looked upon with the same equanimity as was the case several years ago.[14]

All the usual elements in this deterioration can be adduced: Taiwan, textiles, arms and high technology sales, high visibility defectors, even Imperial railway bonds. The more basic question of what the shift means for the PRC's future international orientation and defence policy remains to be explored, possibly because it is still too early to analyse the problem carefully. There is little doubt that Beijing's apparent shift of stance has alarmed Washington.[15] Furthermore it has put the Reagan Administration on the spot – torn between conservative pro-Taiwan political allies and a desire to maintain the support of the PRC in an anti-Soviet strategy.

There are already indications that China is dealing with an America which has downgraded the value of the kind of strategic relationship which seemed so desirable to Washington from 1978 through 1981. The hazard for Beijing is that all this could result in a serious American backlash which might endanger a range of relationships – economic, educational and technological – that are important for China's modernisation, including military upgrading. This could be especially serious for the PRC if the countries of the 'Second World' with close ties to the US are not willing, or able, to compensate for a loss of American assistance in these areas. Furthermore, an anti-US posture, if carried too far, might put at risk the increasingly close and profitable relations which the PRC now enjoys with pro-US regional powers, such as Japan and certain of the states of the Association of Southeast Asian Nations (ASEAN).

Perhaps Americans give undue emphasis to the importance of the PRC's public change of tone toward the US since 1981, producing somewhat exaggerated views of the similiarities between 1983 and the 1960s, when Beijing classified both the superpowers as 'enemies'. In fact, the general atmosphere, or at least the flavour, of Chinese public pronouncements have reverted rather more to the mood of the earlier 1970s, the period between the Nixon-Kissinger breakthrough and the decisive victory of Deng Xiaoping and his policy line in 1978.[16] In this light the 1978–81 period of the 'global international front' can be seen as something of an aberration. It should be considered that while the PRC, in pursuit of the global united front policy, appeared to seek the strategic support of the US in spite of the latter's relative decline in power and influence, this decline, as well as Beijing's disillusionment with American failure to redress the global balance, may also be a reason why China has not promoted this relationship more vigorously. The PRC is in a position to exploit a persistent American psychological need for favourable outcomes which was created by the pattern of America's China policy over many decades, as Professor Tang Tsou so eloquently wrote in his analysis of an earlier era.[17]

There is a quite basic question of how the PRC's defence policy and force dispositions will be affected by the change of US status in Beijing's eyes from demi-ally to quasi-enemy. Since Chinese leaders emphasise that qualification for status as a superpower 'hegemonist' is determined by intent and action rather than capability, there may actually be little change in policy or military dispositions. In any case, considering the state of present PRC military forces, it is unlikely that China will repeat the 1960s error of maintaining two superpower enemies simultaneously.

THE REGIONAL SCENE: BOTH FRIENDS AND ENEMIES

When the PRC emerged from isolation into the world arena in the early 1970s, the subsequent transformation of global international politics was accompanied by an equally dramatic change in regional Asian alignments. Whereas Japan and the ASEAN states were previously considered enemies of China and peace they now, for the most part, enjoy cordial relations with Beijing. On the other hand Vietnam, which had been as close to China as 'the teeth to the lips' (or so Beijing loudly and endlessly proclaimed), has now become the PRC's *bête noire* – the hated 'Cuba of the East'.

Of all the regional relationships, the one with the Socialist Republic of Vietnam (SRV) generates the greatest security concern in the PRC. Several factors underlie this position: (1) the status of the SRV as the strongest military power in Southeast Asia, backed by a long history of militancy, vigour and expansionism; (2) the growth of Vietnamese power and influence in the region in a way that threatens to exclude China from all Southeast Asia, an area which has traditionally been under Chinese influence; and (3) most threatening of all, the linkage of Vietnamese power and policy to the Soviet Union. China's enemy in the north has also become the enemy in the south.

It is well known that the PRC's punitive 'lesson-teaching' expedition into northern Vietnam in early 1979 produced a decidedly mixed bag of results.[18] However, we should not underestimate as a potentially positive result for the PRC the revelations of some critical weaknesses in the PLA – particularly in command, control, and logistical support. These shortcomings, coupled with a demonstration of the effectiveness of Vietnam's Soviet-supplied modern weapons, have underlined the urgent need for PLA reform and modernisation now being pushed by Deng and his followers. China retains the option of striking at the SRV again, and border clashes continue. However, while the security threat posed by a Vietnam allied to the Soviet Union has seriously complicated the PRC's defence problem, the disposition of PLA forces does not match the concerns over Vietnam and Cambodia expressed so strongly and publicly by Chinese officials and media.

Military assistance to the Cambodian resistance against Vietnam remains a basic PRC policy, apparently in the hope that a protracted guerilla war will 'bleed' Vietnam into compromise.[19] There have been some subtle indications, however, that Beijing may be backing off its very harsh line with Vietnam; these included increased emphasis in the media on Hanoi's differences with Moscow rather than on the SRV's role as a stooge of the Kremlin.[20] There are substantial reasons, both historical and in recent economic trends, for the PRC to be less than sanguine about the prospects of a Vietnamese collapse under the strain of a difficult war.

Another possible indicator that Beijing is not overly optimistic about prising Vietnam out of Cambodia is the significant development of a close Sino–Thai relationship since 1981, including the exchange of military missions and what may ultimately emerge as substantial security ties.[21] Although a pledge of Chinese support to maintain Thailand's territorial integrity, made by the PLA Chief of Staff in 1983, does not on its face look like downgrading confrontation with Hanoi, the whole trend of events in the area could mean a significant Chinese readjustment of policy to fit the geopolitical realities of Southeast Asia. Beijing may now have concluded that in order to maintain real influence in this region it must find a replacement for the old links with Cambodia. Thailand is the logical substitute – in fact, a considerably less fragile one. Thailand also happens to be the ASEAN member least suspicious of the PRC and less apprehensive than the others over long-term Chinese objectives in Southeast Asia.

Since Beijing might be willing to acquiesce in predominant Vietnamese influence in Indochina if it were not accompanied by the outflanking link with Soviet military power, Chinese moves to persuade Hanoi to loosen its bonds with Moscow would seem appropriate. The major obstacle, of course, is that the Vietnamese, despite their pride, are on the Soviet hook. They can get off only by ceasing to do what they seem so bent on continuing to do in Indochina.

At the other pole from Vietnam in terms of relations with the PRC is Japan. Not only are Beijing–Tokyo relations exceptionally warm,[22] the content of Japanese history textbooks notwithstanding, but Japan is also an enthusiastic primary source of assistance in China's modernisation. Cooling US–China relations have apparently not altered this state of affairs significantly. Beijing has not revived a challenge to American security links with Japan and supports Japan's own military build-up so long as it remains defensive and does not threaten its neighbours.[23] 'Retired' Japanese general officers are frequent visitors to the PRC,[24] as are representatives of Japanese defence-oriented 'think tanks'. One possible cloud on the horizon, however, is the PRC's increasingly harsh line on Korean reunification and Chinese calls for withdrawal of American forces from the southern half of that country. While Japan would undoubtedly like to see the Korean problem resolved in some equitable manner, its security stake in the *status quo* in South Korea is too high to expect Tokyo to view Beijing's more militant posture with equanimity. Thus the PRC will have to move with considerable caution in Northeast Asia.

China finds herself in a fairly favourable environment in South Asia, despite the threat posed by Soviet forces in Afghanistan. In fact, the Soviet occupation of Afghanistan has made Chinese military aid to Pakistan somewhat more acceptable in regional terms. At least India has warmed somewhat to the PRC, and talks about disputed border questions, while producing no agreements as yet, continue in a reasonably good atmosphere. But China must realise that in Pakistan she is co-operating with a very unstable partner. What does Beijing do if that long-time friend collapses under the weight of foreign and domestic pressures? Is the opening to India a hedge against this possible eventuality?

CHINA AND SOUTH–SOUTH RELATIONS

While the PRC has been distancing itself to some extent from the United States over the last two years, Beijing has stepped up its self-identification with the Third World and its various political and economic concerns. After the hiatus of the 1979–81 period, China is reviving its claim to full-fledged membership in the club of the world's weak and disadvantaged.[25] One fresh element has been the frequent use by Chinese officials and media of the term 'South–South co-operation' as embodying an active mutuality of interests.[26] So far, the renewed campaign appears to have gained some psychological points for China in the Third World, although it is too early to predict how substantial the results may be.

Premier Zhao Ziyang seems to be the 'point man' in this effort, and although he may not yet have the respected stature of a Zhou Enlai or the *panache* of a Deng Xiaoping, he apparently performed well at the Cancun meeting in late 1981 and during his extensive African tour in early 1983. However, his essentially pragmatic approach may lessen the impact of the Chinese approach on the Third World Bloc, with whom grand gestures and a higher level of emotion sometimes carry more weight. For example, during his visit to Tanzania in January 1983, Zhao laid down some pointed and rather sternly practical criteria for the provision of PRC economic aid to the Third World.[27]

Three questions about the renewed emphasis on the Third World emerge: (1) Is it a sincere PRC commitment to a genuinely activist role and toward developing the so-called 'New International Economic Order', or is it largely verbal, an obeisance to what Stephen Cohen terms 'the fetish of international egalitarianism';[28] (2) Can the warm camaraderie of the less developed countries (LDCs) contribute anything significant to the development of China's own defence and security, or to her economic modernisation requirements? (3) Considering the PRC's limited ability to extend aid to the LDCs and Beijing's continued preaching of self-reliance,[29] will the Third World nations give China sufficient diplomatic and psychological support to offset their inability to provide anything more concrete?

DOMESTIC AND INTERNATIONAL LINKAGES

There are several ways in which domestic issues interact with the PRC's international environment and relations. On the most basic level, of course, the policy of the 'Great Leap Outward' and its pragmatic approaches to general foreign intercourse seem to be settled fixtures. However, there is a nagging uncertainty about the capacity of Deng's followers to carry on these policies in the face of opposition from more conservative party leaders after his departure from the scene. Beyond this, there has been considerable concern expressed by PRC leaders in Deng's own camp over growing 'contamination' by Western 'bourgeois values'.[30] These factors are no small matters in a ruling Marxist party suffering a significant crisis of confidence.

Domestic issues revolving around defence policy and the modernisation of the armed forces also have international significance. Tensions between professionalism and ideological purity in the PLA, and between self-reliance and dependence on foreign defense technology, have been widely discussed. Suffice it to say that on the former issue, acceptance of a higher degree of professionalism will mean a wider range of PRC military relationships with the rest of the world. Similarly, the much greater emphasis on self-reliance recently announced by Defence Minister Zhang Aiping[31] will undoubtedly dampen whatever remains of previously over-inflated expectations of large scale purchases of Western weapons systems and military technology.

It is clear that there is considerable opposition to the plans of Deng Xiaoping and his like-minded military colleagues to jettison much of the Maoist tradition and to create a leaner and militarily more effective PLA, shorn of much of its socio-political mystique.[32] While all parties agree on the goal of making China a militarily powerful state by the end of the century, final decisions on how to achieve this objective may either have not been made or have been made without assurance of real permanence.

CONCLUSION: CHINA'S DEFENCE AND THE FUTURE

Both the global and regional environments condition Chinese defence decisions, just as defence policies in turn affect Beijing's foreign policy and international relations. The present shifts in the PRC's global posture are undoubtedly linked, in part at least, to defence issues. Deng Xiaoping and his followers may plan to emulate Japan to some extent in their security policy – by vigorous development of the economy without unduly large expenditures on armaments. If this is the case, and if Beijing continues to avoid actual alliance or bloc commitments, then some sort of assurances on security on a global basis would seem necessary. Among the ingredients of such an arrangement would be maintenance of a good working relationship with the US, a concomitant defusing of tensions with the Soviet Union, and a revival of closer identification with Third World aspirations. But if the past is any guide to the future, analysts should at least have learned humility about predictions, even in such a general way.

NOTES AND REFERENCES

1. This term is used here in a general sense – embodying physical, political, military and economic factors – not in the special category of 'geopolitics' as a school of thought about international affairs.
2. A critique of scholarship allegedly emphasising China as a 'special case' can be found in Robert Boardman, 'Themes and Exploration in Sinology', in Roger Dial (ed.), *Advancing and Contending Approaches to the Study of Chinese Foreign Policy*. (Centre for Foreign Policy Studies, Dalhousie University, 1974).
3. Among many recent works dealing with both basic factors and developing trends are: Onkar Marwah and Jonathan D. Pollack (eds), *Military Power and Policy in Asian States*. (Boulder: Westview Press, 1980); John F. Copper, *China's Global Role*, (Stanford: Hoover Institution Press, 1980); Douglas Stuart and William Tow (eds), *China, the Soviet Union and the West*. (Boulder: Westview Press, 1981); Richard Solomon (ed.), *The China Factor*. (Englewood Cliffs, N.J.: Prentice-Hall, 1981); Richard C. Bush (ed.), *China Briefing 1982*. (Boulder: Westview Press, 1983); Thomas Finger (ed.), *China's Quest for Independence*. (Boulder: Westview Press, 1982); and Herbert Ellison (ed.), *The Sino-Soviet Conflict*. (Seattle: University of Washington Press, 1982).
4. See Jonathan Pollack, 'China in the Evolving International System', in Norton Ginsburg (ed.), *China: The Eighties Era*. (Boulder: Westview Press, forthcoming).
5. However, an article in *Beijing Review* (BR), no. 3 of 1983, on the subject

of the PRC's 'independent foreign policy', rejects the idea of 'equidistance', and reaffirms that PRC policy is based on 'principle' and 'concrete national interests'. See FBIS-CHI, 3 February 1983 at A-1.
6. China's international and domestic problems are well summarised in *Asian Security* (Tokyo), 1981 and 1982 editions.
7. Among a number of recent indications, Wang Bingnan's television interview of 3 January 1983, in FBIS-CHI, 14 January 1983 at A-1; and Wang's radio talk on 'China's Independent Foreign Policy', in FBIS-CHI, 31 January 1983 at A-1 to A-7.
8. This threat is succinctly stated by Kenneth Hunt in his 'Sino–Soviet Theatre Force Comparisons', in Douglas T. Stuart and William Tow (eds), *China, the Soviet Union, and the West*, (note 3 above), 103–114.
9. 'Sino–Soviet Competition in Asia', in Stuart and Tow, *op. cit.*, 180–81.
10. Colin Gray makes this point quite strongly in his *The Geopolitics of the Nuclear Era*. (New York: Crane, Russak & Co., Inc., 1977), 37, 38 and 50.
11. V. G. Kulkarni, 'Seeking a Middle Path between the Superpowers', *Far Eastern Economic Review* (FEER), 31 March 1983, 22. A general PRC view of the Soviet posture in the talks is expressed in an interview with Foreign Minister Wu Xueqian, ibid., 24–26.
12. An excellent summary of trends in the PRC's changing global stance can be found in A. Doak Barnett's 'China's International Posture: Signs of Change', in Richard Bush (ed.), *China Briefing 1982*, (see note 3). The US relationship is well treated in Robert Scalapino, 'Uncertainties in Future Sino–US Relations', *Orbis*, vol. 26, 3, Fall 1982, and Allen Whiting, 'Sino–American Relations: The Decade Ahead', ibid. Statements by Deng Xiaoping and Hu Yaobang to the 12th Party Congress can be found in FBIS-CHI, 1 September 1982, at K-1, 2 & 3 and in FBIS-CHI, 8 September 1982, at K-19.
13. An example is *Renmin Ribao* commentary, 9 December 1982, in FBIS-CHI, 9 December 1982, at A-1.
14. E.g., an anti-US statement re Korea by Hao Deqing, President of Chinese People's Institute of Foreign Affairs, in FBIS-CHI, 1 February 1983, at D-2, and PRC Foreign Ministry Statement condemning joint US–South Korean military exercises as threat to Asian peace and security, FBIS-CHI, 7 February 1983, at D-1. Also Wu Xueqian interview, FEER, *op. cit.* (note 11), 26.
15. In addition to media reports, this point was definitely confirmed in author's recent conversations with a RAND Corporation research official with extensive contacts in Washington.
16. E.g., Zhou Enlai's speech to the 10th Party Congress, *Hongqi*, no. 9, 1973 and Deng Xiaoping's speech to the UN General Assembly on 10 April 1974, in *Peking Review*, vol. 17, no. 16, 19 April 1974, 6–11.
17. *America's Failure in China*. (Chicago: University of Chicago Press, 1963), especially vol. II.
18. The objectives and results are well covered by Harlan Jencks in 'China's "Punitive" War on Vietnam: A Military Assessment', *Asian Survey* vol. XIX, no. 8, August 1979, 801–815. See also David W. P. Elliott, *The Third Indochina Conflict*, (Boulder: Westview Press, 1981), especially Ch. 5.

19. Interview with Wu Xueqian, FEER, *op. cit.* (note 11).
20. Xinhua commentary, 11 January 1983, in FBIS-CHI, at E-4. There are also reports of some 'backchannel' contacts with the Vietnamese in Rumania, perhaps generated to a degree by the Sino–Soviet talks. See Nayan Chanda, 'Romanian Rendezvous', FEER, 17 March 1983, 22–23.
21. John McBeth, 'Close Ties For Comfort,' ibid., 19–21. Also Xinhua stories on Yang Dezhi's visit to Thailand, FBIS-CHI, 2 February 1983 at E-1.
22. An example of the public relations and communication effort of the PRC in this regard was a warm New Years' greeting to Japan, broadcast in Japanese by Liao Zhengzhi, FBIS-CHI, 4 January 1983, at D-3.
23. Wu Xueqian interview in FEER, *op. cit.* (note 11).
24. *Asian Security* (Tokyo), 1981, 100.
25. See note 16, supra.
26. This theme emerges in speeches referenced in note 7, supra.
27. Text of this statement of principles in FBIS-CHI, 14 January 1983, at I–3.
28. Samuel S. Kim, *China, the United Nations and World Order.* (Princeton, N.J.: Princeton University Press, 1979); William R. Feeney, 'Chinese Global Politics in the UN General Assembly', in James Hsiung and Samuel Kim (eds), *China in the Global Community.* (New York: Praeger, 1980), 140–160; and Daniel Tretiak, 'Political Movements and Institutional Continuity in the Chinese Ministry of Foreign Affairs, 1966–1979', *Asian Survey*, vol. XX, no. 9, September 1980.
29. This theme is stressed in a *Hongqi* commentary on Third World debt, FBIS-CHI, 4 February 1983, at A-2 and 3.
30. E.g., General Secretary Hu Yaobang's report to the 12th Party Congress, FBIS-CHI, 8 September 1982, K-18 to 21.
31. FBIS-CHI, 1 March 1983, at K-8.
32. See V. G. Kulkarni, 'A Retreat From Power', FEER, 7 April 1983, 20–22. Maoist opposition in the PLA was bluntly acknowledged by Li Desheng in a *Renmin Ribao* article summarised in *Los Angeles Times*, 14 April 1983, 2.

12 The Soviet Union

DAVID ARMSTRONG

During two decades of bitter Sino–American hostility no serious attempt was made by Beijing to provide for civilian defence in the event of an American nuclear strike. By contrast, within a year of the outbreak of Sino–Soviet hostilities in 1969, the Chinese were enthusiastically following Mao Zedong's instructions to 'dig tunnels deep' throughout China, and if the pace of shelter building fell off after a few years, a concern for protecting the population of China's cities from a Soviet air attack remained in evidence.[1] Yet it is worth recalling that for nearly ten years following the opening rounds of the Sino-Soviet polemics the Soviets did not reinforce their insignificant military establishment in the border regions until 1965, after what they regarded as an assertion of the 'lebensraum' doctrine by Mao in 1964.[2] This was despite the fact that the Chinese, according to Moscow, had been 'systematically violating' the border since 1960.[3] Moreover, the really decisive expansion of Soviet forces did not come until the early 1970s, after a border conflict that some believe was at least in part provoked by Beijing.[4] Although there was a substantial increase in Chinese military spending in the period 1965–71, this seems to have been associated, at least in part, with Lin Biao's bid for power[5] and military spending was reduced after his demise – at precisely the same time as the Soviet build up was reaching its peak. Moreover, at a time when Beijing was experiencing a new 'war scare', during the 1978–79 series of major Soviet initiatives in Vietnam and Afghanistan, the Chinese leadership opted for a policy of according military expenditure a lower priority than general economic development.[6]

So, on the face of it, there is conflicting evidence about Chinese perceptions of a threat from Moscow. The tunnel building suggests that the threat was taken far more seriously than the American equivalent had been, but at other times there was little correlation between Soviet military moves and the attention given to defence matters by China. Furthermore there is evidence which suggests that Moscow was reluctant to transform its dispute with Beijing into a military confrontation. Indeed, if there was no deliberate Soviet intention to escalate the conflict with China, this may have been matched by a Chinese awareness that Moscow had no current designs on China itself. Zhou Enlai's strategic assessment of world affairs in 1973 was that the real target of Soviet 'social imperialism' was Western Europe: its build up on China's borders were merely a 'feint to the East'.[7]

Thus, the question of China's perception of a military threat from the Soviet Union is not as straightforward as it might first appear. The Soviet threat to China was not as inevitable nor as unambiguous as some have suggested, nor was China's response so unequivocal. In China's case, this was in part because the problem of relations with the Soviet Union had become caught up in the factionalism and multi-faceted 'debate' that characterised Chinese politics during much of the 1970s. Although the many sophisticated discussions of this issue have not always reached identical conclusions, there is broad agreement that differences within the Chinese leadership included such matters as the nature of the threat posed by Moscow and the most appropriate means of combating it, the correct order of priorities as between the immediate improvement of China's defence capability and the requirements of a more general modernisation programme, the inevitability or otherwise of war and the role of ideology in domestic and foreign policy formulation.[8] All of these matters had important implications for China's perceptions of and policy towards the Soviet Union.

CHINESE PERCEPTIONS OF THE SOVIET UNION, 1969–82

Only once has Beijing allowed an unmistakeable note of fear to enter its public pronouncements on the Soviet Union. This was in a government statement of 7 October 1969, which came at the end of two months of extreme tension in Sino–Soviet relations, climaxed by a series of moves and signals by the Soviets which appeared to suggest that they were seriously contemplating the possibility of launching a nuclear strike against Chinese nuclear installations, especially those in Xinjiang.[9] In retrospect it appears probable that Moscow was merely engaging in a controlled exercise in brinkmanship: using its overwhelming military superiority to force a less belligerent posture from

Beijing. But China had little option but to treat the Soviet threat as genuine and rapidly stepped up its building of underground shelters. After further signs that Moscow might be seeking a pretext to launch a nuclear attack, Beijing, which at that time could have done little to counter such an attack or effectively retaliate in kind, issued a statement that could only be interpreted as a major climb down. It is true that the statement defiantly declared that China would never be intimidated by war threats, including nuclear war threats.[10] But its overwhelming emphasis was on conciliation: China would never be the first to use nuclear weapons, the difference between the two sides should not prevent normal state-to-state relations on the basis of the Five Principles of Peaceful Coexistence, the boundary question should be settled peacefully and there was no need to fight a war over it.[11]

The Chinese statement was followed by a resumption of border negotiations and a marked toning down by Beijing of its anti-Soviet polemics during 1970.[12] The next five years were dominated by the internal power struggle and the various consequences of China's rapprochement with the United States. Hence Chinese foreign policy has to be seen in the context of the manoeuvring for position in Beijing and the opportunities that had appeared as a result of the Nixon visit to China. The foreign policy 'debate' during these years has been exhaustively discussed elsewhere and cannot adequately be dealt with here.[13] But to the extent that there was a consensus in Beijing about the Soviet threat, this was set out in Zhou Enlai's strategic assessment of 1973. Certain points in his Political Report were constantly reiterated for several years afterwards: China wanted conciliatory actions, not just words from Moscow, the contention between the two superpowers was a good thing,[14] the focus of their contention was Europe, although it was still possible that the Soviets might launch a surprise attack against China and preparations should be made against this eventuality, and finally, détente was a 'temporary and superficial phenomenon' and China should concentrate on warning the rest of the world about the real dangers posed by the hegemonists.[15] Another strand in Zhou's argument was more controversial: that world war could be prevented so long as the world's peoples 'heighten their vigilance, strengthen unity and persevere in struggle'. The standard Maoist position was that war was inevitable and could only be 'delayed', not prevented.

Zhou's line received more general acceptance after the downfall of the Gang of Four in 1976, but it first had to overcome opposition from elements in the army who waged a campaign during 1977 for the modernisation of China's defences to have priority over other claims on China's limited resources. Then, during 1978-80, the Soviet Union itself gave fresh grounds for concern over China's security.

At the end of 1976 two positions were discernible. One, as advanced by China's foreign minister, Jiao Guanhua, maintained that Europe remained the focus of contention between the superpowers: this was determined by their fundamental interests and could not be altered by European 'appeasers' attempting to divert the Soviet Union towards China. As for the Soviet Union it was 'nothing to be afraid of. It is outwardly strong but inwardly weak'.[16] But the more prevalent argument was to the effect that the Soviet Union was a real threat. In June 1977 the *People's Daily* 'Commentator' declared that the Soviet Union 'had become the most dangerous source of world war in the present era. It has swung into a menacing offensive in its rivalry with the other superpower for world hegemony and is preparing in every way to unleash a new world war'.[17] A month later a more ambiguous article accepted that Europe was the chief target of the superpowers, and even that the Soviet build-up on China's borders was primarily aimed at the United States and Japan (though asserting that the Soviet forces posed a serious threat to China's security as well).[18] But the thrust of its argument was that the Soviet Union was overtaking the United States in various aspects of military strength, notably missiles, aviation, shipbuilding and atomic industries. This was 'a striking change demanding close attention'.[19] However, where other articles had called for a 'race against time' to modernise China's defences[20] this one suggested a different order of priorities: a 'race against time to build up our national economy as speedily as possible so as to make ourselves invincible'.[21]

In November 1977 a major article set out in authoritative terms what was either a synthesis or a compromise view. The Soviet Union was indisputably the more 'ferocious, reckless and treacherous' superpower and the most dangerous source of world war.[22] But this was not because the Soviet Union threatened China's security. It was 'determined by a whole set of historical conditions under which the Soviet Union has grown and become an imperialist superpower'. Namely, as a latecomer following on the heels of the US, it was obliged to be more aggressive and adventurous since it was trying to expand whereas the US was merely protecting its position. Because it was economically inferior it needed to place a greater reliance on military power, while its centralised economy made it easier for it to put the country on a war footing. Finally, it was more deceptive because it could 'flaunt the banner of 'socialism' to bluff and deceive people everywhere'. The article also contained a carefully constructed compromise formulation on the issues that had been in dispute over the previous twelve months: 'World war, though inevitable, can be postponed. . . . The key to putting off war lies not in holding talks and concluding agreements, as is vociferously suggested by some people, but in the united struggle of the people of all countries against hegemonism.'[23]

During 1978 there were some signs of renewed apprehensions concerning the degree to which there was a specific and imminent Soviet threat to China. In August Defence Minister Xu Xiangqian delivered the most forthright version of this thesis.[24] Although Xu acknowledged, slightly contemptuously, the view that Soviet policy was 'doubtless' spearheaded against the US and Japan, he was convinced that the facts showed that Moscow had stepped up preparations for a war against China and Chinese policy must be based 'on the assumption that the enemy will launch a war earlier than expected'.[25] Here Xu was clearly engaging in special pleading to try to forestall the cuts in the military budget that were to be made as part of China's retreat from its ambitious modernisation programme.[26] But he was also expressing a genuine concern about the implications of Vietnam's decisive move towards alliance with the Soviet Union and its open rift with China. This was seen by many as giving Moscow important strategic advantages since it enabled the expanding Soviet Pacific fleet to use the Vietnamese port facilities at Cam Ranh Bay and Da Nang. However a less alarmist view of Soviet intentions was put by others who argued that Europe remained the focus of US–Soviet rivalry but because the two sides were 'essentially at a stalemate' there, Moscow had begun a 'large flanking move to encircle Western Europe'.[27] Although China was one target of the Asian aspect of Moscow's global strategy, its more important objective was 'to enlarge its sphere of influence and push out the influence of its arch rival, the United States, from Asia and threaten the peace and security of Japan and other Asian nations'.[28] Moscow was depicted in these analyses as not being about to launch a world war but as gradually building up an invincible 'strategic deployment'.[29]

Although this more reassuring line remained in evidence after 1979, the Soviet invasion of Afghanistan provided a fresh opportunity for those in the army and elsewhere who were, for various reasons, maintaining that the Soviet Union posed a real and imminent threat to China. The first official message from Beijing to Moscow over the invasion said that it posed 'a threat to China's security'.[30] Moreover, although the invasion itself was still regarded as part of the Soviet strategy of outflanking Europe, reference began to be made to a Soviet objective of subjecting China to 'a pincers attack from north and south'[31] and 'a southern seas encirclement'.[32]

After 1980 and the electoral victory of President Reagan, who had signalled his intention of improving the US relationship with Taiwan, the balance shifted back to interpreting Soviet strategy in global (and less immediately threatening) terms. Whereas 'proceeding from temporary, regional interests' was now deemed dangerous, 'proceeding from long term, overall strategic considerations could ease crises, preserve world peace or at least delay the outbreak of a major war'.[33] So, China's analysis of Soviet moves in the Pacific, Southeast Asia and the Indian Ocean was said to be based on 'an overall global strategy rather than China's own interests'.[34] China and other countries should be working to gain time to increase their own strength by uniting to 'upset the Soviet Union's global strategic plan'.[35] It was not that China was not an important target of Moscow but it was far from being the only one, or even the major target and the actual threat from it should be assessed in a more sophisticated way.[36] The threat was essentially political, although military means might be used to attain political objectives: for instance, if the Soviet build-up caused China to spend more on defence, this would endanger China's modernisation plans.

Chinese assessments of the Soviet Union passed through one further, very important, stage before the death of Brezhnev opened the door to the current negotiations. China's rapprochement with the United States had been preceded by a sometimes heated debate as to whether the United States could be considered a declining force, and hence less dangerous.[37] During 1981 a similar, although more relaxed discussion, took place over whether the Soviet Union was on the decline, or at least unable to undertake further expansion because of the many difficulties which now confronted it. Debate focussed first on Brezhnev's report to the 26th CPSU Congress in March. *Renmin Ribao* noted that: 'Compared with the arrogant tone of the report delivered at the 25th Congress, this report seems rather low-key and restrained. This suggests that the Soviet Union is in a tough situation, facing various difficulties'.[38] The article reached a mixed conclusion about prospects for the 1980s: '... the Soviet Union will not abandon its offensive policies and will probably score some achievements as a result of them. Nevertheless, factors that restrict its aggression and expansion will increase at the same time'.[39] However, *Guangming Ribao* concentrated on elements in the speech which it took to imply a proposal to the US to reach a spheres-of-influence agreement; a development that could only be greeted with alarm in Beijing as it would raise again the long feared spectre of a 'joint hegemony' of the superpowers.[40] Other articles found grounds for optimism in the region of greatest interest to China: East Asia. For example, it was suggested that opposition to Soviet policies from Japan, the US, China and the Southeast Asian countries had become '... the chief contradiction in state relations in east Asia and the western Pacific'.[41] This had very important implications for the way in which the Soviet threat in the region was to be assessed:[42]

The debate grew more intense later in the year, following a Soviet offer in September to resume the border talks which China had withdrawn from after the invasion of Afghanistan. There was no real dispute that the Soviet Union had increasingly resorted to 'political tricks' to further its designs[43] but whether this was to be seen as merely a change in tactics or as a fundamental shift was open to debate. Two opposing viewpoints were discussed in an article early in 1982:

> Some people are saying that the Soviets have entered a prolonged period of all-round 'strategic difficulties'. They are convinced that it is declining and therefore cannot afford any more military adventures and can only try to preserve what it has obtained.
>
> Others believe the difficulties are temporary and can be overcome soon. They suggest that concessions and economic benefits are the only things which can be used to curb the Soviet military force and induce it to stop its expansionist adventures.[44]

This article failed to reach any clear conclusions, although it advised caution in interpreting apparent evidence of Soviet weakness, adding that even if the Soviet Union was confronted with greater difficulties, this would not necessarily predispose it to act with prudence. Beijing was particularly encouraged by Moscow's inability to impose order upon Afghanistan which, it was hoped, would deter it from similar adventures elsewhere, at least for sime time.[45]

An interesting contribution in view of the PLA's usually more pessimistic appraisal of the Soviet threat came from the PLA Deputy Chief of Staff, Wu Xiuquan, in an interview in Japan in January 1982. While accepting that China was still behind the Soviet Union in its military modernisation, he expressed his confidence in China's ability to cope effectively with a massive Soviet attack but added, significantly, 'I wonder if the Soviet Union can launch a large-scale assault [on China] at the moment. The situation along the [Sino–Soviet] border area has remained calm and stable over the past one year or two'.[46]

Towards the end of 1982 Chinese analysts seemed to have agreed a tentative consensus viewpoint to the effect that, although the underlying aims of Soviet policy remained the same, 'there are indications that for the present the Soviet Union seems ready to confine itself to using 'détente' in the struggle with the United States for world hegemony'.[47] Particularly promising was the border situation, where, according to a Shanghai magazine, Soviet military exercises had become less frequent and minor border incidents stood a better chance of being resolved in a reasonable manner.[48]

This reassessment of the Soviet Union was clearly part of an attempt by Beijing to develop a more even-handed policy towards the two superpowers. Although the Soviet Union has still to offer the 'actions rather than words' that Beijing had consistently demanded as evidence of Moscow's sincerity, it has none the less kept up a steady barrage of conciliatory signals during 1982. These had included hints about possible troop reductions on the border.[49] Conversely, the United States had shown a tendency to downgrade the importance of its relationship with China and Beijing clearly believed that its interests would be better served if it could establish a position of equidistance between the two superpowers. The Soviet Union was still seen as a threat: after refraining from polemics for some weeks following Mr. Andropov's succession, *Renmin Ribao* reiterated earlier assertions that the Soviet invasion of Afghanistan 'posed a serious threat to China's security'.[50] But when, in the middle of the Sino–Soviet negotiations, that began after the death of Brezhnev, the Soviet magazine *New Times* suddenly accused China of making vast claims to Soviet territory to 'retard the process of normalisation', Beijing replied with an article that was generally interpreted as conciliatory in tone.[51]

THE NATURE OF THE SOVIET THREAT

During China's war scare of 1969, Beijing declared itself to be prepared against China's enemies 'launching a big war, against their launching a war at an early date, against their launching a conventional war and against their launching a large scale nuclear war'.[52] Despite the fact that this formulation may have emanated from the since disgraced Lin Biao, it was repeated on several occasions over the next ten years, and may be seen as some sort of official categorisation of the threats thought to be posed by Moscow. But in reality the Soviet threat to

China is considerably more complex than this simple list suggests. Two examples out of many may illustrate this. If the Soviet Union's belligerent signals of 1969 were meant to be taken seriously, they implied a limited nuclear attack on a few specific targets, with the limited but crucial objective of crippling China's nuclear capacity. Hence, that would have been a 'small scale' nuclear attack of a kind omitted from Lin Biao's list. Ground troops would not have been employed and China's favoured response of people's war would have been unusable. Secondly, since 1969 Beijing has on balance tended to depict the Soviet threat as a long term one, arising less from any specific danger of war (or whatever kind) than from the Soviet Union achieving such a favourable 'global strategic deployment;. Such a threat could not be countered simply through military means. A further complication for China is that the nature of China's resonse to the Soviet threat has always been seen to have important implications for Chinese domestic politics.

Hence, as with the issue of Chinese perceptions of the Soviet threat, complexities abound when considering the precise character of the threat. However, it is possible to distinguish a range of hypothetical scenarios. These include both direct military threats and situations which would have significant, but indirect, security implications.

In order of seriousness, rather than probability, the first such scenario would be general war, combining nuclear and conventional means, with the objective of removing China as a significant factor in the global strategic balance for the foreseeable future by inflicting enormous damage and partitioning what was left. For many reasons, not least the unlikelihood of such a war remaining within its intended bounds, this has to be seen as an extremely remote possibility.

The second scenario would be a large scale conventional war, with nuclear weapons held in reserve by Moscow as a deterrent against their use by China or possibly against an intervention on China's behalf by the United States. Soviet objectives in such a war can be summarised as the 'Finlandisation', 'Mongolisation' or 'Balkanisation' of China' either imposing an acquiescent government on China or separating Manchuria and/or Xinjiang from the rest of the country through annexation or the creation of puppet regimes. This is a low probability at present but one which could increase in certain circumstances, including the emergence of an extremist/unstable government in China. Since the outbreak of the Sino–Soviet dispute, Moscow has kept up a constant barrage of propaganda aimed at encouraging separatist tendencies in China, especially in Xinjiang.[53] It is clear that China does take this threat somewhat more seriously.[54]

One danger of which China has shown a growing awareness is that Soviet development of Siberia would both increase the Soviet stake in protecting the region (perhaps by weakening China in some way) as well as its capacity to do so from locally available resources and, more generally, its ability to project its power in East Asia and the Pacific.[55]

The third scenario is limited nuclear war, which has already been discussed in part. Until recent years, with China's acquisition of something approaching an assured second strike capability, the main deterrent for the Soviet Union was less the fear of China's retaliation than the high risks associated since 1945 with the first use of nuclear weapons in war. As with all scenarios involving major hostilities, the probability of this one is low at present.

The fourth scenario involves the limited use of threat of force in 'pedagogic wars' or 'coercive diplomacy'. China has used force against Vietnam to 'teach a lesson' and it has threatened to use force in order to achieve a desired political end, as in 1965, in support of Pakistan. A 1979 study discovered '29 instances of Soviet coercive military diplomacy in the Third World' between June 1967 and the Angola Crisis of 1975–76.[56] The state faced with either kind of threat will prefer not to be forced into backing down in the case of 'coercive diplomacy' or to 'teach a lesson, back again but without running the risk of the level of violence escalating. But the ability to achieve such an outcome, especially against a superpower, may require the procurement of sophisticated weaponry (and techniques of war) which might in turn have far reaching implications for defence policy and hence internal politics and economics in general.

Two further scenarios may be included, although they do not involve a direct military threat. The first is that China and the Soviet Union might become engaged in a 'proxy war', or a conflict involving an ally. The Vietnamese invasion of Kampuchea was a conflict of this kind, and one which brought a Chinese military response. China has promised to aid Thailand in the event of Vietnamese aggression, and it has a longstanding informal commitment to Pakistan, whose Baluchistan region Beijing sees as a likely future target of Soviet expansion.[57] But Beijing's ability to give significant support to allies might require a capacity to project military power far beyond China's border, which might have unacceptable political and economic implications.

Finally, a major Chinese preoccupation has been with the threat of Soviet subversive activities, especially amongst the minority nationalities. One of many articles on this theme accused the Soviets of 'sending in secret agents to commit sabotage' and of 'buying national splittists to be their lackeys'.[58] To judge from its own propaganda since

1969, Beijing is less concerned about any specific threat to China than with the possibility that Moscow might be able to achieve its alleged objective of global hegemony without actually needing to fight. Weakening China by exploiting separatist tendencies in Xinjiang and elsewhere is precisely the kind of activity Beijing has in mind, and it must not only be considered to have the highest probability of all the scenarios examined here but as being the least susceptible to military solutions.

CHINESE RESPONSES

The basic elements of China's response to the Soviet were set out during 1969–73. They stemmed from a realistic appreciation that China would remain far weaker than the Soviet Union for the foreseeable future and that an attempt to bridge the gap between the two by a 'great leap forward' in defence would entail too great a sacrifice. China was to work towards a more even balance of military power with the Soviet Union but gradually and in a way that would not endanger the more fundamental goal of a self-reliant, socialist nation. But this was a strategy that could take several decades to accomplish. In the meantime there was an immediate and continuing threat. This was to be met by a threefold strategy: undue provocation of the Soviet Union on the border would be avoided; an attempt would be made to compensate for China's military weakness by an improved diplomatic position; if war came a people's war strategy would be employed against it.

This was the theory but the practice was to reveal many problems. Quite apart from complications arising from the factional conflict in China, three main areas of difficulty have emerged over the last ten years. First, the underlying assumption that a gradual, balanced programme of modernisation would eventually bring China to a position of rough military equality with the Soviet Union has increasingly come into question.[59] An American Defence Department report on the Sino–Soviet balance of power in the Far East concluded that 'China's relative low priority military modernisation will mean the balance will increasingly favour the Soviet Union, which steadily improves its forces there'.[60] Given a continuation of Soviet defence expenditure at current levels, there is little or nothing that Beijing can do about this. If the submarine-launched ballistic missile capability that China revealed in October 1982 becomes fully operation in the next few years, China will perhaps have acquired a reliable and accurate deterrent with high survivability that might be sufficient to keep the Soviets at bay. But the cherished Chinese dream of talking with Moscow on equal terms may remain unattainable.

Secondly, although the inadequacies and outdatedness of China's weaponry and military back-up system were fully revealed in the 1979 war with Vietnam,[61] Beijing has come to appreciate that even greater risks might be involved in any attempt to increase the pace of modernisation by stepping up arms purchases from the west. Doubts about over-reliance on the West have come to the fore since 1980 and a recent article by China's Defence Minister, Zhang Aiping, seemed to imply a definite decision to limit military cooperation with the West.[62] This is part of the larger question of the extent to which China should rely on diplomatic manoeuvring, particularly with Western countries, to enhance its security. The Gang of Four made an issue of this, so for some years after their demise it was difficult for a rational case to be put against excessive ties with the West without risking accusations of 'ultraleftism'. But the Reagan administration's Taiwan policy, its delays in approving the sale of various weapons to China,[63] and the proposals in recent arms control talks to move Soviet SS20 missiles currently in Europe to the Far East[64] have all brought this issue once again to the fore. China's 'America card' was played to good effect in the early 1970s when it helped to deter the Soviet Union and to end China's isolation. But in the conditions of the 1980s it is easy to see the attractions for China of playing a 'Soviet card' to ease the border situation and free resources for economic development as well as bringing pressure to bear on the United States.[65]

The third problem concerns the adequacy of a passive people's war as a strategy for all circumstances and the question of how it should be employed in and adapted for modern conditions. As one author has recently pointed out, people's war retains considerable utility: it makes optimal use of China's advantages of territory and population and, perhaps most importantly, it creates conditions which make it impossible for a puppet government to govern effectively.[66] But while it may provide a credible deterrent against a conventional invasion, it is clearly inappropriate in several of the scenarios that have been outlined here. Moreover, it is essentially the strategy of a poor Third World country interested only in defending itself. China clearly aspires to a far higher status, but that would require a demonstrable capacity to employ military power beyond China's borders.

There has also been a debate over several years at to the specific people's war tactics that should be employed in the event of a Soviet invasion. To a purist people's warrior it would not matter if the entire country were overrun by the Soviets, since it would be the long term outcome of the conflict that mattered. But a paradox immediately arises. If China's defences were to be based solely on such a definition of people's war, that might not create a sufficient deterrent against an invader who was intent simply upon achieving certain short term objectives. Indeed it might even tempt him into making an attack if he believed that he could gain his immediate goals without any undue trouble, whatever longer term problems of protracted guerrilla war he might face. Moscow was not deterred from its attack on Afghanistan by the certain prospect of people's war. But once it is accepted that China's strategy against an invasion should include measures to confront the attack with something more immediately effective than guerrilla war, questions arise about how much change the doctrine of people's war can bear before it is changed out of all recognition. Inevitably these issues involve even more fundamental questions about the kind of society China should be: precisely the same questions that caused so much turmoil during the 1960s.

At the level of broad strategic concepts, the Chinese answer to these questions has been a compromise expressed in the term 'people's war fought under modern conditions'. The enemy will be met with both 'active defence' and the people's war tactic of luring him in deep'.[67] In practice, however, the specific and detailed working out of the implications of this strategy have tended to favour an increasing shift to a more conventional defence policy, applied by a more up-to-date professional army. The emphasis is now on producing well trained and technically proficient officers, rather than inducing the right ideological outlook amongst the ranks, on the destruction of tanks and armoured units rather than on man to man combat, and on complex combined operations rather than the kind of separate, semi-independent manoeuvres that would be characteristic of a guerrilla war.[68]

Thus under the intense pressure of planning against potential Soviet threat, China seems to have begun adapting people's war to suit modern conditions. However such changes, as in the case of ideology in general, do not necessarily constitute an abandonment of first principles. People's war, like ideology, has always been flexible, and at its most fundamental meant little more than war with popular support. It is best seen as a strategy, with tactical flexibility left to accommodate change in response to 'modern conditions'. People's war, like Chinese foreign policy as a whole, is more pliable and pragmatic than many had previously recognised.

NOTES AND REFERENCES

1. See for example the speech by Ye Jianying at the Third National People's Air Defence Conference on 1 November 1978, *Beijing Review*, 17 November 1978, 3-4.
2. D. J. Doolin, *Territorial Claims in the Sino-Soviet Conflict*, (Hoover Institutions Studies, 1965), 22.
3. Ibid, 43.
4. See the analysis in Kenneth G. Lieberthal, *Sino-Soviet Conflict in the 1970s. Its Evolution and Implications for the Strategic Triangle*, (Santa Monica: Rand R-2342 NA, 1978), 5-8.
5. Jonathan D. Pollack, 'China's Agonizing Reappraisal', in H. J. Ellison (ed.) *The Sino-Soviet Conflict: A Global Perspective*, (Seattle and London, University of Washington Press, 1982), 55.
6. E. Joffe and G. Segal, 'The Chinese Army and Professionalism', *Problems of Communism*, November-December 1978, 19.
7. Zhou Enlai, Political Report to the 10th National Congress of the Communist Party of China, 24 August 1973, *Beijing Review*, 7 September 1973, 17-25.
8. The best of many sophisticated analyses of these questions include T. Gottlieb, *Chinese Foreign Policy Factionalism and the Origins of the Strategic Triangle*, (Santa Monica: Rand R 1902-NA, 1977); H. Harding, 'The Domestic Politics of China's Global Posture 1973-78', in T. Fingar, (ed.) *China's Quest for Independence: Policy Evolution in the 1970s*, (Boulder Colorado, Westview Press, 1980), 93-146; E. Joffe and G. Segal, *op. cit.* (note 6); K. Lieberthal *op cit.* (note 4); J. D. Pollack *op. cit.* (note 5); and 'Chinese Global Strategy and Soviet Power', *Problems of Communism*, January-February 1981, 54-69; G. Segal, 'China's Security Debate', *Survival*, March-April 1982.
9. K. G. Lieberthal op. cit., 51; note 10, and H. Kissinger, *The White House Years*, (London: Weidenfeld and Nicolson and M. Joseph, 1979), 183-186.
10. *Beijing Review*, 10 October 1969, 3.
11. Ibid.
12. J. D. Armstrong, *Revolutionary Diplomacy: Chinese Foreign Policy and the United Front Doctrine*, (Berkeley, Los Angeles, London, University of California Press, 1977), 98.
13. See in particular K. G. Lieberthal, *op. cit.* (note 4), especially 74-137.
14. After the fall of the Gang of Four, this view was replaced by the line that China needed a peaceful international environment to accomplish its modernisation plans.
15. Zhou Enlai, *op. cit.* (note 7).
16. Speech by Jiao at the UN, *Beijing Review*, 15 October 1976, 13-14.
17. 'Watch How They Are Going to Act', *Beijing Review*, 24 June 1977.
18. 'Soviet Social-Imperialism - Most Dangerous Source of World War', *Beijing Review*, 15 July 1977, 4-10, 21.
19. Ibid. 8.
20. J. D. Pollack, 'China's Agonizing Reappraisal'. *op. cit.* (note 5), 77.
21. Ibid., 21.

22. 'Chairman Mao's Theory of the Differentiation of the Three Worlds is a Major Contribution to Marxism–Leninism', *Beijing Review*, 4 November 1977, 10–41.
23. Ibid. 35.
24. Xu Xiangqian, 'Heighten Our Vigilance and Get Prepared to Fight a War', *Beijing Review*, 11 August 1978, 8.
25. Ibid. 9
26. T. W. Robinson, 'Chinese Military Modernization in the 1980s', *China Quarterly*, June, 1982, 242.
27. 'Social–Imperialist Strategy in Asia', *Beijing Review*, 19 January 1979, 13.
28. Ibid. 16.
29. See, for example, 'Moscow Beefs Up its Pacific Fleet', *Beijing Review*, 10 August 1979, 26–7.
30. *Beijing Review*, 7 January 1980, 3.
31. 'Asian Situation: Developments and Trends', *Beijing Review*, 7 April 1980, 8.
32. 'Increasing Soviet Menace', *Beijing Review*, 25 August 1980, 11.
33. 'The International Situation', *Beijing Review*, 5 January 1981, 11.
34. 'Sino–Soviet Relations', *Beijing Review*, 19 January 1981, 3.
35. 'Global Strategy', *Beijing Review*, 2 March 1981, 3.
36. 'Soviet Strategy for East Asia', *Beijing Review*, 23 March 1981, 20.
37. J. D. Armstrong, *op. cit.* (note 12), 92–102.
38. Y Jao, 'Soviet Foreign Policy as Seen from the 26th Congress of the CPSU', *Renmin Ribao*, 3 April 1981, FBIS-Chi-81-070, 13 April 1981, Cl.
39. Ibid., C4.
40. Di Xin, 'A Sinister Design', *Guangming Ribao*, 31 March 1981, FBIS-81-070 C4–5.
41. Pei Monong, 'The International Situation and Development Prospects in East Asia', *Renmin Ribao*, 27 March 1981, FBIS-Chi-81-067, 8 April 1981, A2.
42. Ibid.
43. Address of Vice Foreign Minister, Zhang Wenjin, to UN General Assembly 23 September 1981, *Beijing Review*, 5 October 1981, 23.
44. 'Is the Soviet Union Declining', *Beijing Review*, 18 January 1982, 12.
45. 'The Recent Soviet Strategic Trend', *Beijing Review*, 22 February 1982, 11.
46. Kyodo in English, 14 January 1982, BBC SWB, FE/6928 A3/8.
47. 'Some Observations on Soviet Detente', *Beijing Review*, 18 October 1982, 19.
48. *Herald Tribune*, 22 December 1982.
49. *The Times*, 16 November 1982.
50. *Herald Tribune*, 2 December 1982.
51. *Herald Tribune*, 24 January 1983.
52. 'The People's Army is Invincible', *Beijing Review*, 6 August 1969.
53. Victor Louis, *The Coming Decline of the Chinese Empire*, (New York, Times Books, 1979), 186.
54. 'Sino–Soviet Relations', *op. cit.* (note 34), 3.

55. 'The Soviet Union's Strategic Intentions in Opening Up Siberia', *Renmin Ribao*, 25 April 1981, FBIS-Chi-81-080 27 April 1981, C1-2.
56. J. M. McConnell and Bradford Dismukes, 'Soviet Diplomacy of Force in the Third World', *Problems of Communism, January–February* 1979, 14.
57. 'Moscow Covets Baluchistan', *Beijing Review*, 10 March 1980, 26–7.
58. 'Socialist Relations Among Nationalities and Regional National Autonomy', *Beijing Review*, 22 October 1976, 16.
59. T. W. Robinson, *op. cit.* (note 26), 246.
60. *Foreign Report*, 2 December 1982.
61. H. Jencks, 'China's "punitive war" on Vietnam: A preliminary assessment', *Asian Survey*, August 1979.
62. *The Guardian*, 5 March 1983.
63. *The Times*, 16 November 1982.
64. *The Guardian*, 9 March 1983 and *Defence and Foreign Affairs Daily*, 17 February 1982.
65. T. W. Robinson *op. cit.*, (note 26) 244 detects signs from late 1980 of army sources advocating 'temporary compromises with the Soviet Union'.
66. G. Segal, *The Soviet 'Threat' at China's Gates*, London, (Institute for the Study of Conflict, 1983).
67. Xu Xiangqian *op. cit.* (note 24), 10.
68. 'Strengthening National Defence', *Beijing Review*, 8 February 1982, 7.

13 The United States

ROBERT SUTTER*

China's foreign policy since 1949 has been continuously obsessed with its relationship to the two superpowers. But like many other obsessions, this one is not without good cause. Only the superpowers have the ability to pose massive threats to China, and in Beijing's perspective both have indeed threatened in the recent past. However, China has rarely seen both superpowers as simultaneous serious threats. More often than not it has perceived one superpower as an ascendant threat, while the other was said to be an ally – tacit or explicit. In the 1970s the United States was said to be in decline as a world power, but still able to serve a useful purpose in helping China defend against the Soviet threat.

Despite the seemingly self-confident rhetoric of Chinese foreign policy in any given period, it is obvious that China's views of the superpowers as threats or 'allies' have changed since 1949. As we move into the mid-1980s it is once again unclear just how China sees the superpowers. Are they both equal threats and to they both offer equal promise in defence of Chinese interests? In the past decade Sino–American relations have been seen as overwhelmingly contributing to China's defence, and posing little or no threat to Beijing's security. However, a shift to a more balanced assessment of threat and promise may be underway. The question needs to be assessed from both the changing United States and Chinese perspectives.

UNITED STATES POLICY UNDER NIXON AND FORD

United States policy began to change in the late 1960s when the Nixon administration fundamentally reassessed American Asian policy in

* The views expressed in this paper are those of the author. They do not reflect the views of the Congressional Research Service or any other U.S. Government agency.

light of the Sino–Soviet split, which had developed into an armed border conflict by 1969. The administration was faced with a continuing massive American involvement in the Vietnam War that weakened its military posture elsewhere, the development of a divisive political struggle in the United States against the war, and the growth of Soviet military power to a point approaching parity with the United States. As a result, it opted to exploit the Sino–Soviet split and improve American relations with China in order to help extricate the United States from the war, while continuing to maintain a balance in Asian and world affairs favourable to the United States.

Improved US relations with China complemented a large scale pullback of American forces from Vietnam and throughout East Asia and allowed American military planners to redesign US strategy in the region, seeing China less as a threat or source of conflict with the United States or its allies. The result was a shift in American military planning by the early 1970s to require military preparedness to deal only with one major conflict in Europe and one minor conflict elsewhere (a 'one and a half war' strategy). The so-called 'two and a half war' strategy – Europe, East Asia, and a third contingency elsewhere – had prevailed when the United States viewed both Moscow and Beijing as major threats.

This change in strategy was seen as enhancing the US ability to deal with the USSR. The opening to China was thought to raise serious doubts among Soviet strategists about the security of the USSR's flank with China in the event of an East–West confrontation elsewhere. Thus the dynamic development of Sino–American reconciliation was seen to give the United States political leverage against the USSR, as it reportedly prompted the Soviets to be more forthcoming toward the US on issues such as SALT and European questions, rather than risk driving the US closer into an alignment with China against the USSR.[1]

Throughout the Nixon and Ford administrations, the United States seemed satisfied with the limited strategic relationship it had established with China, whereby each side was able to view the other largely as an implicit counterweight to the Soviet Union. In these circumstances the focus of the relationship was almost exclusively anti-Soviet in that the most important factor in motivating and preserving the relationship was each side's perception that the other would remain capable and steadfast in opposition to Soviet expansion. The goal for the United States in this type of relationship was to preserve its strategic benefits against the risks of Chinese disillusionment with its value or worse, Sino–Soviet rapprochement. The importance of the

US–PRC bilateral relationship in this context lay in its contribution, through consultations, to the avoidance of misperceptions about policies and intentions, and in its effect on Soviet perceptions of the potential of US–Chinese co-operation.

POLICY DEBATE OVER US–CHINA SECURITY TIES, 1978–1981

American views of China's strategic importance changed appreciably in the late 1970s. In face of the expansion of Soviet military power and political influence in the Third World, American interest in détente with the Soviet Union declined. US policy was also affected by a rising concern over its military preparedness to meet Soviet and other foreign challenges following the collapse of the US-supported governments in Indochina, the fall of the Shah and the capture and detention of the American hostages in Iran, and the acrimonious debate over strategic preparedness during the US Senate deliberations concerning the SALT II Treaty.

As a result the Carter administration, especially in its last two years, shifted away from the policy of 'evenhandedness' that had characterised the American approach to the Sino–Soviet powers in the past. Improved relations with China increasingly came to be seen as an important source of regional and global power and influence for the United States. Officials in the Reagan administration seemed to agree with this basic position. In an effort to consolidate ties with China, Secretary of State Alexander Haig travelled to Beijing in June 1981 and announced that the United States, for the first time, was now willing to consider the sale of weapons to China.

Nevertheless, the seemingly rapid development of US–Chinese security ties were not without serious complications. The new American willingness to move beyond the implicit counterweight strategy with China toward active collaboration against the USSR, notably including the possible sale of American weapons to China, caused US opinion to split. Contending groups within and outside the US Government began actively to debate in public and private whether or not the United States should take what was widely seen as the next step forward in developing Sino–American cooperation – the sale of weapons and weapons-related technology to China. The issue of whether or not to proceed with such sales was not only of military significance but had broader political importance as well. It directly affected the central question in US foreign policy – how far should the United States go in trying to move closer to China in order to improve the American international position against the USSR. Opinion ranged widely.[2]

American proponents of increased transfers stressed the growing need for closer Sino–American co-operation in face of what was seen as Soviet expansionism abroad. (A few of them judged that the United States should soon follow military sales with other forms of security co-operation, leading ultimately to the establishment of a mutual security arrangement between the United States and China.) They acknowledged that although US friends and allies in Asia might be unsettled by the transfers, this need not work completely to American disadvantage. It might actually increase US leverage over some of those states, notably Japan. The proponents claimed that Moscow viewed closer US–PRC ties as inevitable and that the USSR was not likely to act rashly in dealing with either China or the United States.

Trends in the triangular relationship between the United States, the Soviet Union and China were seen by the proponents of increased Sino–American military sales as favouring their case. Pressures for sales to China were seen as likely to build so long as US relations with the Soviet Union remained more hostile than co-operative, US relations with China built toward greater friendship, and Sino–Soviet relations remained stalemated. The Chinese leaders were also seen as likely to continue to press for US military supplies.

In contrast, increased military ties with China were strongly opposed by other US observers. Some believed that negotiations with Moscow were a better way to deal with Soviet power than closer strategic alignment with China. Others saw problems stemming from possible leadership instability in China or excessive Chinese expectations of, or dependence on, US support. They voiced concern over the rise in Chinese influence and decline in US influence in Asia that was expected to follow US arms sales to China, stressing that China might use its new influence to bully its smaller neighbours, especially Taiwan.

In reaction to the US sales, the Soviet Union might increase military pressure throughout China's periphery – a development that would be likely to affect negatively US interests as tensions rose in Asia. Japan might feel compelled to adopt more independent foreign policies that would not necessarily be in US interests. US–Soviet relations would clearly be affected, as the sales to China could lock the United States into a stridently anti-Soviet policy that would preclude progress in arms control negotiations or other important matters.

DIFFERENCES OVER TAIWAN; FOREIGN POLICY ISSUES

Sino-American differences over the sensitive Taiwan issue put at least a temporary cap on the developing US-PRC strategic relationship, and brought the American debate on US arms sales to China to a halt. China made clear in late 1981 that it would not move ahead with increased military co-operation with the United States until the Reagan administration clarified its position on Taiwan. Heavy PRC pressure forced Americans to focus attention on meeting Beijing's demand that the United States agree formally to a gradual cut-off in US arms sales to Tawain. If the United States sold weapons to Taiwan without first agreeing to a gradual cut-off, Beijing asserted that it would downgrade US-PRC relations.[3]

Faced with strong PRC demands, the Reagan administration announced in January 1982 that it had decided not to sell Taiwan jet fighters more advanced that the F-5E already in production there, but it reaffirmed its commitment to sell arms, reportedly including more F-5E fighters, to the island. The administration did not specify the number of US planes to be sold or the duration of the sales. The decision ended months of debate in the United States on whether or not it should agree to sell a more advanced fighter, designated the FX, to Taipei, and it was widely hailed by the Western press as a sign of sensible moderation in American policy towards China.

But China remained dissatisfied with the US stance. After several months of reportedly delicate negotiations, the United States and the PRC, on 17 August 1982, issued a joint communiqué which established at least a temporary compromise over the arms sales question. However, PRC comment showed continued strong sensitivity over the Taiwan issue, demanding strict US adherence to the communiqué and criticising US interpretations of the accord.[4]

CHINA'S CHANGING PERSPECTIVE

Beijing further dampened American enthusiasm for closer Sino-American strategic collaboration when it began a major reorientation of Chinese foreign policy. By 1981, China had begun to move away from its past strident anti-Soviet orientation in foreign affairs in favour of a foreign posture critical of both superpowers. It put aside its emphasis during 1979-1980 on the development of a 'long-term strategic relationship' with the United States. Beijing had been attempting to foster a united front against suspected Soviet international expansion, then viewed as 'the main threat to world peace'. Chinese leaders now seemed to take a more balanced view, arguing that the main threat to world peace came from the competition of the *two* superpowers for international dominance or 'hegemony'. China called on other developing Third World countries to wage unremitting struggle against manifestations of Soviet or US 'hegemonic' behaviour abroad.

Chinese commentators also were less likely than in the past to draw a clear distinction between the threat posed to China and other countries by the two superpowers. In particular, the United States was not as often as in past years characterised as a declining power from whom the rest of the world had less to fear than the advancing, expansionistic Soviet Union.

Chinese Communist Party Chairman Hu Yaobang offered the most authoritative assessment of China's more evenhanded approach at the 12th CCP Congress in September 1982.[5] Hu did not repeat the vivid portrayal of Soviet expansion as the main danger to world peace which was made in the keynote address at the 11th CCP Congress in 1977. He made a more general reference to 'imperialism, hegemonism and colonialism' as the 'main forces' jeopardising peace, and said specifically that the two superpowers' rivalry had become the 'main source of instability and turmoil in the world'. He also strongly reaffirmed China's identification with the Third World against the superpowers, and he repeatedly stressed China's 'independent' foreign policy in which Beijing 'never attaches itself to any big power or group of powers, and never yields to pressure from any big power'.

Hu's treatment of China's bilateral relations with the United States and the Soviet Union, however, did differentiate between the two powers. He expressed hope for forward movement in Sino–US relations, adding that this would require strict US adherence to the US–PRC communiqué of 17 August 1982 concerning US arms sales to Taiwan. He saw the Taiwan issue as a 'cloud' hanging over otherwise beneficial US–PRC relations.

In contrast, Hu portrayed China as directly threatened by Soviet 'hegemonist' policies seen particularly in massed Soviet forces along the Sino–Soviet and Sino–Mongolian frontiers, in Soviet support for Vietnam's invasion and occupation of Kampuchea, and in the Soviet invasion and occupation of Afghanistan.

Hu averred that Sino–Soviet relations could move forward toward normalisation, but on condition that the USSR took certain unspecified steps – presumably involving the issues noted above – to lift its threat to the security of China.

Some other Chinese criticism lumped the United States together with the Soviet Union, claiming that Washington as well as Moscow threatened PRC national sovereignty by insisting on selling arms to Taiwan. Moreover, Chinese media were more outspoken than in the past in condemning US polcies in such sensititive areas as Korea and the Third World, and on such issues as the international economic order, nuclear proliferation and the Law of the Sea. Of course, Beijing had also adopted a tougher line, beginning in 1981, regarding China's demand for a cut-off in US arms supply to Taiwan. Finally, Chinese spokesmen were more critical of alledged US hesitation to sell technical equipment to China and to allow Chinese exports to have freer access to US markets.[6]

Beijing accompanied its interest in improved contacts with the USSR with a moderation – but not a halt – in Chinese polemics against the Soviet Union. China also softpedalled its past antagonistic view of Communist parties and Third World countries that maintained close ties with the USSR, going so far as to improve relations with the pro-Moscow French Communist Party and with Angola, despite the continued presence of Soviet-backed Cuban troops there. China now said that the issue of the Cuban troops in Angola was a matter to be settled by Angola and Cuba – a sharp change from Beijing's harsh denunciation a few years earlier of Andrew Young and other officials in the Carter administration for their interest in improving US relations with Angola despite the presence of Cuban troops.[7]

Behind these adjustments lay broader international and domestic trends that appeared to make China more open to meaningful compromise with the USSR. Beijing was seriously pursuing better relations with the USSR because it had become disappointed with the close relationship it had developed with the United States after the normalisation of diplomatic ties on 1 January 1979. In particular, the Reagan administration at its start appeared intent on following a policy more favourable to Taiwan than that of the Carter administration, suggesting that the United States did not place enough emphasis on PRC nationalistic sensitivities over the Taiwan issue and that the United States was implicitly treating China as a 'junior partner' in the Sino-American relationship.[8]

Beijing also expressed dissatisfaction with the Reagan administration's policy in the Third World, seeing close US relations with such controversial countries as Israel and South Africa, as well as Taiwan, as alienating a wide range of Third World leaders who otherwise might be useful in fostering a common Sino–American interest to offset the spread of Soviet expansionism abroad. And, Beijing saw the United States as inconsistent in applying political, economic and other pressure on the USSR; building up American military power against the USSR; and strengthening unity in the Western alliance. The administration's reversal of the US embargo of grain sales to the USSR and its turnabout regarding restrictions on Western sales for the construction of the new Soviet gas pipeline were seen as two major cases in point. Accordingly, China viewed the United States as an insensitive, maladroit and unreliable partner against the USSR. It saw serious potential costs with little additional benefit in a closer political–strategic association with the United States in opposition to the Soviet Union.

At the same time, it should be noted that US efforts against the Soviet Union, though perhaps marred by some inconsistencies, were basically successful in helping China to contain Soviet powers. Since the Reagan administration showed little sign of substantially easing the pressure against the Soviet Union in the foreseeable future, China could rest assured that even if it were to try to seek its own tactical advantage in establishing a dialogue and developing an accommodation with the US, it would not run the risk of upsetting the US-backed global balance of power favourable to Chinese interests.

Retrenchment and readjustment in China's economic modernisation programme also had a major impact on China's foreign policy, including its dialogue with the USSR. On the one hand, China's more sober development programme reduced the role Western technology and investment would play in China's growth over the next few years. While US and other Western businesses would be important in developing selected areas of China's economy, such as energy, constraints caused by Chinese poverty and technological incompatibility reduced the importance of economic ties with the West for the foreseeable future. Moreover, Chinese leaders expressed disillusionment with US willingness to open American markets to Chinese goods sufficiently to provide for a reduced PRC trade deficit with the United States, or to allow for a freer flow of American advanced technology to China. Accordingly, China was less concerned that a Sino–Soviet accommodation would possibly alienate US and other Western economic support for China's modernisation.

Meanwhile, Chinese military modernisation had moved away from reliance on foreign 'quick fixes'. Chinese leaders continued to wait until China's economy developed to a point where Beijing could afford to invest in a major upgrading of military capabilities. In anycase, the Soviet Union was now seen as less of a threat to China, and therefore military modernisation had become less pressing. The very fear upon which Sino-American détente was based, was fading in importance.

Chinese leaders also have had their own political differences over the close alignment with the United States and strong hostility to the USSR. Some have been arguing that Beijing has more to gain from a more evenhanded policy toward both superpowers that would allow China to play off one against the other. Chinese compromises of nationalistic principles in dealings with the US over Taiwan and other issues have also been sensitive domestic political issues, and have damaged China's credibility with many Third World countries. This has prompted Beijing to move toward a tougher line regarding the United States, a relatively more moderate approach toward Moscow, and a general 'anti-imperialist' foreign policy more consistent with the themes of independent nationalism central to the Chinese revolution of the past century. Meanwhile, placing some distance between China and the United States increased PRC room for manoeuvre in seeking possible concessions from the post-Brezhnev leadership.

On balance, China's recent foreign policy – especially its policy toward the superpowers – has reflected a view of the world that has shifted from one dominated by a perceived serious threat from a strongly expansionistic USSR, to one seeing notably reduced threat from the USSR and, to a much lesser degree, the United States. While all the factors noted above appear to have played a role in explaining this shift, it is important to add that China's current foreign policy remains based on quite shaky ground – any major change in any of these factors would presumably lead to another adjustment in that policy. Thus, for example, if the USSR, belying China's recent view of it as 'bogged down' by internal and external problems, were to launch a major new expansionistic effort – say in the Middle East or the Persian Gulf – it is very likely that China's assessment of the danger posed by the Soviet threat would rise appreciably; this would lend perhaps to greater Chinese interest in closer ties with the United States and the West, and a muting of US–PRC differences over Taiwan and other issues. Meanwhile, any major US effort to reach accommodation with the USSR on issues in East–West relations of importance to China would likely prompt China to reassess its current view of the US–Soviet relationship as an implacably hostile one serving to sap the energies of both superpowers. The result could be a perception of greater danger for China, especially if the US–USSR understanding were seen as freeing Soviet resources for use in dealing with the USSR's 'China problem'.

It is none the less clear that, for the present, Beijing's view of the world as less threatening to China's interests has worked against improved US–Chinese relations and has allowed for some improvement in Soviet–Chinese relations. Thus, China doubtless finds it easier to negotiate and begin a normalisation of relations with the USSR at a time when Beijing sees less chance of the USSR either initiating military action against China or viewing Chinese accommodation as a sign of weakness. The perceived reduced danger posed by the USSR has also served to lessen the immediate importance China attaches to closer US–China relations as a means to counter Soviet expansion. This in turn has made PRC leaders less willing to accommodate principles, nationalistic sensitivities and domestic political pressures – especially over the complicated Taiwan issue – for the sake of maintaining close relations with the United States. As a result, China feels more free to voice its displeasure with US policy toward Taiwan, sometimes going so far as to see the United States as threatening China's sovereignty by helping to keep Taiwan free from mainland control. This is not to say that China sees the United States or Taipei as a substantial dangers to Chinese security, as it no doubt continues to regard the 50-odd Soviet divisions along China's northern border. In fact, with the exception of Taiwan and possibly Korea, Beijing continues to make clear the basic compatibility between its own current security interests and those of the United States in the East Asian region that is so central to Chinese security interests. None the less, during a time of apparent reduced threat from the Soviet Union, China seems to judge that it can more readily afford to raise the profile of issues like Taiwan that seriously offend its nationalistic pride.

PROSPECTS

These recent Chinese actions have clearly sapped American interest in developing a closer strategic relationship with the PRC. Moreover, the urgency felt by US officials in recent years regarding the need to offset the growth of Soviet power has been reduced to some degree by developments in Soviet policy. Many Americans also have come to see the USSR as at least temporarily bogged down in its efforts at international expansion. In particular, Soviet forces are seen as stuck in a protracted and costly conflict in Afghanistan; Soviet planners remain preoccupied with the security of their western flank against potential insurrection in Poland; Soviet resources are extensively committed to far flung client states; and Soviet leaders face important questions of economic development and political succession under a new leadership headed by a fragile Yuri Andropov.

Changes in American military planning to secure against Soviet and Soviet-backed expansion has also affected US enthusiasm for closer security ties with China.[9] An increasingly important objective has been to secure access to the Persian Gulf for the US Rapid Deployment Force in the event of hostilities or major instability there. This objective now seems to have priority in US security plans over East Asian issues. A main threat to US access to the Persian Gulf comes from Soviet naval and air power in the Western Pacific that might be able to harass or cut the long American lines of communication. This threat is to be countered by US and US-backed forces along the periphery of the Western Pacific – a strategy that seems to explain the recently higher profile and greater attention US leaders have given to defence preparedness, co-operaton and co-ordination regarding Japan and several of the ASEAN countries.

This being said, however, it is important to note China's continued and important role in US strategic planning. While cautious about moving closer strategically to China, Americans remain keenly interested in retaining and slowly developing the implicit counterweight strategy that has developed over the past decade. This careful approach seemed manifest during Secretary of State George Schultz's visit to China in February 1983.

In these circumstances one can expect US officials to continue to value greatly the role that China plays in offsetting Soviet power in Asia and in complicating Soviet global military planning. The United States doubtless will also persist in using consultations with China to avoid misperception of policies and intentions and to give the USSR the impression of potential for closer US–China co-operation in the face of challenge from the Soviet Union.

Similar ambiguities in policy, of course, also affect the Chinese side of Sino–American relationship. On the one hand, real differences over important issues of policy, most notably Taiwan, will not fade away. On the other hand, China has not abandoned its view of the Soviet Union as a threat to Chinese security. Thus US power in Asia can serve Chinese interests in important aspects of deterrence.

However, it should be equally clear that much has already changed in China's view of the United States' role. Discussion of arms sales to

China is certainly much less central to Chinese calculations. But more importantly, China seems to have taken itself out of the position of such virulent anti-Sovietism that it found itself lying as Washington's uncomfortable bed-fellow in opposing Third World revolution. China's new and more open criticism of US global policies is certainly a more natural position for Communist China.

Thus the past 15 years has seen China gradually build up notions of a strategic relationship with the United States, and now there seem to be signs that yet another change in policy is under way. It would be simplistic to suggest that China is moving back to the era of the Sino-Soviet honeymoon where Washington was seen as a serious threat. Now the more balanced policy suggests that the United States and the Soviet Union can offer elements of promise to Chinese security, while retaining important threatening characteristics. Obviously the Soviet Union is far more of a threat than the United States, and is likely to remain so for quite some time. But it is crucial to appreciate that both superpowers provide a mix of positive and negative dimension for Chinese policy. This view from Beijing may not be as simple as previous Chinese strategic perspectives, but it is more realistic.

NOTES AND REFERENCES

1. For a recent review of these American calculations, see Richard Solomon (ed.) *The China Factor: Sino-American Relations and the Global Scene.* (Englewood Cliffs, New Jersey. Prenitice Hall. 1981). See also, US Senate, Committee on Foreign Relations, *The Implications of US-China Military Co-operation.* (Washington, D.C., US Government Print Office, 1981).
2. For a review of American opinion see US Senate. Committee on Foreign Relations, The Implications of US-China Military Co-operation. (US GPO, 1981). See also US Library of Congress, Congressional Research service, *Increased US Military Sales to China: Arguments and Alternatives* 20 May 1981. (Report No. 81-121 F, Washington, D.C., 1981).
3. For background, see A. Doak Barnett. *U.S. Arms Sales: The China-Taiwan Tangle.* (Washington, D.C., Brookings Institution 1982).
4. The communiqué and press comment are replayed in US Foreign Broadcast Information Service, Daily Report, China. 17 August 1982.
5. Hu's report is seen in FBIS Daily Report, China, 8 September 1982.
6. See in particular, Foreign Minister Huang Hua's remarks at the UN General Assembly and at the Council on Foreign Relations in New York, reported in FBIS Daily Report, China, 19 October 1982 and 8 October 1982.

7. See FBIS Daily Report, China, 22 October 1982.
8. These differing American views are reviewed in US Library of Congress, Congressional Research Service, *Future Sino–Soviet Relations and Their Implications For the United States.* (Washington, D.C. 30 December 1982 Report No. 83–10 F). 22–25.
9. See in particular recent press reports on the Defence Department's so-called consolidated guidance for US defence policy over the next several years. For example, see *Chicago Tribune*, 17 January 1983.

14 Western Europe

DOUGLAS STUART

There has been a European school of thought, which found its strongest support in France, that Western Europe should develop much closer ties with China for the same basic reason that the United States has reopened its channels to Peking, namely to increase leverage on the Soviet Union. The difficulty is (and it is one of the reasons that invalidates the conception of a pentagonal balance of power) that Western Europe has little to offer China in political terms, with the possible exception of the delivery of Hong Kong ... By the same token, China could afford no real help to Western Europe if the European–American relationship were to degenerate or if it were to come under some new form of pressure from the Soviet Union.

Alistair Buchan
The End of the Postwar Era
(New York: Dutton, 1974) p. 163

Chinese relations with the NATO countries have gone through three phases since Beijing's opening to the West in the early 1970s. During the first half of the 1970s Chinese foreign policy toward NATO was characterised by the late-Maoist theory of the 'strategic differentiation of the three worlds'. This involved a rhetorical distinction between Washington and the European NATO allies, but a high degree of policy co-ordination in Beijing's actual initiatives toward the US and Western Europe. During the latter half of the 1970s Chinese initiatives toward the industrialised democracies were guided by the requirements of the 'global anti-hegemony campaign' against 'Soviet social imperialism'. Rhetorical distinctions between the US and the nations of Western Europe were dropped, and the PRC became the most vociferous supporter of Washington's campaign to encourage stronger defence efforts among the NATO allies. Finally, during the early 1980s, China is moving back toward a policy of differentiating between Washington and the nations of Western Europe, and is downplaying its emphasis upon NATO *per se*. This essay will survey briefly the evolution of Chinese policy toward NATO during the first two periods mentioned above, and then comment on the direction that PRC policy appears to be taking in the 1980s. An attempt will be made to place Chinese policy toward NATO in the context of evolving doctrinal and political disputes within the alliance itself.

LATE-MAOIST POLICIES TOWARD NATO

Mao's well-known theory of the strategic differentiation of the three worlds was formally announced in 1974, although official PRC organs were referring to its theme as early as 1972.[1] The three worlds thesis justified collaboration with the industrialised democracies of Western Europe, Oceania and Canada – the nations of the 'Second World' – in opposition to both superpowers and to the post-World War II bipolar international system.

From the time of its formulation the three worlds thesis was fundamentally flawed in two respects. First, it assumed that the nations of the Second World could be convinced that they had a common interest with the nations of the Third World in contributing to the collapse of the post-1945 order. This assumption was based upon an exaggerated view of the significance of Gaullist and neo-Gaullist initiatives by America's industrialised allies and insufficient attention to the fact that the Second World nations were partners (albeit junior partners) in the management of the bipolar world order, with a considerable stake in the benefits of that system. Thus it is not surprising that China's attempts in the early 1970s to recruit the governments of Western Europe into a campaign of opposition to both superpowers were unsuccessful.

The second flaw in the three worlds thesis was that it was based upon a fiction, since it was preceded by, and in fact contingent upon, China's normalisation of relations with the United States. Just as Willy Brandt discovered in the late 1960s that *Ostpolitik* required the imprimatur of Moscow, the Beijing leadership recognised in the early 1970s that the route to Western Europe still had to pass through Washington. The PRC also needed to insure its security against the 'main enemy' – the Soviet Union – prior to taking any other foreign policy initiatives.[2] The nations of the Second World were 'weak and far away' from China's perspective, and they could not, and would not, provide China with the kind of insurance that Beijing required.[3] It had to come from Washington.

During the early 1970s the fiction of the three worlds thesis was perfectly acceptable to the United States primarily on the grounds of *realpolitik*. Washington also understood that the PRC leadership needed time to move China from the xenophobia of the Cultural Revolution to a position of open collaboration with the United States, and the three worlds thesis served as an interim strategy during this time period. By the end of 1975, however, the PRC leadership had abandoned the fiction of the three worlds thesis and modified its policies and statements to permit a qualitative distinction between Washington and Moscow, with the latter identified as the pre-eminent threat to world peace.

CHINA, NATO, AND THE GLOBAL ANTI-HEGEMONY FRONT

By the late 1970s, Beijing was the most fervent supporter of Washington's campaign to revitalise the NATO alliance to contain Moscow, and China was becoming a central, and perhaps indispensable, component in America's long-term defence plans for Asia. China's rhetoric far exceeded its capabilities or its actions, of course, but the sheer size of the PLA forces, coupled with China's geostrategic location and its commitment to defence modernisation encouraged Washington to believe that China represented at least a partial solution to the problem of the relative decline of US military power *vis-à-vis* the Soviet Union. Certain US advisers (most notably Zbigniew Brzezinski) were also encouraged to increase Sino–American security ties by the fact that Soviet defence planners exhibited a concern about the threat posed by China that was out of all proportion to Beijing's actual military capability.[4] By 1978 the US Department of Defence was considering strategies for Sino–American military co-operation against Moscow. Internal memoranda included plans for the pre-positioning of munitions in the PRC, US/PRC wartime co-operation and other initiatives that Banning Garrett has described as 'remarkably similar to US military arrangements with NATO allies'.[5] During this period the US also encouraged speculation about increased transregional security co-operation between China and NATO, as reflected in the reported assertion by SACEUR General Alexander Haig, 'of course, I am not going to urge China to join NATO. But in a certain sense it is already to some extent the 16th member of NATO'.[6]

Few West European leaders were prepared to share Washington's optimistic view of China's potential contribution to Western security during the latter half of the 1970s. The Chinese claim that control of Western Europe was the ultimate goal of Soviet social imperialism did not generate much of a response after 30 years of relative security and a decade of détente. Indeed, West European leaders were generally more impressed by the argument that the Soviet leadership might be driven to risky and aggressive behaviour toward Europe, the Middle East and/or Southwest Asia if it perceived an increased threat from the US, China and Japan on its eastern front.[7] These European concerns made it difficult for China to convince key West European states of the utility of the 'global anti-Soviet front'.

In France during the late 1970s, the government of Giscard d'Estaing was attempting to manage the often incompatible demands of national independence, Western alliance, and East–West détente. In these circumstances China represented one more potentially destabilising factor in the equation. The French public was also particularly sensitive to the dangers of being drawn into an Asian land war. During 1979, 55 per cent of the French public believed that there is a 'risk that the Chinese–Vietnamese conflict will drag the world into a third world war,' while 40 per cent of the French public listed Southeast Asia as the most likely region for superpower confrontation.[8] Giscard thus treated the PRC with reserve and caution during the 1970s, seeking to close some bilateral arms sales deals without exacerbating Soviet concerns. The only major contracts signed during this period were for helicopters: thirty Alouette and Super-Frelon models in 1977 and fifty Dauphin-II models in 1980.[9]

French concerns about the risks of quasi-military co-operation with China were echoed and amplified by Bonn in the late 1970s. The government of Helmut Schmidt inherited from its SPD predecessor a foreign policy that was inextricably tied to the fortunes of *Ostpolitik*, which China's 'global anti-hegemony campaign' threatened to upset. Among West German political leaders, only Franz Josef Strauss was consistently supportive of China's anti-Soviet campaign during this period. Strauss was also the only major West German politician prepared to accept the logic of China's theory of strategic 'counterweights'.[10]

Herr Strauss's popularity in Beijing encouraged West German pundits to observe that only three Germans had been accorded the honour of having their pictures hung in the Great Hall of the People: Marx, Engels, and Strauss. He was clearly the exception among West German politicians in the 1970s, however. Most of his colleagues were either explicitly opposed to the global anti-hegemony front (Brandt,

Schmidt) or prepared to give it no more than passive support (Kohl). As long as the SPD remained in office, China had no prospect for developing an arms trade relationship with Bonn, and even if a CDU–CSU coalition had come to power in the late 1970s, Beijing would have been frustrated in its efforts to solicit substantial support for its defence modernisation programme or for its global anti-hegemony front.

In Great Britain a similar pattern developed during the late 1970s, with the vast majority of British politicians sharing Prime Minister James Callaghan's fear that China would act not as a counterweight to restrain the Soviet Union but rather as a source of threat along Russia's Asian border that would encourage Moscow to attempt a 'strategic breakout' in some other region.[11] Once again the Chinese had to content themselves with whatever public support they could elicit from military spokespersons (such as Air Marshall Sir Neil Cameron) and selected Conservative Party leaders (most notably, Margaret Thatcher).[12]

Mrs. Thatcher's appointment as Prime Minister in 1979 was considered by China to be a major victory for the global united front against hegemony. The Thatcher government did in fact abandon Mr. Callaghan's policy of rhetorical evenhandedness in favour of a policy of strong support for China and against Moscow. Such rhetoric encouraged many commentators to predict that Thatcher would revitalise the Sino–British arms trade relationship which had been moribund since the purchase of 50 Spey engines in 1975. Since that time, however, the only significant defence-related contract signed between London and Beijing was the March 1982 deal (worth £14 million) for the purchase of avionics and electronic equipment from Marconi Limited. In March 1983, Sino–British arms trade suffered its most serious setback in years, when the Chinese government announced that it was cancelling plans to modernise nine Luda-class destroyers by the purchase of the British Sea Dart Missile and related avionics. Three British companies – British Aerospace, Plessey, and Vosper Thornycroft – were involved in the consortium arrangement for the contract, worth £100 million. China's Minister of Foreign Economic Relations and Trade, Chen Muhua, stated that Beijing's decision to back away from the Sea Dart negotiations was due to PRC dissatisfaction over 'price, technology and production' issues.[13] Chen Muhua's comments notwithstanding, however, China's position on the Sea Dart negotiations is part of a much broader process of policy reassessment relating to the acquisition of defence systems from abroad.[14]

To conclude, Beijing was generally unsuccessful throughout the 1970s in its efforts to convince European governments to support the global anti-hegemony front against Moscow, and the much-vaunted potential for Sino–European arms trade proved to be more theatre than business.

The Soviet Union undermined China's counterweight argument in Western Europe by three very different policies during this period. First, the continuation of a détente relationship with selected West European governments on certain political, economic and social issues. This weakened Chinese and American arguments about the immediacy of the Soviet threat to Western Europe, and increased the West Europeans' stake in the preservation of relations with Moscow.

Second, the invasion of Afghanistan: ironically, this did not result in a long-term increase in alliance solidarity. Nor did it bolster US and Chinese arguments for greater defence build-ups in Western Europe. In fact, the Soviet decision to intervene militarily in Afghanistan tended to be viewed by proponents of the 'strategic breakout' thesis as vindication of their arguments against a global counterweight strategy.

Third, the demonstration of the capability and will needed to cope with a two-front threat. During the 1970s Moscow substantially increased the size of its Asian forces – from approximately 30 divisions in 1969 to between 45 and 52 divisions at present – without making any appreciable reductions in the size or readiness of its forces west of the Urals.[15] The Soviet Union has also responded to the two-front threat by improving the range, accuracy and manoeuvrability of its SS-20 intermediate range missiles, and doubling the number of deployed SS-20s since 1979.[16] Moscow is able to threaten both Western Europe and Asia with SS-20s deployed east of the Ural mountains.

Thus, among NATO nations the US was the principle supporter of the logic of China's anti-Soviet campaign, at a time when Washington was becoming increasingly frustrated with its NATO allies and increasingly interested in developing new containment strategies.

CHINA'S PURSUIT OF A DIFFERENTIATED SECURITY POLICY

Since the beginning of the 1980s China's politico-military relations have been characterised by the gradual abandonment of the global anti-hegemony campaign against Moscow in favour of a more complex and multifaceted strategy based upon bilateral relations. Unremitting opposition to the Soviet Union is no longer the centerpiece of Chinese foreign policy as it was in the 1970s. Instead the PRC is seeking to develop a mixed adversary relationship with both superpowers in order to increase its leverage within the US–USSR–PRC triangle.[17] China has also gradually reduced its support for NATO *per se*, and has attempted instead to distinguish between the Western industrialised democracies in terms of their competing and converging interests with the PRC.

Two NATO allies have been singled out by China for special criticism during the last two years – the US for its policy of support for Taiwan and Great Britain for its post-colonial relationship with Hong Kong.[18] It is not a coincidence that these same two NATO states were the most outspoken supporters of China's earlier campaign of opposition to Moscow. Following the elections of the Reagan and Thatcher governments, China was encouraged to believe that the United States and Great Britain had a much greater stake in the preservation and expansion of quasi-military ties with Beijing.[19]

In these circumstances the PRC felt confident that it could increase its demands on Washington without causing an irreparable rupture in relations. As Robert Sutter discusses in Chapter 13, this PRC strategy of pressuring the US appears to have backfired. Washington appears to have concluded that the domestic and international costs associated with a policy of courting the PRC are simply too great, and the US has toughened its negotiating positions on issues relating to Sino–American trade, the sale of US weapons and dual-use technologies to the PRC, and (most importantly) on US support for the government of Taiwan.

On the issue of Hong Kong's sovereignty, the PRC leadership continues to pressure Great Britain for a favourable negotiated settlement. To date the British government has attempted to communicate flexibility to the PRC, without exacerbating fears in Hong Kong. It remains to be seen whether Mrs. Thatcher will be encouraged by her June 1983 'landslide' victory to take a tougher stand in negotiations with the PRC. For its part, Beijing has already gone too far in linking the sovereignty issues of Hong Kong and Taiwan, and it will be difficult for the PRC government to be either very accommodating or very patient in its discussions with the Thatcher government. It has been reported that during Mrs. Thatcher's visit to China in September 1982, Deng Xiaoping set a deadline of the end of 1984 for the successful completion of UK–PRC negotiations on the Hong Kong issue. Deng insisted that after that date China will 'announce its own solution'.[20]

China's relations with France are also based more on conflict than co-operation at the present time. The major points of dispute between Beijing and Paris involve the latter's policies toward India, Vietnam, and Kampuchea. France has singled out India for special attention in its foreign policy. New Delhi is characterised as one of the 'three pillars' of France's global policy (along with Mexico and Algeria). A central component of French policy toward India is the sale of arms and defence-related technologies. In fact, Paris has recently concluded contracts with New Delhi for the purchase of some of the same weapons systems that France has been attempting unsuccessfully to sell to China – including the Mirage 2000 fighter and Hot and Milan missiles.[21] Although China has been cautiously improving its relations with India in recent months, the PRC is not yet in a position to view significant French contributions to India's defence programme with equanimity.

Beijing has also been frustrated and angered by Mitterrand's policies toward Southeast Asia. In particular the PRC leadership has criticised French support for Vietnam – including the provision of $32 million in aid to Hanoi. During a recent tour of Asia French Foreign Minister Claude Cheysson justified the official French policy of support for Vietnam on the grounds that it contributed to the long-term stability of the region by providing Hanoi with a diplomatic alternative to Moscow.[22] Not surprisingly Beijing has been unimpressed by such arguments and continues to interpret French policy toward Hanoi as giving aid and comfort to the enemy. The PRC has also been angered by Cheysson's vociferous criticism of the Kampuchean coalition. The Kampuchean conflict was reportedly the centerpiece of discussions between President Mitterrand and the Beijing leadership during the May 1983 French state visit to Beijing. Both sides agreed on the goals of peace and self-determination for Kampuchea, but they admitted that there is still ' ... a divergence ... on the means to achieve this'.[23]

The prospects are only slightly brighter for an improvement in Chinese relations with West Germany. The recently elected coalition government of Helmut Kohl is still attempting to establish its basic foreign policy themes, but it is already clear that Franz Josef Strauss will seek to exercise positive and negative influence over West Germany's foreign relations. According to recent reports, Strauss has already taken the initiative in foreign affairs by circulating an internal working paper including a programme for increased Sino-German relations, with special emphasis upon economic co-operation.[24] It would be a mistake, however, to exaggerate the prospects for expanded Sino-German ties. Elite and mass public attention in the Federal Republic continues to be focussed almost exclusively on domestic political and economic issues, and geopolitical realities ensure that when West German foreign policy is discussed, priority will have to be given to Soviet interests and concerns.[25] If China improves its own relations with Moscow and continues to move away from its former policy of pressing Germany and other West European governments to choose between Beijing and Moscow, it will be easier for the Bonn government to develop economic and political ties with China during the 1980s.

CONCLUSION

In spite of the fact that China remains 'weak and far away' in the security calculations of most of the European NATO allies, China's current policy of differentiating between the industrialised democracies of Western Europe is likely to provide the PRC with considerably more opportunities for influence than either the three worlds strategy or the global anti-hegemony strategy. It permits the PRC to manage its bilateral relations and its policy disputes with each NATO ally on a case-by-case basis, without the ideological encumbrances of the 1970s. It is a more modest and therefore a more realistic approach for a middle power such as the PRC. It is a markedly more flexible policy that can be adjusted to accommodate a variety of developments, including crises within the NATO alliance, USSR–PRC détente or US–Soviet cold war jockeying. It permits Beijing to play to a number of different audiences in Europe at the same time – Eurocommunist, social democrat, conservative. It represents one component of a broader pattern of diplomacy that the *Far Eastern Economic Review* has described as 'Friends All Over the World'.[26]

The PRC developed its current policy of bilateral ties after being rebuffed by most West European governments in its efforts to sponsor the global anti-hegemony front based on the theory of strategic counterweights. At least in retrospect, it is not surprising that China failed to convince America's NATO allies of the value of this argument. One need only consider the lengths to which even a superpower such as the US has had to go to reassure West European governments – including the stationing of more than 300 000 US troops in Western Europe – to appreciate the difficulty that any state has in convincing geographically removed allies of the dependability of an extended deterrent commitment. For a medium power such as China, with an essentially defensive military posture based on proportional deterrence and the doctrine of People's War, the problem of convincing West European states to base their security calculations on Chinese assurances of indirect or direct support proved insurmountable.

For its part, Beijing was probably not so unrealistic that it expected to obtain some formal security commitment from NATO during the 1970s. The Chinese anti-hegemony campaign was most probably designed to increase Soviet uncertainty as much as possible at the lowest cost to the PRC. Professor Allen Whiting quotes a 1975 statement by a 'high Chinese official' to the effect that 'the Soviet Union won't attack us until it has defeated NATO'.[27] The comment is better understood as a consolation, devoutly to be wished by the Chinese, rather than as an accurate assessment of existing geostrategic realities. China's effort to align itself with NATO in the later 1970s was at least partly an attempt to bring this situation into existence to the extent that it was possible in view of China's economic, military and political vulnerabilities during this period. In the circumstances China did as well as could be expected. By the early 1980s, however, Beijing had come to realise that its security and its foreign policy were better served by a more moderate and balanced strategy that permitted conditional and cautious reconciliation with Moscow.

NOTES AND REFERENCES

1. Richard Loewenthal mentions that Mao himself is reported to have endorsed the doctrine in 1972 in conversations with a Third World leader. See 'The Degeneration of an Ideological Dispute', in *China, the Soviet Union, and the West*, Douglas Stuart and William Tow (eds), (Boulder, Colorado, Westview, 1982), 69. See also *China's Fascination with Western Europe*, RFE research paper no. 1561, 4 October 1972, and 'Medium Sized and Small Nations Unite to Oppose Two Superpowers', *Peking Review* 15, 18 January 1972, 14–16. The Soviet Union reacted predictably to the announcement of the three worlds thesis, accusing Beijing of being 'ready to strike alliance even with the most reactionary and anti-Communist forces, if their nationalist plans require it'. *Tass*, 2 October 1972.
2. On the importance of the 'main enemy' in Chinese strategic calculus, see D. Bobrow, S. Chan, and J. Kringen, *Understanding Foreign Policy Decisions: The Chinese Case* (New York, Free Press, 1979).
3. See William E. Griffith; 'China and Europe: West and Far Away', in R. Solomon (ed.), *The China Factor* (New York, Council on Foreign Relations, 1981), 159–177.

4. On the psychological component of Chinese deterrence against Moscow, see Michael Pillsbury, 'Chinese Perceptions of the Soviet–American Military Balance', Final Report, Systems Planning Corporation (prepared for OSD/Net Assessment, Washington, D.C., March 1980). See also William V. Garner, 'Soviet Security Policy Towards China: Carrots, Sticks, and US "Alliance" Commitments', ISA conference paper, 25 March 1982.
5. B. Garrett testimony in *The US and the PRC: Issues for the 1980s*. Hearings before the Subcommittee on Asian and Pacific Affairs, Committee on Foreign Affairs, US House of Representatives, 96th Congress, 2nd session, April–September, 1980 (USGPO), 101.
6. See RDM Furlong and LT-Col Al Biegel, 'Chinese Military Links with NATO?: An Assessment of the Kremlin's Concerns', *International Defense Review* 12, no. 9, 1979, 1468; and for Soviet comments, see G. Apolin and U. Mityayev; 'NATO's 16th member', *Militarism in Beijing's Policies* (Moscow, Progress, 1980), 219–226. Also V. Divov; 'China and the NATO Countries', *Soviet Military Review*, no. 4, April 1979.
7. This 'strategic breakout' argument is presented by William Hyland, 'The Sino–Soviet Conflict: A Search for New Security Strategies', *Strategic Review*, Fall 1979, 51–62.
8. Joseph Fitchett, 'Europe and the New China', *International Herald Tribune* (hereafter cited as IHT), 5 March 1979.
9. See Douglas Stuart and William Tow, 'Chinese Military Modernization: The Western Arms Connection', *China Quarterly*, June 1982, 253–270, and W. Tow and D. Stuart, 'China's Military Turns to the West', *International Affairs* (London, Spring 1981), 286–300.
10. Cited in Georges Tan Eng Bok; *La Politique Exterieure de la Chine*, doctoral dissertation, Ecoles des Hautes Etudes en Sciences Sociales, 3 February 1981, 497–498 (translation by the author). For a Soviet analysis of Strauss's popularity in China, see G. V. Astafev et al., *Kitai i Kapitalisticheskie Strany Europy: Sbornik Statei (China and the Capitalist Lands of Europe: A Collection of Articles)* (Moscow, Izdatelstvo Nauka, 1976), 121.
11. Quoted in Joseph Fitchett; 'Europe and the New China', *International Herald Tribune*, 5 March 1979.
12. Sino–British relations are discussed by the author in 'Prospects for Sino–European Security Cooperation', *Orbis*, Fall 1982, 721–746. See also Lawrence Freedman, 'The West and the Modernization of China', *Chatham House Papers*, no. 1, (London, Royal Institute of International Affairs, 1979).
13. See the account of the Sea Dart negotiations in *Defence and Foreign Affairs Weekly*, 4–10 April 1983, 3 and 11–17 April 1983, 3.
14. The gist of Zhang's article was that it was 'not realistic or possible' for the PRC to base its long-term defence modernisation upon technologies or systems from abroad. See V. G. Kulkarni, 'A Retreat From Power', *Far Eastern Economic Review*, 7 April 1983, 20.
15. In recent US Senate testimony, estimates of current Soviet troop strength along the Sino–Soviet border ranged as high as 56 divisions. See 'The Implications of US–China military Cooperation', a workshop sponsored by the Committee on Foreign Relations, US Senate, and the Congression-

al Research Service, Library of Congress (Washington, DC, USGPO, January 1982), 52–56.
16. According to recent US government statements, the USSR has 108 SS-20s facing Asia and 243 targetted on Western Europe. Administration spokesmen contend that Moscow is now constructing four new launching sites in the Asian theatre, enough to double the number of SS-20 launchers aimed at China, (*IHT*, 9 May 1983, 1).
17. This question is discussed by the author in 'China Between the Superpowers', *The World Today*, March 1983, 90–98. See also Robert Sutter; 'Future Sino–Soviet Relations and Their Implications for the United States', Congressional Research Service Report No. 83–10F, 30 December 1982; Bruce Porter; 'The Sino–Soviet–American Triangle', Radio Free Europe–Radio Liberty Research Report, 61/83, 2 February, 1983; and Banning Garrett and Bonnie Glaser; 'Breaking the Iron Triangle', *Far Eastern Economic Review* (FEER), 21 April 1983, 34.
18. This argument is supported by published accounts of the positions taken by Beijing during recent visits to China by US and British government spokesmen, in particular the spring 1983 visits headed by US Secretary of State George Shultz and a Congressional Committee headed by House Speaker Thomas P. O'Neil, and the autumn 1982 visit by British Prime Minister Margaret Thatcher. During the Thatcher visit, the Chinese hosts were anything but subtle in communicating their demands and concerns regarding Hong Kong. On one occasion during the visit, Mrs Thatcher was treated to a performance of a Chinese operetta in which one of the heroes liberates an island occupied by vultures (*South*, November 1982, 33).
19. See, for example, excerpts from a 1982 'strategic guidance' for US Asian security policy during the 1980s, published in *IHT*, 8 June 1982. For a thorough analysis of the evolution and implications of US–PRC security relations, see 'The Implications of US–China Military Co-operation,' (note 15). On the doctrine of horizontal escalation and its implications for the NATO alliance, see D. Stuart and W. Tow, *The Limits of Alliance*, (forthcoming, 1984, Martinus Nijhoff, The Hague).
20. Quoted in an interview by Dr Parris Chang with Hu Yaobang, reported in *Newsweek*, 27 June 1983, 31.
21. Representative reports on Franco–Indian contracts include: 'M. Mitterrand en Inde', *Le Monde*, 29 November 1982, 1; 'Francois' Foreign Affaire', *The Sunday Times* (London), 19 December 1982; 'India is Said to Receive French–German Missiles', *IHT*, 21 December 1982, 2. Regarding ongoing Sino–French Mirage negotiations, see 'PRC Goes Public on Wanting Mirages', *Strategyweek*, 30 August–5 September 1982, 4–5.
22. Nayan Chanda; 'French Foot in the Door', *FEER*, 14 April 1983, 18. See also, *The Asia Record*, October 1982, 4.
23. *IHT*, 6 May 1983, 5, and Nayan Chanda, 'Counting the Cost', *FEER*, 19 May 1983, 18.
24. Rumours relating to the Strauss paper appeared in *Newsweek*, 11 April 1983, 12.
25. According to a voter poll after the March 1983 West German election, only 14 per cent of the West German public were influenced by foreign or defence policy questions in their choice of candidates: David Kramer and

Glenn Yago; 'Germany's Election Solved None of its Deep Problems', *Washington Post*, 13 March 1983. Strauss was recently disciplined by Chancellor Kohl. During a CDU convention in Köln, the Chancellor made it clear that FRG foreign policy would be made in Bonn rather than Münich and that the CSU should not forget that it is a junior partner in the coalition, *United States Information Service Daily Press Review* no. 099, 26 May 1983, 1.
26. *FEER*, 31 March 1983.
27. Allen Whiting, *Siberian Development and East Asia: Threat or Promise?* (Stanford, CA, Stanford University Press, 1981), 163.

15 Japan

JOACHIM GLAUBITZ

Sino-Japanese relations have a long, and not always peaceful tradition. This is one reason why there are strong emotional elements in contemporary Sino-Japanese relations. Another element might be the fact that the two have been at war with each other twice within half a century. China was attacked and invaded by the very nation which owed so much to its culture, and its perception of Japan as well as of Japan's attitude towards China is basically formed by these historic experiences.

Even after Japan was defeated in 1945 it was still perceived by the Chinese leadership as a potential threat. The Sino-Soviet Treaty of Friendship and Alliance concluded in February 1950 was clearly directed against Japan. The preamble and two out of the six articles of the treaty refer in one way or the other to Japan and a potential Japanese threat. Consequently anti-Japanese propaganda of changing intensity began immediately after the Communists came to power and lasted more than two decades. Only in the summer of 1972, just before Premier Kakuei Tanaka visited Beijing did the Chinese government stop charging Japan with neo-militarism and neo-colonial exploitation of South-East Asia.

Instead, Beijing stressed the historic friendship and the perspectives of future co-operation between the two countries and ignored the elements which communist-controlled media tend to criticise in non-socialist societies. This remarkable shift was not mere tactics. It was part of a strategy which first became apparent when, in July 1971, Henry Kissinger during his historic journey to Beijing reached agreement on a visit to China by President Nixon. This event marked a turning point in China's global strategy. Its policy *vis-à-vis* Japan is only one element, although an important one.

As far as Japan is concerned China's policy is determined by three strategic goals. These are, first, strengthening co-operation against

Soviet influence in the Asia–Pacific region; second, utilising Japan's economic power, technology and financial capacity in order to modernise China; third, impeding any development by which Japan could again become a military threat to China – by maintaining military superiority over Japan. What are the instruments or tactics by which China tries to achieve these goals?

THE SOVIET FACTOR

The basic factor which has determined China's foreign policy over the last twelve years is the rivalry with the Soviet Union. Although we notice at present a certain relaxation, rivalry will probably remain the substance of the Sino–Soviet relationship for the foreseeable future. In Beijing the Soviet Union is perceived as an expansionist (or hegemonist) power which tried to fill the vacuum left behind by an indecisive America after its defeat in Indochina. Since 1968–69 the Chinese leaders have regarded the Soviet Union as the main threat to their country and to the world as a whole. In spite of recent strains on Sino–American relations, the US is still regarded as a somewhat more defensive power, whereas the Soviet Union is considered to be more offensive.

China has successfully tried to institutionalise its improved relations with Japan by concluding in 1978 a Treaty of Peace and Friendship, the core of which is an anti-hegemony clause. This clause rejects attempts at hegemony by any third country or group of countries. It is directed first of all, but not exclusively, against the Soviet Union.

When Deng Xiaoping visited Japan in 1978, only two months after the treaty was signed, he frankly admitted the basically anti-Soviet character of China's foreign policy, and tried to involve Japan in this policy by describing the treaty as the cornerstone of a Sino–Japanese alliance. The Japanese leaders, however, denied that the treaty is directed against the Soviet Union or any other country and interpreted it as a purely bilateral instrument. However, since then there are signs that the exclusively anti-Soviet character of China's foreign policy is being replaced by a more balanced policy towards both super powers.

The 1978 treaty intensified Sino–Japanese relations at all levels and in all fields. With the development of close relations with Japan as well as with the US and improved relations with most of the ASEAN countries, China has contributed to détente in the Asia–Pacific region. The Soviet Union rejected this version of détente since it worked against Soviet interests in the Asia–Pacific region. The détente in East Asia can be regarded as part of China's strategy of containing Soviet influence in the region. This development has enhanced China's security as Beijing has won strong new partners for a co-operation of strategic importance. Thus China achieved its first foreign policy goal at very low costs. Its cautious improvement of the relations with the Soviet Union since autumn 1982 can also be seen as a means of diminishing the Soviet threat. China tends to buy its security with diplomatic currency.

There still remain some military threats that are not so easily reduced in importance. Perhaps the most volatile issue is the unresolved Korean problem.[1] It is clear that both China and the Soviet Union have mixed feelings about the necessity for Korean reunification, in large part because Japan would see such a change as a threat. The uncertainties in the Korean balance, especially with the approach of the succession to Kim Il Sung, must raise the possibility that the Korean problem will once again return to plague Sino–Japanese relations. The essentially divergent interests in Beijing and Tokyo as to the type of regime they wish to see in Korea, is only partially masked by the present common desire for stability. But stability built on such marshy ground has a way of collapsing, and thus serious Sino–Japanese Military conflict cannot be ruled out.

JAPAN AND CHINA'S ECONOMY

The second Chinese goal is that of utilising Japan's economic potential and financial capacity. Although all non-socialist partners, the US, Western Europe as well as Japan, are economically highly attractive to China, only Sino–Japanese link developed into a special relationship. There are three reasons for this on the Japanese side. First, cultural solidarity arising out of centuries-old contacts; second, a bad conscience on the part of the political elite in Tokyo because of what Japan has done to China during the second half of the nineteenth and the first half of the twentieth centuries; Third, expectations among business circles that China in the long run will become an important market.

Opinion polls in recent years reflect the extremely positive attitude of the Japanese public towards China. The recent poll of June 1982 has shown the following results: asked with which Asian country Japan should maintain close and friendly (*Shitashii*) relations, 76 per cent of the people named China; China ranks first among ten favoured Asian countries; 73 per cent of those questioned feel an intimate closeness to China, and 89 per cent hold the opinion that the relationship with China is of great importance to Japan.[2]

The leaders in Beijung are probably well aware of this favourable climate; they skillfully helped to create and nourish it, and they make good use of it. China is interested in close relations with Japan mainly because of economic interests. It prefers Japan to the US as a close partner because of two political reasons. First, Japan, although highly developed and industrialised, is strategically too vulnerable to make China dependent; Secondly, politically Japan is rather docile. There is no influential Taiwan lobby in Japan, as in the United States, which could make relations difficult.

Sino-Japanese trade has always had a certain strategic importance. When in the early 1970s the Soviet Union tried to engage Japan in the exploitation of oil in the West Siberian oil field of Tjumen, China offered its own crude oil to Japan. The rivalry was obvious. The Soviet Union asked Japan to grant loans worth $3bn which, after 20 years, should be paid back with crude oil. China, however, offered its oil for cash without demanding financial aid. According to the Chinese proposal Japan would get the same quantity of oil as offered by the Soviets.

The Chinese offer was strategically motivated. China reacted with sensitivity to all projects which would help the Soviets to develop Siberia, and it hinted to the Japanese that it would not like to see Japan engaged in projects connected with the transportation of oil or with the infrastructure of Siberia.[3] In 1974 Japan stopped the discussion of the Tjumen project with the Soviet Union mainly because of the technological and financial risks connected with the project. China, too, might have had some influence on this decision.

Eventually China proved unable to deliver the quantity of oil promised in 1973.[4] A decade later Japan did not get all the Chinese oil it wanted. Nevertheless China's original offer and its displeasure over Japanese participation in certain Siberian projects, had its effect.

Trade between China and Japan increased sharply after the signing of a long-term trade agreement for 1978 to 1985. Until 1977 the volumes of Sino-Japanese and Soviet-Japanese was almost equal (about 3.4bn), but thereafter Sino-Japanese trade grew rapidly; in 1981 it reached $10.3bn whereas Soviet-Japanese trade stagnated around $5.2bn. At present 25 per cent of China's foreign trade is with Japan and, surprisingly, China managed to reach a trade surplus of $1.84bn in its favour in 1982.[5]

A few years ago, however, there were some serious setbacks that created a sober atmosphere on the Japanese side. In 1979 China suddenly decided to slow down the import of industrial plants. Because of this decision 20 to 30 contracts with Japanese companies, totalling a value of $2.1bn to $2.8bn, were under threat. Japan's business circles were shocked. According to official Japanese announcements, however, not a single contract has been violated.

A more serious problem was caused at the end of 1980 by China's second decision, to readjust its programme of modernisation. First China informed Japan that the agreement to increase the delivery of crude oil could not be kept. After that Beijing suddenly informed Japanese companies that most of the contracts for the delivery of plants had to be cancelled. The deals suspended by this decision were worth $1.5bn. In some cases more than 50 per cent of the orders had been already delivered.

Japan was disappointed, to say the least. The very Japanese newspapers on economic affairs which for years had spread optimism about business with China suddenly changed to a more critical tune: 'This Chinese behaviour makes us doubt the country's preparedness to develop relations of peaceful coexistence and mutual dependency with other countries in the international community.'[6]

Shortage of funds might have forced Beijing to take this decision. The strong Japanese reaction, however, had caused the Chinese government to reassess the original decision and to take delivery of equipment already ordered for two projects: the first phase of the Baoshan steel mill and chemical plant facilities in Daqing.

In order to finance these projects China asked Japan for capital assistance of 200bn Yen ($870 Mio) in cheap loans – and got them.[7] These events reduced confidence in a stable development of China's economy and strained the Sino–Japanese relationship, at least temporarily. But Japan neither will, nor can, give up its special relationship, which has already included a certain irrationality. In spite of two readjustments, with their negative impact on the climate of Sino–Japanese economic co-operation, Japan is still prepared to grant extensive loans to China. Between 1979 and 1982 the amount of loans granted reached 366bn Yen, ($1.52bn). In February 1983 China asked Japan for additional loans worth about $6bn in order to finance 12 industrial projects. The decision Tokyo has to make is not an easy one, since Premier Nakasone had already decided to aid South Korea with credits worth $4bn.

In view of the intensive economic relations between China and

Japan, and in comparison with other Chinese partners, Japan has become the most important external element in China's ambitious modernisation programme. China obviously has decided to rely on Japan for this purpose.[8] Whether these Chinese policy assumptions will ever become reality remains to be seen. There are some pessimistic voices in Japan concerning the further development of Sino–Japanese economic relations. They argue that, at least until 1985, China will be unable to increase the export of the two main commodities, crude oil and coal, because of the underdeveloped state of China's infrastructure and its slow progress in prospecting and exploiting new sources. Oil from the Gulf of Bohai will not be able available before the 1990s, and it is still unknown how much can be expected from these finds.[9] And, of course, there was a decline in bilateral trade in 1982 of about 14 per cent compared with 1981. Japanese exports to China went down by 31.2 per cent, whereas the imports from China increased by 1.1 per cent. Nevertheless, in Japan an atmosphere of optimism has replaced the more sober evaluation of the prospects of Sino–Japanese economic relations.[10]

The optimists maintain that the general conditions are very favourable for a positive development of bilateral trade. They point to the net of official treaties between China and Japan on trade, fishery, air and sea transport, to the long-term private trade agreement for 1978–1990 and to the official economic aid to China which reached 65bn Yen ($270 Mio) in the fiscal year 1982. Further, there are semiofficial and private financial sources which actively support the companies engaged in trade with China, and there is a highly efficient commercial policy of Japanese companies and trade houses in planning, carrying out and financing of projects with China.[11]

A growing intensity of Sino–Japanese economic relations could influence China's foreign policy, especially its relations with the Soviet Union. If China continues to concentrate on modernising its economy then it needs Japan for this enormous task. Therefore China is likely to avoid major foreign policy movement that would antagonise Japan.

JAPAN, THE SOVIET UNION AND THE PLA

Therefore Japanese leaders are eagerly watching how the new prospects for Sino–Soviet détente will develop. To Japan, with its strained relations with the Soviet Union, any kind of a Sino–Soviet alliance would have an unfavourable impact on its foreign policy. Even a modest return to Sino–Soviet friendship would be perceived in Japan as a serious threat to the country's security; and might lead to a substantial military build-up. It might also shake the present close relations between Japan and China and could reduce Japan's willingness to assist China with its modernisation. Further, it could force Japan to compromise with Moscow on the territorial issue.

It is doubtful whether the Chinese leaders want to push things in this direction; therefore one could expect that they will carefully confine the improvement of their relations with the Soviet Union to a degree which does not create problems for Japan. The importance Japan has for China's modernisation serves as an additional element which limits the degree of a Sino–Soviet rapprochement.

A field of rather cautious Sino–Japanese co-operation is military security. Although China holds the view that both countries 'share closely related security interests',[12] Tokyo has several times openly rejected any military co-operation with China. China's interest in the exchange of views with Japan on security matters first became obvious when Professor Hisao Iwashima, a member of the research staff of the National Defence College in Tokyo, was invited to China in April 1977. Before he left Japan the Chinese, through their Embassy in Tokyo, let him know the subjects they wished to discuss. According to Iwashima they concentrated on the Japanese appraisal of Soviet intentions in the Far East and on questions concerning the strength of Soviet forces.

Soon after Iwashima's visit a five-member mission of the Research Institute of International Oceanic Problems, comprising active and retired members of the Maritime Self-Defence Force as well as retired members of the old Imperial Japanese Navy, went to China. It was followed in June 1977 by Hideo Miyoshi, the former Chief of Staff of the Ground Self-Defence Force. He was received by Vice Chief-of-Staff Wu Xiuquan and visited various army installations at Luda, Shenyang and Nanjing.[13] The list of military contacts with Japan in 1978, 1979 and 1980 comprises annual visits to China by three groups of Japanese military personnel, including retired generals. In 1981 a team of Japanese military physicians of the three forces went on an inspection tour to China.[14]

The Defence Agency itself, however, was rather reluctant to establish contacts with China's Ministry of Defence. Only in January 1982 did Counsellor Nishihiro of the Defence Agency visit China. This was the first time that a Japanese official who is directly involved in defence planning visited China.

The review of training and exercises of the PLA was announced by the Japanese as the official reasons for Nishihiro's visit. However, in Beijing he met with Vice Chief-of-Staff Wu Xiuquan. Their talks centred on Soviet military strength and the general military posture in the Far East. Wu spoke to his Japanese guest about the global Soviet threat and encouraged Japan to strengthen its defence capability. Wu repeated the Chinese view that the Soviet interest is directed first to Europe and secondly to Asia – but that any country, including Japan, should strengthen its defence forces.[15]

Soon after Nishihiro's visit to China the new Chinese ambassador to Japan, Song Zhiguang, said he believed that Japan and China should increase contacts and interchange in the military field, indicating Beijing's strong wishes to promote security between the two neighbouring countries. He pointed out that there had been exchanges of visits between top ranking military officers of China and Western countries, but there has been little between Japan and China.[16]

Japan, however, showed a cautious attitude in carrying out military contacts with China. In particular the Gaimushō, the Ministry of Foreign Affairs, tried to avoid decisions that could further antagonise the Soviet Union. From the very beginning of Sino–Japanese contacts involving personnel from defence related institutions the Soviet media reacted with fierce criticism.[17] The Soviet Union seemed alarmed about the possibility of a Sino–Japanese military alliance which would augment the already existing alliance between Japan and the United States.

When the Defence Agency in Tokyo decided to send Nishihiro to China in spite of the Foreign Ministry's reluctance it did so because the Agency was interested in an analysis of the general military situation in East Asia, especially concerning the build-up of Soviet forces. Further, it wished to exchange views with the Chinese on the deployment and targeting of Soviet SS-20s in order to complete its own information from US sources and to obtain the Chinese analysis of the matter.[18]

Being well aware of Soviet sensitivity China underlined the anti-Soviet character of the Treaty of Peace and Friendship with Japan when it arranged the visit to Tokyo of a military delegation under Deputy Chief-of-the-General Staff Zhang Caiqian soon after the treaty was concluded, in September 1978. The Gaimusho tried to play down the visit, telling the public that the Chinese delegation was only making a prolonged stop-over on its way to Mexico. But all the desperate moves to blur the purpose of the visit made things even worse.[19]

China further deepened the impression that the signing of the treaty had opened a new phase of Sino–Japanese military co-operation. In September 1978 it invited three military technicians to visit China: the former Generals Mitsunari Okawara and Kanji Tanaka and the technical expert Tomoichiro Ozawa. All three are technicians in various fields of tank development.[20] The Defence Agency declared that it had nothing to do with this invitation.[21]

The whole picture of Sino–Japanese military contacts is somewhat contradictory. On the one hand there is a strong Chinese interest in this kind of contact and there are repeated public statements by high-ranking Chinese politicians and diplomats aimed at encouraging Japan to do more for its defence. On the other hand there are official Japanese statements rejecting any military do-operation with China. Premier Ohira clearly excluded co-operation with China in the military area.[22] The former Premier Takeo Fukuda called a security relationship with China 'unthinkable'[23] and Yasuhiro Nakasone, when he visited China in April 1980, told Wu Xiuquan that Japan will co-operate with China on any field excluding the military area.[24] His position has not changed since he became Prime Minister in November 1982.

At the same time there are Sino–Japanese private-level contacts with military technicians affiliated with companies that produce military-related equipment. The Chinese invitation to Okawara, Tanaka and Ozawa, mentioned above, belongs to this category. Further, Japan's strong interest in trading with China consequently involves strategic goods like computers.[25] Since President Reagan decided in May 1983 to liberalise restrictions on exports of sophisticated technology to China by placing China in the category of friendly or allied countries under the US Export Administration Act, the flow of strategically important goods and technology is also likely to increase from Japan to China.

Analysing all this, one comes to the conclusion that a Sino–Japanese military co-operation in the true sense of the word does not exist. For some time China tried to create the impression of such a co-operation in order to strain the Soviet–Japanese relations and pull Japan closer to the Chinese side. These attempts coincide with China's policy of establishing a United Front against 'Soviet hegemonism' between 1977 and 1981. They become less intensive and finally disappeared when China abolished the United Front policy and decided to improve its relations with Moscow.

There remain, of course, the established political contacts between both neighbours, which include an exchange of views and information on Soviet military activities. It is in this context that Liberal Democratic Party (LDP) Secretary General Susumu Nikaido visited China in February 1983 in order to inform the Chinese government about Premier Nakasone's visit to the United States and to discuss the problems connected with a redeployment of SS-20s. Both sides agreed to co-operate in stopping it, but it is not yet clear what this means in concrete terms.

When China's foreign policy was exclusively anti–Soviet, it was regarded as appropriate to stress the necessity of a stronger Japanese Self-Defence Force. With the slight changes in the Sino–Soviet relations, Beijing has somewhat modified its stated position on this matter. For years China has encouraged Japan to spend more for its defence, and it supported the American–Japanese Security Treaty in order to contain Soviet military expansion in the Asia–Pacific region. Since the second half of 1982, China seems less positive about such spending. At the same time the number of groups of Japanese military personnel travelling to China has decreased drastically.

Concerning the strengthening of the Japanese Self-Defence Forces, China now holds the view that 'Japan is entitled to maintain an armed force for defence against external threats. But such an armed force should be defence-oriented and of appropriate size, so it would not constitute a threat to its friendly neighbours'.[26] From this statement one could conclude that the leaders in Beijing do not want a militarily strong Japan armed with offensive weapons. The Japan–US security treaty is neither criticised nor supported any more; it is simply accepted.

There might be several reasons for these modifications. First, China does not want anymore to antagonise the Soviet Union unnecessarily. Second, it wants to improve further its relations with North Korea, which continues to criticise any military build-up in Japan as well as the Japan–US military alliance. Third, China recognised that other Asian countries, also, do not want to see Japan as a new military power in the region. Finally, China has a historical experience of Japanese imperialism. Therefore it does not want Japan to have the power to become a military threat to Asia. Maintaining military superiority is one of the goals of China's policy *vis-à-vis* Japan. China has so far achieved this, and the leaders in Beijing can be confident that Japan will not be a threat to their country for some time to come.

CONCLUSIONS

The minor levels of Sino-Japanese military contracts seem mainly politically motivated. They were elements of Chinese excessively anti-Soviet foreign policy and therefore they have largely disappeared with the modification of that policy.

Nevertheless the strategic value of Sino-Japanese relations lies in the intensive economic co-operation and in the steadily growing network of all kinds of non-military relations. The possible result of these relations and their impact on the region are a matter for speculation. Judging from the present situation, the special relationship between China and Japan is based on close cultural and historical ties and is characterised by elements of mutual dependence. China needs Japan in order to modernise the country's economy, infrastructure and management. Japan needs friendly relations with China since – in spite of its economic backwardness – it is an influential regional power with increasing international weight. Some day China could have the potential and the position to control the important sea lanes running through the South China Sea and the Taiwan Strait to Japan. It could have the potential to realise its claim to the Tiaoyütai island (or Senkaku) which Tokyo regards as Japanese territory. Further, in any solution of the Korean problem which has an impact on Japan's security China will have a definite say.

Thus, the growing Sino-Japanese relationship is regarded in China as a positive phenomenon. Japan, China's main and most important economic partner, could slowly but effectively help to change China's economic system. This economic link provides the most important grounds why Sino-Japanese relations retain strategic importance.

NOTES AND REFERENCES

1. Gerald Segal 'The Soviet Union and Korea' in Gerald Segal (ed.), *The Soviet Union and East Asia* (London: Heinemann, 1983).
2. cf. Seron-chōsa, Tokyo 1982/12, 17–18
3. cf. Joachim Glaubitz: *Die Politik der UdSSR gegenüber Japan 1974/75.* (Berichte des Bundesinstituts für ostwissenschaftliche und internationale Studien, No. 43/1975, Köln 1975), 23 ff.
4. cf. John P. Putheveetil: 'Strategic options behind Sino-Japanese Trade Relations', *International Studies* (New Delhi) vol. 18, no. 4, October–December 1979, 537 ff.
5. cf. *Neue Zürcher Zeitung*, 8 June 1983.
6. *Nihon Keizai Shimbun*, 2 February 1981.

7. *Asian Security* 1982, 85–87
8. *Beijing Review*, no. 16, 18 April 1983, 16
9. cf. Hisao Maeda: Atama-uchi-no Nitchu-keizai-kankei [Japanese–Chinese Economic Relations at their limits], *Sekai Shuho*, 19 October 1982, 4–5
10. cf. *Neue Zürcher Zeitung*, 8 June 1983.
11. *Neue Zürcher Zeitung loc. cit.*
12. *Beijing Review*, no. 16, 18 April 1983, 16
13. *Japan Economic Journal*, 28 June 1977
14. cf. Asian Security 1981, 100; for more details cf. William T. Tow, 'Sino–Japanese Security Co-operation: Evolution and Prospects'. *Pacific Affairs*, vol. 56, no. 1 Spring 1983, 51ff.
15. *Asahi Shimbun* 6 and 14 January 1982, 1 and 2 resp.
16. *Asahi Evening News* 15 February 1981.
17. cf. *Izvestija* 19 May 1977, 3; *Pravda* 11 June 1977, 5; *Izvestija* 9 September 1978.
18. *Asahi Shimbun*, 6 January 1982, 1
19. cf. *Neue Zürcher Zeitung* 10 September 1978, 3
20. For further details cf. *The International Herald Tribune*, 27 September 1978, 2
21. *The International Herald Tribune loc. cit.*
22. *Asian Security*, 1980, 86
23. *The International Herald Tribune*, 3 November 1981, 2
24. cf. Tadao Kusumi: 'Chugoku to Nichibei to no gunji-kyoryoku-no jittai' [The real situation of the military co-operation between China on the one side and the US and Japan on the other], *Sekai Shuho*, 8 July 1980, 27–29
25. *Asahi Evening News*, 24 May 1982; for further details cf. William T. Tow *op. cit.* (note 14).
26. Wu Xueqian, Minister of Foreign Affairs, to LDP Secretary General Susumu Nikaido. *BBC Summary of World Broadcasts*, FE 7263, 21 February 1983 A3/6–8.

16 Southeast Asia

LARRY A. NIKSCH*

The People's Republic of China has been an active player in the affairs of Southeast Asia since the communists took power in 1949. After unifying China (except for Taiwan), the communist government in Beijing perceived a combination of interests and objectives toward its neighbours to the south. Some were traditional, founded on historical and geographical circumstances. Others were based on communist revolutionary ideology. Finally, certain perceptions stemmed from the involvement of other major powers in Southeast Asia.

Chinese policies since 1949 have reflected multifaceted interests. The emphasis has ebbed and flowed according to conditions inside Southeast Asia and, at certain points, internal political changes in China itself. Nevertheless, the existence of certain interests have remained constant. Most broadly, China views the region as a distinct sphere of Chinese influence. It thus has opposed attempts by other big powers to establish a preponderant presence, particularly if such a presence appears as a threat to China itself. Beijing's projection of its influence has had several aspects: (1) the promotion of revolutionary ideology through support for communist insurgent movements; (2) the assertion of special links with the millions of ethnic Chinese living in Southeast Asian countries; (3) the maintenance of extensive territorial claims, especially in the South China Sea basin; and (4) emphasis on support for Southeast Asian governments that follow policies conducive to Chinese interests.

CHINESE THREAT PERCEPTIONS

China's perceptions of threats to these interests have focussed on the involvement of other great powers in Southeast Asia, but the recent

---

*The views expressed in this article are those of the author and do not necessarily reflect those of the Congressional Research Service of the Library of Congress.

Sino–Vietnamese conflict indicated that Beijing also is wary of the emergence of a regional power that might establish a dominant position. Moreover, during periods when Chinese governments stressed revolutionary ideology, China has looked at all non-communist governments as opponents.

During the 1950s and 1960s, Beijing vigorously opposed the American role in Southeast Asia, especially the system of alliances created by the United States. China correspondingly adopted an attitude of hostility and disdain toward US allies and pro-Western countries in the region. The period of the Cultural Revolution in the late 1960s saw Chinese criticism spread even to neutral states like Burma and Cambodia.

The development of the Sino–Soviet split led to a fundamental change in China's view. The 1968 Soviet invasion of Czechoslovakia and Moscow's formulation of the Brezhnev Doctrine demonstrated to the Chinese government that the USSR might resort to military force against China. Sino–Soviet border clashes in 1969 brought this view closer to home. At the same time, Brezhnev proposed an Asian Collective security system, which China interpreted as a plan for Soviet domination of Asia through Soviet-sponsored alliances. Inside Southeast Asia, China became apprehensive over the growing Soviet involvement in North Vietnam, as Moscow poured in large amounts of heavy weaponry to support Hanoi's intensified campaign to conquer South Vietnam. The specter of Soviet-inspired isolation and encirclement increasingly came to the fore in Chinese perceptions.

Opposition to Soviet policy has dominated the Chinese approach toward Southeast Asia since the end of the Vietnam War. In the period immediately after the war, Chinese statements warned Southeast Asian governments not to allow the Soviets to fill the vacuum left by the apparent exodus of the United States. China proposed to Vietnam that they sign an anti-hegemony clause, which had become the standard PRC statement of anti-Soviet principles in foreign policy. Chinese opposition intensified as the Soviets expanded their presence in Indochina with aid, advisers, and access to military facilities in Vietnam.

China has viewed its rivalry with the Soviet Union in Southeast Asia as a zero-sum game in which it sees a gain for Soviet influence as a loss for China and vice versa. The Soviet presence in Indochina seals off an area of traditional Chinese influence, where Beijing expected to exercise a strong role in the post-Vietnam War period. The Soviet military presence, particularly the permanent naval task force in the South China Sea, could be used against China militarily. Soviet naval forces also pose a potential threat to a realisation of China's territorial claims in the South China Sea. This factor could grow in importance if governments with competing claims, including Vietnam, accelerate the exploration for oil in these waters or build up military forces.

China professes that the Soviet presence in Southeast Asia is part of a larger strategy aimed at establishing Soviet domination of the arc of states extending from Southeast Asia to the Arabian peninsula. PRC analysts have asserted that Moscow's ultimate objective is to control the Southeast Asian straits connecting the Pacific and Indian Oceans, thus isolating the Indian Ocean at its eastern end and controlling the sea lanes from the Persian Gulf to the Western Pacific. This, coupled with penetration of the Persian Gulf region, would be a significant step toward Soviet world domination, according to the Chinese. They further argue that the Soviet invasion of Afghanistan and support for Vietnam's invasion of Kampuchea are components of this grand strategy.[1]

Chinese officials accuse Vietnam of becoming a tool of Soviet strategy in order to realise its own aim of 'regional hegemony'. Beijing's statements indicate a view of Vietnam as a small power, thus reflecting Chinese bitterness over Hanoi's rejection of the big brother-little brother relationship apparently envisaged by China at the end of the Vietnam War. However, China realises that Vietnam challenges key PRC interests. It has ousted the pro-China Khmer Rouge regime in Cambodia, contests Beijing's territorial claims in the South China Sea, and has tried to turn Thai communist insurgents away from China.

POLICIES AND STRATEGY

PRC policies and strategy in Southeast Asia focuses on Vietnam and on the issue of Cambodia. It is very much associated with Vice Premier Deng Xiaoping, whose assumption of authority in 1977 and 1978 coincided with escalated criticism of Vietnam and the USSR. In response to Vietnam's invasion of Cambodia, Beijing has adopted a long-term strategy designed to bring heavy international political and economic pressure on Vietnam; construct a network of deterrence against future Vietnamese aggressions, especially against Thailand, and provide military support for Khmer resistance forces fighting the Vietnamese. Beijing believes that, over a period of several years, this sustained pressure will weaken Vietnam politically and economically, roll back the Vietnamese from Cambodia, and force them to abandon their alliance with the Soviet Union. China has carried this 'bleeding' strategy to the point of calling for the overthrow of the 'Le Duan clique' in Hanoi.[2]

Beijing sees the Association of Southeast Asian Nations (ASEAN), Japan, and the United States as key elements of the international front against Vietnam and its Soviet patron. ASEAN is crucial to mobilising opposition to Vietnam in international fora and in the non-aligned movement and also in extending support to the Khmer resistance forces. ASEAN's adherence to the anti-Hanoi bloc also prevents Vietnam from negotiating a settlement that would recognise its domination of Cambodia. Japan's embargo of aid to Vietnam denies it a key source of Western aid and technology and reinforces the international economic boycott of Hanoi.

The United States plays a multifaceted role in Chinese perceptions. It is vital to the continued international isolation of Vietnam. The United States could provide important aid to the Khmer resistance, a course proposed to Washington by PRC officials. Most importantly, US military power in Southeast Asia balances the Soviet military presence in the South China Sea and near the straits, bolsters the ASEAN states, and helps to deter Vietnam. Thus, despite disputes with Washington over Taiwan and other issues, China has supported continued American access to bases in the Philippines, US steps to upgrade Seventh Fleet capabilities, and increased US security support for Thailand.[3]

The American military presence also reinforces China's military option against Vietnam. This was graphically shown by the timing of China's attack on Vietnam in February–March 1979 immediately after Deng Xiaoping's successful visit to the United States. Deng constantly hinted during the visit that China would take military action against Vietnam. His hints suggested an aim to test the US reaction and portray to the world that Washington backed Chinese policies.

USES OF MILITARY POWER

China has extended its political and diplomatic strategy against the Soviet Union and Vietnam into the use of military instruments. Beijing has employed three kinds of military instruments: (1) the use of military force against Vietnam along the Sino–Vietnamese border and the maintenance of sizeable forces along that border; (2) the extension of arms aid to the Khmer Rouge and other anti-Vietnamese resistance groups in Indochina, and (3) the conduct of military activities in the South China Sea.

The use of military instruments supports Chinese policy objectives in several ways in relation to Vietnam and the USSR. It compels Vietnam to deploy its army on three fronts – in Cambodia, along the Sino–Vietnamese border, and in northern Laos near the Lao–China frontier. Vietnam, moreover, must devote considerable resources to the military, thus adding a factor weakening Hanoi's economy. The Chinese military threat also contributes to a deterrent against a Vietnamese attack into Thailand, giving teeth to Beijing's often spoken pledge of military support to Thailand.

Chinese leaders also view military pressure on Vietnam as ultimately straining Soviet–Vietnamese ties. Vietnam is forced into accepting an ever-growing Soviet military presence on its soil in exchange for Russian arms. The Chinese believe that if Vietnam cannot ultimately attain its goal of domination over Cambodia, Hanoi will find the cost of its alliance with Moscow too high. In short, military pressure is an integral part of the bleeding strategy.

Beijing undoubtedly believes that military instruments also serve broader interests. They remind all of the other parties to the Cambodia issue that China must play a prime role. They help to keep a measure of PRC influence in Indochina, particularly by bolstering the Khmer Rouge.

Military pressure on Vietnam's border

China's attack into northern Vietnam in February and March 1979 initiated a strategy of direct military pressure on Vietnam. China began to plan military action against Vietnam as early as October 1978.[4] Preparations accelerated after Vietnam invaded Cambodia and captured Phnom Penh on 7 January 1979. The PRC's 'self-defence counterattack' began on 17 February 1979. China committed about 20 front-line divisions to the operation and attacked into Vietnam with some 80 000–85 000 men. Total Chinese forces involved ultimately were about 300 000. China did not commit its air force against Vietnam's arsenal of modern Soviet-supplied aircraft, SAMs, and anti-aircraft guns.

Several points can be made about the fighting. The Chinese outnumbered the 75 000–100 000 Vietnamese troops and militia that defended the border. Vietnamese main force units were not involved to an appreciable extent, as Vietnam kept five to seven front-line divisions in the Hanoi–Haiphong area. Nevertheless, China acknowledged that 20 000 of its troops were killed in the one month operation.[5] Chinese forces relied primarily on non-motorised light infantry and human wave attacks. They employed artillery against primary objectives like the provincial capital of Lang Son. Tanks were of limited use in the hilly terrain. Vietnamese weaponry was superior to Chinese arms, reflecting the supply of modern Soviet arms to Hanoi's forces.

China's military aims were limited geographically – a central factor in Chinese successes. The furthest Chinese advance was about 50 kilometres, the outer limit of coverage by its air defence missiles. The Chinese captured five provincial capitals within this zone and began to withdraw its forces after 5 March.[6]

China attained its geographical goals, but it did not inflict the punishing defeat on the Vietnamese it apparently had hoped to do. The attack did not relieve the pressure on the Khmer Rouge, as Vietnam did not withdraw forces from Cambodia, and it did not cause Hanoi to reconsider its occupation of Cambodia. Militarily, PRC leaders including Deng Xiaoping admitted that Chinese forces had displayed serious deficiencies in the operation.[7]

Since the end of the fighting, China has maintained about 250 000 troops near the Vietnamese border to back its warnings of a 'second lesson' if Vietnam expands its aggression to Thailand. The PRC's aim of tying down Vietnamese troops apparently has worked, but Vietnam has built much more formidable defences along the border while deploying up to 200 000 troops in Cambodia. Over 500 000 troops are now stationed in the northern region. They are well-armed with Soviet weaponry and reportedly have constructed extensive fortifications. Vietnamese military leaders confidently state that their preparations would require China to use 50 to 60 divisions in any future attack.[8] Western military analysts reportedly agree. Several have been quoted that China would have to commit at least two million men in a future attack on Vietnam.[9]

Arms Supply to Indochinese Resistance Groups

China had been the sole supplier of arms to anti-Vietnamese resistance groups until late 1982, when Singapore reportedly began shipping weapons to the Khmer People's National Liberation Front (KPNLF). In Cambodia, the bulk of PRC arms has gone to the communist Khmer Rouge force of 20 000–30 000 men, and it has proven essential to the

Khmer Rouge's ability to wage guerrilla warfare against the Vietnamese. The volume of weapons reportedly has increased steadily since 1979. Major items have included man-portable artillery, grenade launchers, mortars, assault rifles, and land mines[10] – in short, proper light infantry weapons for small-unit guerrilla operations. Beijing has also supplied limited amounts of arms to the KPNLF but not enough to arm the group's 9000 fighters. The prospects for expanded KPNLF military strength appear to depend on future access to weapons from other sources.

China reportedly ships the arms through Thailand with covert co-operation from Thai military officials. The arms arrive by sea and are transported to camps on the Cambodia border, where the Khmer Rouge take possession.[11] Peking also has initiated since 1979 military aid to insurgent groups in Laos opposing the pro-Hanoi Lao government and approximately 50 000 Vietnamese troops in that country. The Khmer Rouge, with reported Chinese consent, have provided weapons and ammunition to insurgent elements in the southern part of the Lao panhandle adjacent to Cambodia. China reportedly has established a camp in southern China to train a resistance force. Most reports state that the camp has turned out no more than 2000 guerrillas (Lao resistance sources claim 5000) who conduct raids and intelligence operations in northern Laos.[12] China has also provided sanctuary and assistance in organisation for Lao officials who defected and now oppose the Lao government and its Vietnam connection.

The South China Sea

Chinese military activity in the South China Sea has increased since the Sino-Vietnamese conflict of 1979. The PRC now carries out regular air patrols in the vicinity of the Paracel islands, which Chinese forces seized from South Vietnam in 1974 and which communist Vietnam currently claims. China has reinforced its southern fleet, and naval deployments in the South China Sea have grown in number and in geographical extent. PRC forces have built up their strength on Hainan island, including the installation of missile sites and air bases.

China has several purposes in these actions. The build-up reinforces PRC territorial claims in the South China Sea. These extend 1200 miles south of the Chinese mainland, including the Paracel and Spratley islands, and skirting the coast of Vietnam, the Philippines, Brunei, and Malaysia. The build-up also has a defensive aspect, growing out of Chinese concern over the security of the Paracels in the face of

Vietnamese claims and the permanent Soviet deployment of some 25 naval vessels in the South China Sea.

It also is connected with China's apparent decision to challenge Vietnam's overlapping claims to the waters of the Tonkin Gulf. Here, oil is the key. Multinational oil companies consider the Gulf a potentially fertile ground for oil exploration. China has granted a number of concession zones to American oil companies. Several of these zones include Vietnamese-claimed waters. In July 1979 China declared three zones, comprising several hundred miles south and east of Hainan island, as danger zones. Chinese naval manoeuvres have since intensified in these areas.[13] PRC propaganda organs have asserted that patrolling oil exploration and drilling areas is a task of growing importance to the Chinese navy.

Chinese and Vietnamese naval vessels fought a brief engagement in the Tonkin Gulf on 3 March 1982, and China claimed on the following day the capture of a Vietnamese reconnaissance vessel near the Paracels.[14] These were the worst incidents in the South China Sea since China's seizure of the Paracels in 1974. The Hanoi government has highlighted the importance of the issue by linking its willingness to withdraw from Cambodia with a PRC withdrawal from the Paracels.

RELATIONS WITH ASEAN

As stated previously, China places priority on ASEAN as part of its anti-Soviet and anti-Vietnam strategies. Nevertheless, Chinese relations with ASEAN governments have been unsteady owing to ASEAN suspicions of ultimate Chinese goals in Indochina and throughout Southeast Asia.

ASEAN and China share parallel objectives toward Vietnam and Indochina, but there are also differences. Both want the Vietnamese to withdraw from Cambodia and reduce or end its military ties with the Soviet Union, but unlike China, ASEAN wants a neutral and preferably non-communist Cambodia that limits Vietnamese and Chinese influence and acts as a buffer for Thailand. Thus, ASEAN has promoted non-communist Khmer factions under Son Sann and Prince Sihanouk. China has sought to enhance the Khmer Rouge politically and militarily, which suggests to many in the ASEAN region that Beijing's long term goal is the restoration of the pro-PRC Khmer Rouge regime. ASEAN and China believe in pressuring Vietnam, but ASEAN has shown greater interest in a negotiated settlement that would allow some political role for the pro-Hanoi Khmer and limit the Khmer Rouge. China has opposed ASEAN proposals for a settlement that would disarm the Khmer factions, establish a 'temporary administration' prior to elections, and hold free elections including participation by the pro-Vietnam Heng Samrin elements. Chinese diplomats have argued that such proposals would violate the legality of the Democratic Kampuchea government and weaken the morale of the Khmer Rouge guerrillas. Beijing knows, however, that any diminution of the Khmer Rouge's political role would result in a loss of Chinese influence in Cambodia.

Thai–Chinese relations are another issue of concern in ASEAN. Thailand values the Chinese promise of assistance should Vietnam attack, and the other ASEAN governments recognise that Chinese military power helps to restrain Vietnam. Other ASEAN governments, however, do not want this situation to result in inordinate PRC influence in Thailand, particularly on the Thai negotiating position on Cambodia.

Behind these differences lies a widespread view in ASEAN that China seeks a dominant influence in Southeast Asia, and that it is willing to interfere in the internal affairs of the states of the region in order to attain it. Many ASEAN government officials believe that Chinese overtures to ASEAN represent the Leninist strategy of temporary alliance with ideological adversaries for short-term gains with longer-term struggle held in abeyance until conditions change.

Certain forms of Chinese involvement in the region feed this suspicion. China has supported for years communist parties and insurgents in the ASEAN countries. Beijing has provided political-ideological backing including radio broadcasts from PRC territory. Thai and Burmese insurgents have received arms, training, and money. Beijing has given sanctuary for several hundred communist leaders from ASEAN states and allows them to engage in propaganda and political work. China also continues to show interest in the ethnic Chinese of Southeast Asia, as it displayed with respect to the Chinese community in Vietnam in 1978. Finally, the PRC's claims of sovereignty over large areas of the South China Sea disturbs ASEAN states bordering that body of water.

Chinese strategy since the mid-1970s has thus emphasised relations with ASEAN governments and a corresponding decline in support for communist insurgencies in ASEAN. Material aid to the Thai insurgents has gone down. Chinese media gives less attention to the activities of local communist parties, and Thai and Malay communist radio broadcasts from China have ceased. Chinese leaders have told ASEAN country officials that the PRC will provide 'moral and political' support to local parties but no material aid. There is some evidence that China has encouraged local parties to negotiate with ASEAN governments.[15] China maintains some links, however. The parties remain an instrument of potential Chinese pressure on ASEAN countries, although the declining strength of Malay and Thai insurgencies and ASEAN economic development reduces this potential.

SIGNS OF CHANGE?

Chinese policy towards Southeast Asia has shown itself to be anything but unchanging. While loudly trumpeting one allegedly rock-solid policy, China has been known to shift ground suddenly and proclaim another, with equal power. Indeed, by 1982 it was clear that some important changes were under way in China's policy. The opening of negotiations between China and the Soviet Union in late 1982 produced important changes for Chinese strategy in Southeast Asia. China has made an end to Soviet support of Vietnam's occupation of Cambodia one of three conditions for better relations with Moscow and has indicated a measure of flexibility toward Vietnam at the same time. China offered, in a proposal of March 1983 (secretly proposed to the Soviets late in 1982), to take 'practical steps' to improve relations with Vietnam if Hanoi agreed to withdraw troops from Cambodia and actually began the withdrawal. In emphasising Cambodia as the key to normalisation of relations with Vietnam, China has shelved its more sweeping demands for wholesale changes in SRV policies. It has also dropped calls for the overthrow of the Vietnamese government.

Similarly, in part in response to ASEAN pressure, China's policy on Cambodia also seems to be changing. China has endorsed ASEAN's goal of negotiations with Vietnam, and it consented to non-communist participation in a coalition government with the Khmer Rouge. Chinese leaders have said that they want Cambodia to be a non-communist, neutral country. Beijing, however, held out for a coalition agreement more favourable to the Khmer Rouge than the ASEAN-endorsed Singapore coalition formula, which would have tilted the political balance toward the non-communists. Nevertheless, Chinese military and political backing of the Khmer Rouge seems as strong as ever.

China's strategy on Vietnam and Cambodia has shifted for several reasons. First, the talks with Moscow and pressure from ASEAN create a greater rationale for more 'reasonableness'. In addition, Lao and Vietnamese resistance groups have proven ineffective, and the Khmer resistance forces have made little headway against Hanoi and its clients. Finally, Beijing may recognise that its own military option against Vietnam is less promising. China still maintains these instruments of pressure, but it may have decided to give diplomacy a higher priority in the immediate future.

Obviously the signs of change, such as they are, do not necessarily mean that a revolutionary change is underway in Southeast Asian politics. Evolutionary change seems more likely. For one thing, the Soviet Union is unlikely to facilitate a breakthrough in Sino–Soviet relations by deserting Vietnam. Moreover, Soviet concessions would not necessarily force Vietnam to abandon its goal of dominating Indochina and gaining the status of pre-eminent regional power. The Sino–Vietnamese conflict has a dimension outside of Southeast Asia as a Soviet sphere of influence. Change is possible, but it would seem to require less paranoiac posturing on the part of both China and Vietnam.

However, such reasonableness is not a common quality in the region. There still remain a few conditions under which China might still resort to direct military force in Southeast Asia. China has promised such action to Thailand and has stated so publicly. Chinese statements of this type are similar to PRC pronouncements before intervening militarily in Korea in 1950 and against India in 1962. China's occupation of the Paracels and its granting of oil drilling rights gives Beijing little option if Vietnam moves militarily in the Gulf.

The effectiveness of a future Chinese military push into northern Vietnam is seriously in doubt, and PRC leaders probably realise this. Vietnamese defences are much more formidable than in 1979, and Hanoi reportedly has completed its defensive preparations. Vietnam's superiority in modern weapons appears to have grown. However, China could be compelled to employ more indirect attacks like raids on Vietnam's northeast coast or an incursion into northern Laos.

In short, China's ability to help Thailand may be limited. The slowness of Chinese mobilisation capabilities could allow the Vietnamese to strike into Thailand, with a force of up to ten divisions, bloody the Thai Army, destroy facilities supporting the Khmer resistance forces, and withdraw before PRC forces could react. Vietnam's northern defences gives it the assets to wage a two-front campaign as long as Soviet aid continues. The danger of such a scenario is increasing as Vietnamese military operations in western Cambodia have intensified since January 1982.

The South China Sea may emerge further as a flashpoint between China and Vietnam, especially if oil is discovered in commercial quantities. China can probably defend its claims and oil operations in the Tonkin Gulf against the Vietnamese unless the Soviet navy intervenes. Vietnam's navy of patrol craft and a few frigates is its weakest combat arm, clearly inferior to China's southern fleet; and China's air power on Hainan island probably can match Vietnam's MIG-21s. Chinese operations against the Vietnamese further south, near the disputed Spratley islands, would be more difficult. The Chinese would have surface naval superiority over Vietnam but would lack air cover; and its shipboard air defences are limited. However, PRC amphibious landing assets reportedly are growing. Thus, the Chinese naval presence south toward the straits will probably grow in the next decade; but these deficiencies, plus Philippine involvement in the Spratleys, would give Beijing pause about any overt use of force.

These prospects are predicated on political stability inside China and the continuation of a relatively pragmatic regime in Beijing. The past has shown that instability within China can produce sharp changes in its foreign policy. Equally, there is every reason to suppose that the future will be no different from the past as regards the flexibility of Chinese foreign policy. Beijing has changed its policy in the past in reaction to its altered perception of superpower threats, and the latest signs of some Sino–Soviet détente may yet be another such shift. These myriad potentials for change therefore make any bets on a static Chinese policy most unwise.

NOTES AND REFERENCES

1. See the analysis in *Remin Ribao*, 19 June 1980; and the article by senior Foreign Ministry official Han Xu in the *Asian Wall Street Journal*, 2 December 1980.
2. For a description of the breakdown of Sino–Vietnamese relations, see: US Congress, Senate, Committee on Foreign Relations, *Vietnam's Future Policies and Role in Southeast Asia*. Report prepared by the Congressional Research Service, Library of Congress. 97th Congress, 2nd session, 1982, 42–52.
3. For a favourable Chinese commentary on US military moves and co-operation with ASEAN, see the commentary in *Xinhua*, 3 December 1982.
4. Daniel Tretiak, 'China's Vietnam War and its Consequences', *China Quarterly*, December 1979, 741.
5. *New York Times*, 3 April 1979.

6. For accounts of the fighting, see: Li Man Kin, *Sino–Vietnamese War* (Hongkong, Kingsway International Publications Ltd, 1981); Harlan W. Jencks, 'China's "Punitive" War on Vietnam: a Military Assessment', *Asian Survey*, August 1979, 801–815; and Colonel J. J. Haggerty, 'The Chinese–Vietnamese Border War of 1979', *Army Quarterly and Defense Journal*, July 1979, 265–272.
7. US Congress, Senate, Committee on Foreign Relations, *The Implications of US–China Military Co-operation*. A Workshop. 97th Congress, 1st session, 1982, 10. Statement of Dr June Teufel Dreyer.
8. *Le Figaro* (Paris), 15 May 1981. Interview with Colonel Tran Cong Man, editor of *Quan Doi Nhan Dan*, the official journal of the Vietnamese Armed Forces.
9. Nayan Chanda, 'Diplomacy at Gunpoint', *Far Eastern Economic Review*, 29 May 1981, 10; *New York Times*, 10 June 1980.
10. *London Sunday Times*, 13 December 1979; Steve Heder, 'Democratic Kampuchea: The Regime's Post–Mortem', *Indochina Issues*, January 1981, 4.
11. *London Sunday Times*, 13 December 1979; *New York Times*, 7 February 1979.
12. Nayan Chanda, 'A Defector's Designs', *Far Eastern Economic Review*, 26 March 1982, 44; John McBeth, 'A Chinese Connection', *Far Eastern Economic Review*, 31 July 1981, 9–10; US Congress, House, Committee on Foreign Affairs, Subcommittee on Asian and Pacific Affairs, *U.S. Policy toward Indochina since Vietnam's Occupation of Kampuchea*. Hearings, 97th Congress, 1st session, 1981, 106–111. Testimony of Joseph Zasloff; *Washington Post*, 24 May 1983.
13. Justus M. Van der Kroef, 'The South China Sea: Competing Claims and Strategic Conflicts', *International Security Review*, Fall 1982, 313–314.
14. *Ibid.*; 'A New Gulf Flashpoint', *Far Eastern Economic Review*, 11 June 1982, 26–28.
15. William R. Heaton, 'China and Southeast Asian Communist Movements: the Decline of Dual Track Diplomacy'. *Asian Survey*, August 1982, 779–800.

17 South Asia

YAACOV VERTZBERGER*

At the time of the communist takeover in 1949, China's South Asian borders were among its lesser concerns. The divided and warring subcontinent posed no viable military threat to Communist power. No major border dispute was perceived to exist at the time. Both India and Pakistan were among the first to recognise the new regime. And the re-establishment of Chinese control over Tibet in October 1950 was achieved without resistance by Delhi. Furthermore, India's positions on the Korean settlement, Indo-China and the future role of China in the UN – especially on the Security Council – revealed the potential benefits to China from a closer relationship with India and its prestigious leader Nehru. India's support was a political asset which could serve as a vehicle for achieving a toe-hold in Afro–Asian forums as was the case with the Bandung conference.

These changes paralleled the Soviet turnabout in its attitude toward India in 1953, which made a closer Sino–Indian relationship a logical and practical step. The new policy carried the immediate fruits of the 1954 agreement between China and India in which India gave up the special rights in Tibet which it had inherited from the British Raj. At the same time the thaw in the Sino–Indian relationship served as a warning to Pakistan, which by 1953 had adopted a pro-Western policy which included joining SEATO and the Baghdad Pact. Pakistan, however, went out of its way to convince China that its membership in these alliances was not directed against Beijing but served its legitimate defence needs against New Delhi.

A reassessment resulted from a number of occurrences: deterioration along the Sino–Indian border; the 1959 rebellion in Tibet; the growing estrangement between China and the Soviet Union over the

---

* I am grateful to Jonathan Cohen for research assistance and to the Harry S. Truman Research Institute of the Hebrew University for support.

question of peaceful co-existence with the West; and Soviet–Western diplomatic, military and economic aid to India before and in particular after the 1962 border war.[1] The abandonment of 'proletarian internationalism' by Moscow led to a situation where India was viewed by China as 'a joint stock company with Kennedy as the big shareholder and the Soviet leaders the small shareholders'.[2]

Thus China's assessment concerning South Asia's role and threat potential has been based, since the early 1960s, not only upon the military balance between it and the local powers but also upon the triangular relationship with the superpowers. Over a period China also upgraded its assessment of the benefits to be gained if it handled its South Asian policy properly. This was closely related to China's growing aspirations to a more active role as global power. The rift with the USSR freed China to express strategic aspirations beyond the Asian sphere. In this transformed context South Asia gained a new importance for China. Its geo-strategic location made it an important link to the Middle East, a major area of superpower rivalry for hegemony in which China's main protagonists were perceived to have high stakes.[3]

In South Asia the only country through which China's aims could be pursued was, by the early 1960s, Pakistan. By 1963–64, with the conclusion of the Sino–Pakistani border, aid and trade agreements, the first step was taken toward what would become, in the next two decades, a Sino–Pakistani entente.

PAKISTAN: THE LINCHPIN OF CHINA'S POLICIES

China's strategic threat assessments and security conceptions move along two inter-related lines of thought. One is its assessment of the direct threat from its most powerful neighbours, the USSR, Japan, India and Vietnam; the other is its fear of isolation and encirclement by the two superpowers through their world-wide advances and networks of allies and bases. These precepts have led to the recognition of the importance to China's strategic interests of South Asia as a whole and also of various individual states. It is in the context of this counter-strategy that Beijing has decided that Pakistan could play a useful role in China's relationship with India, the USSR, the US and the Third World.

India constituted a major obstacle to China's road to the status of the dominant power in Asia. These considerations rose in importance with the deterioration of Sino–Indian relations from the late 1950s, the border war of 1962 and the fast build-up of India's military power that followed. China could make things more difficult for India by forming closer ties with Pakistan, India's arch-enemy, presenting India with the prospect of having to fight a two-front war. Another possible option was to undermine India's political unity by capitalising on potential separatist trends in the Indian federation, especially in north-eastern India. East Pakistan was geo-politically best situated for this purpose.

The penetration of Soviet influence into India also constituted a grave threat to China as Sino–Soviet relations deteriorated. It was perceived, in effect, as a Soviet flanking move, and China was worried that in the future the USSR would be in position to open an additional front. A possible riposte to this threat was a Chinese penetration into West Pakistan, which could also serve as a warning to India not to countenance too deep a penetration by the USSR. Regionally, it would also facilitate a counterflanking manoeuvre in the Pamirs – a mountain region of the Soviet Union on the borders of Xinjiang, Kashmir and Afghanistan – an area that the Chinese claimed.

The United States had considered Pakistan a vital link between SEATO and CENTO because of its geo-strategic location. The undermining of Pakistan's links with these alliances could thus be considered valuable to China's defence, as it would limit the ability of the West to contain and encircle China along its southern flank.[4] At the same time, Pakistan's relationship with the US offered the opportunity of opening a reliable and discreet communication channel between Beijing and Washington.

In the 1960s China also realised that it could use Pakistan's help in correcting its image in the Third World as a subversive force and warmonger. In the Islamic context, Pakistan could serve as its bridge to various Muslim countries, primarily those in the Middle East.[5] The strategic position of Islamic states bordering the Soviet Union fitted them for a role in China's long-term plans in the Middle East and in containing growing Soviet influence. Also association with Pakistan, a leading Islamic power, would legitimise China's minorities policy.

Following the defeat of its ally in the Indo–Pakistan war of 1971, China was particularly worried about the possible consequences of India's emergence as the major power in South Asia, as it considered this to be part of a Soviet plan.[6] To restore at least a semblance of balance to the regional power structure, China took upon itself the rehabilitation of Pakistan's armed forces, agreeing to replenish them without cost, and providing large scale economic aid. In the diplomatic arena China encouraged Pakistan and India to reach some sort of accommodation. Beijing's determination to prevent Indian supremacy in the subcontinent entered a new phase with India's nuclear test in 1974. To counter any resultant threat, China assured Pakistan of its 'full and resolute support, including that against nuclear threat and nuclear blackmail'.[7]

The Soviet invasion of and presence in force in Afghanistan came at a time of political and economic instability in Pakistan. Realising the potential threat to its ally, China has committed itself to Pakistan's defence for a number of reasons.[8] Pakistan could become a stepping stone to further Soviet expansion. Moreover, control of Pakistan would give the Soviet Union an avenue of attack into Xinjiang and Tibet from the south, using the connecting road system built by China and Pakistan. Aside from these strategic considerations, there are other reasons for Beijing's need to strengthen Pakistan's defence. In view of China's relatively limited usefulness to Pakistan in its 1971 war with India, China might believe that a repeat performance would do serious harm to its credibility and status in the Third World.

China's commitment to Pakistan's security comes as a natural extension of a relationship which, over the years, has come to include a wide spectrum of co-operative interaction. This has involved economic aid to Pakistan, expansion of trade relations, and extensive road building in their border region, including the Karakoram Highway which has both economic and strategic significance.[9] China has become Pakistan's main supplier of military aid, and arms transfers from China to Pakistan since 1966 come to more than $630 million.[10] These close ties were further strengthened by frequent exchanges of visits and of views as well as the co-ordination of policies at all levels. Since the Soviet invasion of Afghanistan, there have been unusually extensive exchange of visits by the highest ranking officers. It is a reasonable speculation that this indicates a combined planning effort for the eventuality of co-ordinated military activity against external threats.

INDIA: FROM THREAT TO ACCOMMODATION

Following India's defeat in the border war of 1962, its armed forces began a crash build-up programme which gained further momentum in the aftermath of the Indo–Pakistan war of 1965. This has not posed a major military threat to China for several reasons. First, Beijing already had a firm hold over vulnerable Tibet and had efficiently crushed all attempts by the insurgents to destabilise its control. At the same time India's northeast region had been in a state of turmoil and rife with secessionist aspirations which Delhi has never been able to subdue.[11] Second, in the difficult terrain of the Himalayas, any Indian effort to achieve victory over a well-supplied, well-trained and fully acclimatised army which holds superior positions is bound to be a very costly if not an impossible goal. Third, the service which gained precedence in the build-up of India's military power was the air force. It was fully modernised with Soviet aid, but the ability to use air power effectively is asymmetrical. India's bombing capabilities based on outdated Canberra bombers are limited to targets in Tibet, thus enabling it to cause only minor damage to China. The Chinese air force, on the other hand, operating from bases in Tibet, could attack civilian industrial targets in central and northern India, for which India has only limited defences. Fourth, following the 1962 war there was no significant domestic pressure in India to take an adventuristic position concerning its boundary conflict with China. The territorial *status quo* was tacitly accepted, although no Indian government can admit it explicitly because of the Indian public's possible reaction. Fifth, the Indo–Pakistan conflict must have led India's policy-makers to the conclusion that the commitment of India's military resources to a campaign against China could be achieved only at the cost of significantly weakening India's defences along its borders with Pakistan. They have expected Pakistan to take advantage of these circumstances, thus both serving its own interests and at the same time proving a loyal and useful ally to China. Sixth, China's nuclear capability surpasses by far India's potential in this field, because of the headstart China has had in the design and production both of warheads and of delivery vehicles. Furthermore, because of the geo-strategic pattern, Indian targets of major value are within easy reach of China's nuclear forces.[12] This will not be the case with India's nuclear capability *vis-à-vis* Chinese targets, even if India decides to acquire nuclear weapons.

As a result, China seems to view India's military power in the Sino–Indian context as primarily a defensive force, with limited offensive significance. Consequently China's assessment of India's importance in its strategic calculus is related mainly to the Sino–Soviet conflict on the one hand and the Sino–Pakistani entente on the other, two factors which are themselves perceived as inter-related. In the Soviet context, blocking the Soviet encircling strategy, whether carried out directly or by proxies, is seen by China as one of its highest strategic priorities.

China's relationship with India has a spillover effect on Indo-Pakistani relations. Improvement of these relations will lessen India's need for Soviet aid, and will thus reduce Moscow's ability to use India in its grand strategy. Such developments will reduce the risk that China may be drawn into a military confrontation between India and Pakistan, leaving its hand free to concentrate on 'main contradictions' – China's borders with the USSR and Vietnam. Taking into account China's relatively limited resources, this is a significant consideration. It helps explain the diplomatic efforts invested in improving relations with India, and also the Chinese emphasis on the need to settle the Indo-Pakistani conflict. China has been adamantly opposed to letting the normalisation process fall apart.

The key obstacle to improvement of relations is the border issue. The *status quo* is unacceptable to India. A possible approach has been suggested by Deng Xiaoping: 'They [China and India] can shelve those issues on which there actually are differences and take their time in talking them over and do some practical things to develop their relations'.[13] At the practical level, China presents a package deal based on mutual concessions.[14] This will include recognition by China of the McMahon Line in the Eastern sector, and recognition by India of China's right to its holdings and the line of actual control in Aksai Chin, through which runs the access from Tibet to Xinjiang.

While trying to improve relations, China still objects to India's aspiration to pre-eminence in South Asia, emphasising the need for relationships based on the five principles of peaceful coexistence.[15] It also encourages India's neighbours to improve relations with India in order to reduce conflict and the consequent opportunities for outside intervention. These postures are related to Beijing's efforts to convince the smaller countries in the region that China does not intend to allow India to dominate South Asia simply as a *quid pro quo* for resolving its outstanding questions with China.

This applies in particular to China's ally, Pakistan. The Chinese leadership has stressed that the relationship with Pakistan will be unaffected by developments in its relations with other countries, namely India and the USSR. On the sensitive Kashmir issue, China took and retained for two decades the position of support for self-determination and for the UN call for a plebiscite.[16]

The Chinese leadership does not expect to win India over to its point of view regarding the Soviet threat, nor is it likely to reach agreement with India on all outstanding issues in the global, or even Asian, arenas. It would, however, prefer to see India's dependence on the

USSR diminished, and would therefore like to encourage the process, begun under the Janata government and continued under Indira Gandhi, of striking a more balanced path for India's foreign policy.

AFGHANISTAN: RISKS AND OPPORTUNITIES

Afghanistan was until 1978 of low strategic priority to Beijing. Its border with China is short, some 75 kilometres and mostly inaccessible, and the border dispute between the two countries was settled by 1963. The significance it did have was based primarily on three factors: (a) its adjacency to Xinjiang, the strategically sensitive region on China's western border inhabited by China's problematic Muslim minority; (b) the increase of Soviet influence in Afghanistan since the mid-1950s; and (c) Afghanistan's conflict with Pakistan, which at times threatened to erupt into a full-scale war between the two over the question of Pushtunistan.

China's attitude towards Afghanistan changed significantly in the aftermath of the 1978 revolution. Even before the Soviet invasion, the Afghan revolution came to be seen as part of the Soviet grand strategy, thus having global rather than purely regional implications.[17] With the Soviet invasion of Afghanistan in December 1979, the situation became critical. Beijing saw its worst fears realised, pointing to events in Afghanistan as mere steps in a well-orchestrated Soviet master plan for world hegemony.[18]

The Chinese argument is that although in the long run no one is safe from Soviet imperialism, in the short run it is Europe, the US and Japan which are the primary targets of aggression.[19] Thus, most of the responsibility for containing the Soviets should be theirs. In that wider context, the immediate Soviet strategy against China is 'encirclement and isolation', since a nuclear attack would be counter-productive.[20] Isolation is furthered by an all-out effort to disrupt the united front of the US, Japan, ASEAN and China. In the long run this situation poses a possible threat of a multi-directional surprise attack, disrupts the progress of the four modernisations, and thereby weakens China.

Beyond grand strategy the Soviet invasion also highlighted a number of Chinese concerns on the regional, local military levels. One important point is the high mobility of the Soviets by sea and air which (1) enables them quickly and effectively to supply their allies and proxies; (2) enables them to fight along internal lines, due to their ability to move the centre of gravity of an attack as the situation on the battlefield dictates; (3) enables them to concentrate large forces at short notice at any given point along their borders.[21]

Another consequence of the invasion of Afghanistan is that it moves the USSR towards a *de facto* annexation of the Wakhan Salient, an action perceived by the PRC as an attempt to gain a 'strategic edge over China and Pakistan'. The Soviet move has virtually erased the border between Afghanistan and China and made the USSR contiguous to Pakistan.[22] So situated, it can have a direct military impact on the Indian–Pakistani conflict for control of Kashmir, thereby increasing Soviet leverage with India. Finally, annexation and the evacuation of inhabitants from the area sealed off the only direct land route through which the insurgents can receive supplies via China.[23]

Soviet military conduct is also the object of close study by China. Beijing is aware that Afghanistan has become a testing ground for Soviet weaponry and tactics under combat conditions. The fact that the conditions are those of guerrilla warfare is highly relevant to the Chinese. The lesson learned from the relative success of the insurgents in Afghanistan, despite superior Soviet military deployment and fire power, was that 'when a small nation is invaded, its people can mobilise all patriotic forces and adopt military tactics which conform to the specific conditions of their own nation to deal with even such military superpowers as the Soviet Union'.[24] It is reasonable to assume that the conclusions drawn are bound to contribute to the dispute among military and political elites in Beijing over the present relevance of 'people's war'.

Thus the situation in Afghanistan presents not only a grey cloud but also a silver lining. It has revealed the weaknesses of the Red Army, which according to Chinese sources has sustained over 10 000 casualties. Thus the rebels 'have exploded the myth of the invincibility of Soviet hegemonism'.[25] As a result of these factors, China has gained a measure of relief from Soviet pressure and threats; at the same time the situation proves that 'superpowers are nothing to fear'. It also gives the anti-Soviet coalition time to build up its military power and prevent the outbreak of a Third World War.[26] On the diplomatic front the occupation of Afghanistan has put the Soviets on the defensive. Afghanistan is Muslim, Asian and non-aligned, thus exposing the Soviet Union to harsh criticism in all three arenas. From a 'natural ally' of the Third World, the USSR's image has been demoted to that of a threat to the non-aligned movement.

These developments weakened the Soviet position, strengthened China's hand in bargaining both with Russia and the West and checked the momentum of the Soviet drive for world hegemony. Thus the situation in Afghanistan has unexpectedly served China's strategic interests to a degree but at the same time has a serious potential for developing into a major threat.

THE INDIAN OCEAN: NAVAL THREAT AND RESPONSE

As China emerged from the upheaval of the Cultural Revolution and took stock of threats present in its environment, there was not much that was new on her southern flank. Her two arch-enemies, the Soviet Union and the United States, were still colluding with the 'Indian reactionaries' to encircle China.[27] However, there was a new element in the encirclement strategy and that was the 'anti-China sea cordon'.[28] The Soviets were perceived as planning the deployment of their Pacific and Black Sea Fleets in a pincer movement with the co-operation of the coastal states, in particular India. The final goal was seen as naval control over the Indian Ocean and political control over the Asian and African states and their rich raw materials and markets.

Being traditionally a continental power, China had a coastguard-oriented navy. Moreover, the Chinese leadership was concentrating its limited resources on the land threat, unwilling and unable to invest in a blue-water navy. To deal with the naval threat, it had to rely on diplomacy on the one hand, and the congruence of interests with the US on the other.

The diplomatic aspect of China's naval policy was based upon (1) support for Indonesia, Malaysia and Singapore in their efforts to control passage through and above the Malacca–Singapore straits and the Indonesian straits;[29] (2) systematic support for the proposal to declare the Indian Ocean a zone of peace, free of the presence of all foreign navies; (3) efforts to improve relations with India, hoping that this would make India less forthcoming in providing refuelling facilities and other port services to the Soviet navy and (4) a propaganda campaign directed at coastal countries likely to be taken in by Soviet 'high-flown phraseology' which hid naked ambition for hegemony.[30] But the main deterrent to Soviet naval power has been the presence of a powerful Western, primarily American, fleet in this region.

The Chinese method of meeting the Soviet naval threat has been in the main a containment-by-proxy policy aimed at impairing Soviet freedom of naval deployment and mobility. This was in line with the age-old dicta which suggest 'using a barbarian to check another barbarian', and 'co-operate with the far country and strike at the near country'.[31]

With the advent of Deng Xiaoping, the maritimist school gained predominance and attention was shifted toward the building up of blue-water sea capabilities for the Chinese navy.[32] This can be attributed to Deng's outward-looking approach, but one might speculate that it is more particularly related to a reassessment of the adequacy of China's passive approach to the naval power equation in the Indian Ocean. This concern grew when the Soviet Union gained increased access to bases in Vietnam and Cambodia, such as Danang, Cam Ranh Bay and Kompong Som and Ream. The Soviet invasion of Afghanistan was perceived to confirm China's worst apprehensions. Everything seemed to fit a grand plan, in which maritime supremacy in general and in the Indian Ocean in particular was an essential component.

Moreover, the volume of China's seaborne trade has been growing rapidly, and with it China's commercial fleet. This has led to growing dependence on sea lines of communication (SLOC) through the Indian Ocean for trade with Africa, South and Southwest Asia, the Middle East and Europe. Trade not only serves Beijing's economic policy of fast growth but has become of growing importance in its foreign policy of competing for influence in the Third World. At the same time, the Soviet Pacific Fleet has grown to become the largest in the Soviet navy and its presence along SLOC in the Indian Ocean has become a permanent factor. To this must be added the potential threat posed by the fast-growing Indian navy with its sea-denial capabilities.

In the circumstances China, a country aspiring to world power status, cannot afford not to have at least a minimal presence in nearby waters, namely the South and East China Seas and the Indian Ocean. Relying totally on another superpower means losing face. In any event, as US–China relations fluctuate over the Taiwan issue, it becomes even more questionable whether China should rely solely on western navies. Hence a degree of self-reliance, even if only initially symbolic, becomes a pressing necessity.

To counter the Soviet naval threat, China has been moving towards a limited blue-water doctrine for its navy.[33] This is within the PRC's capability both logistically and in terms of ships at its disposal. In the last few years the navy has acquired new guided-missile destroyers, together with some experience in operating at long distances from home ports. It has incorporated an additional 15 000 tons of ocean-going supply ships, and has mastered the technique of resupply at sea.[34] This would make a limited presence in the Indian Ocean feasible.

The Indian Ocean could gain even higher strategic importance in the context of Chinese planning for nuclear deterrence as China builds up its submarine-based ballistic missile force. At this time China only has the capacity to hit targets in European Russia from its launching sites in north-western China. This capability is vulnerable to a Soviet pre-emptive counter-force strike, which will leave China exposed without second-strike capability. The risk of such an eventuality can be countered by following the example of the four other nuclear powers in the establishment of a submarine-based ballistic missile force. A significant step in that direction was recently taken with the successful test-firing of China's first submarine-launched missile in October 1982. Observers assume it was an intermediate-range missile.[35] In order to hit targets in European Russia with SLBM's, the objects will have to be targeted from the Indian Ocean. It is in fact the only realistic deployment area for a Chinese SSBN force.

Moreover, beyond the direct effects on China's strategic relationship with India, a potential Asian nuclear power, there is an important side-benefit to be derived from positioning SLBM's in the Indian Ocean. This relates to Beijing's commitment to its ally, Pakistan, to defend it against blackmail by another nuclear power. A Chinese nuclear presence in the Indian Ocean will confirm the credibility of this commitment both to Pakistan and India. It may also help in convincing Islamabad not to develop its own independent military nuclear capability. China should, however, consider the possibility that deployment of its SSBN's in the Indian Ocean may have the effect of driving India to take the final step toward a nuclear capability. Ironically, such a development would then further justify a presence of Chinese SSBN's off the shores of India on a permanent basis.

China's submarine force is technologically inferior to those of other naval powers, including India's, which means its submarines are slow and noisy. The Indian Ocean offers both a a larger deployment space than the South and East China Seas and also more protection against detection by low frequency modern sonar equipment.

The presence of Chinese submarines in the Indian Ocean will necessitate the permanent deployment of a surface fleet as well, to protect the submarines from the Indian, Soviet or other hostile navies. Logistically such a fleet could rely on the excellent facilities of the port of Karachi in Pakistan. Hence, with a small number of units, a Chinese task force could be maintained for long periods on station. In fact, the development of a capability to threaten the USSR with a relatively immune strike force may increase China's attraction as a useful ally, and therefore increase the willingness of Pakistan to take the risk of providing port services. A surface task force could serve the dual function of shielding Chinese SSBN's and showing the flag in the Indian Ocean. The problem of C^3, which is crucial in deployment far from home shores and in particular for a nuclear strike force, could be resolved in the not-too-distant future using the advances China has been making towards deployment of its own orbiting satellite communications systems.[36]

The growing dependence on the sea for the allocation of its nuclear deterrence force, as well as for commercial purposes, may pose a difficult political and ideological dilemma to Beijing's leadership. Traditionally, China's positions on all matters concerning the law of the sea were in line with those of the Third World countries, and in particular the PRC supported the Zone of Peace proposition concerning the Indian Ocean. The evolution of China's new maritime interests calls for radically different attitudes, much like the ones adopted by other major naval powers. It is highly unlikely that China will change its formal positions, for reasons which need no explanation. However, it will probably adopt a lower profile and hope that the US and USSR stick to their positions and reject any Third-World-initiated plan to constrain their freedom of naval deployment. The ability of the two superpowers to block any such initiative, or to disregard efforts in this direction even if such a plan is adopted in an international forum, will afford Beijing legitimacy to follow in their footsteps without being burdened with the political cost of having to confront Third World countries. Such a gap between China rhetoric and actions is not unknown (see Chapter 18).

CONCLUSIONS: THE COMPONENTS OF CHINA'S POLICY

China began in the 1960s from a position of weakness in South Asia, its only ally, Pakistan, being a state with limited capabilities and uncertain stability. Thus it adopted a multifaceted approach toward the region: First, in order to safeguard the precarious balance of power between Pakistan and India and prevent the emergence of an India-controlled subcontinent, it supplied Pakistan with arms and demonstrated its readiness to intervene directly on Pakistan's behalf. Second, it exercised prudence to avoid the hazard of becoming actually involved militarily in a local war and thus risking a confrontation with the USSR. Third, it managed its alliance with Pakistan skilfully by broadening the base of the relationship. This was achieved through trade and aid policies which benefited Pakistan significantly. Fourth, it advised moderation to Pakistan in the conflict with India and at the same time tried to avoid being considered by India as a mortal enemy. The assumption behind this policy was that the decline in tensions on the subcontinent serves China's interests and damages those of the USSR. Fifth, it developed cordial relationships with the secondary states in the region – Nepal, Bhutan, Bangladesh, Sri Lanka and the Maldive Islands Republic.

Finally, Beijing has supported regional security arrangements. These include Nepal's proposal of declaring itself a Zone of Peace and Neutrality; Pakistan's proposal of a South Asian nuclear free zone; an Indian Ocean Zone of Peace proposal originally suggested by Sri Lanka; Pakistan's offer to discuss a non-aggression pact with India; and other plans for regional co-operation, such as the common use of rivers.[37]

Each of these policies serves the purpose of reducing the danger of conflict in the region and thus limiting the opportunities for penetration by external powers. In addition, reduction of the risk of local conflicts diminishes the danger of China being inadvertently drawn into local conflicts. This prevents it from having to spread thin its limited resources and allows it to concentrate on the 'main contradictions'.

Looking at the evolution of China's policy toward South Asia in perspective, it is clear that Beijing did not approach the region with a predetermined grand strategy. Policy toward the region grew incrementally, was reactive in nature and was shaped in a process of trial and error. The main driving forces were need and opportunity. Events demonstrated to China the growing significance of South Asia. However opportunities were limited and China had to make do with what was available. China's presence in the region became more prominent and widespread, and inter-regional and global developments offered more space for diplomatic manoeuvrability.

Nevertheless, despite this growing Chinese confidence, it would be rash to suggest that there is any new permanent coherence to Chinese strategy. In the light of the importance of China's perception of a Soviet threat as a crucial under-pinning to its South Asian policy, the recent movement towards a degree of Sino–Soviet détente requires observers to adopt a flexible approach. With both China and Pakistan indicating flexibility on the settlement of the Afghan problem in 1983, the old models of inflexible Sino–Soviet conflict seem potentially outdated. What seems most certain is change, but unlike previous times of change, this time China is a far more prominent power in South Asia.

NOTES AND REFERENCES

1. Editorial Department of *Renmin Ribao*, *Peking Review*, vol. 6, no. 45, 8 November 1963, 24-27.
2. *People's Daily* editorial 22 August 1963 in *SCMP* no. 8047, 26 August 1963, 21.
3. Y. Shichor, *The Middle East in China's Foreign Policy 1949-1977*, (Cambridge, Cambridge University Press, 1979), 106-108.
4. *SCMP*, no. 2880, 14 December 1962, 33-34; no. 2933, 3 March 1963, 35.
5. B. L. Sharma, *The Pakistan-China Axis*, (London, Asia Publishing House 1968), 143. N. Entessar, 'The People's Republic of China and Iran: An Overview of Their Relationship', *Asia Quarterly* no. 1 (1978), 82.
6. Statement of the People's Republic of China in *SCMP* no. 5042, 12 December 1971, 83.
7. *Asian Recorder*, 1974, 12168.
8. Xiao Ke, Xinhua in English in *FBIS*, CHI-55, 17 March 1980, F/2, Hua Guofeng 2 May 1980: in *FBIS*, CHI-88, 5 May 1980, F/6-8; Zhao Ziyang, June 1981; *FBIS*, CHI-106, 3 June 1981, F/3.
9. Y. Vertzberger, *The Enduring Entente: Sino-Pakistani Relations 1960-1980*, (Washington, D.C., Georgetown University CSIS, 1983; The Washington Papers Series, no. 95), Ch. 6; *Overseas Weekly Dawn*, 28 October-3 November 1982, 1; 3-9 September 1982, 1.
10. See *Allocation of Resources in the Soviet Union and China - 1981*. Hearings before the subcommittee on International Trade, Finance and Security of the Joint Economic Committee, Congress of the United States, 97th Congress, First Session, part 7, 159; also United States Arms Control and Disarmament Agency, *World Military Expenditures and Arms Transfers 1966-1975 and 1970-1979* (Washington, D.C., 1976 and 1981), 78 and 130; see K. Subrahmanyam, 'Pakistani Credibility Gap', *IDSA Journal*, vol. 14, no. 1, July-September 1981, 114-115.
11. O. Marwah, 'Northeastern India: New Delhi Confronts the Insurgents', *Orbis* 21, no. 2, Summer 1977; Mohan Ram, 'New Anxieties Over Assam', *FEER*, 4 April 1980, 30-31; 'A Gathering Storm in Manipur' and 'New Delhi Tries Conciliation', *FEER*, 2 May 1980, 31-32; 'A Spreading Plague of Violence', *FEER*, 20 June 1980, 33.
12. Radio Moscow to South and Southeast Asia, 24 August 1982; in *FBIS*, SOV-166, 26 August 1982, B/2.
13. Xinhua in English, 14 February 1979; in *FBIS*, CHI-33, 15 February 1979, A/7.
14. Zhao Ziyang to the Editor of *The Hindu*, in *FBIS*, CHI-209, 28 October 1982, F/1.

15. Xinhua in English, 26 June 1981; in *FBIS*, CHI-124, 29 June 1981, F/1–3.
16. *Overseas Weekly Dawn*, 7–13 May 1982, 1; R. Tasker, 'Peace on the Mena', *FEER*, 5 November 1982, 9; *FBIS*, CHI-168, 30 August 1982, F/1.
17. Xue Yuan, 'Turmoil in Afghanistan', *Renmin Ribao*, 11 June 1979; in *FBIS*, CHI-113, 18 June 1979, F/2.
18. *FBIS*, CHI-120, 19 June 1980, C/1–2; also in *Renmin Ribao* 'observer' 19 June 1980; in *FBIS*, CHI-121, 20 June 1980, C/1–3; and Beijing Domestic Service (in Mandarin), 11 July 1980; in *FBIS*, CHI-136, 14 July 1980, C/2.
19. *Beijing Review* 23, no. 4, 28 January 1980, 19; Qi Ya and Zhou Jirong, *Beijing Review* 24, no. 25, 22 June 1981.
20. Beijing Domestic Service (in Mandarin), 18 February 1981; in *FBIS*, CHI-33, 19 February 1981, C/4.
21. See *Beijing Review* 23, no. 4, 28 January 1980, 15–19.
22. *FBIS*, CHI-216, 5 November 1980, F/1; Beijing Domestic Service (in Mandarin), 13 March 1981.
23. China supplies limited amounts of arms for the Afghan rebels mainly through the port of Karachi and thence overland. Direct supply from Xinjiang is considered too difficult and provocative to the USSR (D. Bonavia, 'More Bricks in China's Wall', *FEER* 5 June 1981, 14–15).
24. Yi Li, 'What the Afghan War Tells Us', *Honggi*, no. 1, 1 January 1980, 47–48; in *FBIS*, CHI-14, 22 January 1980, F/2 and CHI-156, 11 August 1980, C/2.
25. Observer's article in *Renmin Ribao*, 26 December 1980 6; *FBIS*, CHI-251, 29 December 1980, C/2.
26. *Renmin Ribao*, editorial, 27 December 1982; in *FBIS*, CHI-248, 27 December 1982, F/1–2; Chen Youwei, 'Why Do We Think About 1939?' *Renmin Ribao*, 16 July 1980, 7; in *FBIS*, CHI-140, 18 July 1980, C/1–2; Y. Vertzberger, 'Afghanistan in China's Policy', *Problems of Communism* vol. 31, May–June 1982, 17–23.
27. *Peking Review*, vol. 12, no. 14, 4 April 1969, 25–27.
28. *Peking Review*, vol. 12, no. 26, 27 June 1969, 16.
29. Y. Vertzberger, 'Malacca–Singapore Straits', *Asian Survey*, vol. 22, no. 7, July 1982; *Peking Review*, vol. 17, no. 26, 28 June 1974, 15.
30. Kung Ping, *Peking Review*, vol. 17, no. 24, 14 June 1974, 14.
31. F. G. Romance, 'Peking's Counter-Encirclement Strategy: The Maritime Element', *Orbis*, vol. 20, no. 2, Summer 1976, 440–441.
32. B. L. Swanson, 'China's Navy and Foreign Policy', *Survival* vol. 21, no. 4, July–August 1979, 147.
33. The theoretical group of the PLA Navy: *People's Daily*, 27 June 1977, 3; in *FBIS*, CHI-126, 30 June 1977, E/4–7; *FBIS*, CHI-200, 17 October 1977, E/11–12.
34. *FBIS*, CHI-119, 22 June 1981, K/14–15; *FBIS*, CHI-152, 7 August 1981, K/9–10; 'China's Navy Advances Rapidly Toward Goal of Modernization', *Zhongguo Xinwen She*, 11 April 1982; in *FBIS*, CHI-71, 13 April 1982, K/6–7; *Ban Yue Tan*, no. 7, 10 April 1982, 32–33; in *FBIS*, CHI-77, 21 April 1982, K/13–14; Beijing Domestic Service in Mandarin,

27 July 1982; in *FBIS*, CHI-147, 30 July 1982, K/5–6; R. Breeze, 'The Wide Blue Yonder', *FEER*, 11 June 1982.
35. Estimates about the range of the test-SLBM vary from 1500 miles to 650 nautical miles. See, M. Weisskopf, 'China Fires a Missile from a Sub', *International Herald Tribune*, 18 October 1982, 1, and D. G. Muller (Lieutenant Commander) 'China's SSBN in Perspective' *Proceedings of US Naval Institute*, March 1982, vol. 109/3/961, 125.
36. On China's satellite programme, see E. Terry, 'China's Long March Has a Military Goal', *FEER*, 24 December 1982, 40, 43–44.
37. See M. Ram 'Neighbours, Keep Out', *FEER* 18 December 1981, 21; *Asian Recorder*, 1979, 14724–14725; *FBIS*, CHI-128, 6 July 1981, F/1–2.

18 The Middle East

YITZHAK SHICHOR

In recent years there have been dramatic developments in China's military relations with some Middle Eastern governments. Mostly behind the scene, the Chinese have undertaken to supply these governments with arms, ammunition and spare parts in quantities unheard of before. The significance of these arms transactions cannot be overstated. For one thing, they testify to China's resumed military production, as well as to better conventional military capabilities than so far realised. For another, they have provided the Chinese with their first worthy foothold in the Middle East, with some tangible strategic advantages over the Soviets and with initial leverage over the local governments. Finally, and most important, earning China not only crucially-needed foreign exchange but also samples of advanced weapons, intelligence and technological information and more intimate understanding of Soviet warfare, these deals have come to play a notable role in China's military modernisation programme. After years of frustration, the Chinese have at last begun to collect Middle Eastern dividends.

China's decision to supply arms to the Middle East was originally motivated by strategic considerations. Although geographically distant and, until recently, practically inaccessible, the Middle East has never been ignored strategically by the Chinese. On the contrary, judging by sheer volume of editorials and commentaries, the Chinese at times seem to have been pre-occupied, even obsessed, by the potential threats involved in this region. To be sure, the Chinese have never perceived the Middle East as an independent source of threat. Rather, their concern derived essentially from the prospects that an outside adversary power (or powers) would seize control over it and use it against China either directly, as a springboard for an eventual encirclement and assault, or indirectly, as a key to global dominance.[1]

Determined by these perceived threats, China's Middle East policy has been geared to a fundamental and immutable goal, namely, that hostile powers should not be permitted to consolidate their presence and influence in, or better still should be kept out of, this crucially important region. In the past, however, there has been very little the Chinese could have, or would have, contributed to the accomplishment of this goal.

Politically, the People's Republic of China had to undergo a painfully slow and tortuous process merely to win diplomatic recognition and to establish official relations.[2] Excluded from the United Nations and from many capitals before 1971, the Chinese could not provide the Arabs with political services. As a matter of fact, it was the other way around. Moreover, despite their admission to the United Nations and to the Security Council and the remarkable expansion of their diplomatic network, the Chinese were neither able nor willing to compete politically with others – not only because of time-honoured habits but also because their newly-acquired political potential, being unsubstantiated by economic and military power, was largely illusory. Indeed, economically the Chinese have had little to offer Middle Eastern countries to attract their goodwill. Both trade and aid have been far smaller than that of other powers and of lower quality and impact. Militarily, the Chinese did a lot worse.

Until the early 1980s, the military dimension had been the least important in China's relations with the Middle East. At best the Chinese provided local national liberation movements with limited numbers of light weapons, rudimentary training and political–revolutionary indoctrination. There is no evidence of any Sino–Arab arms deal of significant scale before 1976. Even afterwards, in the latter half of the 1970s, Chinese arms transfers to the Middle East should be regarded as 'gifts' rather than 'deals', and hardly 'significant': the value of these transfers was estimated (for 1975–1979) at $70 million, a minute 0.2 per cent of the total military supply to this never-satiated region.[3]

This poor performance should be attributed to a combination of domestic and international circumstances. Domestically, the conventional explanation has to do with China's limited capabilities in terms of quantity and, even more so, in quality. Yet these 'limits' have not necessarily or entirely reflected objective constraints. To some extent, at least, they have been conditioned (or rationalised) by self-imposed priorities (for example, nuclear weapons and delivery systems) on the one hand, and by ideological considerations (the human factor, people's war, self-reliance), on the other. Moreover, within these limits and during the same years, the Chinese share in military supplies to other regions (Africa, East Asia and, notably, South Asia) was much higher than in the Middle East.[4] Put differently, China's insignificant role as an arms supplier to the Middle East derived more from regional than domestic circumstances. Saturated by advanced military equipment which they could easily get from the Soviet Union, the United States and Western Europe, local governments had no reason whatsoever to turn to China.

However, by the early 1980s many of these constraints, in both the Middle East and China, had diminished. With Mao gone China embarked upon an ambitious economic and technological modernisation programme to be based on efficient mobilisation of domestic resources and industries, and on massive imports of plant, equipment and know-how. The foreign exchange needed for both had to come primarily from increased exports. These and other policies clearly affected the military. Though assigned the last priority among the Four Modernisations, military modernisation has by no means been neglected. While they seem to disagree on many of its aspects, the Chinese leaders probably share the conclusion that a quick and wholesale transformation of China's military system, to be achieved by large-scale acquisition of sophisticated and updated Western models, is simply impossible. Instead they seem to have opted for a more modest, gradual and selective programme adapted to the Chinese realities, abilities and experience, and in keeping with the principle of self-reliance.[5] These revised requirements and, particularly, the erosion of Maoist righteousness, have enabled the Chinese to overcome their previous reluctance to sell arms.

But, if so, to whom? Traditional small-scale transactions would not do. The Chinese were looking for ideal customers – those who not only need large quantities of Chinese military hardware, commonly regarded as obsolescent, but who are also ready and able to make quick and extensive payments, in cash. There is only one place where China could find such customers: the Middle East.

TOWARDS A NEW POLICY

Far-reaching and inter-related changes in regional circumstances have provided China with opportunities for military transactions on an unprecedented scale. One such change has been the high rate of attrition of Soviet-made weapons in local confrontations, notably the

Yom Kippur war of October 1973 and, much more so, the Iraqi–Iranian war which has been going on since September 1980. Another has been the disruption of Soviet military supplies which had been cut off completely in the case of Egypt, Sudan and Somalia or seriously circumscribed, as in the case of Iraq. This, together with the disastrous effects of the wars, has left Egypt and Iraq with crippled military machines starving for spare parts, ammunition, replacements and maintenance. Given the Soviets' disinclination to satisfy these needs, China has become practically the only country capable of doing so.

And it has. Since 1980 there has been an upsurge in China's military transactions with the Middle East. It is of course impossible to obtain precise information about arms sales anywhere in the world, let alone in the case of China. None the less, an impressive array of data on Chinese military transactions has now been accumulated from a variety of sources, including news-agency dispatches, the Arabic press, speeches and interviews of Arab leaders and various published reports. By no means consistent in so far as their details, these unconfirmed reports do confirm the general outline of unprecedented Chinese arms deals, particularly with Egypt and Iraq.

Sino–Egyptian military relations started out in a rather traditional fashion in early 1976. On 25 March, some ten days after he abrogated the Soviet–Egyptian Friendship and Co-operation Treaty, President Sadat announced that China had supplied Egypt with engines and spare parts for its MiG fighters, free of charge.[6] Within less than a month, on 21 April, a long-term military protocol, the first of its kind, was concluded in Beijing between the Chinese and the Egyptian Vice-President Mubarak. China agreed to supply Egypt with $10 million worth of MiG spare parts and engines, to build a munitions factory and to provide technicians.[7] Later deals indicated that the scope of the April 1976 protocol had been much wider. Yet despite China's barely concealed eagerness to supply arms,[8] that stage in the evolving Sino–Egyptian military relations was quite modest.

The next stage was considerably more impressive. In a number of speeches delivered between early June and early August 1979, Sadat disclosed that China was selling Egypt 50 aircraft as a part of a new arms deal.[9] He gave no further details, and those provided by Arab and international sources were conflicting and confusing in so far as numbers and types of the aircraft supplied.[10] The precise number was probably 90, of which 40 were given as a gift and 50 (those mentioned by Sadat) sold. Their type was given by some sources as F-6 or F-9 (both Chinese versions of the Soviet MiG-19 officially known as J[ian]-6 and Q[iang]-5 respectively), while other sources, not less reliable, insisted on F-7 (or Jian-7, based on the MiG-21).[11] Whatever the details, this deal should be regarded as an intermediate stage in Sino–Egyptian military relations. Related to the 1976 protocol,[12] and partly implemented as a gift, it still reflected traditional patterns. On the other hand, by mid-1979 Maoism had completely eroded and China's new leaders were ideologically and politically free to explore and pursue opportunities which had been unthinkable in Mao's time.[13]

NEW OPPORTUNITIES

Such opportunities emerged in January 1980 when another high-level Egyptian delegation led by Mubarak visited China. A new military protocol was signed of which details were never made public but the size of which can be conceived from scattered unconfirmed data.[14] According to a variety of sources, the Chinese had undertaken to provide Egypt with military vessels, including six newly-built 1800-ton Romeo type diesel submarines (the first two of which arrived in March 1982);[15] military aircraft, including F-6s and particularly F-7s, said to be a 'modified' version with a different engine, better capabilities, easier to maintain and 'equipped with advanced weapons not found in the Soviet model used by the Egyptian air force';[16] CSA-1 surface-to-air missiles (the Chinese version of the Soviet SA-2); spare parts, ammunition and maintenance services.[17] When China's Premier Zhao Ziyang visited Egypt in December 1982, the Egyptian Deputy Premier and Defence Minister used the occasion to state that China had agreed to supply additional F-6s and F-7s (60 to 80, according to other sources), to be assembled in Egypt with the help of Chinese experts.[18] In an interview following the visit, Ding Guoyu, China's newly appointed ambassador to Cairo (himself a major-general),[19] said that in the field of arms 'Egypt can rely on China for all its needs' including information and know-how concerning the production of arms and spare parts.[20]

Sino–Egyptian military relations were discussed yet again when President Mubarak visited China in early April 1983. Asked whether China would increase military aid to Egypt, Foreign Minister Kamal Hasan Ali said: 'It is not aid, it is sales, and I think China is one of the countries that deal with Egypt with very reasonable prices and steady supply'.[21] Mubarak signed a new arms deal valued at $80 million to be repaid over a long period. No further details were given but it was reported that China 'agreed to reschedule Egypt's old military debts, amounting to $100 million'.[22]

Because the information given above is both incomplete and imprecise, it is very difficult to estimate the value of these transactions. Still, assuming that the details collected represent only part of the total of agreements and allowing for the lower Chinese prices, the Sino–Egyptian arms deals might be valued at something between 500 and 700 million dollars. While these figures may be controversial, the fact that China has become Egypt's third largest arms supplier, following the United States and France, is not.

It seems that their experience with Egypt has allowed the Chinese to become even more self-confident and daring. This is evident in the Sino–Iraqi arms deals. Though launched only in 1981, shrouded in secrecy and firmly denied, these deals have reportedly been considerably more extensive than their Egyptian counterparts. The reasons are obvious: the Iraqi–Iranian War, which erupted in September 1980 and is still going on, caused an enormous attrition of the Iraqi Soviet-made weapons and ammunition, which Moscow has been reluctant to replace. It was this predicament, more than anything else, that pushed Iraq into the arms of the Chinese, providing them with a rare opportunity they could not afford to miss.

The first Sino–Iraqi arms deal was signed just a few months after the war had started, probably in early 1981.[23] But it was only in November that information about the deal emerged publicly. Unconfirmed reports said that China would supply Iraq with an unspecified number of T-59 tanks, the Chinese version of the Soviet T-54. The value of the deal was not given but it was said to be financed, at least in part, by a $7 billion Kuwaiti loan.[24] The dimensions of the deal were illustrated a year later. According to United States intelligence officials, China had become a major arms supplier to Iraq: a quarter of Iraq's military acquisitions originated in China while half of China's total military sales were chanelled to Iraq.[25] Assuming that Iraq was spending about $12 billion a year on the war effort,[26] the Chinese share should have been at least $3 billion.

A deal of such scale could not have been limited to T-59 tanks. It probably covered light arms, field artillery and huge amounts of ammunition and spare parts as well.[27] Moreover, in December 1982 it was reported that about a 100 Chinese F-6 fighters had been delivered by sea to Iraq.[28] And in January 1983 intelligence sources in the Far East disclosed that, under a deal estimated at more than $1 billion,

China was supplying Iraq with a substantial number (at least 260) of T-69 tanks. Said to be China's most sophisticated, these tanks are equipped with Chinese-manufactured laser range-finders, infra-red equipment and an improved engine.[29]

Needless to say both the Chinese and the Iraqis firmly denied these reports. The Chinese insisted they have 'not sold any weapons to Iraq because this is incompatible with our principled stand on the war between Iraq and Iran' which is based on 'strict neutrality'.[30] The Iraqi Defence Minister equally insisted: 'Our relations with China are firm and good, but we did not sign any contract with it for the acquisition of weapons'.[31] These denials notwithstanding, all the evidence suggests that Chinese arms have indeed reached Iraq, though apparently indirectly, having been shipped first to Jordan, Saudi Arabia and Egypt and then, after being assembled, overland to Iraq.[32] It might also be possible that, to avoid jeopardising China's 'strict neutrality', these countries, known for their friendship to Iraq and hostility to Iran, have served not only as conveyor belts for Chinese arms but also as signatories to the contracts on Iraq's behalf.

Taken together, the Chinese deals with Iraq, Egypt and other Middle Eastern countries (Iran, either through North Korea or directly,[33] and, to a much lesser extent, Sudan and Somalia) the total value of which can be estimated at approximately $5 billion, represent the largest arms transfers ever undertaken by the PRC, overshadowing all past military transactions put together.

IMPLICATIONS

China's military transactions with the Middle East have far-reaching implications. To begin with, they provide a unique insight into China's defence capabilities, in qualitative as well as quantitative terms.

The decision of some Middle Eastern governments to buy Chinese arms derived no doubt from a variety of considerations, including political (leverage against both Moscow and Washington), economic (low prices) and military (easy integration, second-line capabilities). Yet such considerations by no means justify buying any machine, much less a war machine, known to be defective. Therefore one lesson of these transactions is that China's military models and hardware are not as worthless and inferior as we have been led to believe, often by the Chinese themselves.

Over time, China's weapon systems have undergone considerable modifications that set them apart from, and above, the Soviet models on which they are based.³⁴ For example, 'after nearly twenty years of incremental improvements, the F-6 is surely the most highly perfected obsolescent fighter on earth – vastly better than the best Soviet MiG-19, but two generations behind current technology'.³⁵ Pakistani pilots who have flown the F-6 in combat said it was 'a highly effective ground-attack weapon' and a 'useful air-superiority fighter.' They praised the aircraft for its sturdiness and ease of handling. Its capabilities were comparable to the Mirage IIIE of France and the F-104 Starfighter of the United States. They added that its ability to turn at any altitude and its rate of climb at altitudes below 6100 metres were just as good as the MiG-21.³⁶

The F-6s were also described as 'tough, dependable and highly manoeuvrable – far more manoeuvrable than contemporary Soviet fighters ... capable of out-turning and out-climbing the MiG-21'.³⁷ Similarly the Chinese F-7 has better capabilities than the Soviet MiG-21 from which it was copied.³⁸ And Chinese tanks, when equipped with laser range-finders, infra-red driving lights and spotlights, gun-stabilisers and fire-control systems, are definitely superior to their original ancestors. Therefore, although still a long way behind advanced Soviet and Western weapons, the Chinese models should not be dismissed as useless and ineffective.³⁹ Especially since numbers also count.⁴⁰

This is another lesson. Although conventional military production had been downgraded since the mid-1960s, China's military industries, built in the 1950s with massive Soviet support, still have tremendous excess capacity.⁴¹ This is evident from China's large-scale arms deliveries to the Middle East. It is inconceivable that these deliveries were carried out at the expense of domestic needs. Similarly, the partial diversion of military industries to civilian production could by no means imply a deterioration in defence capabilities, to which the army leaders would never agree. Rather, 'the military industrial enterprises have, *after completing the task for military goods*, increased the production of goods for civilian use by big amounts'.⁴² (Emphasis added). Therefore the Middle Eastern deals do suggest a noteworthy improvement, both qualitatively and quantitatively, in China's current defence capabilities.

No less important, China's future defence capabilities are expected to be upgraded as a result of these transactions, which have made some very significant contributions to the revised Chinese military modernisation programme. Much remains unknown. For example, there is no way to figure out whether the inflow of several billion dollars in foreign exchange has been swallowed up by the thirsty economic system or earmarked to finance defence projects.[43] This much, however, is known: through their relations with the Middle East, the Chinese have gained access to more advanced Soviet, and probably even Western, military technology. In all likelihood they were permitted to inspect and study certain models on the spot and, much more important, also given 'take-away' samples.

According to various reports,[44] these samples included the following: at least two MiG-23S fighters (the Flogger-E export version); MiG-23 engines; an unspecified number of MiG-21MF and Sukhoi SU-20 bomber; at least two types of surface-to-air missiles (SA-3 and SA-6); at least two T-62 tanks; and anti-tank missiles (Sagger). Intercepted on their way to Vietnam or captured in the confrontations with the Soviets in 1969 and the Vietnamese in 1979, some of these models were already familiar to the Chinese. But whereas these models had often been obtained damaged and had to be studied in a hurry, the Middle Eastern samples were more diversified and immaculate and came complete with manuals and spare parts. Their small number should not mislead us into underestimating their significance. 'Western military experts generally agree that in the near future China will be modernising its military not by large-scale import of modern arms but chiefly by purchasing single items or small consignments of weapons and combat equipment as well as their manufacturing technology, the extensive conduct of research and development, and comprehensive development of China's own military industry.'[45]

Indeed, since 1977–1978 there has been growing evidence of Chinese experimentation with the models acquired from the Middle East, primarily from Egypt. Using their proficiency in reverse-engineering, the Chinese have tried to design and produce a new aircraft based on the MiG-23S. Photographs accompanied by a few details of the new aircraft, referred to by some sources as F-12, were first released by Xinhua in mid-1979. It was said to be a 'high-speed and high altitude' interceptor-fighter fitted with Spey afterburning turbofan engine, and was expected to enter service in the mid-1980s to replace outmoded types.[46] While one report indicated that the adaption of the MiG-23 to the F-12 had been unsuccessful,[47] Taiwanese authorities have already displayed anxiety about its potential threat to the island.[48]

Traces of the 'Egyptian' samples can also be found in other fields of China's military development. In 1979 the Chinese began manufacturing a copy of the Soviet Sagger (also captured in Vietnam). As the Chinese Sagger is being deployed in quantity, the PLA's gap in anti-tank weapons will be closed 'significantly'.[49] New surface-to-air missiles, undoubtedly based on the Soviet SA-3 and SA-6, also under development, were expected to become operational in 1982.[50] Finally, it is reasonable to assume that China's new T-69 main battle tank, which appeared for the first time in the summer of 1981, incorporates at least some elements of the Soviet-made T-62, provided by Egypt.[51]

It is unlikely, however, that Egypt has been China's only Middle Eastern source for advanced military technology. Iraq, a recipient of more updated Soviet weapons, should be considered an additional source. Israel may well be yet another. Reports which first circulated in April 1979 argued that Israel and China signed an enormous arms deal, estimated at $2 billion.[52] China would allegedly receive electronic equipment; 52 Kfir fighter-bombers; 'several hundred' Merkava tanks (according to other reports only 16); 108 Tow anti-tank missiles and other types (Lance, Harpoon and Chaparral were occasionally mentioned); and even nuclear co-operation. These reports were again firmly denied by the Chinese,[53] as well as by Israel. Indeed, to a large extent they seem to have been fabricated either by Soviet disinformation agencies or by wild imagination. Still, even if these reports are only partly true,[54] Israel could become an important intermediary in China's military modernisation, capable of providing the Chinese with sophisticated Western technology as well as with a variety of captured Soviet weapons fitted, perhaps, with technological improvements and adaptations.

China's technological benefits should be viewed in a wider perspective. As a testing-ground for Soviet weapons and military doctrines, the Middle East has offered the Chinese not only intelligence in the narrow sense but, important lessons and insights into various kinds of warfare they might themselves be facing in the future. It may be safely assumed that the main Middle Eastern customers of Chinese arms are also China's main sources of information. In addition to intelligence, the Chinese have drawn lessons from the frequent Middle Eastern armed confrontations they have been watching closely. Based on conversations with senior PLA officials in Beijing in May 1979, Thomas Robinson indicated that the October 1973 war, 'where high technology weaponry and well-developed logistical base were critical to the outcome ... greatly influenced the [Chinese] decision not to resort to quantity production of older weaponry'.[55] Others speculated that one reason for the Chinese refusal to commit their air force to battle during the 1979 Vietnam invasion had been the deep impression of the Yom Kippur War, particularly the lethal effectiveness of Egypt's Soviet-made air defence systems.[56] Similarly, in July Deng Xiaoping allegedly warned the CCP Military Commission of the unpredictability of the situation in Vietnam: 'Take the fourth Arab–Israeli War in the Middle East, for example', he supposedly said. 'When the Egyptians crossed the canal and cut the Bar-Lev Line, Sadat had not expected that the outcome of the war would be that the Israelis would cross the canal, cut off the supply lines for the Third Egyptian Army, and encircle it to the extent that they could annihilate it at any minute'.[57] China's 'Middle East watchers' had also been impressed by the effectiveness of the anti-tank missiles in 1973, and even more impressed by their complete ineffectiveness in Lebanon in 1978, after Israeli tanks had allegedly been equipped with what the Chinese called 'an active protective device'.[58]

Finally, there are also important foreign policy implications in this new Chinese Middle Eastern policy that affect the superpowers. Most crucially, it is obvious that China has scored an advantage regarding the Soviet Union, but it is equally obvious that one should not read too much into this advantage. In the first place, the Chinese deals have not met any serious Soviet response, let alone retaliation. On the contrary, it seems as if the Soviets tolerated or even approved the Chinese arms sales which alleviated the never-ending burden of their military supply to the Arabs, prevented a Western monopoly of the market, and helped maintain the infrastructure for future deliveries of more advanced Soviet weapons. Indeed, this coincidence of Sino–Soviet interests has now extended to broader aspects of foreign policy. Since early 1982, having become more irritated by American policies in the Middle East, the Chinese have reduced their hostility towards Soviet policy, while openly stating their at times converging interests against US policy.[59]

As for American policy regarding Chinese arms sales, like the Soviet Union Washington has been silent about recent events. It seems that in the perspective of the Reagan administration's rigid anti-Sovietism, non-Soviet arms deals are better than Soviet ones, even if the new supplier is Communist China. On balance, while the local Middle Eastern states no doubt benefit from the presence of three rather than two great power suppliers, the superpowers have found the new triangle to be yet another frustrating example of relative impotence in the face of intense local conflict.

In sum, almost unperceived, China's military modernisation has already been under way for several years. Although still based on existing Soviet models, defence capabilities have improved through adaptation, new designs and modifications. It is in this context that the Middle East plays an important role. In return for supplying arms, the Chinese have obtained funds, technology and intelligence. But exceedingly more important, they have gained self-confidence and a sense of power. These have already begun to affect their strategic outlook and threat perception. Having achieved for the first time a real advantage over their rivals, the Chinese now appear less pre-occupied by Soviet power in the Middle East than they have for many years.

NOTES AND REFERENCES

1. Yitzhak Shichor, *The Middle East in China's Foreign Policy 1949–1977* (Cambridge University Press, 1979).
2. In May 1956, more than a year after the Bandung Conference, Egypt became the first Middle Eastern government to establish diplomatic relations with the PRC, to be followed quickly by Syria and Yemen. Since 1970 the rest of the Middle Eastern countries have established relations with China, except for Saudi Arabia, Qatar, Bahrein, the United Arab Emirates and Israel.
3. US Arms Control and Disarmament Agency, *World Military Expenditures and Arms Transfers 1970–1979* (Washington, March 1982), 129.
4. Ibid., 127–129.
5. Thomas W. Robinson, 'Chinese Military Modernization in the 1980s,' and Douglas T. Stuart and William T. Tow, 'Chinese Military Modernization: The Western Arms Connection,' *The China Quarterly*, No. 90, June 1982.
6. Middle East News Agency, 25 March 1976; *Financial Times*, 26 March 1976.
7. AFP (Beijing), 29 April 1976; in Foreign Broadcast Information Service, *Daily Report: People's Republic of China* (Washington, DC – hereafter FBIS-CHI), 29 April 1976, A/11; also, *al-Ahram*, 27 April 1976, 1; in FBIS, *Daily Report: MIddle East and North Africa* (hereafter FBIS-MEA), 30 April 1976, D/5; Middle East News Agency, 24 April 1976; in FBIS-MEA, 26 April 1976, D/6.
8. 'Major Gains Seen in China–Arab Ties,' *New York Times*, 23 April 1976. Mubarak said he was 'surprised' that China had offered Egypt far more aid than the Egyptians had expected: 'Not only did China promise to give us what we wanted free of charge, but also *volunteered* to assist us in connection with various types of weapons which are considered vital to Egypt and the Arab nation' (emphasis added). AFP (Beijing), 22 April 1976; in FBIS-CHI, 22 April 1976, A/12; *International Herald Tribune* (Paris), 22 April 1976; AP (Cairo), quoted in *Japan Times*, 27 April 1976, 5.

9. Cairo Domestic Service, 5 June 1979; in FBIS-MEA, 6 June 1979, D/8, and 5 August 1979; in FBIS-MEA, 6 August, D/10.
10. *Al-Ahram*, 7 June 1979, 1, said the deal included 'a number' of F-6s and spare parts. 'Informed diplomatic and news agency sources' spoke about 60 F-6s: Bernard Gwertzman, 'Sadat Reports Accord with China for Arms', *New York Times*, 6 June 1979, A/1, A/6; Robert Bailey, 'China to Supply MIG-19s', *Middle East Economic Digest* (London) (hereafter *MEED*), 8 June 1979, 23; *An-Nahar Arabe et International* (Paris-Beirut), No. 110, 11–17 June 1979, 5, mentioned 60 MiG-19s 'or 60 F-9s which are closer to the more developed MiG-21'. Finally, according to French military sources, the deal covered MiG121s, tanks, missiles, light weapons and spare parts, *Al-Sharq al-Awsat* (London), 8 June 1979.
11. *October* (Cairo), no. 140, 1 July 1979, 4; Middle East News Agency, 1 July 1979; in FBIS-MEA, 2 July 1979, D/5; *al-Hawadess* (London), No. 1201, 9 November 1979, 13; UPI (Cairo), 4 August 1979.
12. The Chinese ambassador to Kuwait said that the arms had been given to Egypt in accordance with previous agreements signed in 1976, 'but we are only now able to implement them'. *Al-Watan* (Kuwait), 10 October 1979; also in FBIS-CHI, 16 October 1979, A/3. See also Middle East News Agency, 6 June 1979; in FBIS-MEA, 7 June 1979, D/4–D/5.
13. After meeting Mao, Mubarak reported that the Chinese leader had 'confirmed China's principle which is based on aiding states in liberating their lands without charge' and 'explained that *his* principle was that China should not be an arms merchant' (emphasis added). Middle East News Agency, 24 April 1976; in FBIS-MEA, 26 April 1976, D/6.
14. For example: *MEED*, 29 February 1980; *Strategic Mideast and Africa* (Washington), 21 January 1980; Stockholm International Peace Research Institute (SIPRI), *World Armaments and Disarmaments 1981 Yearbook* (London, 1981), 220; *al-Musawwar* (Cairo), 11 February 1980.
15. In a special interview (*al-Musawwar*, 11 January 1980, p. 47), the commander of the Egyptian navy, emphasised 'China's noble assistance' not only to the navy but also to the air force. Two years later he told reporters (Reuter's from Alexandria, 18 February 1982), that two Chinese-manufactured submarines were due in mid-March as a part of a larger military agreement to strengthen the Egyptian navy. According to London's *Daily Telegraph*, 1 November 1982, this agreement included six newly-built submarines, spare parts and Chinese technicians who had already been busy overhauling Egypt's old and inoperative submarines. *MEED*, 24 December 1982, 10, reported that the two submarines were delivered in November and that China provided technicians to refit four of the Egyptian navy's six other Romeo-class submarines.
16. *al-Gumhuriyya*, 27 April 1980, 1–11. *MEED*, 24 December 1982, 10, said that Egypt has had more than 30 F-7s in operation since 1981.
17. *Al-Kifah al-'Arabi* (Beirut), 21 January 1980, 4, reported that 'a large number of Chinese military advisers began arriving in Egypt following Mubarak's visit and as a part of the military agreement signed by him'.
18. Middle East News Agency, 21 December 1982; in FBIS-MEA, 22 December 1982. D/9. See also: *Japan Times*, 23 December 1982; *al-*

Watan al-'Arabi (Beirut), 31 December 1982; *al-Hawadass*, 31 December 1982, 12; *Financial Times*, 22 December 1982; *MEED*, 24 December 1982, 10. According to *Japan Times*, 5 April 1983, 1, Egypt had more than 90 Chinese-built F-6s and F-7s in operation.
19. See Wolfgang Bartke, *Who's Who in the People's Republic of China* (Brighton: The Harvester Press, 1981), 55–56.
20. *Akhir Sa'a* (Cairo), 19 January 1983, 8.
21. AP (Beijing), 2 April 1983; also in *MEED*, 8 April 1983, 11.
22. *Al-Musawwar*, 8 April 1983, 6. Also AP (Cairo), 6 April 1983 and *MEED*, 8 April 1983, 11.
23. Reports, circulated in late January, said that China had agreed to supply Iraq with enriched uranium and were firmly denied by the Chinese. See: *Wen Wei Po* (Hong-Kong), 31 January 1981; in FBIS-CHI, 3 February 1981, U/1, and *Beijing Review*, No. 8, 23 February 1981, 3. It is possible that the arms deal was signed then.
24. 'China Poised to Send Tanks to Iraq', *Arab–Asian Affairs* (London), No. 104, November 1981, 1–2.
25. *Newsweek*, 22 Novmeber 1982, 7.
26. *Newsweek*, 29 November 1982, 21.
27. Michael Weisskopf, 'China Plays Both Sides in Persian Gulf War', *The Washington Post*, 13 January 1983.
28. *Far Eastern Economic Review* (Hong Kong), 17 December 1982. Iran is named incorrectly.
29. *MEED*, 21 January 1983, 24 (also in *Far Eastern Economic Review*, 3 February, 9).
30. *Beijing Review*, No. 48, 29 November 1982, 3.
31. Interview in *al-Hawadess*, 11 February 1983.
32. *MEED*, 21 January 1983. At least 30 F-6s were assembled in Jordan and delivered to Iraq. Fewer aircraft, including some F-7s, were delivered by Egypt. See: Clarence A. Robinson, Jr., 'Iraq, Iran Acquiring Chinese-Built Fighters,' *Aviation Week & Space technology*, 11 April 1983, 16–18.
33. See note 27 above and C. Robinson, ibid, 16–18.
34. Jonathan D. Pollack, 'Defense Modernization in the People's Republic of China', *A Rand Note*, N-1214-1-AF, October 1979, 6–7.
35. Harlan W. Jencks, 'The Chinese "Military-Industrial Complex" and Defense Modernization,' *Asian Survey*, vol. XX, no. 10, October 1980, 968.
36. 'The PRC Air Force', *Xiandai Junshi* (Contemporary Military Affairs), (Hong Kong), no. 33, July 1979, 36; in Joint Publications Research Service, *China Report, Political, Social and Military Affairs* (hereafter JPRS, *China Report*), no. 14, 7 September 1979, 17. See also: Charles H. Murphy, 'China: An Emerging Military Superpower,' *Air Force*, July 1972, 55, and 'China Air and Missile Forces,' *Flight International*, 22 September 1979, 952.
37. R. K. Campbell, *The Military Potential of the People's Republic of China* (South African Institute of International Affairs, April 1980), 5.
38. *Aviation Week and Space Technology*, 10 September 1979, 19; 'The PRC Air Force,' 21. See also note 16 above.

39. *al-Musawwar*, 8 April 1983, 6, Foreign Minister Kamal Hasan Ali also disclosed that Egypt had increased the cambat efficiency of Chinese-supplied warplanes by 'introducing some changes'.
40. Jonathan D. Pollack, 'China's Potential as a World Power,' *International Journal*, vol. XXV, no. 3, summer 1980, 585.
41. Jencks, (note 35), 986; Pollack (note 34), 'Defense Modernization,' 7–8.
42. Beijing Domestic Service, 22 January 1981; in FBIS-CHI, 27 January 1981, L/24. There are numerous indications that military production was by no means neglected. 'National Defense Science and Technology, National Defense Industry Achieve New Successes', *Nanfang Ribao*, 2 January 1982; 1; in JPRS, *China Report*, no. 276, 3 March 1982, 53; Beijing Domestic Service, 11 February 1982; in JPRS, *China Report*, no. 273, 23 February 1982, 52.
43. The Chinese Defence Minister wrote in March 1983 that 'from now on, with development of the country's economic construction and flourishing of science and education, more favourable conditions will be created in turn for national defence modernisation. This means ... that funds for building national defence will be increased ...' Zhang Aiping. 'Several Questions Concerning Modernization of National Defense', *Hongqi* (Red Flag), no. 5, 1 March 1983, 21–24; in FBIS-CHI, 17 March, 1983, K/6.
44. Data assembled from the following sources: KYODO (Tokyo), 19 January 1978; in FBIS-CHI, 20 January 1978, A/1–A/2; AFP (Beijing), 6 June 1979; in FBIS-CHI, 7 June 1979, I/1; *Events* (Beirut), no. 41, 21 April 1978; Research Institute for Peace and Security (RIPS), *Asian Security 1980* (Tokyo, 1981), 90; Pollack, 'Defense Modernization', 13; Robinson, 'Chinese Military Modernization', 240; Campbell, *The Military Potential*, 7; Jencks, 971–973.
45. K. Borisov, 'Modernization of China's Armed Forces', *Zarubezhnoye Voyenoye Obozreniye* (Foreign Military Survey), no. 10, October 1981, 15; in JPRS, *China Report*, no. 277, 8 March 1982, 65.
46. KYODO (Tokyo), 14 November 1977; in FBIS-CHI, 15 November 1977, E/1; KYODO (Tokyo), 19 January 1978; in FBIS-CHI, 20 January 1978, A/1–A/2; *MEED*, 2 December 1977, 28, and 27 January 1978, 18; *The Washington Post*, 3 November 1978; AFP (Beijing), 7 June 1979; in FBIS-CHI, 7 June 1979, I/1; US Government sources quoted by UPI (Washington), 23 December 1979; *Ta-kung Pao* (Hong Kong), 7 September 1979; in JPRS, *China Report*, no. 19, 25 September 1979, 67; 'The PRC Air Force', *Xiandai Junshi*, 22 (see note 36); *International Defense Review* (Switzerland), April 1980.
47. Shu Yao, 'The Yun-7, China's Newest Passenger Airplane', *The China Business Review*, November–December 1982, 41.
48. Zong Shengzhi, 'The Balance of Armaments on Both Sides of the Taiwan Strait', *Bashi Niandai* (The 1980s), (Taipei), 15 January 1983, 50; in JPRS, *China Report*, no. 384, 31 January 1983, 93, in an interview, *Far Eastern Economic Review*, 27 January 1983, 29–30. See also: Lin Jianguo, 'Suggestions on the Modernization of Taiwan's Three Services–Section on the Airforce', *Lianhe Yuekan* (Unity Monthly), Taipei, no. 8, March 1982, 88–97; in JPRS, *China Report*, no. 386, 2 February 1983, 141–142; Far Eastern Economic Review, *Asia 1981*

Yearbook, 35, and *Asia 1983 Yearbook*, 29; Bill Sweetman, 'Chinese Air Forces,' this volume, Ch. 5.

49. Jencks, p. 971. See also RIPS, *Asian Security 1980*, 90. A photograph showing Chinese anti-tank missiles, apparently identical to the Sagger, is given on the outside back cover of *Bingqi Zhishi* (Ordnance Knowledge), no. 5, 1981, reporduced in JPRS, *China Report*, no. 236, 12 November 1981, 38.
50. RIPS, *Asian Security 1981*, 104.
51. *Defense and Foreign Affairs Daily* (Washington), vol. XI, no. 142, 23 July 1982, 1–2. See also Zong Shengzhi, *op. cit.* (note 48), 93.
52. Radio Peace and Progress, 21 April 1979; *al-Anba'* (Kuwait), 21 December 1979, 10 February 1980; *Akhir Sa'a* (Cairo), 30 July 1980; *'Uruba wa 'l-'Arab* (Beirut), 29 August 1980; *Pravda*, 15 August 1980, 17 November 1980; *Economist* (London), 22 November 1980; *Newsweek*, 24 November 1980; *al-Qabas* (Kuwait), 14 December 1980; *al-Ra'i al-'Am* (Kuwait), 21 January 1981.
53. 'An Absurd Rumor', *Renmin Ribao*, 22 July 1980, 6; in FBIS-CHI, 28 July 1980, I/2–I/3; 'The Sinister Motives of the Rumor Monger', *Renmin Ribao*, 25 January 1981, 4; in FBIS-CHI, 26 January 1981, C/1.
54. For a sceptical analysis see Gerald Segal, 'Israeli Arms for China – Wishful Thinking?' *Soviet Jewish Affairs*, vol. II, no. 2, 1981, 23–37.
55. Robinson, 'Chinese Military Modernization,' 238–239.
56. James B. Linder and A. James Gregor, 'The Chinese Communist Air Force in the "Punitive" War against Vietnam', *Air University Review*, vol. XXXII, no. 6, September–October 1981, 72.
57. *Issues and Studies* (Taipei), vol. XVI, no. 8, August 1980, 90–91.
58. Shan Lin, 'A Shield in the Budding Stage – Active Protective Devices for Tanks', *Bingqi Zhishi*, no. 3, 1982, 8–9; in JPRS, *China Report*, no. 334, 3 September 1982, 65–68.
59. For example: Mu Mu, 'Do Not Use the Wolf to Expel the Tiger', *Renmin Ribao*, 16 January 1982, 6; in FBIS-CHI, 22 January 1982, I/1. On this issue see: Yitzhak Shichor, 'In Search of Alternatives: China's Middle East Policy after Sadat', *The Australian Journal of Chinese Affairs*, no. 8, June 1982, 105.

Index

active defence 9, 11
aeronautics research, joint Chinese–US 153
Aero-Technology Import and Export Corporation 126
Afghanistan
  China's attitude to 236, 253–5
  Chinese–Pakistan relations and 250
  Soviet invasion and occupation of 75, 149, 170, 175, 184, 186–7, 201, 205, 214
Africa 128, 170, 175
agricultural decentralisation 32
Air Army, Divisions and Groups 42
Air Force (PLA) 42–3, 44, 71
  aircraft designations 83n
  bombers 43, 76–7
  fighters 77–9
  inferiority to Soviet Union's 71–80, 83
  SAM missiles 79
  size of area to be defended 71–3
  tactical support by 42, 78
air power decisiveness 73
aircraft production, Chinese 73, 80–2, 135
  based on Soviet models 271–2
  military 73, 80–2, 135, 269–70
airlift capability 43
Ali, Kamal Hasan 267
American Motors 154
Amoy 92
Andropov, Yuri 187, 206
Angola 189, 202
Arabat 155
Arab–Israeli wars, lessons of, for China 272–3
arms
  Chinese exports 128–9: to Middle East 78–9, 263–9, 272; to Pakistan 250; Soviet and US attitudes to 273
  Chinese self-sufficiency policy 151–2, 168, 191
  sales to China 191, 198–9: cost problem 156, 157–8, 213; from W. Europe 155–8, 213; Japanese 230; obstacles to 151–6, 159; second grade rejected 157; US attitude to 149–55, 198–200, 202; *see also* Taiwan
art, military 6–8, 10
Artillery Control Equipment 63
Asian collective-security scheme 170
Association of Southeast Asian Nations (ASEAN) 237, 241
  attitude to Soviet Union 186
  Chinese relations with 96, 141, 172–4, 223, 241–3
  US relations with 206

Bai Hua: *Unrequited Love* 31
Baldridge, Malcolm 153
Baoshan 134
bauxite exports 143
Bechtel Corporation 141
Beijing Military Region 66
Belgium: computer deal with China 157
biological warfare capability 65
Brandt, Willy 210
Brezhnev, L. I. 170, 185, 235
British military sales to China 155–6, 213
budget, military 56, 94–5, 119–20

Callaghan, James 213
Cameron, Sir Neil 213
Carter Administration 198, 202
Changzhi–Nantong coal slurry pipeline 141
chemical warfare capability 65
Chen Muhua 153–4, 213
Chen Zaidao 23
Chengdu 61

Index

Chinese Communist Party 7, 60
  army modernisation and 28–9
  Central Committee: military directive 55; Military Commission 119; Science, Technology and Arms Commission 125
  controls in armed forces 20
  disagreements within 176, 181
  Mao's alienation from 20–1
  military attacks on leadership 19, 30–3
chromium exports 144
civil control of military 18–20
civil defence 99, 180, 182
coal industry
  foreign capitalist co-operation in 141–2
  slurry pipeline projects 141
coastline sovereignty disputes, offshore oil and 140–1
Cohen, Stephen 175
combined arms operations 36, 39, 40–1, 43–5, 47, 53–4, 58–9, 62, 192
Commands, Specified and Unified 44
Commission in Charge of Science, Technology and Industry for National Defence 125
communications satellite, Chinese 154
Composite Army 42–4
computer-aided manufacture 123
computerised simulation 57–8
Cultural Revolution 21–3, 27, 61, 118, 135
Czechoslovakia 235

Davenport, Alice A. 141
Deng Xiaoping 27, 30–3, 61, 95, 120, 136, 152, 176–7, 256
  on Soviet Union 88, 223
  on United States 150, 171–2
  on other foreign affairs 175, 215, 236–7, 252, 273
deterrence 41
  by denying enemy victory 104–6
  by offensive action 7, 105
  nuclear 38–9, 90–1, 102, 104–6: massive or minimum 107–9
  proportional 218
Ding Guoyu 267

East Asia, détente in 223–4
economic development five-year plan 140

economic zones 86
Egypt 81
  Chinese military exports to 78–9, 266–8
  Soviet arms acquired by Chinese in 271–2
electronic warfare capability 63, 93
Electronics Import and Export Corporation 126
electronics industry 80, 123–4, 128, 134
energy
  conservation 140
  production 140–2
  see also coal; oil
Europe, as superpowers' target 183–4
Europe, Western, and anti-hegemony front plan 211–15, 217–18, 230
Exocet missile 94
expenditure, military 28, 94–5
export and import corporations 126–7
exports, Chinese
  arms 128–9, 250: to Middle East 78–9, 263–9, 272–3
  ships 86
  strategic minerals 142–3

fishing 87
Fluor Corporation 141
force projection 44–5, 46
foreign investment 86, 92, 141
foreign trade
  balance 95
  corporations 126–7
France 202, 212
  military sales to China 156–7, 212
Fukuda, Takeo 230

Gang of Four 29, 31, 135, 140, 181
Garrett, Banning 211
Gaullism 210
General Logistics Department 61
geography
  factor in nuclear strategy 101, 108
  military 7, 37–8
German Federal Republic 157, 216–17
germanium exports 144
Giscard d'Estaing, V. 212
Great Leap Forward 19, 118
Great Leap Outward 176
Great Wall Industry Corporation 127
Guangming Ribao 139, 185

Index

guerrilla warfare 6, 53, 55, 192, 254
  strategic task of 9
Guo Huaruo 5

Haig, Alexander 149–50, 198, 211
Hainan Island 92
Hebei field exercises 58
Hong Kong 92, 140, 215
Hong Qi 37
Hong Xuezhi 46, 61
Hu Yaobang 201
Hua Guofeng 26–7, 31, 119, 125
human wave, tactics 9
Hunan 5

ideological differences and resemblances, Soviet–Chinese 102, 105, 247–8
ideological policy in Southeast Asia 241–4
ideology and nuclear strategy 101–3
import and export corporations 126–7
imports of strategic minerals, by countries supplying 144
  see also arms sales to China
India 73, 81, 175, 244, 247, 252–3
  Soviet attitude to 247, 251
  threat to, nuclear 251, 257
  threat to China 99, 248–9, 250–1
  war with Pakistan 249–50, 251–2
Indian Ocean
  Chinese submarine-based ballistic missile force in 257
  Zone of Peace 258–9
Indonesia 96
industry, defence 117–30
  civilian *v.* military control 124–5
  constraints on 117–18, 119, 133–4, 146
  design capability 135
  economic cost of 122
  excess capacity 270
  growth 119, 121
  management deficiencies 133, 135, 138, 137, 146
  manpower 121–3, 146
  ministers in charge 126–7
  modernisation 119–20, 122, 129–30, 145
  new projects 118–19, 123, 135
  output 29–30, 117, 120–1: civilian 121–2, 124–6, 128, 139–40, 146; and military, by products 126–7

procurement, growth of 121
  reform and restructuring 134–5, 138–40, 146
  research and development 123, 128, 133, 135–8, 145–6
  scientists and technicians in 137–8
  technological weaknesses 122, 133
intercontinental ballistic missiles (ICBMs) 37–8, 85, 99–100, 107, 109
International Atomic Energy Agency 155
Iran 198, ch. 18 *passim*
Iraq, Chinese military supplies to 29–30, 83, 268–9, 272
Islamic states, role in China's plans 249
Israel
  arms deal with China 272
  combat aircraft manufacture 81
Italy 157
Iwashima, Hisao 228

Japan 186, 198–9, 206
  Chinese relations with 10, 95, 99, 101, 149, 158, 172–4: economic 141, 224–7, 230, 232; military talks 228–32; strategic aims in 222–32; Treaty of Peace and Friendship 223, 229
Jencks, Harlan 48
Jiao Guanhua 183
Jiefang Ribao 32
Jiefangjun Huabao 11–12
Jingli Guanli 135
Jugoslavia 81
Jungar Qinghuangdao pipeline project 141–2

Kampuchea 87, 173–4, 189, 201, 236–9, 241–4
Keyworth, George 153
Khmer People's National Liberation Front (KPNLF) 239–40
Khmer Rouge 236–9, 241–4
  Chinese arms supplies to 239–40
Khrushchev, N. 102
Kissinger, Henry 222
Kohl, Helmut 216
Korea 202, 231
  reunification 174, 224
Korean War 46–7, 244
Krupp Corporation 142

land-border defence strategy 11
Lao Zi 4
Laos 240, 244
leftist guerrilla mentality 61
Liberation Army Daily 31–2
Liberation Army Pictorial 58–9
Lin Biao 3, 21–4, 48, 181, 187
  fall of 25–6, 119
Liu Huaqing 46, 89, 153
logistics modernisation 61–2
Luo Ruiqing 21

Mao Zedong 4, 25, 67, 105, 267
  alienation from Party 20–1
  evaluation of role of 31
  military directives 10, 181
  on defence 107–8
  on protracted war 4–5
  succession struggle 26
  three-world thesis 210–11
machine-tools 123, 134–5, 138
Manchuria 11, 188
Marconi Ltd 155, 213
merchant marine build-up 86
metallurgy 134
Middle East 170
  Chinese arms agreements with 129, 263–9
  Soviet military supplies disrupted 266
  Soviet arms technology transfer from, to China 270–2
Middleton, Drew 62
Military Control Committees 22
militia, modern, functions of 55–6
minerals
  Chinese marketing policy 143–4
  exports 140, 143: strategic 142–3
  imports, strategic, by countries supplying 144
mines
  at sea 93–4
  artillery-deliverable 64
Ming Fan 5
Miyoshi, Hideo 228
mobile warfare 9, 11–12, 53, 62
mobility
  strategic, limited 40–1
  tactical 40, 44, 64
modernisation, China's 62–5, 190, 265
  armed forces 66, 263: advocates of 46–7; Air Force 81–3; logistics 61–2; military elite's view of 45–7; naval 85, 89, 94–5; Soviet models for, from

Middle East 270–2, 274; technological 28–9, 26–7, 38–41, 129–30, 273–4
  defence industry 119–20, 122, 129–30, 145
  economic 120, 185, 203
  foreign policy and 172, 184
  Japanese element in 226–8
  opposition to 66, 184
  ports and shipping 86
  scientific and industrial 66–7
  Zhou's plan 119
Mubarak, President 266–8

Nakasone, Yasuhiro 230–1
Nanhua Power Machinery Research Institute 138, 139–40
National Defence Industry Office (NDIO) 124–5
National Defence Science and Technology Commission (NDSTC) 125
naval forces 38, 44
  air support 91, 94
  defensive role 91
  education and training 88, 90, 92, 94
  electronic systems 93
  expansion in southern seas 240–1, 255–6
  extended operations at sea 90
  mine warfare 93–4
  modernisation 85, 89, 94–5
  ship-based helicopters 90
  strength 85, 91
  see also submarine-based ballistic missiles
naval policy, diplomatic aspect of 255
Netherlands 157
New International Economic Order 175
Nian rebellion 5
Nikaido, Susumu 231
Nimrod 94
Nishihiro, Counsellor 228–9
Nixon, Richard 182, 196–7, 222
North Atlantic Treaty Organisation 11
  change in China's attitude to 209–10, 217
Nuclear Energy Industry Corporation 126
nuclear forces, Chinese 99, 257–8
  theatre 12
nuclear missiles, sea-launched 37–8, 85, 88–91, 93

see also submarine-based ballistic
    missiles
nuclear research, joint Chinese–US   153
nuclear strategy   37–9, 45, 100–4
  deterrence in   38–9, 90–1, 102,
    104–9
nuclear submarines   93
nuclear threat to China   98
nuclear weapons
  'assured destruction' policy   107
  first use of   99, 106–7, 182, 189
  indecisiveness of   107–9
  limited war assessment and   108–9
  production of   73
  range of   106–7, 109
  tactical   106–7, 109

Occidental Petroleum   141
Ohira, Premier   230
oil exports, China's   225–7
oilwells, offshore   86–7, 140, 236, 241, 245
Okawara, Mitsunari   230
Ordnance Ministry   138
Ozawa, Tomoichiro   230

Pakistan   99, 128, 175, 246, 258
  Chinese aid and support   250, 257–9
  linchpin of China's South Asia policy
    248–50, 252
  threat to   77–8, 189, 250
  war with India   249–50, 251–2
Pamirs, China's claim to   249
Paracels Islands   92, 240–1, 244
Peng Dehuai   5, 55
  dismissal   19–20
People's Police   54
People's War   3, 5–6, 37, 48, 191–2, 218
  defensive essence of   7
  doctrine and applications   6–10
  modern   53, 65, 192, 254
People's Liberation Army
  agricultural production by   55
  Beijing's authority over   23, 25
  biological and chemical warfare
    capability   65
  cadres   56–71
  Capital Construction Engineers units
    54
  command changes   60
  Command, Control, Communication
    and Intelligence (C^3I) capability
    12, 40, 53, 63, 65–6

computers in   62
discipline   61
educational levels   57, 65
field exercises   58
force projection capability   45, 46
General Political Department   30, 32
intervention in Cultural Revolution
  22
involvement in politics   20–5, 30
logistics modernisation   61–2, 66
Mao succession struggle and   26
nuclear strategy and   103–4
officer training   47, 66
police powers   55
political quiescence   18–20, 27
political representation reduced   25–6
provincial political and administrative
  supremacy   22–3, 24
Railroad Engineer units   54
rifts within   23, 27–8, 30–1
Second Artillery   103
simulators in   58
standardisation   54
technological modernisation   28–9,
  36–7, 38–41, 44, 63–6, 176,
  182–3, 203–4, 270: based on
  Soviet models from Middle East
  271–2
training   30, 47, 53, 56–61, 66, 145,
  192
Perry, William   154
Persian Gulf   206
Philippines   87, 96, 237, 245
Pingsuo coalmines   141
Poland   206
police, armed   54–5
Politburo
  advocates of military modernisation
    in   46
  military representation in   26
political commissars   30
positional warfare   9, 12, 53
precision-guided missiles   41, 64, 79
production, military   *see* industry,
  defence
protracted war   9, 11, 37–8

radar equipment   79
radio-electronic warfare   63
ranks, military   61
Reagan Administration   150, 152, 171,
  185, 198, 200, 202–3
Red Guards   21–3

Renmin Ribao (*People's Daily*) 183, 185, 187
research and development institutes 136–7
Revolutionary Committees 22, 24
Robinson, Thomas 169, 272
Rolls-Royce Spey engine 79, 81, 134–5, 149
Romania 81

Sadat, Anwar 266
satellite-tracking station sale to China 154
Schmidt, Helmut 212–13
Schultz, George 152–3, 155, 206
science, military 6–7
Sea Dart 93
   sales to China cancelled 156, 213
sea-launched ballistic missiles (SLBM) 37–8, 85, 88–9, 93, 100, 103, 106, 109, 190–1
Sea Treaty Law 87
semiconductors 134
Shanghai 137
Shanxi militia 55
Shell Oil 142
Shenyang 66
Shipbuilding Trading Co. Ltd 127
Si Kexuexue 137
Sloan, John J. 66
Song Shilun 11
Song Zhiguang 229
South Asia
   Chinese claims in 242
   Chinese military activity in 240–1, 245
   Chinese strategic assessment of 247–52, 258-60
Southeast Asia
   Chinese policy in 234–6: military 236–41, 244; political-ideological 241–4
   Chinese-Soviet rapprochement and 243–4
   see also Association of Southeast Asian Nations
Soviet Union 10
   air power 71–6
   border situation 180, 187, 197, 205, 214
   Chinese charges against 87, 183–4, 201–2, 223, 236, 253–5
   coercive military diplomacy 189
   Command, Control, Communications and Intelligence (C^3I) resources 76
   Communist Party 6
   defence against 39–40, 53, 62–3, 65, 91, 106, 190–2, 212: in the air 76–80
   Frontal Aviation 74–5
   ideology, resemblances and differences with China 102, 105, 247–8
   influence 6, 9, 42–3, 170
   keeping cost of war high for 80–2, 90–1
   military aid to China 28–9, 118, 123
   naval expansion: Indian Ocean 256; Pacific 87–8, 95, 184, 206, 235–6, 241, 255
   naval provocation 88
   offensive doctrine 12, 91
   Pacific region, détente and 223–4
   rapprochement with China, search for 158–9, 169–71, 182, 187, 229, 231–2, 243–5, 259, 273: Japan's attitude to 227–8
   security concessions sought from 170
   Siberian development 169, 189
   subversive activities 189–90
   threat from 10, 71–6, 98, 141, 169, 180–90, 201, 204–7, 211, 213, 223, 235
   threat to 211
   US policy towards 198–9, 202–3
   war objectives 188, 212
   weaponry: overtaking US 183, 197, 211; SS-20s 74, 214, 229
State Scientific and Technological Commission (SSTC) 125
steel output 134
strategic mobility 40–1
strategic self-reliance policy 151–2, 168, 191, 213, 265
strategy, Chinese 3–6, 9–12, 38
   balanced 48, 200–1, 204, 207, 218, 223
   doctrine 3–6, 10–12
   gaps in 12
   Japan in 223–32
   land-border defence 11
   Middle East 263
   new 36, 66
   nuclear 37–9, 45, 100–4: deterrence and 38–9, 90–1, 102, 104–9
   social dimension 5
   South Asia 247–55, 258–60
   Southeast Asia 236–45
   thought, military, formation of 4–6, 9

see also Soviet Union; United States
Strauss, F. J. 212–13, 216
structural changes, military 40–1, 42–5, 47–8
Su Yu 108–9
submarine-based ballistic missiles 37–8, 85, 88–91, 93, 100, 103, 106, 109: deployment area for 257–8
Sun Zi 4–5
superpowers
  China's view of 196, 204–5, 210, 254
  hegemony 185–6, 200–1, 212–13, 230, 248
Sutter, Robert 215
Systems and Applied Sciences Corporation 154

Taiping rebellion 5
Taiwan 45
  threat to 73, 92, 95, 101, 199
  US arms sales to 152–3, 200–2
  US policy towards 150–2, 154, 171, 200–2, 205, 215
Tanaka, Kakuei 222
Tanaka, Kanji 230
Tang Tson 172
technical schools, military 57
technology
  foreign military 119, 123, 129, 134, 150–1: sold to China 154
  training in 123, 134
  transfer 149, 152–3, 155, 159, 203: from Middle East 270–2
  see also modernisation
Thailand 174, 236–8, 242, 244
Thatcher, Margaret 213, 215
Third World 142, 175, 201–3, 207
  Chinese aid to 128–9, 175–6
Tibet 247, 250–1
titanium exports 143–4
Tjumen oil project 225
Tonkin Gulf 241, 245
training, military 30, 47, 53, 56–61, 66, 145, 192

United States
  arms sales to China: attitude to 149–55, 198–200, 202; support for W. European 149, 152
  co-operation with China: aeronautics research 153; coal industry 141–2; imports from China 142–3, 203; joint jeep

  production 154
  defence against 98–9, 106
  import restrictions 144–5
  nuclear export rules, modification of 155
  policy towards Soviet Union 198–9, 202–3
  relations with China 10, 149, 155, 185, 191, 197–9, 202, 206–7, 210–11, 215: Chinese naval expansion and 96; deterioration of 150–2, 171–2, 187, 202–5; military 211; Taiwan and 150–4, 171, 200–2, 205
  role in China's Southeast Asia strategy 237
  strategy 197–20, 205, 211
uranium, enriched, sales of 155

vanadium exports 143
Vickers Ltd 155–6
Vietnam 87, 91, 129, 212
  Chinese disagreements with 91–2, 101, 173–4, 236
  Chinese strategy against 236–40, 243
  Chinese threat to 73, 173, 189, 244–5
  Chinese war with 45, 80, 87, 149, 173, 189, 191, 235, 238–9
  Soviet support for 87–8, 173–4, 184, 235–6, 238–9, 244
  War, US in 78, 197

Wei Guoqing 32
Wei, Rulin 4
Whiting, Allen 218
Woodward, Kim 141–2
Wu Xiuquan 156, 186, 228–30
Wuxi 128

Xiangtan 125
Xiao Ke 46–7
Xinhua 152–3
Xinjiang 11, 181, 188, 190, 250
Xu Xiangqian 11, 184

Yang Dezhi 46, 55, 61
Yang Yong 107–8
Ye Fei 89
Ye Jianying 30–1, 89, 108, 119
Yu Qiuli 60

Zhang Aiping 46, 88–9, 95, 151, 157, 176, 191
Zhang Caiqian 229
Zhang Tingfa 46
Zhanjiang 92

Zhao Ziyang 175, 267
Zhou Enlai 25, 106–7, 119, 175, 181–2
Zhu De 5
Zhuang Zi 4